Death and Meaning

ROYAL INSTITUTE OF PHILOSOPHY SUPPLEMENT: 90

EDITED BY

Michael Hauskeller

CAMBRIDGE
UNIVERSITY PRESS

PUBLISHED BY THE PRESS SYNDICATE OF THE UNIVERSITY OF CAMBRIDGE
The Pitt Building, Trumpington Street, Cambridge, CB2 1RP,
United Kingdom

CAMBRIDGE UNIVERSITY PRESS
UPH, Shaftesbury Road, Cambridge CB2 8BS, United Kingdom
32 Avenue of the Americas, New York, NY 10013–2473, USA
477 Williamstown Road, Port Melbourne, VIC 3207, Australia
C/Orense, 4, planta 13, 28020 Madrid, Spain
Lower Ground Floor, Nautica Building, The Water Club, Beach Road,
Granger Bay, 8005 Cape Town, South Africa

Printed in Great Britain by Bell & Bain Ltd, Glasgow.
Typeset by Techset Composition Ltd, Salisbury, UK

A catalogue record for this book is available from the British Library

ISBN 9781009187862
ISSN 1358-2461

Contents

Notes on the Contributors

Havi Carel is Professor of Philosophy at the University of Bristol. She recently completed a Wellcome Trust Senior Investigator Award, the Life of Breath. She was awarded the Health Humanities' Inspiration Award 2018 for this work. Her third monograph, *Phenomenology of Illness*, was published by Oxford University Press in 2016. She was selected as a 'Best of Bristol' lecturer in 2016. Havi is the author of *Illness* (2008, 2013, 2018), shortlisted for the Wellcome Trust Book Prize, and of *Life and Death in Freud and Heidegger* (2006). She is the co-editor of *Health, Illness and Disease* (2012), *New Takes in Film-Philosophy* (2010), and of *What Philosophy Is* (2004).

Drew Chastain received his Ph.D. from Tulane University and has published a number of articles on spirituality and meaning in life, some forthcoming, appearing in journals such as *The Journal of the Philosophy of Life, Sophia, Philosophia, Ethical Perspectives* and *Overheard in Seville*, and also in *The Philosophy of Spirituality: Analytic, Continental and Multicultural Approaches* and *Deep Space Nine: Essays*. His work explores what it means to be spiritual but not religious and also how to better understand the subjective, experiential aspect of meaning in life.

Michael Cholbi is Chair in Philosophy at the University of Edinburgh. He has published widely in ethical theory, practical ethics, and the philosophy of death and dying. His books include *Suicide: The Philosophical Dimensions* (Broadview, 2011), *Understanding Kant's Ethics* (Cambridge University Press, 2016), and *Grief: A Philosophical Guide* (Princeton University Press, expected 2021). He is the editor of *Immortality and the Philosophy of Death* (Rowman and Littlefield, 2015) and *Exploring the Philosophy of Death and Dying: Classic and Contemporary Perspectives* (Routledge, 2021). He is the founder of the International Association for the Philosophy of Death and Dying.

Michael Hauskeller is Professor of Philosophy and Head of the Philosophy Department at the University of Liverpool, UK. He specializes in moral and existential philosophy, but has also done work in various other areas, most notably phenomenology (the theory of

doi:10.1017/S1358246121000199   © The Royal Institute of Philosophy and the contributors 2021
Royal Institute of Philosophy Supplement **90** 2021

Notes on the Contributors

atmospheres), the philosophy of art and beauty, and the philosophy of human enhancement. His publications include *Biotechnology and the Integrity of Life* (Routledge 2007), *Better Humans? Understanding the Enhancement Project* (Routledge 2013), *Sex and the Posthuman Condition* (Palgrave Macmillan 2014), *The Palgrave Handbook of Posthumanism in Film and Television* (ed. with T. Philbeck and C. Carbonell, Palgrave 2015), *Mythologies of Transhumanism* (Palgrave Macmillan 2016), *Moral Enhancement. Critical Perspectives* (ed. with L. Coyne, Cambridge University Press 2018), and *The Meaning of Life and Death* (Bloomsbury 2019).

Daniel Hill was educated at Birkenhead School, Oxford, and King's College, London. He has taught philosophy at the University of Liverpool since 2000. He is the author or co-author of four books: *Divinity and Maximal Greatness* (Routledge, 2005), *Christian Philosophy: A-Z* (Edinburgh University Press, 2006) with Randal C Rauser, *The Right to Wear Religious Symbols* (Palgrave Macmillan, 2013) with Daniel Whistler, and *Does God Intend that Sin Occur? We Affirm* (Palgrave Macmillan, 2021, forthcoming) with Matthew J Hart. He is currently working with Stephen McLeod and Attila Tanyi on a book on entrapment, virtue testing, and temptation. He is the Chair of the Tyndale Fellowship's Study Group for Philosophy of Religion, and the Secretary of the University of Liverpool's Staff Christian Fellowship.

Guy Kahane is Professor of Moral Philosophy at the University of Oxford, and Fellow and Tutor in Philosophy at Pembroke College, Oxford. He is also Course Director of Oxford's MSt in Practical Ethics programme, Director of Studies at the *Oxford Uehiro Centre for Practical Ethics*, and Associate Editor of the *Journal of Practical Ethics*. Kahane is the author (or co-author) of nearly 100 articles on a wide range of topics in meta-ethics, applied ethics, moral psychology and philosophy of religion.

F. M. Kamm is the Henry Rutgers University Professor of Philosophy and Distinguished Professor of Philosophy, Department of Philosophy, Rutgers University. She is the author of nine books including *Morality, Mortality*, Vols. I (OUP, 1992) and II (OUP, 1996); *Intricate Ethics: Rights, Responsibilities, and Permissible Harm* (OUP, 2007); *Bioethical Prescriptions* (OUP, 2013); *The Trolley Problem Mysteries* (OUP, 2016), and her most recent *Almost Over: Aging, Dying, Dead* (OUP, 2020). She also has published many articles on normative ethical theory and practical ethics.

Antti Kauppinen is Professor of Practical Philosophy at the University of Helsinki, and PI of the Academy of Finland Research Project *Responsible Beliefs: Why Ethics and Epistemology Need Each Other*. Prior to taking up his current position, he worked at the universities of St Andrews, Amsterdam, Dublin, and Tampere. His research focuses mostly on ethics and metaethics, on topics like normativity, meaning in life, well-being, and moral sentiments. With Jussi Suikkanen, he is the editor of *Methodology and Moral Philosophy* (Routledge, 2019).

Teodora Manea studied philosophy in Romania and Germany, specialising in hermeneutics, existentialism, and bioethics. She worked as a medical interpreter and presently is lecturer in applied clinical ethics at the University of Liverpool, School of Medicine. Between 2010 and 2018 she taught medical humanities, philosophy and ethics at the Medical School, University of Exeter and she has been working as an ethics expert for the European Commission since 2011. Her latest project, *The Other Voice of Medical Consultations*, is a sociological analysis of emotion work in medical interpreting.

Thaddeus Metz is Professor of Philosophy at the University of Pretoria in South Africa, and is often credited for having helped develop life's meaning as a distinct field in Anglo-American philosophy over the past 20 years. Influential works of his on meaning in life include: 'The Concept of a Meaningful Life', *American Philosophical Quarterly* (2001); 'Recent Work on the Meaning of Life', *Ethics* (2002); and *Meaning in Life: An Analytic Study* (Oxford University Press, 2013). His most recent notable contribution is *God, Soul and the Meaning of Life* (Cambridge University Press, 2019).

Sven Nyholm is Assistant Professor of Philosophy at Utrecht University, a member of the Ethics Advisory Board of the Human Brain Project, and an Associate Editor of the journal *Science and Engineering Ethics*. Much of his recent work has been about the impact of emerging technologies on our opportunities to live meaningful lives, have meaningful relationships, and do meaningful work. He is particularly interested in how life in the contemporary world – with technologies like robots and artificial intelligence – affect traditional ideas about ethics and our human self-understanding. Nyholm's publications include *Revisiting Kant's Universal Law and Humanity Formulas* (De Gruyter, 2015) and *Humans and Robots: Ethics, Agency, and Anthropomorphism* (Rowman & Littlefield International,

Notes on the Contributors

2020). He is currently writing his third book, *This is Technology Ethics: An Introduction* (Wiley-Blackwell, 2022).

Thomas Schramme is Professor of Philosophy at the University of Liverpool. He has published widely in the philosophy of medicine and psychiatry, mainly on the concepts of health and disease. He also specialises in moral psychology and political philosophy. Most recently he has published the textbook *Theories of Health Justice* (Rowman & Littlefield Int.). He has edited several collections of essays, for instance *Being Amoral: Psychopathy and Moral Incapacity* (MIT Press, 2014) and the *Handbook of the Philosophy of Medicine* (co-edited with Steven Edwards; Springer 2017). His interest in the philosophy of death and meaning in life mainly stems from earlier work on suicide and theories of wellbeing.

Fredrik Svenaeus is Professor of Philosophy at the Centre for Studies in Practical Knowledge, Södertörn University, Sweden. His main research areas are philosophy of medicine, bioethics, medical humanities and philosophical anthropology. Current research projects focus on existential questions in association with various medical technologies and on the phenomenology of suffering in medicine and bioethics. He has published widely in these fields, the most recent book is *Phenomenological Bioethics: Medical Technologies, Human Suffering, and the Meaning of Being Alive* (Routledge, 2017).

James Stacey Taylor is a Professor of Philosophy at The College of New Jersey. He is the author of three books, all published by Routledge: *Stakes and Kidneys* (2005), *Practical Autonomy and Bioethics* (2010), and *Death, Posthumous Harm, and Bioethics* (2015). He is also the editor of two collections: *Personal Autonomy* (CUP, 2005) and *The Metaphysics and Ethics of Death* (OUP, 2013). He is currently working on two new manuscripts: *Bloody Morality* argues that it is ethically necessary to offer compensation to the donors of blood and blood products, while *The Bottle Imp and Other Unnatural Goods* develops a theoretical framework to identify the limits (both moral and otherwise) of markets.

Introduction: Death and Meaning

MICHAEL HAUSKELLER

Due to the Covid pandemic, the *Royal Institute of Philosophy Annual Conference 2020* had to be postponed and was eventually held online in July 2021. The conference, on which this volume is based, was meant to explore the connection between death and meaning (in life).

What motivated me to host a conference on that particular theme was initially my interest in the philosophical debate on human enhancement and the possibility and desirability (or undesirability) of radical life extension. Naturally, that debate is complex and touches on many different aspects of the human condition. However, there is one claim in particular that captured my attention because the question it raised struck me as being of fundamental importance for the entire discussion. It is the claim, occasionally made by transhumanists and other proponents of radical life extension, that *death undercuts meaning*, in the sense that as long as our lives will have to end someday, our lives cannot possibly be meaningful (More, 1990). Even religion with its promise of a life after death, it is alleged, can only ever achieve the illusion of meaning, but never the real thing. This is mainly because true meaningfulness cannot be derived from being part of somebody else's (in this case God's) plan, which supposedly has the inevitable effect of stifling a sense of our own personal value. Yet it is claimed that without such a sense of personal value our (individual) lives must lack true meaning, for what gives our lives (true) meaning is 'the continuation of the process of improvement and transformation of ourselves into ever higher forms' (More, 1990, p. 10). Since this process is understood as open-ended, it is clear that death, by bringing it to an end, destroys not only the meaning that any individual life can have up to the point of its termination, but the very possibility of meaning. If our lives can only have meaning if we can pursue 'our own expansion and progress without end' (More, 1990, p. 12), then life can only be meaningful if it never ends. That connection to meaning may well play a part in why death is often perceived and described as the greatest evil.[1] It is the greatest of evils not merely because it sets an end to

---

[1] See for instance Bostrom (2005), de Grey and Rae (2007).

doi:10.1017/S1358246121000205   © The Royal Institute of Philosophy and the contributors 2021
Royal Institute of Philosophy Supplement **90** 2021

our life, to our aspirations, hopes and plans,[2] or because it deprives us of all future pleasures (Bradley, 2004), but because it is, rightly or wrongly, believed to render all we do meaningless. For this reason, the argument goes, we need to do everything in our power to stop the presently inevitable decline of our bodies and find a way to extend human lifespan indefinitely.

This is certainly an extreme view because it assumes that nothing but a life without end can satisfy our desire for meaning. Simple life extension will not be enough. But even though it is an extreme view, it is not wholly implausible. It is easy to feel that if one day, however far in the future that may be, everything is over for us and, worse still, nothing will remain of what we have done and achieved in this life, then our hopes and aspirations are actually quite pointless. If there will come a day when nothing we ever did matters anymore, then it seems that it doesn't really matter already. It may matter *to us*, but not in itself. And that is what meaning (or at any rate the kind of meaning we desire) seems to require: that our lives have some objective and permanent significance (Hauskeller, 2017).

Yet it is of course far from obvious that our lives can only have such objective and permanent significance if they do not end. What we do in this life may well matter in the sense that it makes a difference, that it contributes to shaping the future of other people (so that the future would be different had we never existed or had we acted in a different way), and if it does matter in that sense, then it seems that it does so whether or not we will still be around to witness and appreciate it. Not all we do we do for ourselves, and only what we do for ourselves might retrospectively appear pointless when we die. The meaningfulness of what we do for others, however, remains unaffected by our own death, though it may plausibly be thought to be affected by *their* deaths. But perhaps that kind of meaningfulness is not what those who claim that there can be no meaning in a mortal life are talking about. So what kind of meaning is it exactly that is threatened by our mortality – if it is indeed threatened by it? Does it perhaps depend on a particular world view, so that, if we do not share that world view, we can easily do without it and find a different, but perfectly sufficient meaning-fulness in a mortal life? Or is it really the case that even if what we achieve in this life will not someday be lost to the world, if it will indeed make a lasting difference (presumably for the better), that

---

[2]   See Thomas Nagel's 'Death' in his (1970, pp. 1–10); Nussbaum (1994, updated edition 2009, pp. 207–210).

even then our life will have been meaningless if it has ended or is going to end?

It would seem, though, that the view that meaningfulness in life requires an infinite life span (or, even stronger, a de facto never-ending life) implies, rather implausibly, that no human that has ever lived has had a meaningful life. The common belief that some (mortal) lives are more meaningful than others (or are meaningful while others are not) would thus be mistaken because all (mortal) lives would in fact be equally meaningless. This raises the interesting (and puzzling) question whether meaningfulness is a quality that a life either does or does not have, or rather one that a life can have to a greater or lesser extent. If the latter, then we could concede that mortal lives can have some meaning, and at the same time insist that only an immortal life can be completely meaningful, or meaning-ful at the highest level. But does that even make sense? Are there indeed lower and higher orders of meaning (of which the higher orders are only accessible in an immortal life), or lives that are 100% meaningful and others that are only, say, 50% meaningful?

It has also been argued, by Leon Kass and others, that far from re-quiring immortality the meaningfulness of our lives, on the contrary, directly *depends* on our mortality (Kass, 2002; 2003; Nussbaum, 2013, pp. 225–32). According to this view, it is mortality that makes life matter in the first place. It is the knowledge that we will have to die, and not too far in the future, that makes things and people precious to us, that inspires love and a sense of beauty and the good, and that is ultimately the source of human dignity or self-worth. And without self-worth a meaningful life is not possible. Kass also stresses the importance of the natural life cycle, which must necessarily include a phase of rise, a peak, and a phase of decline if our lives are to have (a humanly understandable) meaning: 'A flourishing human life is not a life lived with an ageless body or untroubled soul, but rather a life lived in rhythmed time, mindful of time's limits, appreciative of each season and filled first of all with those intimate human relations that are ours only because we are born, age, replace ourselves, decline, and die – and know it' (Kass, 2003, p. 27). One might say that life, in order to have meaning, must have a 'significant shape' (Eagleton, 2008, p. 38), not unlike a piece of art or a dramatic performance, which no one would want to go on forever.

Others have objected that although life must indeed have a certain narrative shape to be truly meaningful, there is no reason why this shape should not extend beyond what is now the natural human life cycle and why we should not enjoy it indefinitely (Fischer, 2009). Even an immortal life can have a narrative structure and an aesthetically satisfying form if the events of one's life are suitably connected, if things do not just happen to us, but can plausibly be regarded as resulting from our own free decisions and as reflective of and informed by our own previous experience. Life is like a story (and has, for this reason, meaning or 'narrative value') if there is an intelligible connection between its parts, if it creates a kind of 'emotionally suffused' understanding. Although we would normally expect a story to have an ending, this is not necessary. 'Whereas the life as a whole could not be considered a narrative, the parts could be, and this would seem to render immortal life recognizably like our current human lives and also potentially desirable (in a distinctive way). The literary analogue for such a life is not the novel, but perhaps a collection of short stories' (Fischer, 2009, p. 158). What seems to matter most here is not really that our life has a certain definite shape, but that I can plausibly see myself as the author of my own life story, that my life reflects what I am (rather than the accidents of my existence).

However, this account is not without problems either, for it is not always clear to what extent the direction our lives take is a result of our own (free) agency rather than the result of dumb luck (good or bad), nor is it entirely clear why we should prefer the former. Usually it is an inextricable, happy mix of both. Moreover, we tend to be very good at making sense of what happens to us. Even something as unpredictable as a major win in the lottery can be easily integrated into our own personal life story and seen as resulting from our own agency. I can tell myself that I deserve this more than anyone else, that I was 'meant' to have all that money because of all the good that I can and will do with it, that I was the one who had the hunch that made me buy that lottery ticket on that particular day, which wouldn't have been possible if I hadn't made other decisions before, and so on and so forth. It is hard to imagine a life that is so accidental and causally unconnected that the one who lives it cannot possibly see it as a story unfolding.

Whether death interrupts that story or brings it to a satisfying conclusion probably depends on the kind of story it is. And whether or not we believe that our life story needs an ending to have a narrative value or be meaningful probably depends on what we think constitutes meaning. If we lay particular emphasis on agency and autonomy, if we insist on being the sole author of our own life story, then it is hard not to see death or rather mortality (the fact that we have to die sometime) as destructive of meaning. Yet if we are prepared to let things happen to us and to find meaning in what Michael Sandel calls 'the unbidden' (Sandel, 2007, pp. 45–47), then mortality (which makes death the ultimate unbidden) may well be regarded as, perhaps not necessary for, but certainly conducive to, a meaningful life. That would also solve the problem of purpose, which in an unending life would have to be permanently renewed, so that no final purpose could ever be achieved. And nothing would appear worth doing because we could always just as easily do it tomorrow (Baggini, 2002, pp. 28, 54). Thus there is the danger of postponing one's own life indefinitely instead of living it in the present.

Now obviously death, or more precisely mortality, cannot be both a precondition of a meaningful life and an obstacle to it. So which is it? In order to find out, we would have to answer a number of questions, starting with those concerning the meaning of meaning: What does actually constitute meaning? What do we mean when we talk about meaning? Are there different kinds of meaning (perhaps one for mortal lives and a different one for immortal lives)? Are there different degrees of meaning (so that a life can be more or less meaningful)? How does meaning relate to happiness or well-being? Is a happy life necessarily a meaningful life (and vice versa, a meaningful life necessarily a happy life, and if not, why should we then care about meaning in the first place?).

I am not going to try to answer all these questions here. Each of them would merit a separate investigation. However, let me say a bit more about the last point, the connection between meaningfulness and happiness, to provide some context for the question. After being ignored by psychologists for a long time, meaningfulness has only recently become a topic of interest in the discipline. Even after the paradigm shift to a 'positive' psychology that slowly took place in the second half of the twentieth century, which led researchers away from the study of mental illness and towards the study of positive emotions, meaningfulness was hardly ever regarded and treated as an essential aspect of psychological well-being. Instead, researchers remained largely preoccupied with happiness and its variants. However, recent studies have shown that there are important differences between happiness and meaningfulness (Baumeister, Vohs, Aaker and Garbinsky, 2013), as has also been argued by various philosophers (Wolf, 1997; Metz, 2009; Kauppinen, 2013). Whereas, for instance, happiness seems to depend on the extent to which our needs and wants are satisfied, such satisfaction does not affect our sense of living a meaningful life. Thus it seems entirely possible for someone to live a happy but meaningless life, or, at the opposite end, one that is unhappy, but highly meaningful. It appears that meaningfulness has a very strong temporal dimension connecting past, present and future (whereas happiness is firmly rooted in the present), is more linked to giving rather than taking, and is also positively related to the extent of our engagement both with loved ones and strangers (Debats, 1999), all of which suggests an expansion of personal identity into forms of social solidarity (or more generally into larger, trans-individual units). This expansion is likely to affect also people's attitude towards their own death: what it means for them, how much they fear it, and how appealing the prospect of radical life extension is for them.

However, although these considerations can certainly bring us closer to an adequate understanding of the distinct nature of meaning, there are still other questions to be answered before we can claim to have a clear picture. For instance, what is the difference between meaning and value? Can a life be meaningful, but bad, even morally obnoxious (as for instance Steven Luper 2014 suggests)? Can it be devoid of meaning, but still valuable and worth living? Does there have to be an objective dimension to meaning or is it just a question of giving ourselves a purpose in life, no matter how trivial that purpose may be? Is my life meaningful whenever I regard it as such or do I have to connect with something that is intrinsically valuable? Susan Wolf has claimed that 'meaning arises from loving objects worthy of love and engaging with them in a positive way' (Wolf, 2010, p. 8). Is she right?

In addition, there are other questions that pertain more directly to the immortalist position. In what way exactly can the fact that we have to die be thought to undercut meaning? Or is it the knowledge or belief that we have to die that has this effect, as some have argued (Swenson, 2000)? And if an immortal life is really necessary for meaning, why would a life after death, as it is promised by some religions, not be sufficient? What exactly is the difference between (real) meaning and the mere illusion of meaning? And if we don't really need immortality, but merely more time, then how much more time exactly do we need in order to render our lives meaningful? How much is enough?

Thaddeus Metz has pointed out that it is not enough to ask whether only an immortal life can be meaningful (Metz, 2003). We will also have to specify what *kind* of immortality is required for what kind of meaning, because we can imagine various forms of immortality and various forms of meaning. Thus an immortal life can be one that does not *have* to end (because of the absence of ageing or other forms of material deterioration, its general resilience, or its transferability to other substrates), a life that does not have any *de facto* end, a life that *cannot* end, a life that ends, but is then renewed, a life after death in some world-transcendent realm, a life in heaven, or a life in hell. Presumably it makes a difference for the meaningfulness of life which of these immortalities we are talking about. Likewise, it is quite possible some of these different immortalities are compatible with some understandings of meaningfulness, but not with others, so it needs to be clarified what kind of meaning, if any, requires what kind of immortality. However, to answer this question, it needs to be examined what exactly it is that those different forms of immortality would allow us to do or be that we would not be able to do or be without them, and how whatever that will turn out to be is related to a meaningful life.

Yet it is not only the position of the immortalist and radical life extensionist that is in need of clarification. The claim that death and a natural (that is currently normal) human lifespan are in fact prerequisites of a meaningful life also faces difficulties and gives rise to certain questions: Will life *inevitably* become meaningless at some point in an indefinitely extended life? Will it then really be too late to end one's life (in the sense described above)? Can we see the (intrinsic) value in things and other people (and indeed life itself) only if those things are fragile and bound to perish? Why should something eternal (even something that is by its very nature indestructible) not be seen as valuable in itself? (Isn't God highly valued by many people?) Why should it be necessary for life to have not only a beginning, but also an end? Would that imply that for the world as a whole to have meaning, it too will have to end one day? And why should we need a final purpose, instead of an open-ended sequence of purposes, to make our lives meaningful?

Now why is important to explore the issue and to answer all those questions? I can think of at least three good reasons. First, radical life extension is an area of scientific research that increasingly attracts interest and funding, as those working in the area, encouraged by the rapid development of new biotechnologies and recent progress in genetic manipulation, feel that they are close to 'rejuvenation breakthroughs that could reverse human aging in our lifetime' (de Grey and Rae, 2007, subtitle). This is supported by a growing number of philosophers and ethicists who argue that nothing is more important than that we figure out how to defeat ageing and death.[3] Yet we cannot properly assess the desirability of radical life extension without answering the above question about the exact connection between meaning and death, and how we answer it will make a considerable practical difference if meaningfulness is indeed a quality that a life must have in order to be regarded as good and worth living. Arguably a meaningless life is not worth living.

---

[3] See for instance Harris (2007).

Consequently, if death does indeed undercut meaning, then it can be plausibly argued that nothing is more urgent than to find a cure against it. If, on the other hand, meaning depends on having a limited human life span, then it seems that there is hardly anything more dangerous for humanity than radical life extension.

Second, radical life extension is central to the human enhancement project, which dominates the direction of technological development in the 21st century and whose main goal it is to increase human freedom and control and thus make human life better (or, which is considered the same, make us happier than it is currently possible for us to be). It is all about overcoming limitations. Death, however, can plausibly be regarded as the ultimate limitation, which explains its centrality to the enhancement project. But if that is so, then the above question about the connection between death and meaning can be given a wider scope covering the entire human enhancement project by rephrasing it as: do our *limitations* (that is, the fact that there are limits to what we can do and be) undercut meaning, or does, on the contrary, meaning depend on those limitations? Currently the debate about the pros and cons of radical human enhancement very much focuses on autonomy, happiness, and the requirements of human nature. This would have to change if meaningfulness could be shown to be an aspect that deserves to be taken seriously in its own right, alongside, or perhaps even trumping, autonomy, happiness and naturalness.

Third, investigating the connection between death and meaning potentially has wide-reaching consequences for the way we frame ethical problems arising from situations in which we have to deal with the dying and the dead, especially if it can be verified that meaningfulness and happiness are quite distinct from each other. The standard theoretical framework used to analyse ethically challenging situations in medicine is formed by the four principles proposed by Beauchamp and Childress (2009), namely autonomy, beneficence, non-maleficence and justice. This not only leaves no room for wider considerations relating to the notion of a good life that we seek to address through the concept of 'meaningfulness', but in doing so it also threatens to undermine the very applicability of those principles. What it means not to harm somebody (non-maleficence) and to act in someone's best interest (beneficence) cannot be properly understood independently of what is required to live a meaningful life (or die a meaningful death). Regarding, for instance, the ethical, still hotly debated problem of euthanasia, rather than asking whether people have the right to determine how, and when, they want to live and die (principle of autonomy), it might be more illuminating to ask how the ability to decide upon the manner and time of one's death contributes to a meaningful life.

University of Liverpool
m.hauskeller@liverpool.ac.uk

References

Julian Baggini, *What's It All About? Philosophy and the Meaning of Life* (London: Granta Books, 2002).

Roy F. Baumeister, Kathleen D. Vohs, Jennifer L. Aaker and Emily N. Garbinsky, 'Some Key Differences between a Happy Life and a Meaningful Life', *Journal of Positive Psychology* 8 (2013), 505–516.

Tom L. Beachamp, and James F. Childress, *Principles of Biomedical Ethics* (Oxford: Oxford University Press, 2009).

Nick Bostrom, 'The Fable of the Dragon Tyrant', *Journal of Medical Ethics* 31 (2005), 273–277.

Ben Bradley, 'When Is Death Bad for the One Who Dies?', *Nous* 38 (2004), 1–28.

Dominique Louis Debats, 'Sources of Meaning: An Investigation of Significant Commitments in Life', *Journal of Humanistic Psychology* 39 (1999), 30–57.

Aubrey de Grey and Michael Rae, *Ending Aging* (New York: St. Martin's Press, 2007).

Terry Eagleton, *The Meaning of Life* (Oxford: Oxford University Press, 2008).

John Martin Fischer, *Our Stories. Essays on Life, Death, and Free Will* (Oxford: Oxford University Press, 2009).

John Harris, *Enhancing Evolution. The Ethical Case for Making Better People* (Princeton and Oxford: Princeton University Press, 2007).

Michael Hauskeller, '"Something that Matters". The Religious Dimension of Moral Experience', *Revista Filosofia Aurora* 29/46 (2017), 309–323.

Leon Kass, 'L'Chaim and its Limits: Why not Immortality?', in: Leon Kass, Life, *Liberty and the Defence of Dignity: The Challenge for Bioethics* (San Francisco: Encounter, 2002), 257–274.

Leon Kass, 'Ageless Bodies, Happy Souls: Biotechnology and the Pursuit of Perfection', *The New Atlantis* 1 (2003), 9–28

Michael Hauskeller

Antti Kauppinen, 'Meaning and Happiness', *Philosophical Topics* 41/1 (2013), 161–185.

Steven Luper, 'Life's Meaning', in: *Cambridge Companion to Life and Death*, ed. Steven Luper (Cambridge: Cambridge University Press, 2014) 198–212.

Thaddeus Metz, 'The Immortality Requirement for Life's Meaning', *Ratio* 16 (2003), 161–177.

Thaddeus Metz, 'Happiness and Meaningfulness: Some Key Differences', in: *Philosophy and Happiness*, ed. Lisa Bortolotti (London: Palgrave Macmillan, 2009), 3–20.

Max More, 'Transhumanism. Towards a Futurist Philosophy', *Extropy* 6 (1990), 6–12.

Thomas Nagel, 'Death' in Thomas Nagel, *Mortal Questions* (New York: Cambridge University Press, 1970).

Martha Nussbaum, *The Therapy of Desire: Theory and Practice in Hellenistic Ethics* (Princeton: Princeton University Press, 1994, updated edition 2009).

Martha Nussbaum, 'The Damage of Death', in: *The Metaphysics and Ethics of Death*, edited by James Stacey Taylor (Oxford: Oxford University Press, 2013), 225–243.

Michael, Sandel, *The Case Against Perfection. Ethics in the Age of Genetic Engineering* (Cambridge, MA/London: Belknap Press, 2007).

David F. Swenson, 'The Transforming Power of Otherworldliness', in: *The Meaning of Life*, ed. E.D. Klemke, 2nd ed. (New York: Oxford University Press, 2000), 31–39.

Susan Wolf, 'Happiness and Meaning: Two Aspects of the Good Life', *Social Philosophy and Policy* 14 (1997): 207–225.

Susan Wolf, *Meaning in Life and Why It Matters* (Princeton and Oxford: Princeton University Press, 2010).

Meaning and Anti-Meaning in Life and What Happens After We Die

SVEN NYHOLM

Abstract
The absence of meaningfulness in life is meaninglessness. But what is the polar opposite of meaningfulness? In recent and ongoing work together with Stephen Campbell and Marcello di Paola respectively, I have explored what we dub 'anti-meaning': the negative counterpart of positive meaning in life. Here, I relate this idea of 'anti-meaningful' actions, activities, and projects to the topic of death, and in particular the deaths or suffering of those who will live after our own deaths. Connecting this idea of anti-meaning and what happens after our own deaths to recent work by Samuel Scheffler on what he calls 'the collective afterlife' and his four reasons to care about future generations, I argue that if we today make choices or have lifestyles that later lead to unnecessarily early deaths and otherwise avoidable suffering of people who will live after we have died, this robs our current choices and lifestyles of some of their meaning, perhaps even making them the opposite of meaningful in the long run.

On September 26 of 1983, a nuclear early-warning system in the Soviet Union mistakenly indicated that a missile had been launched from the United States, that it was heading in the direction of the Soviet Union, and that the missile had been followed by five more. According to Soviet military protocol, it was the job of the duty officer of the command center to report the indications of the satellite warning system to officers higher up on the chain of command. The responsible lieutenant colonel of the air defense forces – Stanislav Petrov – decided to disobey his orders, however. He did so because he deemed this to be a false alarm. If he had relayed the message generated by the missile detection system in accordance with protocol, this might have triggered a large-scale retaliatory nuclear attack by the Soviet Union on the United States. A nuclear war might have broken out. Because he refused to convey the warning created by the faulty detection system, Stanislav Petrov is thought to have helped to prevent a nuclear war, with all of the devastation that it might have caused to large parts of the world. Petrov died in 2016 at the age of 77. During his lifetime, he was not reprimanded by the Soviet powers for what he had done, but nor was he rewarded for it. He retired early, and at one point suffered a nervous

doi:10.1017/S1358246121000217

Sven Nyholm

breakdown. During his lifetime Petrov did not gain much recognition for what he had done. In fact, it was mostly unknown to the rest of the world. Now that this has become more widely reported, however, we can all rejoice in what Petrov did for the world in disobeying his orders and, thereby, helping to prevent a nuclear war (Aksenov, 2013; Chan, 2017). Even if it might not have led to happiness and public recognition for him during his lifetime, this can be seen as a very meaningful thing to have done in one's life.

Consider next a much more well-known person, who is still alive, but whose actions might also potentially benefit people living in the further future: the Swedish teenager Greta Thunberg, who for the last few years has worked tirelessly to raise awareness about the urgency of taking decisive action to try to prevent further human-created damage to the climate. It is too early to tell whether Thunberg's actions and campaigning to fight climate change will help to turn the tide and thereby benefit future generations, who are currently at great risk of having to live in a world with a severely damaged climate. However, if Thunberg indeed manages to play a key role in helping to create a better world for people of future generations, as she might do, then this would certainly be another example of actions in the here and now that could be thought to be tremendously meaningful because of the good they do for future generations.

Others, in contrast, do things during their lifetimes that might seem to be the opposite of positively meaningful because of the harm or risk of harm that they bring about to people living after they are gone. Early during his presidency, for example, the former US president Donald Trump was all but outright challenging Kim Jong Un of North Korea to a nuclear war, when Trump was appearing in front of the UN's assembly and threatening the 'little rocket man' with 'fire and fury'. That could potentially have provoked a nuclear war and led to destruction on a massive scale, which might have led to suffering for many people who would live after Trump would no longer be around. Such actions – as well as other examples of actions and policies carried out by the Trump administration, such as actions denying the reality of climate change and seemingly threatening the future of US democracy – can seem like they are not simply meaningless as in being devoid of meaning. Rather, they can seem like actions that are the polar opposite of positively meaningful. In terms of the legacy that is left behind to those who will come after him, former president Trump's legacy will strike many of his critics as in no way being a positively meaningful one, but as something better described in the opposite terms.

Meaning and Anti-Meaning in Life

These are three rather extreme cases. Most of us do not have opportunities to have such clear effects or possible impacts on those who will live after we are gone. But these examples nevertheless help to illustrate the topic I will discuss in this paper: namely, the question of whether what happens after we are dead might help to make what we do in our lives more or less meaningful. I will be particularly interested in whether harm that we might do to future generations of people who will exist after we are dead might be thought to bring what I will call 'anti-meaning' (viz. the polar opposite of positive meaning) into our lives. The suggestion I will be discussing is that yes, indeed, what happens after we die – especially if it depends on our actions, projects, or lifestyles – might detract from the positive meaning of what we do and how we live our lives.

Discussions about meaning in life and its relation to death usually take a different perspective. They are usually about whether the fact that we will all die should be taken to threaten the possibility of living a meaningful life. Some philosophers – e.g., some transhumanists[1] – have argued that because we will ultimately all die, nothing we do in life can be truly meaningful, since it will all come to an end. Other philosophers – such as Leon Kass[2], to pick just one example – have argued that the fact that we will die and that our time on Earth is limited is better viewed as something that can help to make what we do with our lives much more meaningful than it would be if our lives just went on and on and we never died. On this second way of seeing things, our mortality creates a certain urgency to everything we do, and helps to make each day we are alive and each project we undertake matter more. As I noted above, in contrast, I am here going to connect meaning in life and death in a very different way: I will discuss whether what happens after we are dead might affect how meaningful what we do during our lives can and should be thought to be. I will do so in a slightly gloomy way by focusing, as also mentioned above, on how bad things that happen after we are dead might threaten the meaningfulness of what we do during our lives.

The discussion below divides into the following sections. First I will briefly say a little more about meaningfulness in life and the idea of 'anti-meaning', i.e. the idea of the polar opposite of positive meaning in life, a topic I have written about before together with Stephen Campbell and, more recently, Marcello di Paola

---

[1] See, for example, More (1990).
[2] See Kass (2017).

Sven Nyholm

(section 1).[3] Next I will bring up some ideas that might already have come to mind to some readers, namely, Samuel Scheffler's work on what he calls the 'afterlife conjecture' (Scheffler, 2011; 2018). I will highlight some key features of Scheffler's fascinating ideas about the importance of what happens after our deaths for what matters to us in our lives, and I will relate those ideas to some of the ideas my co-authors and I have discussed regarding what we call 'anti-meaningful' actions or activities (sections 2 and 3). This will lead me to my main claim, which is that our effects on people who live after we are gone can impact the meaningfulness of what we do during our lives, including in negative ways in case our activities negatively affect those who come after us. I will briefly suggest some examples, like issues to do with climate change, potentially devastating wars and other conflicts, as well as risks related to powerful AI technologies (section 4). Next, I will very briefly discuss some philosophical distinctions I think we should pay attention to when we reflect on these kinds of ideas (section 5), and then I will end with a concluding discussion (section 6).

1. The Notion of Anti-Meaningful Actions and Activities

Shelly Kagan has an interesting article in which he discusses what he calls 'ill-being' (Kagan, 2015). By this Kagan means the opposite of well-being. For example, if one accepts a hedonistic theory of well-being, on which well-being consists in experiencing pleasure or happiness, ill-being would amount to pain and suffering. On a preference satisfaction theory of well-being, ill-being would consist in preference frustration. In the same way, some authors writing about meaningfulness in life have found it useful to not only distinguish positive meaningfulness from meaninglessness (viz. the absence of meaningfulness), but to also distinguish meaningfulness from its polar opposite.

Different philosophers who have been interested in this idea have used different terms to pick out the same general notion. Typically, they use examples to make this idea intuitively plausible to readers. Thaddeus Metz, for example, talks about what he calls 'anti-matter'. To make this idea seem intuitive, Metz asks his readers to contemplate the following:

---

[3]   See Campbell and Nyholm (2015), Nyholm and Campbell (in press) and di Paola and Nyholm (manuscript).

14

Consider a life composed of actions such as killing one's spouse for the insurance money or blowing up the Sphinx for fun. Does this life merely lack meaning or does it contain antimatter? Is it more akin to an impoverished life, one that lacks money, or to an unhappy life, one that contains misery? (Metz, 2002, pp. 806–807)

Metz expects us to think that such a life is more like the second of the two options: it is more like an unhappy life that contains misery than a life lacking in wealth.

Similarly, Iddo Landau discusses the importance of ethics and moral considerations for meaning. According to Landau, if some activity is immoral, this not only means that it may lack positive meaning. It may be the 'inverse' of meaningful. Take, as an example, Adolf Hitler's role in the mass murder of millions of people and other crimes against humanity during World War II. Landau writes:

Hitler's life is not merely meaningless, a life in which meaning is absent, but instead a life in which the converse of meaning is present. To use an arithmetic analogy, the meaningfulness of lives such as Hitler had should not be evaluated at around zero or even as simply zero, but in negative numbers. The scale of meaning of life should be conceived as stretching into that negative sphere as well. (Landau, 2011, p. 317)

Ingmar Persson and Julian Savulescu, in turn, use the phrase 'bad meaning' to refer to a similar idea (Persson and Savulescu, 2019). They suggest that, in general, we should understand meaningfulness in a person's life in terms of what the person intentionally does and what effects the person intentionally produces. If the effects of a person's intentional actions are good, then this gives good meaning to the person's life. In contrast, if what a person intentionally does has negative consequences, then this gives bad meaning to the person's life.

Together with Stephen Campbell, and more recently also with Marcello di Paola, I have written about this topic as well.[4] We have used the term 'anti-meaning'. Our main claim in these papers is that, as citizens of the modern world, it is very hard for most of us not to participate in activities that, in some fashion or other, adversely impact present or future people and/or serve to cement various forms

---

[4]   Campbell & Nyholm (2015), Nyholm & Campbell (in press), Di Paola & Nyholm, (manuscript).

of social injustice. This is not to say that ordinary people's lives are always or even typically anti-meaningful on the whole. Rather, the point is that various aspects of participating in modern society can serve to counteract, if not undermine, the meaningfulness of some aspects of our lives or lifestyles.

2. Scheffler on the Afterlife

In my discussion about anti-meaning in this paper, I am particularly interested in whether what happens after we die might make some of the things we do while we are alive less meaningful or perhaps even to some extent anti-meaningful. Readers familiar with Samuel Scheffler's recent work (Scheffler 2011; 2018) might be reminded of it here, and I am indeed also strongly influenced by Scheffler in my thinking about this. Scheffler uses the term 'the afterlife' to refer to what happens to people who live after we ourselves die. And he uses the following types of scenarios to motivate what he calls the 'afterlife conjecture' regarding the importance of the afterlife:

The Asteroid Scenario: a gigantic asteroid is traveling through space towards the planet Earth. It is a little bit like in the motion picture *Armageddon*, in which an asteroid is traveling towards Earth and the only way to save the planet is to blow up the asteroid. In the film, Bruce Willis portrays a hero who is able to destroy the asteroid and save everyone. In Scheffler's scenario, there is an asteroid approaching, but no Bruce Willis-type of hero, and we know that everyone will soon die because the world will be hit by the enormous asteroid. So, there is no future for human life on Earth.

The infertility scenario: in a second, less violent scenario, there is no giant asteroid that is about to dramatically collide with Earth and thereby immediately kill everyone. Rather, just like in the novelist P.D. James's book *The Children of Men*, everyone on Earth has been unable to conceive any children for the last 25 years. Otherwise, everyone is apparently healthy and appears to be living out a normal lifespan. Since nobody is having any new children, the world's population will eventually die, and there will be no future people coming after us. We are the last generation – not because of a nuclear war or because of an explosion killing everyone in one go – but rather because we simply are no longer having any children.

Scheffler expects us to react with horror and dismay, or at least sadness and a sense of resignation, when we contemplate these kinds of scenarios. His 'afterlife conjecture' is that what happens to other people after we ourselves die matters much more to us than we may know. Interestingly, that is the sort of language Scheffler uses when he talks about this idea. He talks about how what happens to people after we die 'matters' to us more than we perhaps realize. He says that we 'care' about this. And he says that 'our capacity to value things' here and now depends on our thinking that there will be an afterlife after we are gone. We can accept, Scheffler thinks, that we ourselves will die. But we would find it much harder to accept a situation where there is no afterlife, viz. when there is nobody who lives after us in the future.

Strikingly, Scheffler does not use the language of what is 'meaningful' in life when he talks about this topic. Instead, he talks primarily, as just noted, about what is valuable to us, what we care about, or what matters to us. But it seems like it would have been a natural choice of terminology to put things in terms of what is meaningful to us, or what helps to make our current activities meaningful to us. Perhaps this is just a matter of what terminology Scheffler is comfortable with or prefers to use, and what fits best with the terminology of a lot of his previous work, for instance on what is involved in valuing something.[5] At any rate, it appears very intuitive to interpret what Scheffler is talking about in terms of what helps to give meaning to what we do in our lives.

When it comes to what Scheffler is aiming to do, he presents his project as being one of finding reasons to care about future generations that are (i) non-experiential, (ii) non-utilitarian, and (iii) personal in nature. Since we care about what happens to people in the future after we die, and we will have no experiences of the future after we die, our reasons for caring must be of a non-experiential kind, Scheffler argues. He is also trying, he says, to present an alternative to the sort of broadly utilitarian or altruistic reasons for caring about future generations that Derek Parfit discusses in his monumental last part of *Reasons and Persons* (Parfit, 1984). The reasons Parfit discusses to care about future generations are related to how we can benefit future generations – but Scheffler is interested in different kinds of reasons, of a non-utilitarian character. Lastly, Scheffler is trying to steer away from impersonal concern with the future and towards more personal reasons for concern, which have to do with things that we care deeply about in our own lives. Another thing

[5]   E.g. Scheffler (2010).

Sven Nyholm

that could be noted here is that 'reasons' here seems to refer to what Bernard Williams has famously called 'internal reasons' (Williams, 1979). That is to say, the reasons Scheffler is concerned with are reasons that derive from what we care deeply about, as opposed to 'external reasons' that are not grounded in our own internal cares and concerns. Scheffler does not himself explicitly pledge allegiance to a Williams-inspired internalism about reasons. But he nevertheless bases his whole line of argument on attempts to show what we care about deep down, whether or not it is immediately obvious to us. That is the hallmark of an internal conception of reasons for action of the sort Williams has articulated.

In his second book on this topic, Scheffler goes on to articulate four such reasons to 'worry about future generations' (Scheffler, 2018). I will not discuss them in great detail here, but just quickly explain what they are. They are:

1: *Reasons of interest:* many of our projects that we take an interest in, Scheffler thinks, assume that others will carry on these projects after we are gone. If we, for example, are doing research about how to cure cancer (to use one of Scheffler's examples), or if we are building bridges or other things it takes a long time to complete, then part of what we implicitly think gives value to these projects is that others will carry on these projects or benefit from what we do in the future, including after we are gone.

2: *Love of humanity:* When we are sad or dismayed about the prospect of their being no future generations, this shows, Scheffler thinks, that we have a deep 'love of humanity'. We love humanity and therefore we would find it very sad and unfortunate if humanity would die out soon and there would be no humans shortly after we are dead. It is comforting to us, Scheffler thinks, that people will still be there after we are gone, because we harbor a deep love of humanity.

3: *Reasons of value:* It matters to us, Scheffler thinks, that there are people around in the future who can value the sorts of things that we value. There can be no value without valuers, as Scheffler sees things. And so, in order for the future to be a future of value, there need to be human beings – or other valuing beings – around who can value things and thereby carry on our traditions of valuing certain things or kinds of things.

4: *Reasons of reciprocity:* Lastly, since our lives derive some of their value from the existence of an afterlife in Scheffler's sense, it is not only the case that future generations can benefit from what we do for them. We can and do also benefit from their existence – e.g. they can carry on projects that we have an interest in and they can continue valuing things we find important. Therefore, it is mutually beneficial for us and future generations that we exist and that they are able to exist as well.

Like I said, I am not going to discuss in any great detail the reasons named by Scheffler for why we worry about future generations. Hopefully the short summaries of the reasons Scheffler articulates that are provided above are clear enough for the reader to get a sense of the sorts of concerns that Scheffler points towards. What I want to do here rather than discuss further Scheffler's own suggested reasons is to suggest that we should add a fifth general reason for caring about what happens to future generations. We should add what might be called a *reason having to do with meaningfulness*. That is to say, my suggestion is that what happens to other people after we are already dead might help to make our own lives more or less meaningful. Thus, a further reason to care about future generations – in addition to those formulated by Scheffler – is a reason related to how future generations can help to make our own lives more or less meaningful. Why? In short, this is because meaningfulness in life has to do, among other things, with how what we do fits into a larger picture.

In other words, as I see things, things we do in life get their meaning, in part, from the larger context(s) of which they are part. This can be understood in different ways. For example, Antti Kauppinen has discussed a 'narrative' theory of meaningfulness in some of his work, on which meaning in life partly depends on the overall narrative of our lives.[6] On another view – defended by Ben Bramble – meaning in life has to do with whether we live in ways that produce good overall consequences (Bramble, 2015). I do not here mean to necessarily commit myself to one or the other of these views, but I think they are both on to something true about how it makes sense to think about meaningfulness: namely, to repeat, that it has to do with, among other things, how what we do fits into a larger picture.[7]

[6]   E.g. Kauppinen (2012).
[7]   In general I adhere to Susan Wolf's 'hybrid' theory of meaning in life, whereby meaning in life is achieved when we are passionate about things that have a non-subjective value. This view has both a 'subjective' and 'objective' component. The latter can plausibly be related to the idea of doing things

Sven Nyholm

To briefly summarize the main claims of this section: firstly, although Scheffler himself uses other terminology when he discusses how it matters to us what happens to other people after we are gone, I suggest that what Scheffler is talking about can very plausibly be translated into claims about what makes a difference to how meaningful our lives are. Secondly, in addition to the sorts of personal reasons that Scheffler articulates for caring about what happens to future generations – reasons of interest, love of humanity, reasons of value, and reasons of reciprocity – we should also include reasons of meaningfulness in our accounts of what different kinds of reasons we have for caring about people in the future.

3. Anti-Meaning and Activities that Harm – or Risk Harm to – Future Generations

Let's return again to the two scenarios from Scheffler's discussion that I outlined above: the asteroid scenario and the infertility scenario. In the former, there will be no people in the near future because an asteroid is about to collide with Earth and kill everyone. In the latter, there will be no people in the near future because all people have become infertile through no fault of our own. As noted above, Scheffler thinks that such scenarios pose a threat to our capacities to find value in the activities we engage in now, the idea being that our capacity to find value in our activities importantly depends on our assumption that others will come after us. If we follow the suggestion I made above and we think about these scenarios and Scheffler's 'afterlife conjecture' in terms of the concept of meaningfulness, the category related to meaningful that suggests itself is that of meaninglessness. That is, the way that Scheffler describes the reactions he thinks most people would have – and would justifiably have – to the scenarios he discusses seems to suggest that he is talking about reactions that indicate that we would view many of our activities as losing their meaning or becoming less meaningful if there is no 'afterlife' in Scheffler's sense.

Notably, the scenarios Scheffler primarily discusses are ones in which it is not human agency that lies behind the discontinuation of human life on Earth. In one scenario, there will be no more human life because an asteroid is about to kill everyone. In the

---

that are part of something 'bigger than us', as Wolf and many others put things. See Wolf (2010).

other, there will be no more human life because people have become infertile through no fault of their own. In neither scenario is it human agency – viz. anything that we have done – that has brought about the bad outcome that Scheffler thinks we will view as sad or disheartening. It is of great interest in this context, however, to also consider scenarios in which the reason why the future will have certain bad features is because of human agency. I therefore think that we should also consider scenarios such as these two broad kinds:

> *Scenarios involving what Ingmar Persson and Julian Savulescu (2012) call 'ultimate harm' that is caused by what people do who live now*: there is something that we do in the present that prevents the future possibility of human life on Earth (or any other form of life that we find highly important).

> *Scenarios that involve what we might call 'irreparable harm' that is caused by what people do who live now:* there is something that we now do that makes life for people living after us very unpleasant, risky, or bad in other highly significant ways.

Again, what makes these two kinds of scenarios radically different from the ones Scheffler focuses on is that in these two broad kinds of scenarios, the reason why there is either ultimate harm (no possibility of life on Earth) or irreparable harm (greatly decreased quality of life) is that people who live now act in some way, have certain forms of lifestyles, or in other ways cause these outcomes through our human agency.

We can here imagine various different kinds of ways in which these kinds of scenarios could come about. The literature about so-called existential risks is a great source of possible ways in which these scenarios could come about.[8] For example, we can think of human-created climate change and excessive resource-depletion caused by the ways in which we live in the modern world. We can imagine cases in which we elect leaders who start or provoke nuclear wars. Or we can imagine scenarios in which powerful artificial intelligence (AI) systems or other technologies get out of hand and cause great damage.

Some of these scenarios might also be related to each other. For example, Aimee van Wynsberghe, Mark Coeckelbergh, and others argue that many current AI technologies are highly environmentally unsustainable by having a very big carbon footprint.[9] Another comment about risk of ultimate or irreparable harm caused by

---

[8] See, for instance, Ord (2020).
[9] See van Wynsberghe (2021) and Coeckelbergh (2021).

powerful AI that we may lose control over: one possible scenario is the sort discussed by Nick Bostrom in his (2014) book *Superintelligence*, i.e. where AI systems become much more intelligent than human beings but where the goals they have been given are most easily achieved by them in ways that pose existential risks to human beings. However, this is not the only kind of out-of-control AI systems that we need to worry about and that could do great damage to us now or to people living after we are gone. So long as an AI system gets out of control and is powerful enough, it might cause a great deal of damage, even if the system is by no means super-intelligent. Consider again, for example, the nuclear attack detection system that generated the false alarm discussed in the Stanislav Petrov example in the introduction. That was by no means a super-intelligent AI system. However, if Petrov had followed the recommendation from the detection system and warned his superiors of an on-coming (but actually non-existent) American nuclear attack on the Soviet Union, this might potentially have created a devastating nuclear war. The philosophically inclined computer scientist Roman Yampolskiy describes many such potential AI risk scenarios in his work that do not involve any superintelligence.[10]

If these kinds of scenarios occur – i.e. we do certain things now that make things extremely bad for people living after we are gone, or that make it impossible for there to be any more people after we are gone – what categories related to meaningfulness then suggest themselves? Here I want to submit that it is not only meaninglessness that seems to be the right category to think in terms of. That is, our doing things that cause ultimate or irreparable harm to future generations does not only seem to be devoid of positive meaning. Rather, the category of 'anti-meaning' seems to suggests itself as a better category to use here. In other words, if people living after we are gone will have it very bad or will not be able to live at all because of what we do now, then what we do now can appear to become the opposite of meaningful for this reason, at least when considered in light of these future effects of what we do now. In other words, the bad effects our current lifestyles, projects or choices might have on other people who will or would live after we die can add a dimension of anti-meaning to the things we do now while we are alive. When we put the effects of what we do now into the larger perspective of how it will affect those who come after us, this could give what we do a very positive meaning, but it

---

[10]   See, for example, Yampolskiy (2018).

could also give a negative meaning – or anti-meaning – to what we do now.

4. Relevant Distinctions Related to Potentially Anti-Meaningful Aspects of Our Lifestyles and Projects

When we think about whether what happens after we die – and especially when we think about what happens after we die because of what we do now – there are some philosophical distinctions that might help to make it easier to specify what our conclusions about this issue should be when it comes to meaningfulness and anti-meaningfulness in life. I will not discuss all possible distinctions that might be helpful here, but simply focus on a sub-set I find particularly relevant.

Firstly, Dale Jamieson and Marcello di Paola (2016) draw an interesting distinction between what they call the 'episodic' and 'systemic' life of our actions and activities. The episodic aspects of our actions are those that are most immediately obvious to us, and the most immediate effects of our actions. For example, when driving a car, what is obvious to us might be the fact that it gets us quickly to the destination we want to go to. But the act of driving cars is part of a practice that pollutes the climate and has various other effects that are problematic in nature, potentially both for current and future generations. Some acts are in themselves perfectly harmless – e.g. taking a long warm shower – but might be part of a system that uses up resources in an unsustainable way – e.g. lots of people taking lots of long warm showers.

This distinction is not exactly the same as but similar to the distinction between the short-term effects and the long-term effects of our actions, lifestyles, or projects. Again, the short-term effects may be relatively harmless. But the long-term effects of having lots of people engage in some lifestyle, use some technology, or having certain projects might have very bad effects, both for the people currently living and potentially also for future generations not yet living.

This, in turn, can be related to the distinction between foreseen (or perhaps unforeseen), but definitely unintended or at least not directly aimed-at consequences or side effects of our activities, lifestyles, or projects. Insofar as we live our lives in ways – or have projects – that might make things worse for people living after we are gone, this is highly likely to be unintended or at the very least not a directly aimed-at effect of how we conduct ourselves. Of course, there are some people who do wish to harm current and future people. For example, there are doomsday cults with leaders who devise plans for how to bring about the end of the world. But most people – the vast majority of people – are not like that. When we do things that bring harm to others (whether people in the present or people in the future), these are typically unintended side effects of what we are doing.

This, to bring up one last distinction, relates to risks associated with what we are doing, as opposed to the potential benefits or goods we are seeking to bring about. When we harm other people (present people or future people), this is often because we were doing something risky while pursuing some potential benefit or good that itself might not be harmful to others or that carries with it risks of harm to others as a side effect of achieving the good or benefit for ourselves.

With these distinctions drawn and concepts highlighted, I can now restate the point I was making towards the end of the previous section in somewhat more precise terms. My claim is that if our current ways of living/our projects have side effects whereby bad outcomes occur after our deaths (e.g. devastating climate change or AI disasters), then this can make our ways of living/projects less meaningful, to the point that they might partly become the opposite of meaningful ('anti-meaningful'), at least to some extent. Some activities (e.g. trying to develop certain AI technologies) might be meaningful in the short term (because of their potential to do good), but anti-meaningful in the long run (e.g. because they are highly unsustainable and risk leading to devastating crises in the further future). By imposing great risks on people who will live after we are dead, we are in effect risking to make our own activities less meaningful.

In suggesting this claim, I am assuming the following three things about meaningfulness in general. Firstly, I am assuming, as noted above, that meaningfulness – as well as anti-meaningfulness – has to do with how our activities fit into a larger picture. Secondly, I am assuming that whether our actions turn out to be meaningful or anti-meaningful depends on what actual effects our activities end up having. Thirdly, I am taking it that having good intentions is not enough, so to speak, in order for our actions and activities to end up being meaningful and avoid being anti-meaningful. Kantians are right, as I see things, that whether we have a good will and are good people depends on what our intentions are and what we are trying to do. If we act with the best of intentions and with good motives, then we are good people with a good will even if things do not turn out in a good way. But when it comes to meaningfulness, I am taking it, things are different. When it comes to this issue, whether what we are doing and how we are living our lives can be seen as positively meaningful or ends up being partly anti-meaningful does depend on how things ultimately turn out.

5. Concluding Discussion

Above, I started with the example of Stanislav Petrov and how he might have 'saved the world' when he disobeyed Soviet protocol by refusing to relay the information from the satellite detection system that seemed to indicate that the United States had launched a nuclear attack on the Soviet Union. This, I suggested, can be seen as a tremendously meaningful thing to have done, since so many people potentially benefited from this action, since this might very well have prevented an all-out nuclear war. Let us suppose now, instead, that Petrov had followed his orders, that this might have triggered a nuclear war, and that this would have led to damage on a massive scale for the people who lived after Petrov and those around him were gone. And let us consider the people who had worked to develop the faulty nuclear attack detection system. Their intentions might have been good. But they would have developed a technology that led to suffering on a large scale both during their lifetimes and after their lifetimes, since a large-scale nuclear war is likely to cause damage that several generations might suffer from. In this counterfactual version of the example, what the engineers who developed this technology did, and what Petrov in this version of the story did when he passed on the information generated by the technology, can be seen as being the opposite of positively meaningful. It can be seen as anti-meaningful.

The worry I have been trying to formulate in this paper is that we – or some of us – might potentially be doing similar things. People developing powerful AI technologies might potentially be developing technologies that people will lose control over and that might lead to damage and destruction on a large scale. This might not be because the AI technologies are 'super-intelligent', as noted above, but simply because they are highly unsustainable from an environmental point of view. Or it might be because they lead people to act in destructive ways, like in the example above with the counterfactual story about how things might have gone in 1983 in the Stanislav Petrov case. To use a less dramatic example: the fact that we are using up the world's resources at an alarming rate, and that we are doing so while polluting the climate, might also lead to very harmful effects for future generations, who will then need to suffer greatly after we are dead because of how we lived our lives while we were alive. This can be seen as detracting from the positive meaning of how we live our lives in the modern world, and as introducing – at least to some extent – the polar opposite of positive meaning into our lives in the modern world.

This can seem more likely to be the case when it comes to people who have a lot of influence over others, and who can therefore do more harm to current and future generations. To go back to another one of the opening examples: somebody like the former US president Donald Trump might have succeeded in convincing lots of people that climate change is 'fake news'. While the actions of somebody like Greta Thunberg might help to inspire many people to live in more sustainable ways, the actions of somebody like Trump might discourage many people from trying to live their lives in more sustainable ways. The actions of a Greta Thunberg can seem highly meaningful in a positive sense with respect to how they might impact people who live after she is no longer around, while the actions of a Donald Trump are likely to end up being the opposite of positively meaningful – or anti-meaningful – in the long run, because of the harm they might cause to people who will live after Trump is no longer alive. Most of us do not have the kind of influence that Thunberg and Trump have. So, we might not have opportunities to do meaningful things during our lives whose positive meaningfulness depends on great benefits enjoyed by those who are here after we are gone nor opportunities to do things that are strongly anti-meaningful because of great harms to those who will live after we are gone. However, by participating in the modern world – with all that this means in terms of depleting resources and causing climate change through the systemic effects of our actions and activities – we all face the risk of introducing anti-meaningfulness or negative meaning into our lives because of the ways in which we live our lives now will affect those who will live after we are no longer around.[11]

Let us now also briefly return to the relation between what I have been suggesting and the ideas in Samuel Scheffler's fascinating books about what he calls the 'afterlife' in which he discusses 'why to worry

---

[11]   Some readers might be willing to grant that actions and activities that might harm future generations can be viewed as potentially being anti-meaningful to some extent in theory, but wonder why exactly this should be taken to matter in practice. In other words, why care about anti-meaning? I do not have enough space to discuss that important issue here, but I discuss it in some detail in Campbell & Nyholm (2015), Nyholm & Campbell (in press) and Di Paola & Nyholm (manuscript).

about future generations'. How does what I have suggested above contrast and compare with what Scheffler puts forward in his work on this topic?

Firstly, as noted above, Scheffler does not put his claims in terms of what is meaningful or anti-meaningful. Rather, Scheffler is discussing what we 'care' about, what 'matters' to us, and what we 'value'. Of course, this does not mean that there is any necessarily very sharp distinction to be drawn between what Scheffler is interested in and what I have been interested in above. What we care about, what matters to us, and what we value are very closely tied to what appears meaningful to us or, more generally, to meaningfulness in life.

Secondly, I noted above that when Scheffler articulates reasons to care about future generations, he seems to be trying to identify what Bernard Williams calls 'internal reasons' to care about future generations. That is, Scheffler is articulating reasons that are closely – if not essentially – tied to our cares and concerns. This is contrasted with 'external reasons', which are reasons that we might be thought to have for doing or caring about things, which are wholly independent of what we actually do care about or would care about in certain counterfactual circumstances. It might be asked whether what I have been talking about – viz. reasons to care about future generations related to meaningfulness in our own lives – should also be viewed as a form of 'internal reasons' tied to what we already care about, or whether they can also be interpreted as 'external reasons' that we have whether or not we do care. Regarding this issue, I intend my discussion above to be neutral with respect to whether we should think of reasons as being 'internal' or 'external' in Williams' senses. That is to say, while Scheffler seems, at least as I am reading him, to be particularly interested in identifying internal reasons to worry about future generations, the claims I have formulated above are not meant to necessarily be of that nature. I want to side-step the issue of how we should understand normative reasons. The only thing I need for my purposes is the premise that we can make value judgments about whether the effects of our current actions and activities on future generations are good or bad. How exactly this is to be interpreted from a more meta-philosophical point of view I wish to leave open here.

A third comment about the relation between what I have been saying above and what Scheffler says in his work: when I suggested above that in addition to the four reasons to care about future generations that Scheffler discusses, we should also add a fifth reason related to meaningfulness, I did not mean to suggest that such a further reason would be completely independent of or different from the four reasons to worry about future generations that Scheffler articulates. As a reminder, Scheffler's reasons are reasons of interest, love of humanity, reasons of value, and reasons of reciprocity. These can in different ways be seen as being related to how meaningful our actions and activities are. And so the idea I am suggesting – viz. that what happens to future generations because of what we do matters to how meaningful our actions and activities in the here and now are – can be seen as a form of or alternative formulation of one or more of the reasons Scheffler has articulated. Or it might be seen as a type of corollary of Scheffler's conclusions about what reasons we have to care about what happens to future generations. The statement that our actions and activities might have good or bad effects on people who live after we are gone and that this might make those actions and activities more or less meaningful – and that this gives us a reason to care about what happens to future generations – fits neatly with the reasons to worry about future generations that Scheffler articulates, and is an alternative way of explaining the importance of the kinds of reasons that he puts forward.

A fourth and last comment about the relation between Scheffler's discussion and mine: as I noted above, but as bears repeating, what Scheffler is interested in is simply the possibility that there will be no future generations soon after we are dead and the question of what this means for us. To bring this out, Scheffler focuses particularly on scenarios where it is not our fault that there will be no future generations. In contrast, I have been particularly interested in scenarios in which what we do here and now significantly impacts the lives of those who will live after we are gone. I have joined Scheffler in partly being interested in scenarios in which there are no more future people shortly after we are dead (e.g. because we start a massive nuclear war), but there too I have been primarily interested in such cases where this depends on what we do. And I have also been interested in cases in which there will be people living after we are dead but where the quality of life of those people has been significantly impacted – perhaps in a bad way – because of how we live our lives here and now. Scheffler is more narrowly interested in whether the mere existence or non-existence of future generations should be taken to matter to us now. My concern has been primarily with the impact of our actions and activities on people who live after we are gone – both in terms of whether our actions might make it impossible for there to be many more future generations and in terms of whether we might have good or bad effects on the lives of people who are able to live after we are gone. This is a key difference between my focus above and Scheffler's focus in his work.

Let me lastly also note that I do not mean to suggest that meaning and anti-meaning in life only or even primarily depends on what happens after we are dead. Just like what we do while we are alive can be very meaningful because of what happens while we are still alive, what we do while we are alive can be, in certain respects, anti-meaningful because of what happens while we are still alive. None of what I have discussed above has been meant to suggest otherwise. I am in agreement with authors like Thaddeus Metz, Iddo Landau, and others that destructive and immoral actions and activities, for example, are among the things that might be anti-meaningful because of the negative value of these actions and activities in the here and now. Although my focus in this paper has been on how what happens after our deaths might have positive or negative impacts on how meaningful our activities turn out to be in the long run, this is not to deny that we can and should also concern ourselves with how meaningful our activities are in the short run. Both issues are very important. But the one I have focused on deserves more attention, which is why I have highlighted it in this paper.[12]

Utrecht University
s.r.nyholm@uu.nl

References

Pavel Aksenov, 'Stanislav Petrov: The Man who May have Saved the World', *BBC News*, (26 September 2013), https://www.bbc.com/news/world-europe-24280831 (accessed on July 30, 2021).

Nick Bostrom, *Superintelligence* (Oxford: Oxford University Press, 2014).

Ben Bramble, 'Consequentialism about Meaning in Life', *Utilitas* 27 (2015), 445–459.

[12] For helpful feedback on this material, many thanks to Michael Hauskeller and the participants of his 'Meaning in Life and the Knowledge of Death' *Royal Institute of Philosophy* annual conference, especially Frances Kamm and Antti Kauppinen. My work on this article is part of the research program Ethics of Socially Disruptive Technologies, which is funded through the Gravitation program of the Dutch Ministry of Education, Culture, and Science and the Netherlands Organization for Scientific Research (NWO grant number 024.004.031).

Sven Nyholm

Stephen Campbell and Sven Nyholm, 'Anti-Meaning and Why It Matters', *Journal of the American Philosophical Association* 1 (2015), 694–711.

Sewell Chan, 'Stanislav Petrov, Soviet Officer Who Helped Avert Nuclear War, Is Dead at 77', *New York Times*, (18 September 2017), https://www.nytimes.com/2017/09/18/world/europe/stanislav-petrov-nuclear-war-dead.html (accessed on July 30, 2021).

Mark Coeckelbergh, *Green Leviathan or the Poetics of Political Liberty: Navigating Freedom in the Age of Climate Change and Artificial Intelligence*, (London: Routledge, 2021).

Marcello di Paola & Sven Nyholm, 'Climate Change and Anti-Meaning', (manuscript).

Dale Jamieson & Marcello di Paola, 'Political Theory for the Anthropocene', in David J. Held and P. Maffettone (eds.) *Global Political Theory* (Cambridge: Polity Press, 2016), 254–80.

Shelly Kagan, 'An Introduction to Ill-Being', *Oxford Studies in Normative Ethics* 4 (2015), 261–88.

Leon R. Kass, *Leading a Worthy Life: Finding Meaning in Modern Times* (New York: Encounter Books, 2017).

Antti Kauppinen, 'Meaningfulness and Time', *Philosophy and Phenomenological Research* 84 (2012), 345–77.

Iddo Landau, 'Immorality and the Meaning of Life', *Journal of Value Inquiry*, 45 (2011), 309–17.

Thaddeus Metz, 'Recent Work on the Meaning of Life', *Ethics* 112 (2002), 781–814

Max More, 'Transhumanism: Towards a Futurist Philosophy', *Extropy* 6 (1990), 6–13.

Sven Nyholm and Stephen Campbell, 'Meaning and Anti-Meaning in Life' in Iddo Landau (ed.), *The Oxford Handbook of Meaning in Life* (in press).

Toby Ord, *The Precipice: Existential Risk and the Future of Humanity* (London: Bloomsbury, 2020).

Derek Parfit, *Reasons and Persons*, (Oxford: Clarendon Press, 1984).

Ingmar Persson & Julian Savulescu, *Unfit for the Future* (Oxford: Oxford University Press, 2012).

Ingmar Persson & Julian Savulescu, 'The Meaning of Life, Equality and Eternity', *Journal of Ethics* 23 (2019), 223–38.

Samuel Scheffler, *Equality and Tradition: Questions of Value in Moral and Political Theory*, (Oxford: Oxford University Press, 2010).

Samuel Scheffler, *Death and the Afterlife* (Oxford: Oxford University Press, 2011).

Samuel Scheffler, *Why Worry about Future Generations*, (Oxford: Oxford University Press, 2018).

Aimee van Wynsberghe, 'Sustainable AI: AI *for* Sustainability and the Sustainability *of* AI', *AI and Ethics* (published online ahead of print, 2021).

Bernard Williams, 'Internal and External Reasons', in Ross Harrison (ed.), *Rational Action* (Cambridge: Cambridge University Press, 1979), 101—113.

Susan Wolf *Meaning in Life and Why it Matters* (Princeton: Princeton University Press, 2010).

Roman Yampolskiy, *Artificial Intelligence Safety and Security* (Boca Raton: CRC Press 2018).

Importance, Fame, and Death

GUY KAHANE

Abstract

Some people want their lives to possess importance on a large scale. Some crave fame, or at least wide recognition. And some even desire glory that will only be realised after their death. Such desires are either ignored or disparaged by many philosophers. However, although few of us have a real shot at importance and fame on any grand scale, these can be genuine personal goods when they meet certain further conditions. Importance that relates to positive impact and reflects our agency answers a distinctive existential concern for one's life to matter. And since what is important merits wide appreciation, the step from wanting to be significant and wanting that significance widely appreciated is small. Still, desires for importance and fame can take a more vicious character when they are not properly structured, and when they are not dominated by more impartial aims. If we accept the personal value of importance and fame, it is hard to see why that value cannot extend beyond our death. The temporal distribution of glory is actually irrelevant to its value. But it is also a mistake to identify a concern with posthumous glory with the wish to leave a trace after our death.

1. Stendhal's Gamble

Henry Bayle died on the streets in Paris in 1842. The circumstances were ignoble: Bayle died of a seizure while the street children jeered, thinking he was just a drunkard. At the time, he was a relative unknown – none of his works was in print when he died. Bayle - more famous under one of his assumed names, Stendhal – described his audience as 'the happy few'. But he also predicted in 1830 that he will be 'understood about 1880'.[1] Elsewhere he wrote that he is 'putting a ticket in a lottery the grand prize of which consists in this: to be read in 1935'.[2] Stendhal obviously won a grander prize than he ever imagined. He remains widely read and will be for a while.

The grand prize, I take it, was literary glory – or what some call literary immortality.[3] Stendhal presumably didn't merely want to be

---

[1]   Stendhal first made this prediction in a letter to Balzac. See Gauss (1923, pp. 76–78).
[2]   Cited in Smith (1942, pp. 44–49).
[3]   Canetti wrote of Stendhal that 'nowhere in modern times is a belief in literary immortality to be found in a clearer, purer and less pretentious form'

doi:10.1017/S1358246121000229   © The Royal Institute of Philosophy and the contributors 2021

Guy Kahane

read by someone, anyone, in the year 1935, but to be widely known, to be considered a major, trailblazing literary figure. And if this is what Stendhal was hoping for, his hopes were fulfilled and more. Stendhal became, and remains, an important literary figure: his novels are classics, and Stendhal is seen as a key connecting link between Classicism and Romanticism. Not all important figures are famous, or even widely known. But Stendhal is a popular author, known to anyone with a passing knowledge of European literature, even if we cannot describe him as famous today in the sense in which a current celebrity is famous.

Stendhal's gamble succeeded, but I suspect that there will be those who find his ambition puzzling, even deeply irrational. For some, this will be because they think that seeking glory and recognition is itself foolish, a misguided goal. For others, what is puzzling is not the desire for glory, but for posthumous glory – for glory that you will never enjoy, that you will not even know about. It is good, they will think, that Stendhal's work was eventually recognised and widely enjoyed. But there is nothing in any of that for *him*, for Stendhal himself.

So some will find Stendhal's gamble puzzling. Others will find it perfectly intelligible. Now, few of us aim for glory of any kind, let alone posthumous literary glory. But this is because, for most of us, that is just preposterously out of reach. But many aim, or at least wish, for achievement and appreciation on a smaller scale. The wish to do, or at least link to, something of genuine importance, and to enjoy wide recognition, is common, even very common.[4]

There is something else that many people desire. Many people want their lives to be meaningful. But the desire for meaning is seen in a much more positive light than the desire for importance and fame. It is admirable to want your life to be meaningful, even if you ultimately fail. But wanting to be or do something important – to do it *because* it is important (as opposed to aiming to do something

---

(Canetti, 1962). I take it as obvious that Stendhal's gamble was primarily self-focused – that he did not write simply out of concern for, say, the future state of French literature or out of some other purely moral or aesthetic aim; Stendhal was, after all, also the author of *Memoirs of An Egotist*.

[4]   Samuel Johnson went so far as to assert that '[e]very man, however hopeless his pretensions may appear, has some project by which he hopes to rise to reputation; some art by which he imagines that the attention of the world will be attracted; some quality, good or bad, which discriminates him from the common herd of mortals, and by which others may be persuaded to love, or compelled to fear him' (Johnson, 1751).

that also *happens* to be important) is, I think, treated much more ambivalently, even with suspicion. We certainly feel uncomfortable about those who act *as* if they are important – even if this self-importance isn't entirely groundless. As for craving fame, this is widely seen as shallow, even embarrassing.

These rather different attitudes may help explain the rather different attention that meaning, importance, and fame have received from philosophers. At least more recently, there is much attention to the conditions under which a life might be said to be meaningful.[5] There is far less written on importance (with some notable exceptions[6]) though this is also probably in part because it's not always properly distinguished from meaning (and some views come close to identifying the two).[7] As for fame, there is nowadays very little philosophical interest in this topic, though there is of course a very long philosophical tradition of denigrating fame and those who crave it. The Epicureans, for example, recommended that we 'live unknown' (or unnoticed),[8] and in Boethius's *Consolations of Philosophy*, Philosophy tells Boethius that fame is 'a shameful thing' (Boethius, 1969). A similar line is taken by Richard Kraut, one contemporary philosopher who does discuss fame. He describes fame as one of the 'vanities', those things that are widely desired despite being worthless in themselves; one of the aims of philosophical reflection on the good is precisely to release us from the grip of such vanities (Kraut, 2007).

Importance and fame would deserve philosophical attention simply in virtue of being commonly desired, even if they lacked genuine value. But I will argue that once we get clearer about what importance and fame are, and how they are related, a case can be made that they both possess final value – final value *for* the person who possesses them – at least when they meet certain conditions. We should distinguish this question about the value of importance and fame from the further question of how we should evaluate desires that aim at them: even if importance and fame are worth having, it won't immediately follow that wanting them is worthy. Whether such desires are appropriate or vicious depends, I will argue, on how they relate to each other and to other, more selfless aims.

---

[5] See e.g. Wolf (2012); Metz (2013).
[6] See e.g. Frankfurt (1999); Nozick (1989). For an insightful discussion of glory, see Chappell (2011).
[7] For discussion, see Kahane (forthcoming).
[8] Roskam (2007). Plutarch criticised this doctrine in in Plutarch (1967).

I will end by returning to Stendhal, and the desire for posthumous glory. To write a book takes time, and effort. There are other ways Stendhal could have spent his time, other projects he could have pursued. Even if he sought literary success, he could have tried to write in a style his contemporaries were more likely to appreciate. The desire for so-called literary immortality is often interpreted as reflecting the wish to somehow overcome death. But whether leaving a trace in this way is worthwhile or utterly pointless, it is distinct, I will argue, from both importance and fame (though the three can interact or overlap). The desire for posthumous glory is perfectly sensible not (or not only) because it is a way to transcend death, but because the value of glory – the value of importance and fame – is simply independent of one's life and its limits. It is a value – a value for oneself – that can transcend death, but whether or not it transcends death is simply irrelevant to its value.[9]

2. Importance

We can start with importance. What does it take for something to be important (or significant, consequential, noteworthy, seminal, key, and so forth)? I will draw here on an account of importance that I have developed in more detail in other work.[10] I call it the *value impact* view of importance. It starts from the thought that to be important is to *make a difference*. Now, there are all sort of differences one can make, and many of these would be trivial. But the kind of difference that is genuinely important – the kind of difference that is worth making – is, perhaps unsurprisingly, a difference to what matters, that is to say, to what has final *value*. So importance is a function of final value, yet something's importance isn't the same as how much final value it has, or even how much final value it brings about.

[9]   I will be speaking about the personal value of glory, including posthumous glory, but I don't think it is useful to see it as adding some further quantity to a person's pile of 'well-being'. So I don't want to say that by reading Stendhal today, we are literally benefiting him or that Max Brod would have gravely harmed the recently deceased Kafka if he had destroyed his written work as requested. But I still want to say that there was something in it – in later glory – for them, for Stendhal and Kafka themselves, not just for their readers. For a similar distinction between well-being and meaning, see Metz (2013).

[10]   See Kahane (2014), and in particular Kahane (2021, forthcoming a) where I also discuss purely 'descriptive' senses of importance that aren't linked to value in this way.

To begin with, unlike final value, a thing's importance is *relative* to a domain or context. Quine is an important philosopher but he is not an important political figure or even especially important in the context of, say, late 20th century US history. In many cases, the relevant domain will be at least partly defined in spatiotemporal terms, though this need not be so.

Another way in which importance operates differently from final value is that it is *relational*: it involves a comparison (implicit or explicit) with what else is in the domain – with *other* difference-makers. This is another reason why how important one is depends not on how much final value one brings about absolutely, but how much final value one brings about compared to other things: a disfiguring skin condition might be a pretty important thing in a person's life, but its importance would instantly shrink against the background of a catastrophic plague. Similarly, a simple doodle that would be of no significance whatsoever if inscribed on a cave wall today may be of momentous importance if it is the work of a Neolithic craftsman.

I have offered a sketch of what *makes* something more, or less, important. We can next ask what *follows* from importance – ask about its normative upshot. Put simply, to be important is to merit being treated *as* important. And to be treated as important, I say, is to receive proportional attention, and to be given sufficient weight – though the specifics can vary depending on the domain and the kind of value involved. Put differently, we can say that to be important is to matter objectively, and to be treated as important is to matter subjectively, to matter to others. And things go well, normatively speaking, when the two align.

So people, things, events and acts can be more or less important by making more or less of a difference to the overall value of some domain, and in virtue of that merit more or less of the attention of those concerned with that domain. Some people are resistant to the idea that some people are more important than others. They want to insist that all people are equally morally important.[11] But by this they just mean the idea that all of us have equal moral value, and equal moral status. This, however, is a different notion of importance, roughly relating to the *moral weight* that each of us should get in moral deliberation.[12] But it remains the case that, say, Confucius,

---

[11] Nagel speaks of the sense in which, from an objective standpoint, 'no one is more important than anyone else'. See Nagel (1986, p. 171).
[12] As this example shows, there is a further normative sense of importance not covered by the value impact account – the difference something should make in the context of deliberation.

Guy Kahane

Napoleon, Queen Victoria, Adolf Hitler, and Nelson Mandela are figures of immense importance on the largest scale, while you and I are not. And as some of these examples bring out, the impact that makes someone or something important may be incredibly negative.[13] Importance in this sense is not a moral notion.

3. Fame

Fame is primarily used as a categorical term in the sense that you are either famous or you are not. But we can also say of someone that they are more famous than another. So to be famous in the categorical sense is to be famous enough in the degree sense. It is this degree sense that interests me, even when it applies to cases we won't describe as famous, categorically speaking.

I don't think we have a good label for this much broader property, so I will still use 'fame' (in the degree sense) to describe it. This property is, in the first instance, a cognitive one – it relates, roughly, to how much someone or something is known. As with importance, there is relativity at work, whether implicitly or explicitly, since we can have in mind different populations of potential knowers. Someone can be famous in France but obscure in the US, famous in cancer research but obscure to the general public, a global sensation this week but forgotten in a month's time, etc.

The relevant cognitive property is complex and involves multiple dimensions.[14] Focusing on the case of persons, there is, for example, *how* many people know about someone, to what extent they know *who* that person is, how much they know *about* them and what they did, and the degree to which this knowledge is dormant (simply something they could recall, if the occasion arose) or regularly salient (something that is often on their minds). These variables can come apart in multiple ways – most of us know Stendhal via his assumed name, and far fewer would recognise his real name; Homer and Shakespeare are among the most famous of literary

---

[13]   The example of Napoleon raises a worry. Napoleon was obviously of great historical importance, but can we confidently say that his impact was overall positive or negative? One way to go is to point out that Napoleon's life made a great difference to *what things* had value (both positive and negative) even if it, say, turns out that his positive and negative impacts largely cancel each other out. But I'm not sure this solves the problem.

[14]   In thinking about fame, I have benefited from Halberstam (1984) and Lackey (1986).

figures, yet we know nearly nothing about the first, and rather little about the second, etc. But I won't offer an account of the weight that these different factors have in determining the degree of someone's fame.

But while fame is primarily a cognitive property, very often – and in the sense that people typically desire – fame involves more than bare cognition. There is also an affective, evaluative aspect. This is brought out when, for example, we describe people who are famous for unpleasant things as infamous – and clearly that implies a degree of contempt, a negative attitude. Conversely, celebrities are those that are, in one sense, celebrated. People closely follow celebrities because, in at least some minimal sense, they care about them and what happens to them; they do not report the latest scandal in a matter of fact tone. Conversely, if someone's name and key facts of their lives are used in a textbook grammar exercise used by millions of schoolchildren, who recite these facts in monotone, not even as the butt of some recurring joke, then this person enjoys fame only in an attenuated sense even if they possess the purely cognitive property to a considerable degree.

4. Importance and Fame

At this point the relation between importance and fame should be obvious. Roughly, *fame is what importance merits*. The famous receive a great degree of attention and concern. Whether or not they are important, the famous are treated *as* if they are important. Now one of the very oldest complaints is the complaint that the two rarely align, that what is truly important is ignored or overlooked, that people pay most attention to the trivial, and celebrate the superficial, frivolous, and shallow. Famously, some people are 'famous for being famous'.[15] Though we shouldn't exaggerate. What is really important and what is actually famous (in the broad sense) aren't

---

[15] Martin Amis's short story 'Career Change' dramatizes this by portraying a counterfactual world where Hollywood actors recite poetry to great crowds, and poets are feted and receive vast salaries for their latest sonnet, while sci fi screenwriters languish, publishing their scripts in obscure underground magazines. But Amis's aim is presumably ironic: one point of the story is that poetry would be degraded if it were linked to fame in this way and turned to a mass market product and vehicle for star vanity projects. But this is compatible with thinking that this counterfactual world is superior to ours. See Amis (1998).

completely unrelated. Very many truly important things receive a great deal of attention – a global epidemic, a war, a recession.

Moreover, even when the two do align, it is not correct to say that fame is simply what rightly follows (recognised) importance. The relation is more complex: often people and things acquire importance by being famous, and their importance is sustained by their fame. The more widely Stendhal was read and appreciated, the greater was his influence, and his importance grew. And his influence over time largely depended on him being continually read, discussed, etc., and in this way, having further impact. While it is possible to have great impact in complete obscurity, even, in some cases, with the difference you made being completely unknown, this is fairly rare. Napoleon wouldn't have achieved the impact he had in his own life without being known by numerous people, indeed, without being incredibly famous. And a great deal of his posthumous impact was mediated by this continuing fame.

Return, finally, to the idea of being famous for being famous. The idea here is of someone who is famous despite clearly *not* meriting such fame – despite being unimportant. But to begin with, you obviously cannot *first* become famous *because* you are famous. You become famous in some other way, and because of that initial fame you become even *more* famous. Conversely, although you may be famous, to begin with, without meriting any such attention, fame, as we have just seen, can generate importance of a sort. The celebrity influences millions on a daily basis, affecting their mood and bank accounts. So there is bootstrapping here: by being famous, one acquires a degree of importance, and thereby begins to actually merit a degree of fame. (Although, all the same, the importance one acquires in this way is relatively modest and won't justify receiving *that* degree of attention over many other, more important things.)

5. The Value of Importance

I have said something about what importance and fame are, and about their relation. I now turn to ask whether they are at all worth having.

Let us start with importance. No doubt, in many contexts, greater importance has its instrumental benefits, though these are rarely directly brought about by importance itself – they are typically the social upshots of *perceived* importance (and in some cases, even of fame). Still, I take it as plain that at least some people desire importance non-instrumentally, even in the absence of such reward. They desire, for example, to find a cure for cancer or a vaccine that protects against COVID-19 and desire to do so, at least in part, *because* by doing so they will have done something important, something noteworthy.

An obvious way to show that importance is desired for its own sake are cases of desire for posthumous importance – think again of Stendhal. He did become an important figure in French literature, an influence on Nietzsche, etc. But those posthumous events could not make Stendhal happier or help him with his debts.

Now some people may want importance because they see it as a *path* to fame (even to posthumous fame). We cannot rule out this was the case with Stendhal. So for such people importance is still instrumental, and whether it has value will depend on whether fame has value – something we will turn to below. But at least some people value importance even in the knowledge that no one will ever know about it. Think of a cold war mole of whom nothing is known even by her handlers.[16] The mole would probably (though not necessarily) prefer to be known and celebrated at some point. But this is not a condition for the value, for them, of their critical historical role. And in some cases, people may actively seek to avoid fame. Think of anonymous philanthropists.

Now the cold war mole, the anonymous philanthropist, may have powerful impartial, or at least not self-centred reasons to do what they do. They want the good side to win, to save many lives, etc. And no doubt in such cases, these reasons are also overwhelmingly sufficient for doing what they do. But I submit that, in at least some such cases, these people don't merely want that independently valued, more impartial outcome to be realised. They also want to be the *ones* realising it, or at least playing a big role in doing so. There's an agent-relative, self-centred element here, something rewarding to *them* – they don't just want to make that impartial difference to value, which will also happen to endow their act with importance; they also want to do something that *is* important. In at least some cases, people may even start out desiring the latter, abstract property, and look for feasible first-order ways of realising it.[17]

So I claim that at least some people desire importance for its own sake, and desire it for *their* own sake.[18] It doesn't follow that

---

[16] For a similar example see Benatar (2017).
[17] Effective altruists tell us to ask ourselves: 'how I can do the most good?'. But we can put the emphasis both on 'most good' and on 'I'.
[18] Some will no doubt respond that it is the instrumental benefits of importance (or fame) that lead people to care about them, but that some people

importance of any kind is desirable. Think of a lab technician whose lazy negligence launches a deadly global epidemic. This would be an incredibly important event. If it spells the end of humanity, the negligent technician would arguably be one of the most important people who had ever lived. But this kind of importance doesn't seem worth having. There are two things are work in this example: whether the difference one makes is positive or negative, and whether that difference reflects one's directed agency. With respect to the first, I think that it is attractive to hold that it is worth making a difference, for one's own sake, only if that difference is positive; it needs to be impartially good to be also personally good. But it is hard to deny that at least some people seem to seek importance, and even make great personal sacrifice to do so, even though they are well aware that the difference that they make is purely negative (think of those who try to become important by assassinating a political leader or cultural figure – who hope to achieve something important by killing someone who is *already* important). I suspect that these people are making a mistake in thinking that there is anything for them in such acts. But an alternative view would be that making such an impact is a personal good even if the moral reasons against acting in this way are overwhelmingly decisive. The line we take on this question will presumably depend on the line we take about parallel questions about, for example, the personal value of taking pleasure in others' suffering, or of so-called 'anti-meaning'.[19]

Even those who think there is value in importance of any kind would presumably still accept the further condition that this impact should be properly traced to one's directed agency, and perhaps also be consonant with one's attitudes. But again, I suspect that at least some would hold that there is at least *something* for us in, say, being the person with the rare genetic mutation whose discovery made it possible to eradicate a serious disease.[20]

---

confusedly come to desire them for their own sake. I don't have space to assess such a debunking strategy but for my purposes here it is enough to point out that it is just as easy to mount such an attack on altruist or non-hedonic aims.

[19] See Campbell and Nyholm (2015).

[20] To the extent that one accepts that importance has value only when it involves positive difference and one's directed agency, then one comes close to holding that importance has value only when it meets criteria that some see as grounding meaningfulness (see especially Metz, 2013). But while I think there may be a case to be made that importance has final value only when it is also meaningful, I don't think the value of importance is merely

I have so far tried to show that at least some people value importance for its own sake, and explored some conditions importance
might need to meet to be a candidate for value. This leaves it open
why importance has that value, even when it meets these conditions.
Here is a sketch of an account. The basic idea is this. I think that importance can address a distinctive existential concern: the *wish for
one's existence to matter*. When people worry that they, or their
lives, are utterly *insignificant*, they worry, I believe, that what they
do, that even their very existence, makes little or no difference to
the world around them. As Nagel puts it, '[l]ooking at [one's life]
from the outside, it wouldn't matter if you had never existed'
(Nagel, 1987). Importantly, your existence might not matter, in
this broader way, *even* if you are happy, if your life possesses considerable value, *even* if your life is *deeply meaningful*.

To see the how meaningfulness and importance can come apart,
think of Bill and Hilary Clinton. The Clintons remain important political figures. But since he left the White House, Bill Clinton is not
remotely as important as he was when he was president. And
Hilary Clinton is not remotely as important as she would have been
had she won the 2016 US elections. Perhaps, in a range of respects,
their lives are more meaningful compared to that prior or counterfactual life. But we will easily understand if they nevertheless feel a sense
of loss, even deep loss.

Several authors link meaningfulness to certain fitting attitudes, including third person attitudes such as admiration.[21] Think of
someone who lives a life of quiet decency, bravely facing adversity
and, despite many obstacles, rearing a flourishing family. When we
meet such a person, or reflect on such a life, we should respond
with admiration. Yet it is not true that there is a reason for everyone
to know about and admire that life, or that their name should be em-
blazoned on the front pages. Meaningfulness doesn't, on its own, call
for general attention – it isn't especially noteworthy. It's important
for the person, but it isn't important in the everyday sense we are
talking about. If that life is removed from the world, something valuable and meaningful is removed, but the world is nevertheless not

---

that of meaning (unless, of course, we prefer to think of desirable importance
as a distinct *kind* of meaning; but I don't find such an expansive terminology
helpful). For further discussion of the relation of importance and meaning,
see Kahane (forthcoming).

[21] See Kauppinen (2012); Metz (2013).

substantially different overall.[22] In other words, because it doesn't make a significant overall difference to value, such a life doesn't objectively matter such that it should subjectively matter to (relevant) impartial observers.

6. The Value of Fame

The value of fame is harder to defend – if anything, it is widely seen as a paradigm of something that is desired despite having no inherent value. Why should it matter whether one is known (even favourably known) by numerous strangers? This is compatible with valuing fame instrumentally, for its typical causal benefits. Yet it again seems clear that some people desire fame independently of such benefits and even when they don't expect them. If anything, people make considerable sacrifices, even absurd sacrifices, to get even a long shot at a moment in the limelight. And again, there are those cases, even if uncommon, of people who make considerable sacrifices – sometimes even risking their lives – in the hope of obtaining posthumous fame.[23] Such acts are clearly done without instrumental intent or expectation.

If fame and importance aligned often enough, then fame might have epistemic value – offering collective support to one's own perhaps shaky judgments about the impartial value of what one has achieved, and thereby also externally validating its importance; contrast the epistemic loneliness of the misunderstood artist. But such epistemic significance would only be a way to track the prior personal value of importance, and won't add further personal value, nor would such a role justify a concern with posthumous fame. And of course in many cases the relation between importance and actual fame is flimsy at best.

Another way in which the value of fame may derive from that of importance we already saw: I said earlier that fame often plays a role in amplifying and sustaining importance, especially posthumous

---

[22] Though this needs to be qualified in two ways. First, our imagined removal can still make a difference (remove something of importance) on much smaller scales and, for some, that would be enough. Second, while our individual removal may not make a real difference this need not be true of our collective removal. For discussion of our potential collective significance on the largest, cosmic scale, see Kahane (2014; 2021, forthcoming a).

[23] Perhaps the most famous example is Herostratus who burned down the temple of Artemis at Ephesus in order to be remembered by posterity.

importance. If importance has personal value, then fame that promotes one's impact can acquire critical instrumental value.

We are asking, though, whether fame itself might have final value. There is actually a straightforward way to argue that fame has *impartial* value when it is merited and proportional. I have in mind here the view that it is good to love the good, and to hate the bad.[24] To the extent that fame is accompanied by fitting attitudes,[25] then on such a view fame (as well as infamy!) arguably has final value – the world is better when acts and events of importance are fittingly appreciated. I say arguably since the view that it is good to love the good typically focuses on fitting appreciation of final value, and importance often supervenes on instrumental value – the importance of a declaration of war derives not from the value it directly realises (e.g. the moral cowardice or courage it reflects) but from its wide further effects – all those lives or freedoms saved or lost. It is less clear that we add final value to the world simply by appreciating the things that bring about final value as opposed to appreciating that final value itself. Notice also that if we accept that such responses themselves possess impartial value, then we must also accept a kind of feedback loop: fame is not only a conduit for further importance, through the value impact it enables, but is itself directly a value impact, and thereby directly amplifies a thing's importance, meaning that such fame calls for yet *further* fame, which then calls for yet more, and so on.

If this is right – and I don't pretend to have shown that it is – then we have impartial reasons to promote merited fame (and infamy) – say, to rediscover an overlooked singer-songwriter or inventor or make more widely known a forgotten atrocity, and uncover its perpetrators – even if this won't help any of its long dead victims. Still, this doesn't show there is anything in that *for* that now fashionable singer-songwriter.

But it seems to me that if importance has personal value, and if it calls for a certain kind of response, then it is a small step to thinking that it is a further personal good if that importance is acknowledged and fittingly appreciated (or we can say instead that the personal value of importance is more fully realised when it is thus appreciated).

---

[24]　See especially Hurka (2000).

[25]　In other work, I have suggested that when we attend to value from a great temporal distance, fittingly responding to it may require not much more than cognitive response, so long as that response is governed by one's recognition of the thing's value. See Kahane (2021, forthcoming b)

Even if we accept this further step – that it is good for us not just to be such that we merit a certain response, but also that we in fact receive that response – there is still a gap from ascribing any final value to fame. This depends on how we understand the relevant merited response. To begin with, responses can come in different *forms*, ranging from superficial approval to close, deep engagement. Nor is it obvious that the *numbers* should count. Thus, why isn't it enough if a handful of people appreciate the importance, appreciate it deeply and from up close, as opposed to the offhand knowledge of millions?[26] It might be thought, in particular, that it is not the fickle opinion of the masses that should matter but that of a few close intimates (or perhaps, even, just of oneself).[27]

We need not deny that degree of evaluation, and its depth, matters. But that such responses count for more is compatible with thinking that the numbers matter. That, for example, an exquisite response from a wide, highly educated musical audience is better than such a response from a single listener.[28] And while often the nearby receives deeper, more sustained response, this isn't always the case. Distant future critics may devote an entire life to studying Stendhal's work, they may see things that contemporaries (let alone close friends) cannot. Things that even Stendhal himself could not see.

7. Worthy Motivation

Even if importance and merited fame possess final value, it doesn't follow it is always admirable to aim to have these things. Concern for one's importance, and even more so for fame, is seen as embarrassingly egocentric, even narcissistic. It is no doubt self-focused, but in this respect it is no different from the desire for happiness or even meaning in one's life. We don't desire merely that there be more happiness out there. We may desire that, but we also desire our own

---

[26] Responding angrily to a very favourable journalistic piece on his work, Degas remarked that 'one works for two or three living friends, and for others one has never met or who are dead' (quoted in Muhlstein, 2016).

[27] Valéry thought that Stendhal was 'divided between his immense desire to please and to become famous, and the opposite mania, his delight in being himself, in his own eyes, in his own way. He felt, deeply embedded in his flesh, the spur of literary vanity; but he also felt a little deeper down the strange sharp pricking of an absolute pride determined to depend on nothing but itself' (Valéry, 1989).

[28] I set aside, though, the question of how to weigh few deep responses against many more shallower ones.

happiness. And while people often enough aim to do certain things selflessly – things such as helping others – that also endow their lives with meaning, often enough they also directly seek meaning. And here they don't just seek there to be more meaning out there. They want *their* life to be meaningful. Wanting to be linked to something important, to do something important and even, in virtue of that, to oneself possess a degree of importance aren't different. Now importance does have an inherent relational, comparative dimension that happiness and meaningfulness do not. But this doesn't mean that aiming at importance is essentially competitive. You can want to stand out without wanting others to stand out less.

The desire for others' attention, for everyone's eyes to be on you, can again seem harder to defend. However, we are not talking about wanting others' positive attention *regardless* of whether that is merited, or even when it is actually undeserved. When something important happens, others *already* have reason to attend to it. The claim is just that there is an agent-relative reason to want some others to respond to that independent impartial reason.

Our evaluation of the desire for personal importance and fame is complicated by the obvious point that the vast majority of people have little or no shot at importance or fame on a large scale. It is straightforwardly irrational to devote considerable efforts to a goal that is out of reach. Even mere longing for such things will typically be demoralizing or worse, and such fantasies are therefore best kept out of mind by most of us. And because glory is out of reach for most of us, there may be a reluctance to admit its value and to respect its pursuit by those who do have a shot; Nietzschean ressentiment may be at work.

This is not to deny that the pursuit of such things, especially when it is all-consuming, is often associated with attitudes and dispositions that are deeply unpleasant; the narcissist may obsessively seek others' admiring attention as a way of dulling his underlying sense of insignificance.[29] Even setting aside such psychological associations,

[29] In his short story 'Good Old Neon', one of David Foster Wallace's characters described what he calls the 'fraudulence paradox': the more he succeeds in impressing others – in winning their admiring attention – the less he impresses himself, and the more empty he feels inside – a spiral of self-loathing that ends in suicide. The story doesn't make clear whether this character thinks that the admiring attention is deserved. It would not be surprising if immense skills in manipulating others into admiring you despite not being worthy of such admiration is ultimately unsatisfying. But it is hard to consistently impress others without offering them something that is genuinely impressive, at least to a degree. Why then loathe

Guy Kahane

desiring glory *can* be problematic if the relevant desires are not structured properly.[30]

In the *Analects*, the Master is recorded as saying 'A man should say… I am not concerned that I am not known, I seek to be worthy to be known'.[31] In one way, Confucius doesn't go far enough here. We should be concerned, it might be argued, about doing the things we ought to do and doing them well; we should aim to bring about what has value simply because it has value. Not even because it *merits* an appreciating response. On the other hand, while a completely selfless attitude might be especially admirable, once we allow self-centred attitudes into the picture – again, desiring one's own happiness or a meaningful life being examples – it is hard to see why we can't *also* be concerned, for our own sake, with the importance of what we do, and with that importance receiving wide fitting appreciation. These more selfless and self-centred attitudes are perfectly compatible. It is just a question of how they are ordered in our motivational set.

Take the cliched example of finding a cure for cancer. For a scientist who has a shot at finding such a cure, the primary aim should be the impartial one of finding such a cure because of its extraordinary moral value – the untold suffering it will prevent. But it seems perfectly acceptable to *also* wish, more weakly, that this cure be found by oneself, or one's team; that *you* will be the one to realise that impartial value (what is vicious is not to want that, but to want that either you find the cure, *or no one will*). You may further (even more weakly) prefer that one's contribution to that impartial goal stands out in some way – that you make some distinctive, decisive contribution as opposed to moving things slightly forward alongside a small army of other researchers. You may next prefer that, if you make such a contribution, it will be widely and fittingly appreciated, as well as (even more weakly) that it be appreciated as *your* contribution (again what is vicious isn't that but wanting to make a contribution only *in order to be* widely appreciated, or even to be widely

---

oneself for receiving merited appreciation? The problem, I think, is that the focus remains on others' attitudes, with what merits these attitudes serving merely as a means. So even when there is genuine value being produced, it is not only playing a derivative role but, for that reason, also arguably being *devalued*. See Foster Wallace (2014).

[30] For a different account of the motivation for glory, see Chappell, 'Glory as an Ethical Ideal'.

[31] Confucius (1861, IV.14).

appreciated for no good reason, or even on fraudulent grounds). You may also, moreover, wish to be in a position to *know* that you did something important, and that this was fittingly appreciated. In this way you must, at each point, give priority to the more fundamental motivation.

The question of motivation may also be affected by the kind of value in question. It is easiest to see such motivations in approving terms in the aesthetic case. After all, a fitting response is likely required to even generate aesthetic value. And even if we hold that works of art have value even if not appreciated by anyone, few would deny that far more aesthetic value is realised once we add the fitting aesthetic response. Accordingly, it would seem odd for an artist not to be at all concerned whether anyone comes to appreciate their work, and positively perverse for them to prefer no one to so appreciate it, or even for it to be misunderstood or ridiculed. When we turn to achievement, including intellectual achievement, the value in question is more plausibly seen as independent of further appreciation. But it doesn't seem especially problematic to desire to be the one making that achievement and even for it to be fittingly appreciated as one's own. The trickiest case is probably the moral domain. It is common to see any element of self-regard as undermining moral praise. To the extent that moral acts merely aim at such praise, such undermining would certainly follow. Still, when the different motivations – impartial and self-concerned – are properly ordered, it is not obvious that the mere presence of the latter must besmirch the former.

8. Death

We can finally turn to the question of the relation between importance, fame, and death. Suppose we accept that importance is a final personal good, as is deserved fame, in the sense of wide positive recognition of positive importance (to simplify things, I will continue to speak of importance and fame, simply assuming these qualifications). To the extent that we accept this, the idea of the value of posthumous importance and fame seems perfectly straightforward. How important or famous someone is need not have anything to do with how long they live or whether they are even alive. And to the extent that these things possess value, it is hard to see why that value should be cancelled when the person dies. If so, this is a personal good that can extend beyond our death (and in some cases, such as Stendhal's, even largely *begin* after our death). In that way, it is a personal good that can transcend the limits of human life. Yet, at the same time, its final value is in no way derived *from* or even amplified by this death-defying feature. How important or famous you are, and whether or not you are alive, are simply independent.

If importance and fame are independent of one's life, can they also extend *before* one's birth or conception? The idea of pre-conception fame seems straightforward. Think, for example, of a long-antici-pated messiah, the object of longing for centuries before his arrival. That anticipation may utterly shape the course of history, though it is less obvious that we want to say that messiah's importance extends before his actual appearance (as opposed to the importance of people's anticipation).

In fact, so far as I can see, the temporal (and spatial) distribution of one's impact, or fame, is simply unimportant.[32] What matters is what comparative difference to value you make to a domain, not *where* or *when* you make it – whether during life or after your death, over a minute or over centuries. In practice, of course, one can typically have more of an impact if one's causal effect on value extends further in space and time. But that is just contingent. The same for fitting appreciation: most of the potential 'audience' for what people do probably lies in the future and, of course, we cannot reach a past audience. But these are contingent matters. Imagine a spiritual leader who emerges in humanity's last decade, helping guide it to final enlightenment before it peacefully bows out. Such a leader would be both maximally important and famous. Yet that importance and fame may be concentrated over a relatively brief period of time, perhaps just a few years.

This is a point about the spatiotemporal spread, and the distribu-tion, of one's importance and fame.[33] What matters, I suggested, isn't where that importance and fame is located, spatiotemporally, but how much difference to overall value one makes, and how many people ap-preciate that difference and to what degree. That difference to value, for example, may be highly concentrated spatiotemporally, as in the

---

[32]   See also my (2021, forthcoming a). For a tentative defence of the view that temporal (as opposed to spatial) distribution may *impersonally* matter, see Temkin (2015).

[33]   These are distinct variables given that one may, for example, be re-membered for several centuries but most of one's fame may be located a century after one's death before dramatically tailing off. Another person may be overall just as known – in terms of, e.g., the number of people knowing them, the aggregate intensity of their engagement, etc., but that fame might be more evenly spread and concentrated over a shorter period.

spiritual leader example above. At the same time, if we say that this leader was an extraordinarily important figure in the history of humanity as a whole, then this leader just is important on that grand scale, even though her *causal* impact is incredibly narrow in reach.[34]

People sometimes desire to leave a mark; we could interpret Stendhal's gamble in such terms. But to describe someone as aiming to leave a mark is ambiguous. To leave a mark can refer to doing something important on a grand enough scale. But it can also refer to leaving a lasting trace.[35] These are different things. To begin with, one can leave a trace that goes on for a long time but isn't important. Think of being remembered within one's family for many generations. Or even the forward impact people believe they can have via having a long line of descendants. Neither need count as important in any interesting sense. Conversely, as we saw, even importance on a truly grand trace need not be especially temporally (or spatially) extended – think again of the example of the final spiritual leader. It is true, though, that one way to leave a robust lasting trace is by doing something truly important, and thereby becoming posthumously famous for a long time. But if there is further value to leaving a trace it seems to me to go beyond, and be independent of, the value associated with importance and (merited) fame. And it seems to me odd, even lopsided, to want to do something grandly important only, or even primarily, because that would leave a lasting trace.

Woody Allen famously quipped, 'I don't want to achieve immortality through my work; I want to achieve immortality through not dying. I don't want to live on in the hearts of my countrymen, I want to live on in my apartment' (Allen, 1995). Galen Strawson somewhere similarly writes that 'It's not being forgotten by others that matters, it's eternal future non-existence' (Strawson, 2003).

I think that both Allen and Strawson have in mind the idea of leaving a trace. But it seems natural to extend this objection to a concern with posthumous importance and fame. However, as we saw, *if* importance and fame are at all valuable, then they won't stop having (or adding to) that value when one dies. Conversely, if one is simply rejecting that final value altogether, then the issue of death is irrelevant since one should also reject it when the person in question is alive. Moreover, the personal value of importance and fame are simply distinct from the value to us of our continued life.

---

[34]   See again my (2021, forthcoming a).

[35]   For a discussion of the desire to leave a trace, and especially to be remembered, see Margalit (2002).

Guy Kahane

Once we stop thinking of posthumous glory in terms of a kind of substitute afterlife,[36] it makes no sense to complain that it cannot compensate for what we are deprived of by death, or that posthumous glory doesn't make our mortality any less definite and depressing. In fact, even if the personal value of importance to you can extend beyond your life it remains the case that death puts a severe limit on how much impact you can make on the world. Thus, to recognize the value of importance and fame can make death *even worse*. But notice, conversely, that even if we had lived forever, this wouldn't in itself address the existential concern to make a difference, and for that difference to be fittingly recognized. One could exist for eternity in insignificant obscurity. In fact, I have elsewhere argued that if God exists, then His incomparable value and impact would make all of us humans insignificant on the grander scale, even if some of us will also enjoy eternal bliss.[37] This is an implication that is recognized by many religious traditions, even if it is obscured by the common conflation of meaning and importance.

The things that we regularly describe as 'universal' are really preposterously parochial. Talk of literary immortality is similarly hyperbolic. Stendhal had a good run, better than he expected in his wildest dreams. But can we say with confidence that he'll be read much in two hundred years? And even in the unlikely event that, say, Shakespeare somehow remains a vital cultural influence until the last days of the solar system, this will still fall far short of anything approaching literal literary immortality.

The concern to be remembered by posterity is often ridiculed on this count. To quote Galen Strawson again: 'what's the timescale of remembrance? In the end Ecclesiastes is right. In the end there is "no remembrance of former things, nor will there be any remembrance of things that are to come amongst those who shall come after"' (Strawson, 2003).

Let us suppose that Shakespeare would realize the personal good of glory to some ideal extent if his work was enjoyed and admired forever. It wouldn't remotely follow that it wouldn't be better, from his point of view, if *Hamlet* was admired for thousands of years rather than for several hundred, let alone for just a few

---

[36] Unamuno famously described the urge to perpetuate one's name and fame as the 'shadow of immortality' – see Unamuno (1921).

[37] See Kahane (2014). Conversely, we humans might be of immense cosmic importance – though not enjoy cosmic fame! – if God doesn't exist *and* we are alone in the universe, despite the fact that humanity will eventually go extinct, *even* if we go extinct in the not so distant future.

decades, just as a life lasting two hundred years is better than one lasting twenty, even if both pale in comparison with immortality. Though recall that it is not temporal extension per se that matters here but the size and quality of the audience, so to speak. It would make no difference, in terms of glory, whether Shakespeare's audience extended for a million years further on a sparsely populated Earth or for only a thousand more years in a more densely populated planet.

Moreover, there are two rather different ways of thinking of that audience. On the first, more is literally better: the ideal situation (focusing on fame) is getting appreciation from an indefinitely large potential audience. But an alternative view takes the potential audience as fixed. The best situation is getting as much appreciation from *that* audience (however big or small) as is fitting. On this second view, if Shakespeare or Einstein will be properly recognised till humanity's end, they will have realised this personal value to the maximal degree. I am not sure whether the latter view is correct with respect to fame, but I have argued elsewhere that something like this *is* true of importance – importance is always relative to the *actual* world, meaning that importance is always relative to the fixed amount of value that the world overall contains (or will end up containing).[38] It is actually the idea of infinite value that makes it hard to see how anyone could make a difference to overall value and thus threatens the very idea of importance on the grandest scale.[39]

University of Oxford
guy.kahane@philosophy.ox.ac.uk

References

Woody Allen, *The Illustrated Woody Allen Reader* (New York: Random House, 1995).
Martin Amis, 'Career Move', in his *Heavy Water and Other Stories* (London: Jonathan Cape, 1998).
David Benatar, *The Human Predicament* (Oxford: Oxford University Press, 2017).

[38] See again my (2014) and (2021, forthcoming a).
[39] This chapter was presented at the *Meaning in Life and Knowledge of Death* conference at the University of Liverpool. I am grateful to the participants for very helpful comments.

Guy Kahane

Boethius, *The Consolation of Philosophy*, trans. V.E. Watts, (London: Penguin Books, 1969).

Stephen M. Campbell and Sven Nyholm, 'Anti-meaning and why it matters', *Journal of the American Philosophical Association* 1 (2015), 694–711.

Elias Canetti, *Crowds and Power*, (New York: Viking Press, 1962).

Timothy Chappell, 'Glory as an Ethical Idea', *Philosophical Investigations* 34 (2011), 105–134.

Confucius, *The Analects of Confucius*, translated by J. Legge, (Oxford: Clarendon Press, 1861).

David Foster Wallace, 'Good Old Neon', in his *Oblivion: Stories* (New York: Little, Brown, and Co, 2014).

Harry Frankfurt, 'The Usefulness of Finals Ends', in his *Necessity, Volition, and Love* (Cambridge: Cambridge University Press, 1999).

Christian Gauss, 'Prophecies by Stendhal', *Modern Language Notes* 38 (1923).

Joshua Halberstam, 'Fame', *American Philosophical Quarterly* 21 (1984), 93–99.

Thomas Hurka, *Virtue, Vice and Value* (Oxford: Oxford University Press, 2000).

Samuel Johnson, *The Rambler* (1751).

Guy Kahane, 'Our Cosmic Insignificance', *Noûs* 48 (2014), 745–72.

Guy Kahane, 'Importance, Value, and Causal Impact', *The Journal of Moral Philosophy* (2021, forthcoming a).

Guy Kahane, 'The Significance of the Past', *The Journal of the American Philosophical Association* (2021, forthcoming b).

Guy Kahane, 'Meaningfulness and Importance', in Iddo Landau (ed.), *The Oxford Handbook of Meaning in Life* (Oxford: Oxford University Press, forthcoming).

Antti Kauppinen, 'Meaningfulness and Time', *Philosophy and Phenomenological Research* 84 (2012), 345–77.

Richard Kraut, *What is Good and Why* (Cambridge: Harvard University Press, 2007).

Douglas Lackey, 'Fame as a Value Concept', *Philosophy Research Archives* 12 (1986), 541–51.

Avishai Margalit, *The Ethics of Memory* (Harvard: Harvard University Press. 2002).

Thaddeus Metz, *Meaning in Life* (Oxford: Oxford University Press, 2013).

Anka Muhlstein, 'Degas Invents a New World', *The New York Review*, (12 May 2016).

Thomas Nagel, *The View from Nowhere* (Oxford: Oxford University Press, 1986).

Thomas Nagel, *What Does It All Mean?* (Oxford: Oxford University Press, 1987).

Robert Nozick, 'Importance', in *The Examined Life* (New York: Simon & Schuster, 1989).

Plutarch, *Moralia, XIV* (Cambridge, MA: Loeb Classical Library, 1967).

Geert Roskam, *Live Unnoticed: On the Vissicitudes of an Epicurean Doctrine* (Leiden: Brill, 2007).

Maxwell Smith, 'Stendhal, Hyphen-Mark in the History of French Fiction', *The French Review* 16 (1942).

Galen Strawson, 'Blood and Memory', *The Guardian*, (4 January 2003).

Larry Temkin, 'Rationality with Respect to People, Places, and Times', *Canadian Journal of Philosophy* 45 (2015), 576–608.

Miguel de Unamuno, *The Tragic Sense of Life* (London: Macmillan and Co, 1921).

Paul Valéry, 'Stendhal', trans. M. Turnell, in Harold Bloom (ed.), *Stendhal* (New York: Chelsea House, 1989), 7–30.

Susan Wolf, *Meaning in Life and Why It Matters* (Princeton: Princeton University Press, 2012).

Dying for a Cause: Meaning, Commitment, and Self-Sacrifice

ANTTI KAUPPINEN

Abstract

Some people willingly risk or give up their lives for something they deeply believe in, for instance standing up to a dictator. A good example of this are members of the White Rose student resistance group, who rebelled against the Nazi regime and paid for it with their lives. I argue that when the cause is good, such risky activities (and even deaths themselves) can contribute to meaning in life in its different forms – meaning-as-mattering, meaning-as-purpose, and meaning-as-intelligibility. Such cases highlight the importance of integrity, or living up to one's commitments, in meaningful living, or dying, as it may be, as well as the risk involved in commitment, since if you die for a bad cause, you have only harmed yourself. However, if leading a more rather than less meaningful life benefits rather than harms you, there are possible scenarios in which you yourself are better off dying for a good cause than living a longer moderately happy life. This presents a version of a well-known puzzle: what, then, makes dying for a cause a self-sacrifice, as it usually seems to be? I sketch some possible answers, and critically examine relevant work in empirical psychology.

> Choose to die well while you can; wait too long, and it might become impossible to do so – Gaius Musonius Rufus
>
> All men must die, but death can vary in its significance – Mao Zedong

On the 18th of February 1943, members of the anti-Nazi resistance group White Rose distributed copies of their sixth leaflet at the University of Munich. Before they left, one of them, Sophie Scholl, flung the remaining copies into the atrium from the top floor. She was seen and taken into Gestapo custody with her brother Hans. Being a young woman, Sophie was given the option to recant and save herself, but she refused. In court, she explained their actions as follows:

> Somebody, after all, must make a start. What we said and wrote is also believed by so many others. They just don't dare to say it out loud.[1]

---

[1] See http://www.mythoselser.de/texts/scholl-urteil.htm for the original German.

doi:10.1017/S1358246121000230
© The Royal Institute of Philosophy and the contributors 2021

Antti Kauppinen

Predictably, the Scholls were sentenced to death for treason and executed. While in prison, Sophie discussed her coming execution with a cellmate, Else Gebel, who reported her saying the following:

> What does my death matter, if through our actions thousands of people will be shaken and awakened? ... I could also die of illness, but would it have the same meaning?[2]

Well, probably not. Dying for a cause can be more meaningful than dying from an illness, including in the sense of giving meaning to one's life. What I want to explore in this paper is exactly what this means and why and when it is the case. For much of it, I will be mapping out the conceptual space rather than giving arguments, since I don't think philosophers have written much directly on the topic, though of course Stoics and others have addressed issues in the ballpark, as the quotes from Rufus and Mao suggest.

I will proceed as follows. First, I will distinguish between three varieties of meaning in life, drawing in part on psychological research on experiences of meaning. Next, I will define what I mean by a 'cause', and distinguish between the different ways one can be said to die for a cause. I also consider examples of both successful and failed cases of promoting a cause by risking or facing death. Third, I draw on the previous sections to set out conditions for when dying for a cause contributes to the different varieties of meaning in life. In the final section, I turn to the question of how dying for a cause can amount to self-sacrifice even when it makes one life more meaningful and is therefore, on my view, in an important way in one's self-interest in the right circumstances.

1. Three Meanings of Meaning in Life

I am going to start by clarifying what it means to say that someone's life is meaningful or is made meaningful by something. I am going to argue that there are at least three different philosophically interesting things this could amount to.[3]

My argument begins with the assumption that someone's life is meaningful if and only if it is *fitting* to *experience* it as meaningful.[4]

---

[2]   From Else Gebel's letter to Sophie Scholl's parents, online in the original German at http://www.mythoselser.de/texts/scholl-gebel.htm.
[3]   For more details, see Kauppinen (forthcoming).
[4]   For a defense of this assumption, see Kauppinen (2012, pp. 352–55).

58

The reason this connection matters is that if there are many distinct experiences of meaning, it follows that there are many different ways for life to *be* meaningful. And indeed, in recent work in psychology, it has become common to think that there are indeed a number of distinct experiences of meaning. To be sure, quite often psychologists speak as if there are just three different aspects of meaning, as Login George and Crystal Park do in the following: 'We define MIL [meaning in life] as the extent to which one's life is experienced as making sense, as being directed and motivated by valued goals, and as mattering in the world' (George and Park, 2016, p. 206).

But as Frank Martela and Michael Steger rightly emphasize, these experiences of intelligibility, purpose, and mattering can and do come apart and have different practical roles (Martela and Steger, 2015). Let's start with intelligibility. I have recently argued that psychologists tend to exaggerate the role of intelligibility in experiences of meaning, especially when it comes to merely perceiving patterns of some sort rather than randomness (Kauppinen, forthcoming). But there is something to the thought that for our own lives to make sense to us, we must see in their twists and turns some recognizable variation of culturally available models (see especially the work of de Bres 2018). What I emphasize is that for us to find our lives intelligible in the sense that is linked to having a *reason* to live and not merely as something that fits into an explanatory framework, we must also regard the choices we've made as having been aimed at something sufficiently *good* that offers a kind of narrative justification for them.[5] This sort of intelligibility can be called into question in cases of subjectively irrational life choices, personal loss, or radical cultural change, which may result in disorientation – I don't know who I am or where I am going any more.

Even if you do find your life intelligible in this way, you may experience it as meaningless in the sense of lacking *purpose*. As I use the term, experiencing our lives as purposeful is a matter of having some orienting aim which we take to provide reasons for action and which we believe our actions to serve. Sense of purpose is thus manifest in enthusiastic motivation, and missing in boredom or depression. While it normally goes together with intelligibility, there is such a thing as newfound purpose that you can have even while experiencing your life as a whole as not making sense.

---

[5] See MacIntyre (1981) for a classic account of this kind of view.

Antti Kauppinen

Finally, for us to experience our lives as meaningful in the sense of *mattering* is for us to find that actions that express our authentic selves successfully serve some objective or intersubjective value – that we purposefully make a positive difference to something or someone important to us when it is challenging to do so. (Note that our lives can be *important* without mattering in this sense.[6]) I think this kind of experience consists primarily in feelings of fulfilment, agential pride, self-esteem, and confident hope, which affectively construe our past or on-going actions in such manner. Evidently, we can find our lives intelligible or purposeful without experiencing such feelings. Experiences of meaninglessness in this respect consist in feelings of failure or angst, which I take to be an existential feeling involving the thought that nothing is ultimately worthwhile.[7]

While these experiences are distinct, I do think that there is what I call a *negative rational dependence* among them. What I mean by this is that while you can have a sense of comprehension without a sense of purpose, if you experience your life as *lacking* purpose, it is not rational for you to experience it as (fully) intelligible either, because leading up to something worth pursuing is an important part of the experience of intelligibility. Similarly, if you think that your life doesn't and won't matter, it is not rational to experience a sense of purpose, because it entails thinking that you won't realize an objectively or intersubjectively valuable aim. In this sense, experiences of mattering seem to me to be the most fundamental experiences of meaning – existential anxiety rationally, and typically, undercuts sense of purpose and the intelligibility of one's life as a whole.

The table below (modified from Kauppinen forthcoming) summarizes the discussion so far:

---

[6] For importance, see Kahane (forthcoming). Briefly, the two key differences between importance and mattering are that a life or an action can be important without mattering in virtue of making a large *negative* difference to intrinsic value (Stalin's actions were important), and in virtue of *accidentally* making a large positive difference to intrinsic value (if, unbeknownst to me, my breathing out happened to produce chemicals that would stabilize the world's CO_2 levels, my life would be important!).

[7] For existential feelings, see Ratcliffe (2014).

Dimension / Experience Type	Sense-making: contribution to a desirable pattern	Purpose and resonance: contribution to aims	Mattering: contribution to value beyond the self
Experience of meaning	Sense of comprehension and narrative justification	Enthusiastic future- or present-oriented motivation	Feelings of fulfilment, pride, and self-esteem
Experience of meaninglessness	Disorientation	Demotivation, boredom, depression	Angst, feelings of failure

Next, if our lives are meaningful to the extent that it is *fitting* for us to experience them as meaningful, distinguishing between these three kinds of experience suggests there are the following three forms of meaning in life, or three ways in which experiences of meaning may be *warranted* or *correct* in the light of opinion-independent facts about value and reasons:

Meaning$_I$: S's life is meaningful$_I$ to the extent that the actions and events that comprise it fit into a culturally recognizable narrative of pursuing some sufficient good.[8] (For example, you might be a knight errant seeking the Holy Grail, or a former addict trying to make amends.)

Meaning$_P$: S's life is meaningful$_P$ to the extent that she pursues high-level ends she has subjective and objective reason to pursue. (For example, you might organize your activities around the aim of preventing coral bleaching, or just taking care of aging parents.)

Meaning$_M$: S's life is meaningful$_M$ to the extent that her actions over time merit fulfilment and pride, which entails (at least) non-accidentally successful pursuit of challenging aims that she identifies with and has objective reason to pursue.[9] (For example, by

[8] As Michael Hauskeller highlighted for me, this definition implicitly relativizes meaning-as-intelligibility to culture. I think this is the right result – some lives that made perfect sense in the 13th century wouldn't make sense now. But those who think that intelligibility should not be relative can remove the word 'culturally' from the thesis.

[9] As Thaddeus Metz pointed out to me (personal communication), meaningfulness-as-mattering is compatible with a degree of outcome luck – indeed, often projects that yield exceptional meaning when successful

Antti Kauppinen

the sweat of your brow, you might succeed in finding a way to prevent coral bleaching.)

We might say that what ties all of these notions together is that they have to do with having a reason to go on living or there being a point to one's life. These are presumably the kind of things people wonder about when they ask if their lives have meaning. We might also say that a life is *superlatively meaningful* to the extent that it is meaningful in all these ways.

For our purposes, it is important to say how *events* can be meaningful in the sense of contributing to meaning in life. In ordinary talk, to be sure, we talk about meaningful events more broadly, so that an event that has any kind of emotional resonance, or makes a significant difference to what happens later, can be said to be meaningful. But here we are interested in how an event like death can contribute to meaning in life. Given the earlier distinctions, my proposal is the following:

> An event contributes to meaning$_I$ to the extent that it promotes or constitutes one's life fitting into a culturally recognizable narrative of pursuing some good. (For example, getting fired after a transgression contributes to intelligibility – a *lot* of events fit into culturally recognizable narratives of pursuing some good. Getting fired without a discernible cause, in contrast, can be disorienting and puzzling.)
> An event contributes to meaning$_P$ to the extent that it promotes or constitutes having a high-level aim that there is sufficient subjective and objective reason to have. (For example, a moral insight or religious conversion might contribute to purpose in life.)
> An event contributes to meaning$_M$ to the extent that it promotes or constitutes the successful realization of a challenging identity-defining aim that there is sufficient objective reason to pursue. (For example, doing research that turns out to result in a new scientific discovery might contribute to mattering.)

2. Varieties of Dying for a Cause

With these distinctions in hand, let us turn to dying for a cause. Let's start with the question of what a 'cause' in the relevant sense is. I will

---

are particularly *risky*, like organizing a union in a repressive political environment. Not everything that requires luck is accidental.

say that when you take up a cause you *commit to trying to right a wrong*. In paradigm cases, there is some group of people who are at least perceived to be treated seriously unjustly by some other group of people who benefit from the status quo, so that there is a strong (apparent) reason for anyone in a position to change this intrinsically bad state of affairs to do so. The injustice could be denial of rights, denial of national self-determination, or discrimination on a morally irrelevant basis. That is why there is the cause of civil rights and Palestinian and women's causes. Of course, not all causes involve injustice to people – there are also environmental causes, and more broadly pursuit of some important impersonal value that some people fail to respond to. Note that it follows that when you have a cause, you have an *antagonist*, some group of people who benefit or at least think they benefit from the way things are, and that antagonist is likely to be powerful, since otherwise things wouldn't be such as to favour their perceived interests over those of others. And that means you have to *fight* for a cause, which will involve risk and thus require courage. It is no wonder that successfully acting in the service of a good cause is a prime candidate for leading a superlatively meaningful life – after all, people like Mandela and Gandhi are paradigm examples of meaning.

2.1. Death and Intentionality

Turning to *dying* for a cause, then, the first basic distinction I shall make is between different aims in relation to death. For the most part, when we think of someone dying for a cause, we think of people who *risk their lives* in the service of some cause they are committed to. This includes people like Hans Scholl, or the Parisians who set up barricades in 1870, or human rights activists in many former parts of the Soviet Union. Such people do not in any sense *aim* to die for their cause – indeed, they typically try their best to avoid death, as long as that is compatible with working for their cause. But their commitment to it is so strong that they would rather act and die than fail to act and live. Hans Scholl knew that he could easily be caught for writing and distributing leaflets critical of the Nazi regime, and that he would be executed if he were, but it was more important for him to follow his conscience than to live in the relative safety of silence. While such people do not choose to die, they do choose to act in the face of significant risk of death rather than betray their values, and can thus appropriately be said to have died for their cause if they are killed in its service.

Antti Kauppinen

However, there are also people who do *choose* to die for a cause, and not merely risk their lives for it. Perhaps the purest example of *aiming* to die for a cause are people who publicly kill themselves to redirect the attention of the public to their cause. Think here of the Buddhist monk Thích Quảng Đức who burned himself to death during the Vietnam War to call attention to religious inequality in the country, or the Tunisian street seller Mohamed Bouazizi, who likewise set himself on fire to protest arbitrary and humiliating treatment by authorities, sparking the Tunisian revolution of 2011.[10] Psychologists interested in self-sacrifice often focus on suicide bombers as an example of this category, and it does seem that some of them specifically seek martyrdom (see Section 4). However, I suspect that many suicide bombers simply use themselves as guidance devices for explosives and would save themselves if they could – their aim is to kill *other* people, and their own death is a side effect rather than a means to their aims.

Not all who can be said to choose to die unambiguously aim at death, however. Consider hunger strikers like the Irish Republicans Terence MacSwiney in 1920 and Bobby Sands in 1981. Roughly speaking, they demanded recognition as political prisoners rather than mere criminals. They didn't aim to die as such, but neither did they just accept a risk of dying – after all, they knew they *would* die if they continued to reject nutrition.[11] We might say they placed their lives in the hands of their antagonist, forcing the British government to choose between outrage at their deaths or yielding to their demands. Still, at the point at which it became clear to them the British would not in fact yield, they did choose to do something – refuse nutrition – which they knew would result in their death in the belief that by doing so they would serve their

[10] For information about Đức and Bouazizi, I'm relying on their Wikipedia entries, respectively https://en.wikipedia.org/wiki/Th%C3%ADch_Qu%E1%BA%A3ng_%C4%90%E1%BB%A9c and https://en.wikipedia.org/wiki/Mohamed_Bouazizi.

[11] Since both MacSwiney and his comrades were Catholic (and fighting for the cause of predominantly Catholic Irish people), the Catholic Church was forced to take a position on their hunger strikes. This resulted in interesting theological debates about whether starving oneself to death in such circumstances was suicide (and thus prohibited) or not (see Scull, 2016). For example, Father P.J. Gannon pointed out in 1920 that in a hunger striker 'There is nothing of the mentality of a suicide, whose object is to escape from a life that has grown hateful to him' (quoted in Scull, 2016, p. 293).

cause.[12] Indeed, Sophie Scholl stands out among the members of the White Rose in making a similar choice in virtue of declining to recant, and thus choosing to be killed rather than only risking being killed. (Of course, unlike the hunger strikers, she didn't kill herself.)

2.2. Death, Success, and Failure

Besides kinds of intentionality, we can also make an orthogonal distinction between death successfully serving a cause and failing to do so. Sometimes a person's death does have an instrumental role in furthering a cause. The very fact that Bouazizi died in his self-immolation in all likelihood played a role in the impact his act had. Similarly, Đức's act really did shock the conscience of the world and led to the US forcing the Vietnamese to improve the treatment of Buddhists. MacSwiney's death from hunger strike increased sympathy for the Republican cause and inspired future revolutionaries from Gandhi to Ho Chi Minh.[13] Even the Scholl siblings had at least some reason to believe that if they were to be caught and martyred, it would further the cause of resistance to the Nazis at least by breaking the illusion of uniform support for the regime, though in fact the immediate effects were minor.[14] In all of these cases, the mechanism of promoting the cause is something like the death redirecting the attention and motivation of other people in a way favourable to the cause. If third parties are at all charitable, news of such deaths easily leads them to wonder what is so wrong with the way that Buddhists or the Irish are being treated as to make some of them willing to give up their lives to change it, or make the relevant injustice salient. Such thoughts and inquiries can lead to anger and then action. And the very courage and willingness to sacrifice displayed by people who take the risky first steps against some powerful antagonist (recall Sophia Scholl's insistence that 'someone had to make a start') can itself inspire others to act on their convictions.

[12] As MacSwiney wrote during his strike, 'If I die I know the fruit will exceed the cost a thousand fold. The thought makes me happy'.
[13] See Perlman (2008).
[14] Hanser describes the group's aims as follows: 'For them, an immediate, visible result was not an important consideration. What was important was to launch a moral protest, to send out a cry of conscience. They wanted to make a start at eroding the faith of the German people in their leadership, to let their fellow dissidents know that they were not alone and that the monolith of public support for the regime was a propaganda myth' (Hanser, 2012, p. 167).

Of course, dying for a cause doesn't always serve the cause in any way. It is not a coincidence that it is not as easy to think of concrete examples of this – going unnoticed or being soon forgotten is constitutive of failing to make a difference by dying. But take Joseph Murphy, who was captured along with MacSwiney and also went on hunger strike in Cork Gaol, dying on the same day as MacSwiney (Perlman, 2008). As it happened, his sacrifice went nearly unnoticed in the shadow of the more famous man's death and can hardly be said to have made any difference. Or, for a case of aiming to die, consider the death of Irina Slavina. Who? She was a Russian journalist who burned herself to death in 2020 in protest at the constant harassment of independent journalists by the authorities.[15] Very sadly, her death doesn't seem to have made a difference, and I would wager that few of us have heard of it. When it comes to cases in which people accept the risk of death for a cause, they don't usually even think death would promote the cause, but simply accept it as a potential price to pay without allowing themselves to be deterred by it. For example, Rosa Luxemburg's death at the hands of the Freikorps in January 1919 didn't help along a communist revolution in Germany. We can summarize these distinctions and examples in the following table:

	Death serves the cause	Death doesn't serve the cause
Death is accepted for the cause	Hans Scholl	Rosa Luxemburg
Death is chosen for the cause	Sophie Scholl, Terence MacSwiney	Joseph Murphy
Death is sought for the cause	Thích Quảng Đức, Mohamed Bouazizi (?)	Irina Slavina

3. Living Meaningfully and Dying for a Cause

With this understanding of the varieties of dying for a cause, let us turn to the issue of how death for a good cause might contribute to different kinds of meaning (I will discuss bad causes later). Given what I said earlier about contributing to meaning as *mattering*, we get the following principle:

[15]   *The New York Times*, October 2, 2020.

> Death contributes to meaning$_\text{M}$ to the extent that it non-accidentally promotes or constitutes the successful realization of a challenging and identity-defining aim that there is objective reason to pursue.

Clearly, we must look here to cases in which death does end up serving the cause in some way. Start with aiming at death. As far as I know, Đức was deeply committed to the presumably good cause of religious equality in Vietnam, and resorted to self-immolation only when nothing else worked. Promoting the aim in this way was certainly challenging, and took a lot of courage. And as I noted above, his death really did make a difference as a result of the bad publicity for the government, and was meant to do so. So it can be said to have contributed significantly to his life being meaningful in the sense of mattering. It seems to me that very much the same goes for cases of choosing to die without aiming at death, like those of Sophie Scholl and Terence MacSwiney.

Where death is merely accepted, however, and thus only comes about as a side effect of other efforts, it becomes in a relevant sense less expressive of who one is. It is not itself either a part of the plan or a foreseen consequence of one's choice. That is why I would suggest that Hans Scholl's death contributed somewhat less to meaning$_\text{M}$ than his sister's, since he didn't get to make the choice about whether or not to die after being caught.

However, here it is good to remember that often the actions of people who fight for a good cause at the risk of losing their lives make a greater positive difference than their deaths – if you die in the course of blowing up the last bridge across the river to allow refugees to escape, it is blowing up the bridge that makes your life matter, not your dying. Similarly, even if Hans Scholl's death as an event in itself contributed less to meaning than his sister's, he was the founder and leader of the White Rose and the main author of most of their pamphlets, and those valuable activities chosen in spite of high risk of dying certainly were expressive of his identity and gave considerable meaning to his life.

What about meaning as *purpose*, then? The earlier discussion suggests the following criterion:

> Death contributes to meaning$_\text{P}$ to the extent that it is a high-level aim that there is subjective and objective reason to pursue.

Again, we see that dying for a cause does contribute to purpose in life for people who aim to die for a cause and whose death serves it. But an important difference here is that dying for the cause of free journalism can contribute to the meaningfulness$_p$ of Irina Slavina's life, for example, even if it doesn't end up serving the cause. Consequently, it can make motivation and striving for it fitting. Some might protest here that someone like Slavina could also take pride in her actions and is a rightful target of admiration, in spite of her death's instrumental inefficiency, which suggests that her death also contributes to meaning as mattering. I think there's some truth to this, but what it ultimately points to is just that we can see it as part of the aim of someone like Slavina to show that there are still some people in Russia who have the moral integrity to choose death rather than submission to autocracy. Her action certainly realized that valuable aim and was to that extent successful even if it didn't shake the autocracy itself.

What about people who choose death without strictly aiming at it – does dying for a cause contribute to purpose in their lives? I think it follows from what I have said that it doesn't. But I am not yet sure, because I am not quite sure what to say about the intentionality of their dying for the cause, since it doesn't seem like a mere foreseen side effect of, say, refusing nutrition. In contrast, death itself clearly doesn't provide purpose for those who merely accept a significant risk of it for a cause. Other things being equal, their actions would be just as meaningful were they miraculously saved. Imagine that rebel elements within the German armed forces had rescued Hans Scholl at the last minute, and he would have survived the rest of the war in Switzerland. That wouldn't have in any way undermined the purposefulness of his White Rose activities.

Finally, what about intelligibility and dying for a good cause? The principle looks something like the following:

> Death contributes to meaning$_I$ to the extent that it promotes or constitutes making the actions and events that comprise one's life fit into a culturally recognizable narrative of pursuing some good (a hero narrative).

Here, I think it is good news all around for dying for a good cause. There definitely is a hero narrative shared among a wide range of cultures, in which people sacrifice themselves for the sake of the common good. For such a death to add to the arc of one's life making sense, it need not be in any way successful – dying in vain for a good cause is a common variant of tragedy. Nor does it matter from the point of view of intelligibility if the death is an unwelcome side effect of fighting a more powerful enemy. It will still provide a recognizable closure that may be missing if one merely wastes away from illness.

The downside is that intelligibility is a low bar. Other things being equal, a life that makes sense may be better for a person than a life that doesn't. For example, Helena de Bres argues that intelligibility allows for the goods of mutual understanding and community (de Bres, 2018). But these alone are not the kind of values for the sake of which it is a good idea to give up an otherwise good life – especially since it *also* makes sense to give up your cause instead to save your life.

One question you might have at this point is that while it may be plausible enough that events *during your life* contribute to its meaningfulness in something like the way I have suggested, just *when* could death possibly make your life more meaningful? Seemingly, it can't do so once you die, and before that it hasn't even happened. I don't think this puzzle can be solved without endorsing retrospective value change. Luckily, then, I have defended such a view in various places.[16] Roughly speaking, I believe that death can change the teleological significance of prior actions that lead to it, and consequently make them more (or less) meaningful (Kauppinen, 2020, p. 668).

4. Meaning, Self-Interest, and Self-Sacrifice

In his book on the White Rose resistance movement, Richard Hanser says that for the members of the movement 'there was something worse than arrest, trial, and execution. What was worse was living without protest under a system that, by its nature, was the enemy of all decencies on which civilized intercourse among human beings rested'[17]. This is a very natural thing to say about the cases we are interested in. But if it had been worse for Sophie Scholl to live under the Nazis than to die, we are faced with a kind of puzzle. After all, it seems that one of the reasons we admire people like her and are grateful to them if we are among the beneficiaries of their act is that they *sacrificed* themselves for a good cause. Some may even think that it is precisely sacrificing their lives for a cause that made them meaningful (although I think this is a mistake – roughly, it's doing objectively good things in the face of challenges that gives meaning to their lives). But if dying for protesting was better for the Scholls – most likely in virtue of making their lives more meaningful than otherwise – than living much longer without protest, it seems they *didn't* after all sacrifice themselves, since they

[16] Such as Kauppinen (2015) and Kauppinen (2020).
[17] Hanser (2012, p. 20).

chose what was best for themselves. On the face of it, this is so implausible that it calls into question the thesis that dying for a good cause can make one's life meaningful.

To examine this challenge, let us start by defining self-sacrifice more precisely. As it is standardly understood, self-sacrifice involves knowingly and voluntarily choosing an option that is all-things-considered bad for yourself, and worse than other available alternatives, because you regard something else as more important than your self-interest.[18] Why are all these things required? Clearly, if you are *forced* to do something that is good for others and bad for you, you are not sacrificing yourself (though you may be sacrificed), so it must be a free choice. Similarly, if you choose to do something that is in fact all-things-considered bad for you and good for a cause because of falsely believing that you are serving your interests, you are not self-sacrificing, and merit little gratitude, so you must believe that it is all-things-considered bad for you. Call this the *subjective condition* of self-sacrifice. (It is evidently no self-sacrifice either if you do something you think is in some way bad for you, but in other ways good for you, and the good outweighs the bad – it is no self-sacrifice to go to a dentist.) On the other hand, if you falsely believe that serving some good cause is bad for you when it in fact benefits you, that is not self-sacrifice either, though in this case you may merit some admiration. So you must correctly believe, and better yet know, that serving the cause is all-things considered worse for you. Call this the *objective condition* of self-sacrifice. It must plausibly also be something positively bad and not just a less good option – at least, it is not much of a self-sacrifice to holiday on Corfu rather than Santorini because it happens to provide some benefit to refugee children.

It follows that there are two basic ways in which dying for a cause can fail to amount to self-sacrifice, setting aside the issue of positive badness:

Failure of subjective condition. If S believes she can either a) die for her cause or b) give up her cause and live, and *believes* that a is all-things-considered better for her than b, and chooses a *because* she believes so, she doesn't sacrifice herself by choosing a.
Failure of objective condition. If S can either a) die for her cause or b) give up her cause and live, and a *is* all-things-considered better for her than b, she doesn't sacrifice herself by choosing a.

---

[18]   See Overold (1980) and Heathwood (2011).

4.1 The Subjective Condition of Self-Sacrifice

Let us start our examination of when dying for a cause amounts to self-sacrifice with the subjective condition. It is certainly possible for someone to reason in the following fashion: 'Dying for the cause will make my life significantly more meaningful than giving it up to live. Meaning is a really important good in a life. So, it is in my overall self-interest to lead a significantly more rather than less meaningful life, even if it means losing many years of happiness and other goods. So, I will fight for my cause at the risk or price of death'. A person who thinks this way will fail the subjective condition of self-sacrifice. Their reasoning is relevantly similar to someone who thinks it is in her overall self-interest to go to a dentist, even though it means enduring some unpleasantness for a while. But for our purposes, the key question is whether someone who dies for a good cause *must* think in this way. And of course, for each particular individual, such as Sophie Scholl, we can ask whether they *did* think in this way.

The question of whether people who die for a cause in fact meet the subjective condition is an empirical one. Psychologists have studied people's motives for (apparent) self-sacrifice or martyrdom (Bélanger et al., 2014) especially in the context of suicide terrorism in places like Palestine, Sri Lanka, and Chechnya. Interestingly for our purposes, the leading hypothesis, defended by, among others, Arie Kruglanski and his colleagues, does seem to be that suicide bombers are typically motivated by 'quest for significance' (Kruglanski et al., 2009), or 'the desire to count, to be someone, to be recognized, to matter in the eyes of one's group, according to its (sacred) values' (Webber et al., 2017, p. 853) – roughly, a desire for meaning-as-mattering and living on in the collective memory of one's group – that is postulated to be a basic human motive, even a need. As Kruglanski and colleagues put it,

> On this analysis, the underlying motivation for suicide terrorism involves the coupling of a quest for significance with a collective crisis situation, involving a perceived threat to one's group, and a terrorism-justifying ideology whereby a suicide attack is portrayed as an act of heroic sacrifice (martyrdom) lending one's existence and demise an aura of supreme glory. (Kruglanski et al., 2009, p. 337)

This claim is supported by various sorts of empirical studies. Many are conducted in the tradition of Terror Management Theory, according to which, very roughly, fear of death and insignificance motivates people to attach themselves to groups and embrace cultural worldviews or 'ideologies' that promise them at least symbolic immortality, a role in something greater than themselves.[19] Consequently, being reminded of mortality (for example, when one's family members are killed by an occupying power[20]) or being made to feel insignificant increases people's motivation to support their group and make a mark on the world in ways endorsed by the prevailing ideology, including by participating in suicide missions when there is a grievance that calls for violent retaliation. And indeed, unsurprisingly, many would-be suicide terrorists justify their actions by appeal to defending their religion or nation (Kruglanski et al., 2009, pp. 340–44). Conversely, people who strongly identify with their religion or nation are more supportive of terrorism than others and are less anxious about their own death (Orehek et al., 2014).

Of course, it doesn't follow that people willing to die for a cause are at bottom on a quest for personal significance – they could care about defending the honour or safety of their ethnic group for its own sake and not only instrumentally. So the important question is whether people would choose or risk death for a cause if there was a possibility to gain (or restore, or avoid the loss of) significance in some other way, or if they didn't see it as a means to personal significance in the first place. The best evidence I have been able to find for significance motivation comes from two sources: first, some suicide terrorists seem to have turned to it after personal failure (doing something shameful, losing a job) (Webber et al., 2017), and second, some deradicalization programs, such as the one targeting incarcerated Tamil Tigers in Srik Lanka, appear to succeed in virtue of offering people alternative routes to significance by way of vocational education (Kruglanski et al., 2013, pp. 572–73). While this evidence is inconclusive, it suggests that in some cases risking one's life for a cause is motivated by a deeper desire to gain or restore a sense of mattering.

---

[19] See e.g. Solomon et al. (2015).

[20] Spekhard and Akhmatova (2006) found that all Checzhen suicide attackers in the 2002 Moscow theatre siege had had family members killed or tortured by Russians or their cronies, which Kruglanski and colleagues interpret as supporting the death reminder theory (Kruglanski et al., 2009, p. 339). One wonders, though, if arousing righteous anger or desire for vengeance isn't a simpler explanation – family deaths by natural causes should also remind one of mortality, but would they motivate suicide terrorism? Similarly, Webber et al. (2017) code terrorists who have lost a loved one to violence as being motivated by loss of one's own personal significance, which again ignores the simpler emotional explanation.

So, there is some psychological evidence that some people who die for a cause fail to meet the subjective condition for self-sacrifice, since if you do something ultimately because you think it will make your life more significant and therefore better in one way, you are not knowingly choosing the option that is worse for you. But evidently the empirical results come nowhere near showing that this *must* be the case. It is perfectly possible and is supported by what we know about the Scholl siblings that somebody reasons along the following lines: 'Getting ordinary Germans to rise up against tyranny is supremely important. This moral evil must be stopped, even if it means losing many years of happiness and other goods for me. So I will pursue rebellion against the regime even at the risk or price of death'. Someone who reasons in this way chooses an option they think is *morally* better in the belief that it is or may easily be *prudentially* worse. She doesn't aim at making her own life meaningful, but at making the world less bad. She need not at all think about the meaning of her own life or her self-interest, or how others will think of her afterwards. But whether she as a matter of fact does so – and clearly, there is evidence in the quotations I started with that Sophie Scholl, for example, wasn't insensitive to meaning[21] – the crucial thing is that she doesn't make her choices *because* she thinks it is best or most meaningful for *her*. She at least *would* act the same way even if she didn't think so.

To put it differently, what people seek whose choices meet the subjective condition of self-sacrifice are things that make their lives meaningful *de re*, not things that make it more meaningful *de dicto*. That is to say, it is true *of* the aims that they pursue, such as resisting the dictatorship, that pursuing them makes their lives meaningful (that is the *de re* reading), even though they don't pursue them *under the description of* making their lives meaningful (as the *de*

---

[21] There is even more to suggest that Hans Scholl was motivated to some extent to make his life matter. According to the biographer Richard Hanser, his favourite book as a boy was 'a collection of article-essays by Stefan Zweig called *Sternstunden der Menschheit*, a title that loses something in English – 'Stellar Hours of Mankind'. In it Zweig described a variety of crucial moments from which some enduring significance for coming generations flowed' (Hanser, 2012, p. 53). It is unsurprising, then, that Hans 'felt that he himself was being summoned to act heroically' and had 'a deep strain of idealism that demanded that life have a meaning, that activity have a basis in purpose' (Hanser, 2012, p. 38). Perhaps it could be said that the felt need for mattering initially got Hans to look for some way to make a valuable contribution, but most likely once he had committed to the cause of undermining the regime, any self-directed motives faded into the background.

dicto reading would have it). It is only if they pursued what makes their life meaningful *de dicto* that they would be motivated to engage in self-focused reasoning about which option would best promote meaning, and be prepared to change their project if another, less costly option were to emerge. It is worth noting that such reasoning is at least to some extent self-defeating, since if you, say, try to bring down a tyrannical regime just in order to make your life more meaningful and just as long as you think it will do so, you are not genuinely committed to bringing down the regime (since commitment would entail that you wouldn't trade it for another option just because it looked better from the perspective of your personal meaning). And if your actions don't express your commitment, they are not as deeply rooted in who you are as they could be, and therefore contribute less to making your life meaningful even if they are successful.

4.2 The Objective Condition of Self-Sacrifice

I have argued that we don't have reason to think that people who die for a cause always or generally fail the subjective condition of self-sacrifice. But what about failing the objective condition? With some plausible additional assumptions, this is a real challenge to my view. I have argued that dying for a cause can indeed make a person's life more meaningful. If that is combined with the assumption that meaning in life is a very important prudential good – that it is very much in our self-interest to lead a more rather than less meaningful life – it follows that it can relatively easily turn out that it is better for someone to die for a cause rather than to live a longer, less meaningful life. And if that is so, then my view entails that even a person who subjectively sets her self-interest aside may end up doing what is best for her, and thus won't sacrifice herself, because she fails the objective condition. This is a challenge to my view, since people who die for a cause often *do* sacrifice themselves for it. So I must explain why acts that give great meaning to our lives can nevertheless be all-things-considered bad for us.

An easy way out would be to deny that meaning in any of three varieties I have mentioned is in our self-interest. And there certainly are theories of well-being, such as forms of hedonism and subjectivism, according to which it is only instrumentally or contingently good for us, respectively, either by way of contributing to pleasure or happiness or by being something we desire or value. If that were the case, it would be easy to show that in most cases of dying for a cause the person would get more pleasure or satisfy desires better by saving themselves. And even if some more objectivist theory of well-being is true, it could be that meaning in life is a value that is distinct from well-being or self-interest. Some of the things Susan Wolf says are in this vein, especially when she highlights the contrast between reasons of self-interest and reasons of love, when the latter are involved in many meaning-generating activities according to her (Wolf, 2000, p. 51). But if we look at her work more carefully, the real contrast she tends to draw is between meaning and happiness (Wolf, 2000, p. 49). And plausibly, there is more to self-interest than happiness.

Most famously, the idea that happiness is not all that matters for well-being is supported by the often misunderstood Experience Machine thought experiment (Nozick, 1974). As Eden Lin notes, properly construed it involves two subjects who lead experientially identical lives and thus are equally happy, but while one of them derives her happiness from actual achievements and interactions, the other's experiences are surreptitiously generated by a supercomputer she is plugged into while passively lying in a tank (Lin, 2016). If happiness were the only thing that matters, the lives of these two people would necessarily be equally good for them. But they are not – other things being equal, it is better for you to feel the same amount of joy for actually winning a prize than for having the perfect illusion of doing so – so there must be more to self-interest than happiness. But what else? I can't argue for it here, but I believe that meaningfulness (as mattering or purpose or both) is a good candidate for a feature that unifies such things as valuable achievements and successful personal relationships. Indeed, as many from Nozick onwards have suggested, the most appealing explanation of why a perfectly happy life in an Experience Machine is not the best possible one is that it is notably lacking in meaning. All the standard tests for what kind of life is prudentially good also point to meaning being among welfare goods – other things being equal, we *wish for our children* to grow up to lead meaningful rather than meaningless lives, and not just because we think that would be instrumentally beneficial to them; other things being equal, we *envy* people who lead more rather than less meaningful lives, and so on. And it is not just hedonism but also subjectivism that struggles to explain this, since for a subjectivist meaning is only good for us if we desire or value it.[22] Yet it seems all the more tragic if a child grows up not valuing the things that would *de re* make her life meaningful.

[22] For sophisticated subjectivism, see Tiberius (2018).

So, there is at least a good prima facie case for thinking that meaning is a welfare good, something in itself and non-instrumentally good for us. But that means we must take head-on the challenge of showing how a significantly more meaningful life resulting from dying for a good cause and thereby (or as a result of) successfully promoting it can be all-things-considered worse for you than saving oneself. Given that on any plausible theory of well-being, meaningfulness is not the *only* welfare good, there are two possibilities: either the losses in terms of other goods outweigh the gains in meaning, or there is a net loss of meaningfulness. Fortunately for meeting the objective condition of self-sacrifice, we find both of these in our paradigm cases.

Let us start with the more straightforward case, the greater loss of other goods. It is probably not a coincidence that when we think about cases of self-sacrifice, we tend to focus on the young who would otherwise have a lot of good life ahead of them. While it is difficult if not impossible to give anything like precise weights to different components of any pluralist conception of well-being, it seems clear that sixty years of a happy life that is neither meaningless nor particularly meaningful is better for you than a very meaningful life that lasts only twenty years. The Scholl siblings, for example, might well have survived the war and gone on to live ordinary happy lives filled with friendship, achievement, and culture, despite quite possibly occasionally feeling ashamed for having been quiet during the Hitler regime. On the other hand, if a very old person goes out in a blaze of glory, her act may be admirable for its inherent or instrumental value and the courage it takes to face pain, but may well not amount to genuine self-sacrifice, if the alternative is joylessly withering away.

But wait – what if Sophie Scholl had, unbeknownst to all, a congenital heart condition that would have caused her to die in March 1943 anyway? My account would then entail that it is, after all, in Sophie's best interest to die for her cause, so that it doesn't amount to self-sacrifice. But that, to me, is the right thing to say. An informed advisor concerned only for Sophie's good would have good reason to tell her to choose the more meaningful option rather than the marginally longer life that would be considerably less meaningful, even if it contained somewhat more happiness. If you are not convinced, suppose that Sophie *knew* that she was going to die soon anyway. Her choice of sticking with her group would look a lot less like a self-sacrifice in that case.

A different kind of protest might start from the idea that even if Sophie would have died a week later anyway, as long as she *didn't* know that, her choice is admirable in virtue of being an instance of self-sacrifice. My response is to grant that her choice would indeed be admirable, but not because it would be a case of self-sacrifice, but because of her *willingness* to sacrifice herself for a good cause. It would be analogous in this respect to jumping in front of a raging bull in order to rescue some unknown children only for the bull to fall into a trap just before it gets to you. In such a situation, you wouldn't have in the end sacrificed yourself to save the children – indeed, if a grateful billionaire mother granted your every wish as a result, your action might well turn out to have been very much in your best interests. Still, the gratitude wouldn't be misplaced, since your action would nevertheless have manifested a virtuous willingness to sacrifice yourself for the sake of a great value.

I take it that it should be fairly obvious that the more meaningful choice can result in overall worse consequences for a person even if meaning counts towards self-interest. But it can also be the case that the more meaningful choice results in overall loss in terms of meaning itself. Consider the following possible lives for someone like Sophie Scholl:

> Life A: Sophie gets caught for distributing anti-Nazi leaflets; Sophie refuses to renounce her opposition; Sophie gets sentenced to death and executed on February 23, 1943.
> Life B: Sophie gets caught for distributing anti-Nazi leaflets; under pressure, Sophie recants and is sentenced to community service; immediately after the war, Sophie begins collecting evidence of Nazi atrocities, and for the next five decades, keeps the memory of the horrors alive for new generations, before succumbing to cancer on June 7, 1997.

For reasons discussed earlier, life A is more meaningful than life B until February 23, 1943 (and indeed for a considerable time after). But as Sophie in life B begins her important work in making sure that later generations never forget, her life gradually gains in meaning, and may eventually overtake life A in that respect. What this shows is that even choices that significantly contribute to meaning in life need not make the life more meaningful than it would otherwise have been.[23] They can thus amount to sacrifice in terms of meaning itself, and not just in terms of other prudential goods.

---

[23] This is structurally similar to Valerie Tiberius's observation that living up to one's values right now can result in net loss of value fulfillment in the long run, and thus amount to self-sacrifice. See Tiberius (2018, p. 43).

5. Conclusion

To sum up, I have argued that dying for a good cause can contribute to meaning in life in its various senses. If death itself is chosen and serves the cause, it plays a part in making one's life leading up to it matter. If death is a worthwhile aim in service of the cause, it can give purpose to earlier efforts, even if it doesn't have good consequences. And dying for a good cause can make for a good ending to a heroic narrative, though that is not in itself worth dying for. Insofar as having meaning in life is a good thing for an individual, there is thus something to be said for dying for a cause from the perspective of prudence. This raises the issue of how it nevertheless often amounts to self-sacrifice. The answer is that one need not choose to risk or face death because one thinks it is best or most meaningful for one, and even if such death contributes to meaning, this benefit may be outweighed by other losses, including those in terms of meaning itself.

While there thus *can* be something to be said for dying for a cause from the perspective of meaning, morality, and self-interest, I do want to finish by cautioning against it by pointing out three distinctive major risks. First of all, you might end up dying for a bad cause. People can, notoriously, fool themselves into thinking that their own group, religion, or race is objectively superior to others, and commit to righting perceived wrongs that are not genuine wrongs. The cause of the Southern Confederacy is a paradigm example. Such causes can, unfortunately, give one a sense of purpose and mattering. But they don't, for all that, make one's life meaningful, because the ends one pursues are not objectively worth pursuing. Second, even if the cause is genuinely good, it is almost always highly uncertain whether one's death will promote it, thus calling into question whether it will make one's life matter. And even if the action that leads to your death does promote the cause, it may be morally wrong, as happens in the rare cases of suicide terrorism that kills innocent civilians in pursuit of a genuinely good cause. Such wrongness may be a kind of undercutting defeater for a contribution to meaning.[24] And finally, even if the cause is good and one's death would promote it without moral wrong, it might not be good enough to make dying for it a proportionate response. It may be important to protect neighbourhood parks against greedy property developers, but you shouldn't sacrifice your life for it. So if you wish to

---

[24] I owe this intriguing suggestion to Frances Kamm.

lead a meaningful life and are lucky enough to be able to do so without risking your life, there is much to recommend in living for a cause.[25]

University of Helsinki
antti.kauppinen@helsinki.fi

References

Jocelyn Bélanger, Julie Caouette, Keren Sharvit, and Michelle Dugas, 'The Psychology of Martyrdom: Making the Ultimate Sacrifice in the Name of a Cause', *Journal of Personality and Social Psychology* 107 (2014), 494–515.

Helena de Bres, 'Narrative and Meaning in Life', *Journal of Moral Philosophy* 15 (2018), 545–71.

Login George and Crystal Park, 'Meaning in Life as Comprehension, Purpose, and Mattering: Toward Integration and New Research Questions', *Review of General Psychology* 20 (2016), 205–220.

Richard Hanser, *A Noble Treason: The Story of Sophie Scholl and the White Rose Revolt Against Hitler Vs the Revolt of the Munich Students Against Hitler*, (Ignatius Press, 2012).

Chris Heathwood, 'Preferentism and Self-Sacrifice', *Pacific Philosophical Quarterly* 92 (2011), 18–38.

Guy Kahane, 'Importance, Value, and Causal Impact', *Journal of Moral Philosophy* (forthcoming).

Antti Kauppinen, 'Meaningfulness and Time', *Philosophy and Phenomenological Research* 84 (2012), 345–77.

Antti Kauppinen, 'The Narrative Calculus', *Oxford Studies in Normative Ethics* 5 (2015), 196–220.

Antti Kauppinen, 'Prudence, Sunk Costs, and the Temporally Extended Self', *Journal of Moral Philosophy* 17 (2020), 658–81.

Antti Kauppinen, 'The Experience of Meaning', in Iddo Landau (ed.), *The Oxford Handbook of Meaning in Life* (Oxford: Oxford University Press, forthcoming).

Arie Kruglanski, Xiaoyan Chen, Mark Dechesne, Shira Fishman, and Edward Orehek, 'Fully Committed: Suicide Bombers' Motivation and the Quest for Personal Significance', *Political Psychology* 30 (2009), 331–57.

[25]   I'd like to thank participants in the Meaning of Life and Knowledge of Death workshop for useful discussion, especially Michael Hauskeller, Daniel Hill, Frances Kamm, and Thaddeus Metz, who sent me written comments. I also owe a debt for Lilian O'Brien for her insights on several drafts of the paper.

Antti Kauppinen

Arie Kruglanski, J Jocelyn J. Bélanger, Michele Gelfand, Rohan Gunaratna, Malkanthi Hettiarachchi, Fernando Reinares, Edward Orehek, Jo Sasota, and Keren Sharvit, 'Terrorism: A Love Story: Redirecting the Significance Quest Can End Violence', *American Psychologist* 68 (2013), 559–75.

Eden Lin, 'How to Use the Experience Machine', *Utilitas* 28 (2016), 314–32.

Alasdair MacIntyre, *After Virtue: A Study in Moral Theory* (Notre Dame, IN: University of Notre Dame Press, 1981).

Frank Martela and Michael Steger, 'The Three Meanings of Meaning in Life: Distinguishing Coherence, Purpose, and Significance', *Journal of Positive Psychology* 11 (2016), 531–45.

Robert Nozick, *Anarchy, State, and Utopia* (New York: Basic Books, 1974).

Edward Orehek, Jo Sasota, Arie Kruglanski, Mark Dechesne, and Leianna Ridgeway, 'Interdependent Self-Construals Mitigate the Fear of Death and Augment the Willingness to Become a Martyr', *Journal of Personality and Social Psychology* 107 (2014), 265–75.

Mark Overvold, 'Self-Interest and the Concept of Self-Sacrifice', *Canadian Journal of Philosophy* 10 (1980), 105–118.

Jason Perlman, 'Terence MacSwiney: The Triumph and Tragedy of the Hunger Strike', *New York History* 88 (2008). Online at https://web.archive.org/web/20081204101849/http://www.historycooperative.org/journals/nyh/88.3/perlman.html

Matthew Ratcliffe, *Experiences of Depression: A Study in Phenomenology* (Oxford: Oxford University Press, 2014).

MM Scull, 'The Catholic Church and the Hunger Strikes of Terence MacSwiney and Bobby Sands', *Irish Political Studies* 31 (2016), 282–99.

Sheldon Solomon, Jeff Greenberg, and Tom Pyszczynski, *The Worm at the Core: On the Role of Death in Life* (New York: Random House, 2015).

Anne Spekhard and Khapta Akhmatova, 'The Making of a Martyr: Chechen Suicide Terrorism', *Studies in Conflict and Terrorism* 29 (2006), 1–65.

Valerie Tiberius, *Well-Being as Value Fulfillment: How We Can Help Each Other to Live Well* (New York: Oxford University Press, 2018).

David Webber, Kristen Klein, Arie Kruglanski, Ambra Brizi, and Ariel Merari, 'Divergent Paths to Martyrdom and Significance Among Suicide Attackers', *Terrorism and Political Violence* 29 (2017), 852–74.

Susan Wolf, *Meaning in Life and Why It Matters* (Princeton, NJ: Princeton University Press, 2000).

Promises to the Dead

JAMES STACEY TAYLOR

Abstract

Many people attempt to give meaning to their lives by pursuing projects that they believe will bear fruit after they have died. Knowing that their death will preclude them from protecting or promoting such projects people who draw meaning from them will often attempt to secure their continuance by securing promises from others to serve as their caretakers after they die. But those who rely on such are faced with a problem: None of the four major accounts that have been developed to explain directed promissory obligation (the Authority View, the Trust View, the Assurance View, and the Reliance View) support the view that we are obligated to keep our promises to persons who are now dead. But I will provide hope for those who wish to use such promises to protect the meaning with which they have endowed their lives. I will argue that while we cannot wrong a person who is now dead by breaking a promise made to her during her life, we could wrong the living by so doing. We thus (might) have reason to keep the promises that we made to those who are now dead.

1. Introduction

Many people attempt to give meaning to their lives by pursuing projects that they believe will bear fruit after they have died. Knowing that their death will preclude them from protecting or promoting such projects, people who pursue them to give their lives meaning might attempt to secure their continuance by securing promises from others to serve as their caretakers after they have died. A mother might, for example, secure a promise from her child that he will never sell their farm as she has devoted her life to keeping it in the family, or a philanthropist might secure a promise from her trustees that they will abide by the original terms of her Trust.[1] Securing such promises often reassures those to whom they are

---

[1]   Daniel Hill holds that for a life to be meaningful it is necessary that it 'be freely lived, at least in significant part, for a valuable purpose, and that, *to a significant degree, the life achieve that purpose*' (Daniel Hill, 'God, the Meaning of Life, and Meaningful Lives,' in this volume; emphasis added.) On this view a person who lived for a purpose that would be realized after her death might attempt to ensure that her life was meaningful by

doi:10.1017/S1358246121000242   © The Royal Institute of Philosophy and the contributors 2021

James Stacey Taylor

made, for it is widely believed that to break a promise that was made to a person who is now dead would be to wrong her, just as to break a promise to a person during her lifetime would be to wrong her.[2] Indeed, it is popularly believed that breaking a promise made to someone on their deathbed is somehow *worse* than breaking promises made to them at other times.[3]

This belief is not only held by laypeople: it is also widely (and largely uncritically) accepted by philosophers. So entrenched is the view that breaking a promise that was made to a person who is now dead would be to wrong them that it is often treated as being axiomatic within the debates over whether it is possible to harm or to wrong the dead. In defending the view that posthumous harm is possible against the charge that there was no subject for such harm to befall, for example, Joel Feinberg rhetorically asks 'When a promise is broken, someone is wronged, and who if not the promisee? ...If there is no problem of the subject when we speak of wronging the dead, why should there be when we speak of harming them...?' (Feinberg, 1993, pp. 182–83). Yet Feinberg's rhetorical flourish glosses over the fact that it is not obvious just *why* breaking a promise to someone wrongs her. Prior to accepting that breaking a promise to a person who is now dead would wrong her, then, one must first establish why it is that promises obligate, and hence why it is that breaking a promise to a person in the standard case (i.e., when she is still alive) might wrong her. Then, with this account of promissory obligation

---

having someone promise to ensure that the plans that she had set in place to fulfill her intended purpose would be followed.

[2] Widely, but not universally; James Griffin, for example, is skeptical that promises made to persons long dead are binding on the promisor; see Griffin (1986, pp. 194, 362, n.34). Henry Sidgwick also doubts that promises remain binding once the promisee has died, writing that 'It appears that a clear *consensus* can only be claimed for the principle that a promise, explicit or tacit, is binding, if a number of conditions are fulfilled: viz, if the promiser has a clear belief as to the sense in which it was understood by the promise, *and if the latter is still in a position to grant release from it.*... If any of these conditions fails, the *consensus* seems to become evanescent, and the common moral perceptions of thoughtful persons fall into obscurity and disagreement' (Sidgwick, *The Methods of Ethics*, 3.6, sec. 9; Italics on 'consensus' in original, italics added to pertinent clause.) Sidgwick's view has an affinity to David Owens' Authority View of promissory obligation that will be discussed below; see Owens (2006; 2007; 2012).

[3] Popularly, but not necessarily philosophically; see Norcross (2011, p. 220).

82

in hand, one would need to show that it would *also* support the claim that breaking a promise to a person who is now dead would wrong her. And there's the rub for those who rely on such promises to support their pursuit of meaning in life: None of the four major approaches to explaining such directed promissory obligation (the Authority View, the Trust View, the Assurance View, and the Reliance View) support the view that we are obligated to keep our promises to persons who are now dead.[4]

That none of the major accounts of how promises obligate supports the view that breaking a promise that was made to a person who is now dead would wrong her does not show that the dead cannot be wronged. It might be that another account of promissory obligation is both correct *and* supports the view that we are obligated to keep our promises to the dead. Or it might be that while the dead cannot be wronged by the breaking of the promises made to them in life they could still be wronged in other ways.[5] But until sound arguments supporting one or more of these positions are forthcoming, the common claim that a person can be posthumously wronged should not be accepted.

But despite this conclusion I will provide hope for those who wish to attempt to protect the meaning with which they have endowed their lives by securing promises from the living to be fulfilled after their deaths. I will argue that while we cannot wrong a person who is now dead by breaking a promise made to her during her life, we could wrong the living by so doing. We thus (might) have reason to keep the promises that we made to those who are now dead.

---

[4] The issue is how breaking a promise to a person would be to wrong her, and so only those accounts of promissory obligation on which the obligation to keep one's promises is an obligation owed to one's promisee are relevant. The prominent Practice-Based accounts of promissory obligation developed by Hume and Rawls will thus not be addressed here for on those accounts of promissory obligation one's obligation to keep one's promises is not owed directly to one's promisee, but instead is owed generally to the persons who participate in the practice of promise-keeping. See Hume (1978, pp. 522–24) and Rawls (1999, pp. 301–307).

[5] Arguments in favor of the view that the dead can be wronged that are not based on the claim that one has an obligation to keep promises to the dead have been developed by Belliotti (1979); Lande (1990) and Blustein (2008, Ch. 5). An alternative promise-based argument for the view that the dead can be wronged has been developed by Wisnewski (2009, pp. 58–60). These arguments are all criticized in Taylor (2012, ch. 4).

James Stacey Taylor

2. The Standard View: To Break a Promise to a Person Who is Now Dead Would Wrong Her

Feinberg is the most well-known proponent of the view that since a promisee can be (putatively) wronged by the breaching of a promise after her death then persons can also be harmed by events that occur after their deaths. But he was not the first to use this analogy to motivate the view that posthumous harm is possible. This approach to motivating the idea that posthumous harm was possible was earlier pursued by George Pitcher (Pitcher, 1984, p. 183), while Thomas Nagel held that to break a promise after the promisee's death would be 'an injury to the dead man' (Nagel, 1970, p. 78). Indeed, by the time Feinberg drew on the claim that breaching a promise to a dead person would wrong her to support the view that posthumous harm was possible, Barbara Levenbook had noted that that analogy was widespread and had 'persuaded a few philosophers' of the possibility of posthumous harm.[6]

The view that to break a promise to a person who is now dead would wrong her is not only treated as axiomatic in the debate over whether posthumous harm is possible.[7] Loren E. Lomasky and Daniel Sperling have drawn on this view to establish that the dead have rights,[8] while Harry S. Silverstein has noted that the view that

[6]   Levenbook (1984, p. 407). Levenbook was not herself convinced by '[t]his sort of reasoning' and so provided an alternative account of how posthumous harm was possible. However, other philosophers (such as Dorothy Grover, Anthony Serafini, and J.J. Thomson) continued to be persuaded that posthumous harm was possible because they believed that it was possible to wrong a person after her death by breaking a promise that had been made to her during her life. See Grover (1989, pp. 339, 351–52); Serafini (1989–90, p. 335), J.J. Thomson (1992, pp. 318–19). Not all philosophers have been convinced by this analogy between posthumous wrongs and posthumous harms; Richard Kraut, for example, accepts that a person would be wronged by the posthumous breach of a promise but denies the possibility of posthumous harm (Kraut, 2007, p. 139, n.9).
[7]   Those who use the claim that to break a promise to a person who is now dead would be to wrong her to motivate the view that posthumous harm is possible cannot use this strategy unless they believe that the reason that breaching such a promise is wrong independently of any harmful effects it might have on the dead promisee.
[8]   Lomasky (1987, p. 212); Sperling (2008, p. 170). Ashley Dressel argues that the dead cannot have rights as they do not exist and so 'rights based' accounts of promissory obligation cannot support the view that there is an obligation to keep promises to persons who are dead (Dressel, 2015, pp. 326–27). But this argument misunderstands the view that it

84

it would wrong a person to break a promise to her after her death has been widely discussed 'as a possible counter-example to utilitarianism'.[9] And it is not merely philosophers who take it as axiomatic that to break a promise to a person now dead would wrong her. As Susan Wolf has recently observed, the idea that it would be acceptable to break a deathbed promise (even where this breach could not affect the practice of making promises to be executed after the promisee was dead) departs 'radically' from 'common sense' and is a view that 'ordinary morality' 'recoils' from.[10]

3. The Problem of Directed Promissory Obligation

Yet while Feinberg's claim that 'When a promise is broken, someone is wronged....' is both widely accepted and relatively uncontroversial there is a longstanding puzzle as to why the breaking of a promise would wrong the promisee. This is the Problem of Directed Promissory Obligation: How can one acquire an obligation to a person P to do X just by promising P that one will do X? More precisely, how can one's mere utterance of a performative verb place one under an obligation to another person to perform the act that one has communicated to her that one will perform? Hume, famously, found the putative acquisition of an obligation in this way to be utterly 'mysterious and incomprehensible,' comparing it to 'transubstantiation or holy orders, where a certain form of words, along with a

---

addresses for those who hold that the dead have rights ascribe these rights to their putative possessors as they were while alive. For example, consider that in 2018 P promises to Q that she will perform act X in 2020 and then breaches this promise after Q dies in 2019. On the rights-based account of promissory obligation P's breach of her promise to Q would have made it true that the right that Q held *during her lifetime* that P do X was violated by P (See Lomasky, 1987, pp. 213–17.) While Dressel recognizes that her argument does not hold against those rights-based views of promissory obligation that are not based on the claim that non-existents have rights she fails to recognize that *all* rights-based views of promissory obligation are of this sort (and so her argument does not address any of them).

[9] Silverstein (1972, p. 448). For examples of this discussion see Smart (1956, p. 350); Hare (1963, pp. 132–36) and Cargile (1964, pp. 23–24). Since in this context the breaking of a deathbed promise is used as a (putative) example of harmless wrongdoing, those who deploy this example to criticize utilitarianism reject harm-based accounts of promissory obligation.

[10] Wolf (2016, p. 125); see too Hare (1963, p. 133).

certain intention, changes entirely the nature of an external object, and even of a human creature' (Hume, 1978, p. 524). Yet unlike the supernatural mysteries of transubstantiation and holy orders. Hume believed that an account could be given of the basis of promissory obligation.[11] Noting that there is a problem of how one's making a promise could place one under a new obligation to the person to whom one has made the promise should thus not be construed as an objection to the existence of such obligation but as an indication that it needs to be explained and justified.[12]

Not surprisingly, those who have addressed this issue have focused on explaining how promises can generate obligations in standard cases of promising – those where one person A promises to another, B, to perform some act X at some point in the future at a time when B will still be living. This focus on standard cases of promising leaves open the possibility that *non*-standard cases of promising (such as promises to oneself, or a promise made by A to B to do X at a time when B would be dead) would not generate any promissory obligations to the promisee for the non-standard cases might lack the obligation-generating features of the standard cases.

4. Four Accounts of Directed Promissory Obligation

As noted above, Hume's own account of promissory obligation is an attempt to answer the general question of why persons are obligated to keep their promises rather than the more specific question of how making a promise to a person places one under an obligation to that person to keep one's promise to her.[13] As such, even if his account of promissory obligation is correct it cannot support the claim that

---

[11]   Although, as noted above, Hume did not provide an account of why making a promise placed one under an obligation to one's promisee to keep one's promise, but an account of why one was obliged to keep a promise *simpliciter*. He was thus not addressing the Problem of *Directed* Promissory Obligation that is at issue here but a less restricted Problem of Promissory Obligation that does not require an explanation of how a promiser could have an obligation to her promisee.

[12]   This point was made by Sheinman (2011, p. 7).

[13]   For Hume we are first motivated to keep our promises out of self-interest, and then, when we recognize the social utility of promise-keeping, we keep them out of a sense of obligation. We are thus obliged to keep our promises because breaching them would undermine the useful social institution of promising. According to Hume, then, breaking one's promise does not wrong the promisee, but is a wrong done to the

breaking a promise to a person who is now dead that was made to her while she was alive would be to wrong her.[14] However, four other prominent accounts of promissory obligation have been developed to account for the view that in making a promise to B, A incurs an obligation *to B* to keep that promise: the Authority View, the Trust View, the Assurance View, and the Reliance View.

The Authority View of promissory obligation (as developed and defended by David Owens) is based on the claim that persons have both an 'authority interest' (an interest 'in having the right to oblige others to do certain things') and 'an interest in being able to satisfy the needs of others should we so wish' (Owens, 2012, p. 146). When A promises to B that he will do X, he communicates to her that he has granted her authority over him with respect to his performance of X. If B communicates to A that she will accept this authority over him, thus bringing into existence their relationship as promisor and promisee, A's interest in being able to grant this authority to her is satisfied, as is B's interest in acquiring authority over A. If A then breaches his promise to B, he will have wronged her by thwarting her authority interest over his performance of X (Owens, 2012, pp. 146–47).

The Trust View of promissory obligation is based on 'the idea of *inviting someone to trust one to do something*' (Friedrich and Southwood, 2011, p. 278). On this view, the making by A of a promise to B to do X signals to B that A recognizes that X is important to her by inviting her to have faith in A's character with respect to A's performance of X. If this invitation is accepted, and the promise made, then the relationship between A and B will be transformed, such that were A not to do X he would not only have failed to do something he knew was important to B but would have betrayed the trust that he invited her to place in him. A person is thus obligated

---

participants in the practice of promising as a whole. See Hume, (*Treatise*, pp. 522–23).

[14] That practice-based accounts of promissory obligation cannot support the view that a promiser's obligation is to his promisee has led to them being widely criticized with their detractors holding that these accounts fail to capture something crucial about the nature of promissory obligation. See, for example, Feinberg, who offers a general criticism of practice-based accounts of promissory obligation along these lines (Feinberg, 1993, pp. 188–90), and (in the context of criticizing Rawls' account of promising), Scanlon (1998, p. 316) and Darwall (2011, pp. 262–64).

to keep the promises that he has made out of a moral duty not to betray the trust that he invited the promisee to place in him.

A similar account of promissory obligation is offered by the proponents of the Assurance View. On this account a person is obliged to keep her promises because in making them she has intentionally and voluntarily created in the promisee the expectation that she will X, where X is something that the promisee values and hence whose occurrence she wants to be assured of, and, moreover, both the promiser and the promisee know that this assurance has been created, and they both know that the other knows this, and so on.[15] On this view, a promiser will wrong the person to whom she has promised to X if she fails to X, and hence fails to live up to the assurance that she had created within him that she would X. While this account of promissory obligation is similar to the Trust View, it is also distinct from it. One might create assurance without inviting trust, by, for example, simply imparting information concerning one's future plans (Friedrich and Southwood, 2011, p. 283). Conversely, one might invite trust without thereby creating assurance – a philandering spouse might attempt to do this as she protests (once again!) that she is mending her ways.[16]

Both the Trust and the Assurance Views of promissory obligation are similar to the Reliance View. On this view, a person is obligated to keep her promises since in making them she has invited the promisee to rely on her performing (or refraining from performing) some action, and this invitation has (at the very least) not been rejected, thus leading the promisee to rely on the promisor.[17] This account of promissory obligation differs from the Trust View since a person might invite another to rely on her to perform or refrain from performing an action without thereby inviting her to trust her so to refrain or perform. In a repeated Prisoner's Dilemma game with an unknown number of iterations, a person might, for example, invite her partner to rely on her not to defect by signaling this through her actions. But this invitation stops short of an invitation to trust, for this would require an optimism in the signaler's good character that would be alien to the game. The Reliance View of promissory obligation also differs from the Assurance View, which lacks its invitational element.

---

[15]   See, for example, Scanlon (1998, p. 304). A similar account of promissory obligation has been proposed by Narveson (1971).

[16]   A similar point was made by Friedrich and Southwood, (2011, pp. 283–84).

[17]   See, for example, Thomson (1992, esp. Chapter 3).

If correct, any one of these four accounts of promissory obligation would establish that in the standard case of a promise broken to a person who is still alive, the promiser would wrong the promisee.[18] But that this is so does not entail that they would *also* show that in a *non*-standard case in which a promiser broke a promise to a person after her death that he made to her while she was still alive he would thereby wrong her. And, as will be argued below, none of these accounts of promissory obligation support this further claim.

5. The Authority View

It is clear that on Owens' Authority View of promissory obligation one cannot wrong a person who is now dead by failing to fulfill a promise that was made to her while she was alive.[19] On this account of promissory obligation, a person's obligation to fulfil her a promise stems from the value of satisfying the authority interests of the persons to whom she has made the promise in question. A person acquires an authority interest in the actions of another when a promise is made, with this placing the promisee in authority over the promisor with respect to the act that the promisor promised to perform. Having acquired this authority over the promisor, the promisee can either oblige the promisor to perform the promised act or else release her from this obligation. It is the promisee's ability to choose whether to oblige performance or release her promisor from this obligation that satisfies her authority interest. The promisee's authority interest is thus not satisfied by the promisor being bound to perform the promised act, but by the promisee being in a position to choose whether or not she is obliged to do so. If it is not possible for the promisee to choose whether to oblige the promisor to perform his promised act or to release him from this obligation, then she will lack the authority interest that grounds promissory obligation. The promisor will thus have no obligation to fulfil his promise to her and so will not have wronged her if he fails to do so. The dead clearly cannot exercise authority in this way over those

[18] Note too that none of these accounts would support the view that a promissory obligation is generated by an attempt to make a promise to a person who is dead at the time that the promise was made. That there is no promissory obligation to the dead in this sense was noted by Roth (2016, p. 101, n.26).

[19] This was recognized by both Woods (2017, p. 80) and Liberto (2017, pp. 109–110).

who made them promises during their lifetimes. There is thus, on Owen's Authority View of promissory obligation, no obligation incumbent on a promisor to fulfil the promises that she made to person who are now dead. A promisee's death thus releases her promisors from their promissory obligations to her (Owens, 2012, pp. 198, 201). Hence on the Authority View of promissory obligation a dead promisee can never be wronged by her promisors' failure to fulfil their promises to her.

6. The Reliance View

The Reliance View of promissory obligation also appears to fail to support the view that one can wrong a person who is now dead through breaking a promise that was made to her while she was alive. On the Reliance View of promissory obligation, a person will wrong the individual to whom he has made a promise if he invites her to rely on him to do something and then fails to do it. The wrong involved in breaching a promise is thus the wrong of leading another person to order her actions on the basis of the belief that one will X, and then not doing X. It is accordingly a requirement of the Reliance View of promissory obligation that the promisee be able to make plans on the basis of the promises that were made to her. One will thus not, on this account of promissory obligation, have any obligation to keep promises made to persons just before they died, for in such cases one will be unable to issue the requisite invitation to the promisee to rely on one in making her plans. On this view, then, deathbed promises will have no obligatory force.[20]

But one should not conclude from this that the Reliance View could not recognize any posthumous breach of a promise as a wrong to the promisee. Not every promise made to a person now dead was made when she was unable to make any further plans. My promise to my mother to ensure that her collection of dolls remains intact after her death is one that she is currently relying on in making plans concerning the disposal of her estate. If I were to breach this promise after she dies, then I would have breached a promise that she relied on in making her plans. My promise is important to my mother because she is making decisions concerning her doll collection based on the belief that I will ensure that it remains intact after her death and because she believes that my promise will

---

[20] Friedrich and Southwood consider this to ground an objection to the Reliance View (2011, p. 285).

ensure that this belief will be true. If I breached this promise after my mother's death, I would make it the case that some of the beliefs that she relied upon while acting were false. Thus, one could hold that on the Reliance View the wrong of breaching a promise is the wrong of bringing another person to order her actions based on a false belief. And since breaching a promise after the promisee's death could make it the case that, while alive, she ordered her actions on a false belief, it seems that one could, on the Reliance View, wrong someone after their death by breaching a promise that was made to them while they were alive.

But why would falsifying some of a person's beliefs, the truth of which she relied upon in deciding how to act, be to wrong her? One reason could be that in leading a person to act on false beliefs one would be undermining her ability to achieve her goals, thereby compromising her well-being. This might ground a plausible account of why on the Reliance View breaking a promise to a person while she is still alive would be to wrong her. However, if it is offered as an account of why on this View breaking a promise to a person after she is dead would be to wrong her it would commit its proponents to the claim that persons can be harmed by events (e.g., the breaking of a promise) that occur after their deaths. And there is good reason to believe that posthumous harm is impossible.[21] However, rather than relying on a concern for the well-being of promisees, one could instead draw hold that the falsification of a person's beliefs through breaching a promise to her could undermine her ability to make her

---

[21]   Taylor (2012, ch. 3). The classic arguments in favor of the view that persons can be harmed or benefitted after their deaths have been developed by Pitcher (1984, pp. 157–68) and Feinberg (1993). For objections to the Pitcher-Feinberg account of posthumous harm and arguments in favor of the view that that the dead cannot be harmed, see Taylor (2005) and Portmore (2008). In *Death, Posthumous Harm, and Bioethics*, Chapter 2, I also criticize the defenses of the possibility of posthumous harm that have been developed by Levenbook (1984), Grover (1989), Sperling (2008), and Griseri (1987). Dressel also offers objections to the view that posthumous harm is possible to establish that there is no harm-based obligation owed to persons who are now dead to keep promises that were made to them while they were alive (Dressel, 2015, pp. 327–334. Dressel's objections are very similar to Taylor's.) Since she (mistakenly; see note 8) believes that she has shown that no rights-based account of directed promissory obligation could ground the obligation to keep promises to the dead, she (mistakenly) believes that undermining the possibility of any harm-based obligation to keep such promises will establish that there is no such obligation at all.

own decisions. From this, one could then develop an autonomy-based account of how on the Reliance View breaching a promise to a person would be to wrong her. On this analysis breaches of promise would be wrong on the Reliance View because in rendering false those of a person's beliefs that she is using to make her decisions one would be compromising her autonomy – and to compromise a person's autonomy is *prima facie* to wrong her.

It is true that in some cases rendering a person's beliefs false could compromise her autonomy. However, this would not be because she is making her decisions on the basis of false beliefs. Rather, it would be because it is through this falsification of her beliefs that another person usurps control over the decisions that she makes by manipulating her beliefs so that she will make the decisions and perform the actions that her manipulator desires of her. Thus, for a person's autonomy with respect to her decisions and consequent actions to be compromised through the falsification of her beliefs, this falsification must be deliberately brought about by another. And this must have been done with the aim of motivating the person whose beliefs have been falsified to make the decisions that her manipulator desired her to make. This falsification of belief must thus occur *prior* to her making the decisions in question. Since this is so, breaching a promise that was made to a person who is now dead could not wrong her by undermining her autonomy with respect to the decisions that she made in consequence of relying on her promisor's word. The falsification of her relevant beliefs would have occurred *after* the decisions that they were relevant to had been made. Thus, if on the Reliance View the breaching of a promise wrongs the promisee through compromising her autonomy, then this account of promissory obligation cannot support the claim that to breach a promise to a person who is now dead would be to wrong her.

7. The Trust and Assurance Views of Promissory Obligation

The Reliance View of promissory obligation thus does not support the claim that one could wrong a person who is now dead by breaking a promise that was made to her while she was alive. What, then, of the Trust View and the Assurance View of promissory obligation? As with the Reliance View, to determine whether these accounts will support the view that breaching a promise to a person who is now dead would be to wrong her will require an analysis of just why a betrayal of trust or a violation of an assurance would be to wrong the person whose trust was betrayed or whose confidence in the assurance she received was misplaced. One possible answer is simply that a betrayal or the violation of an assurance *just is* a wrong – that both betrayals and violations of assurances are wrongs in themselves, independently of any effects that they might have.[22] But without further argument there is no reason to accept this response, for it is not analytically true that a betrayal of a trust or a violation of an assurance is necessarily a wrong. One can certainly ask whether a particular betrayal, or the violation of a particular assurance, wronged the person who was betrayed or whose confidence in the assurance she received was misplaced without evincing a misunderstanding of the terms. The Rev J. Llewellyn Davies, for example, was not obviously mistaken when he noted in response to Mill's utilitarianism that the betrayal of a person's trust by a friend should not be called a 'crime' if it was done in order to avoid fatally harming either the man betrayed 'or someone belonging to him'.[23]

Moreover, there is reason to believe that the view that betrayals or violations of assurances *just are* wrongs to the persons betrayed, or whose confidence in the assurances they received was misplaced, is mistaken. If betrayals or violations of trust are bare wrongs then breaches of promises that involved them would be wrongs even if they had no effect on anything. If this were correct, then if a person P did not do X when she had not promised to do X then she would not have breached a promise, and so would have done no wrong. However, if P had promised to do X but did not, then she would have breached a promise, and so would have done wrong. But if breaching a promise would be a wrong *even if it had no effect on anything*, then it would be the case that P would do wrong in failing to do X only if she had *declared* that she would do wrong if she failed to do X. And, as Hume noted, it is mysterious as to why merely declaring something a wrong would make it a wrong (Hume, 1978, p. 524).

But if it is implausible to believe that betrayals and violations of assurances are bare wrongs what accounts for their wrongness? Two possible answers to this question can be drawn from the above discussion of the Reliance View of promissory obligation. A betrayal or a violation of an assurance could wrong someone through falsifying

---

[22] Nagel appears to think this; see Nagel (1970, p. 76). The notion of a 'bare wrong' was introduced by W.D. Ross in the context of his criticism of the utilitarian account of promissory obligation and his argument in favor of 'the *intrinsic* rightness of a certain type of act'. See Ross (2002, pp. 37–39, 46–47).

[23] Quoted by Mill (1978, p. 18, n.2).

some of her beliefs that guided her decision-making. If this falsification through betrayal or the violation of an assurance occurred either before *or* after she made her decisions, then it could have wronged her by unjustly harming her through thwarting her interests. If, however, it only occurred *prior* to the promisee making her decisions related to the broken promises, then she would have been wronged through having her autonomy with respect to her decisions (and consequent actions) compromised. As was noted in the above discussion of the Reliance View, there is no reason to believe that posthumous harm is possible. There is thus no reason to believe that a person who is now dead could be wronged by being harmed through having her trust betrayed or the assurances that she was given violated. The above discussion also makes clear breaking a promise to a person who is now dead cannot wrong her by compromising her autonomy with respect to those decisions that she made as she trusted her promisor to perform a certain action or accepted his assurance that he would do so. There is thus no reason to believe that on either the Trust View or the Assurance View to break a promise to a person who is now dead would wrong her.

8. Respecting the Autonomy of the Dead

There remains, however, one final argument that could be offered by a proponent of the Reliance View, the Trust View, or the Assurance View who believes that one can wrong a person who is now dead by breaking a promise that was made to her while she was alive: that such a breach could evince a failure properly to respect the autonomy of the promisee.[24] To fail to respect a person's autonomy is to fail to adopt the attitude towards her autonomously-formed desires and actions that they are *prima facie* worthy of consideration simply in virtue of their being a person's autonomously-formed desires and actions. One could fail to respect another person's autonomy *without* compromising her ability to exercise it. (This position is thus not undermined by the argument – outlined above – that one could not wrong a person who is now dead by compromising the ability that she had while alive to exercise her autonomy by breaking a promise that one made to her while she was alive.) One might, for example, fail to respect another person's autonomy and so be

---

[24]   This view is endorsed by Charles Fried, who writes that 'the obligation to keep a promise is grounded not in arguments of utility *but in respect for individual autonomy* and in trust' (1981, p. 16). (Emphasis added.)

disposed to ignore or override her autonomous decisions as though they had no weight but never actually do so since they happen to be congruent with one's own plans. In such a case one would fail to respect the other's autonomy but would not compromise it in any way. The breaking of a promise to a person who is now dead could hence evince a failure to respect her autonomy even if it would not compromise her ability to have exercised it while she was alive. Thus, if to fail to respect a person's autonomy is to wrong her, then the breaking of a promise to a person who is now dead could wrong her by evincing a failure properly to respect the autonomy that she possessed while she was alive. This could be so even if a posthumous breach of promise would not compromise the promisee's autonomy while she was alive.[25]

For this argument to establish that breaking a promise to a person who is now dead could wrong her by evincing a failure properly to respect her autonomy, it must be the case that the promise-breaker appropriately respected the autonomy of the promisee while she was alive. If he did not, then a person who believed that breaking a promise to a person who is now dead would *not* wrong her could simply claim that the breaching promiser's wrongdoing lay not in the posthumous breaking of the promise but in his failure to respect the promisee's autonomy during her life. (He would have wronged her during her life both by failing appropriately to respect her autonomy and also by deceiving her by representing himself to her as a sincere promise-maker even though he made a promise to her that he did not consider himself to be bound by.) For it to be clear that the (putative) wrong of breaking a promise to a person who is now dead would occur *after* the death of the promisee *and* that this wrong was grounded on a failure of respect for the promisee's autonomy, then, the promise-breaker must both have appropriately respected the autonomy of the promisee while she was alive, and then, at some point after her death, ceased to do so, with this leading to his breaking his promise to her.

An example of such a situation would be that of a person who promised a friend that he would always look after her prized maple tree. After her death he developed a sexist streak and ceased both to respect her wishes and (in consequence of this) to look after the tree. This example appears to show that breaking a promise to someone after their death could evince a failure to respect the autonomy of the person to whom the promise was made, and hence could wrong them. But to draw this conclusion would be too hasty. If the

---

[25]   See Robins (1984, p. 120).

posthumous breaking of a promise evinces a failure on the part of the promise-breaker to respect the autonomy of the promisee, and for this reason is held to wrong her, then the wrong in question is based not on the promise-breaking itself, but on *the promise-breaker's attitude towards the promisee.* The posthumous breaking of the promise would thus not itself be wrong. Instead, it would merely provide evidence of a wrongful attitude. The wrong in this case would not be the wrong of the breaking of a promise. It would be the (putative) wrong of holding a particular attitude towards the autonomy of another.

This respect-based argument thus fails to show that the breaking of a promise to a person who is now dead would be to wrong her. But it does lend support to the view that the dead can be wronged by being the objects of morally inappropriate attitudes. Perhaps, then, persons could be wronged by actions or events that occur after their deaths, even if there is no reason to believe that they could be wronged by the breaching of promises that were made to them while they were alive?

But despite the appearance that the dead could be wronged by persons adopting attitudes towards them that evince a failure to respect their autonomy, one should still ask why an apparent failure to respect the autonomy of another would be to wrong her. One possibility is that a failure to respect another's autonomy could lead one to mistreat her, or else to discount her interests in ways that adversely affect her well-being. If this is the basis for the moral concern with respect for autonomy then for one to be concerned about putative failures to respect the autonomy of persons who are now dead, one would have to believe that the dead, like the living, could be subject to harms or benefits. But, as has already been noted, there is reason to believe that the view that posthumous harms and benefits are possible is mistaken.[26] Alternatively, one might hold that a failure to respond appropriately to the value of autonomy would be a wrong in itself. To hold this view, one must hold that autonomy is of more than prudential value. But, if this is so, then unless an argument to show that autonomy is valuable in itself is forthcoming, there would be no reason to believe that a failure to respect it would constitute a moral wrong.[27] Moreover, even if one could show that autonomy was intrinsically valuable, one would also have to show why merely *adopting a particular attitude* towards it would constitute a moral wrong, independently of any effects that such an attitude might have. And since this would

[26] See note 21.
[27] For an argument that autonomy is not valuable in itself see Valdman (2010).

involve holding such an attitude to be a 'bare wrong', it is unlikely that this line of argument would succeed. Thus, not only does a concern for respecting the autonomy of the dead fail to support the view that breaking a promise to a person after her death would be to wrong her, but, absent further argument, there is no reason to believe that the dead can be wronged by the living failing to respect the autonomy that they possessed while alive.

9. Meaningful Lives and Keeping Promises to the Dead

It was noted at the start of this paper that some people might secure promises from others to perform (or refrain from performing) certain actions to ensure that their projects whose achievement they believe to be a necessary condition for their lives to have meaning come to fruition.[28] From the point of view of someone who both believes that the lives of such persons would not be meaningful unless such promises were kept, and who is concerned that persons' lives be meaningful, the arguments developed in this paper might appear worrisome. If correct, they establish that one cannot wrong a person who is dead by breaking a promise to her that was made while she was alive. Moreover, as noted above, one cannot harm a person through posthumously thwarting her interests. One thus cannot harm someone by posthumously thwarting her interest in having a meaningful life by breaking the promise that one had made to her to secure the achievement of the projects that would give meaning to her life. One could thus not wrong a dead person by harming her. Since one could thus neither wrong a dead person by breaking a promise that one made to her while she was alive nor by harming her through thwarting her interests, it might appear that there is no moral obligation to keep promises made to persons who are dead at the time that the promise should be fulfilled. Persons who wish for their lives to be meaningful might thus appear to be well advised to ensure that the ends of the projects that they pursue to give meaning to their lives could be achieved within their own lifetimes. This is because it appears that if they were to pursue projects whose ends would be achieved after they die, then they would be risking the meaningfulness of their lives for those who promised to ensure that the ends of their projects were achieved would have no moral obligation to keep these promises.

[28] See note 1.

James Stacey Taylor

But – and fortunately for those who aim to give their life meaning by pursuing projects whose ends will only be achieved after they are dead – even though a promisor would not wrong a promisee by, after her death, breaching a promise that was made to her while she was alive, this does not entail that he would thereby do no wrong. While the Practice-Based Views of both Hume and Rawls do not justify the claim that breaking a promise to a person who is now dead would wrong *her* (for they do not address the Problem of *Directed* Promissory Obligation but simply the Problem of Promissory Obligation), they could still support the claim that *it would be wrong to* break such a promise. Persons are likely generally to desire that the promises that were made to them to perform (or refrain from performing) some action after they die be kept (e.g., to enable them to render their lives meaningful by pursuing projects whose ends would only be achieved after they are dead). If this is so, then even though breaking such promises would not wrong the persons to whom they had been made it could undermine what is taken to be the useful social practice of keeping promises to the dead. It would hence wrong the (living) participants in that practice.[29]

The Reliance, Trust, and Assurance Views of promissory obligation would also (in certain circumstances) support the keeping of one's promises to persons even after they die. While this might appear counterintuitive, note that at the time that one makes these promises one should not be intending to breach them. Making a promise to do (or refrain from doing) X with the intention of breaking it after the death of the promisee would, if one thinks that the promisee believes that one will not break one's promise to her to X after her death, constitute deception. Since to deceive someone is (at least *prima facie*) to wrong her, it would be wrong to make a promise to a person with the intention of breaking it.[30] Thus, to avoid the wrong of deception one should either refrain from making a promise to a person that one has no intention of keeping after she is dead, or

---

[29] On this account one should keep promises made to the dead to establish a practice of promise-keeping that persons in general would find valuable. For development of this view see Partridge (1981), Wellman (1995, p. 156) and Taylor (2012, pp. 66–68).

[30] The wrong of deception could be explained by (e.g.) the adverse effect on a person's autonomy with respect to the actions that she was deceived into performing, its evincing a failure to respect the autonomy of the person deceived, or the likelihood that successfully subjecting a person to deception would adversely affect her well-being.

make it clear to her that one will not consider the promise binding after she dies, or else intend to keep the promise after she dies.[31]

Finally, one might have a reason to keep promises that is independent of the moral requirement to avoid wrongdoing through their breach. One might believe that being a particular sort of person (e.g., 'a gentleman') required that one keep one's promises independently of any consequences that this might have for others. If one both believed that one was this sort of person, and endorsed this self-conception, this could provide one with a non-instrumental, self-directed, reason to keep one's promises – whether these were made to persons still living or persons now dead.[32]

Thus, while there is no reason to believe that the dead can be wronged by the breaking of promises that were made to them while they were alive, there *is* reason to believe that even after a promisee dies persons should keep the promises that they made to her while she was alive. This might give comfort to people who wish to protect the projects whose posthumous achievement will give meaning to their lives through securing promises from others to ensure that this occurs after they die.

10. Conclusion

Although the belief that breaking a promise to a person who is now dead would wrong her is both widespread and entrenched, none of the four major analyses of directed promissory obligation support it. This is important for the metaphysics of death, for this belief has been taken as an axiomatic foundation for arguments that have been developed in favor of the views that the dead can be subject to

[31] It might be that the latter possibility is only available to persons who believe that the account of promissory obligation that they endorse establishes that it would be wrong to breach a promise after a person's death that was made to her while she was alive. It is not clear that one can intend at time T1 to keep a promise at T2 when the only reason one would have for keeping the promise at T2 was that one intended to do so at T1, especially if there would be costs associated with keeping the promise at T2. (The question of whether one can at T1 intend to keep a promise at T2 where the only reason for failing to breach it would be to establish one's intent at T1 is thus structurally similar to Kavka's Toxin Puzzle (Kavka, 1983).
[32] I thank Teodora Manea for bringing this point to my attention. I discuss this type of non-consequentialist prescriptive expressivist reason for action in Chapter 6 of Taylor (forthcoming).

both wrongs and harms. It is also important for those discussions of utilitarianism that draw on the view that to breach a deathbed promise would wrong the promisee.[33] Yet while showing that there is no reason to believe that breaching a promise that was made to a person who is now dead when she was alive would wrong her shifts the burden of proof onto those who believe that such wronging is possible, the implications of this burden-shifting should not be overstated. The conclusion of this paper is a relatively modest one: It is that *there is no reason to believe* that one can wrong a person who is now dead by breaching a promise that was made to her while alive. It is not the stronger claim that breaching a promise to a person who is now dead could *not* wrong her. And while the claim that breaking a promise to a person who is now dead wrongs her is often used to support the view that the dead can be wronged, the argument in this paper does not directly take issue with the latter, broader, claim. Showing that there is no reason to believe that the dead could be wronged through breaching the promises made to them is compatible with there being *other* (as yet undefined) ways in which they could be wronged.

However, that a person cannot be wronged by the posthumous breach of a promise that was made to her while she was alive does not entail that it would not be wrong to breach such a promise after her death. Nor does it entail that a person would have no reason (i.e., independent of morality) to keep the promises that she made to someone who is now dead. These observations might give comfort to one who wishes to render her life meaningful by the pursuit of projects whose ends would be achieved after her death, and who wishes to ensure that these ends are achieved through securing a promise from someone to oversee this. And although a person cannot be benefitted by an event that occurs after her death (just as she cannot be harmed by an event that occurs after her death) the belief that one's life will be made meaningful through the posthumous achievement of the aims of one's projects (with this being secured by someone who has promised to do so) might still be comforting to the living.[34]

The College of New Jersey
jtaylor@tcnj.edu

---

[33] See note 9.

[34] I thank the participants in the Royal Institute of Philosophy conference on 'Meaning in Life and the Knowledge of Death' hosted by the University of Liverpool in July 2021 for their very helpful and thoughtful comments on this paper. I especially thank Michael Hauskeller, both for his excellent feedback on this paper and for all of his efforts in making

References

Raymond A. Belliotti, 'Do Dead Human Beings Have Rights?' *The Personalist* 60 (1979), 201–210.

Jeffrey Blustein, *The Moral Demands of Memory* (Cambridge: Cambridge University Press, 2008).

James Cargile, 'Utilitarianism and the Desert Island Problem,' *Analysis* 25 (1964), 23–24.

Stephen Darwall, 'Demystifying Promises,' in Sheinman, ed. *Promises and Agreements*, (Oxford: Oxford University Press, 2011), 255–74.

Ashley Dressel, 'Directed Obligations and the Trouble with Deathbed Promises,' *Ethical Theory and Moral Practice* 18 (2015), 323–35.

Joel Feinberg, 'Harm to Others,' in John Martin Fischer, ed., *The Metaphysics of Death* (Palo Alto: Stanford University Press, 1993).

Charles Fried, *Contract as Promise* (Cambridge, MA: Harvard University Press, 1981).

Daniel Friedrich and Nicholas Southwood, 'Promises and Trust,' in Sheinman, *Promises and Agreements* (Oxford: Oxford University Press, 2011), 275–92.

James Griffin, *Well-Being: Meaning, Measurement, and Moral Import* (Oxford: Clarendon Press, 1986).

Paul Griseri, 'Can a Dead Man be Harmed?' *Philosophical Investigations* 10 (1987), 317–329.

Dorothy Grover, 'Posthumous Harm,' *The Philosophical Quarterly* 39 (1989), 334–53.

R. M. Hare, *Freedom and Reason* (Oxford: Clarendon Press, 1963).

David Hume, *Treatise on Human Nature* (Oxford: Oxford University Press, 1978).

Gregory S. Kavka, 'The Toxin Puzzle,' *Analysis*, 41, (1983), 33–36.

Richard Kraut, *What is Good and Why: The Ethics of Well-Being* (Cambridge, Mass.: Harvard University Press, 2007).

Nelson P. Lande, 'Posthumous Rehabilitation and the Dust-Bin of History,' *Public Affairs Quarterly* 4 (1990), 267–286.

Barbara Baum Levenbook, 'Harming Someone after His Death,' *Ethics* 94 (1984), 407–419.

---

this conference such as success in the face of the slings and arrows of outrageous fortune.

James Stacey Taylor

Hallie Liberto, 'Promissory Obligation: Against a Unified Account,' in Timmons., ed., *Oxford Studies in Normative Ethics, Volume 6* (2017), 102–122.

Loren E. Lomasky, *Persons, Rights, and the Moral Community* (New York: Oxford University Press, 1987).

J. S. Mill, *Utilitarianism* (Indianapolis, Ind.: Hackett Publishing Co., 1978).

Thomas Nagel, 'Death,' *Nous* 4 (1970), 73–80.

Jan Narveson, 'Promising, Expecting, and Utility,' *Canadian Journal of Philosophy* 1 (1971), 207–233.

Alastair Norcross, 'Act-utilitarianism and Promissory Obligation,' in Hanoch Sheinman, ed., *Promises and Agreements: Philosophical Essays* (New York: Oxford University Press, 2011), 217–36.

David Owens, 'A Simple Theory of Promising,' *Philosophical Review* 115 (2006), 51–77.

David Owens, 'Duress, Deception, and the Validity of a Promise,' *Mind* 166 (2007), 293–315.

David Owens, *Shaping the Normative Landscape* (Oxford: Oxford University Press, 2012).

Ernest Partridge, 'Posthumous Interests and Posthumous Respect,' *Ethics* 91 (1981), 259–264.

George Pitcher, 'The Misfortunes of the Dead,' *American Philosophical Quarterly* 21 (1984), 183–88.

Douglas Portmore, 'Desire Fulfillment and Posthumous Harm,' *American Philosophical Quarterly* 44 (2007), 27–38.

John Rawls, *A Theory of Justice: Revised edition* (Cambridge, MA: Harvard University Press, 1999).

Michael R. Robins, *Promising, Intending, and Moral Autonomy* (Cambridge: Cambridge University Press, 1984).

W.D. Ross *The Right and the Good*, ed. Philip Stratton-Lake (Oxford: Clarendon Press, 1930, 2002).

Abraham Sessu Roth, 'Intention, Expectation, and Promissory Obligation,' *Ethics* 127 (2016), 88–115.

Thomas Scanlon, *What We Owe to Each Other* (Cambridge, MA; Harvard University Press, 1998).

Anthony Serafini, 'Callahan on Harming the Dead,' *Journal of Philosophical Research* 15 (1989–1990), 329–39.

Hanoch Sheinman, 'Introduction: Promises and Agreements,' in Sheinman, ed., *Promises and Agreements* (Oxford: Oxford University Press, 2011), 3–56.

Henry Sidgwick, *The Methods of Ethics*.

Harry S. Silverstein, 'A Note on Hare on Imagining Oneself in the Place of Others,' *Mind* 81 (1972), 448–50.

J.J.C. Smart, 'Extreme and Restricted Utilitarianism,' *The Philosophical Quarterly* 6 (1956), 344–54.

Daniel Sperling, *Posthumous Interests: Legal and Ethical Perspectives* (New York: Cambridge University Press, 2008).

James Stacey Taylor, 'The Myth of Posthumous Harm,' *American Philosophical Quarterly* 42 (2005), 311–22.

James Stacey Taylor, *Death, Posthumous Harm, and Bioethics* (New York: Routledge, 2012).

James Stacey Taylor, *Markets with Limits: How the commodification of academia derails debate* (New York: Routledge, forthcoming).

J.J. Thomson, *The Realm of Rights* (Cambridge, Mass.: Harvard University Press, 1992).

Mikhail Valdman, 'Outsourcing Self-Government,' *Ethics* 120, 4 (2010), 761–790.

Carl Wellman, *Real Rights* (New York: Oxford University Press, 1995).

J. Jeremy Wisnewski, 'What We Owe the Dead,' *Journal of Applied Philosophy* 27 (2009), 54–70.

Susan Wolf, 'Two Concepts of Rule Utilitarianism,' in Mark Timmons, ed., *Oxford Studies in Normative Ethics, Volume 6* (New York: Oxford University Press, 2016), 123–44.

Jack Woods, 'The Normative Force of Promising,' in Timmons., ed., *Oxford Studies in Normative Ethics, Volume 6* (2017), 77–101.

Comparing the Meaningfulness of Finite and Infinite Lives: Can We Reap What We Sow if We Are Immortal?

THADDEUS METZ

Abstract
On the rise over the past 20 years has been 'moderate supernaturalism', the view that while a meaningful life is possible in a world without God or a soul, a much greater meaning would be possible only in a world with them. William Lane Craig can be read as providing an important argument for a version of this view, according to which only with God and a soul could our lives have an eternal, as opposed to temporally limited, significance since we would then be held accountable for our decisions affecting others' lives. I present two major objections to this position. On the one hand, I contend that if God existed and we had souls that lived forever, then, in fact, all our lives would turn out the same. On the other hand, I maintain that, if this objection is wrong, so that our moral choices would indeed make an ultimate difference and thereby confer an eternal significance on our lives (only) in a supernatural realm, then Craig could not capture the view, aptly held by moderate supernaturalists, that a meaningful life is possible in a purely natural world.

1. New Religious Thought about Meaning in Life

In the West, philosophers sympathetic towards a religious account of what is central to meaning in life have changed their account of late. For much of the modern era, up until about 20 years ago, the dominant view amongst those who believe that life's meaning depends crucially on God or a soul (as characteristically conceived by the Abrahamic faiths) has been that such spiritual conditions are *necessary* for any one of our lives to be meaningful. Positions have included the claims that: a meaningful life is a purposeful one, where God alone could provide an objective purpose; only God could ground a universal morality without which life would not make sense; living up to a universal morality, and hence living meaningfully, would require having an indestructible spiritual nature that is able to overcome the physical laws of nature; meaning in life consists of coming close to God or of God meting out justice, which can be done only if we have immortal souls. Call these rationales instances

doi:10.1017/S1358246121000254   © The Royal Institute of Philosophy and the contributors 2021

of 'extreme supernaturalism', for entailing that, if neither God nor a soul exists, all our lives are meaningless, which involves denying that anything about the course of our existence merits pride, admiration, or awe or that there are any values in it higher than animal pleasures and satisfactions.[1]

However, in the 21st century, many western religious thinkers – beyond those inclined towards a naturalist approach to meaning in life – have found objections to extreme supernaturalism compelling. One powerful intuition has been that at least the lives of Gandhi, Einstein, and Mandela were meaningful, even on the supposition that there exists only a physical universe.

Supernaturalism has not died out, but instead has morphed into a more 'moderate' version. A salient view amongst religious philosophers of life's meaning has become that, while a meaningful life is possible in a world without God or a soul, a *greater* or *ultimate* meaning would be possible only in a world with (at least one of) them. Explicit adherents to this view include thinkers such as Philip Quinn (2000), John Cottingham (2016), Richard Swinburne (2016), Timothy Mawson (2016), and Clifford Williams (2020).

There have been a variety of specifications of what constitutes a great or ultimate meaning, with moderate supernaturalists yet to debate amongst themselves which is most promising.[2] In this article, I critically discuss temporal and quantitative interpretations of greatness or ultimacy, according to which it is the longest or largest amount of meaning. According to this sort of moderate supernaturalism, on which I focus here, while an earthly life could offer a limited or finite meaning, only a life with a soul and God could offer an eternal or infinite one.

William Lane Craig can be read as providing an important argument for the view that only with God and a soul could our lives have an eternal, as opposed to temporally limited, significance.[3] According to him, without such spiritual conditions, our moral decisions make no ultimate difference, neither to the world nor to our

---

[1] Perhaps most recent analyses of the concept of meaning in life (or definitions of the phrase) are cluster or amalgam accounts, which include these kinds of properties (even if not solely them). For my own, family resemblance analysis, see Metz (2013, pp. 24–35).

[2] For an overview of the variety of ways greatness has been conceived in the literature, with some suggestions about their logical implications, see Metz (2019, pp. 27–28, 43–44).

[3] Craig (2009a), Craig (2009b) and Craig (2013, pp. 158–61, 166–67).

lives, whereas if those conditions do obtain, then our moral decisions do make an ultimate difference.

After briefly expounding this argument in the following section (2), I present objections to it. I contend that if God existed and we had souls that lived forever, then, in fact, all our lives would turn out the same (section 3). One central rationale is that, if God and a soul exist, then we cannot make any difference to the quality of others' lives, since, in terms of harms, God would compensate others for any that befell them and, in terms of benefits, we could not improve on the infinity in Heaven coming to them from God. After that I maintain that, if this objection is wrong, so that our moral choices would indeed confer an eternal significance on our lives (only) in a supernatural realm, then Craig could not capture the view, aptly held by moderate supernaturalists, that a meaningful life is possible in a purely natural world (section 4). Basically, an eternal significance would be 'too big', reducing any meaning possible during an earthly life to nothing by comparison. I conclude that moderate supernaturalists would probably be wise to avoid appealing to eternal or infinite meaning when spelling out the respect in which God and a soul could alone impart a great meaning to our lives; some other notion of greatness should be considered (section 5).

2. Craig on Life Mattering through Making a Difference

It is not clear that it is right to view Craig as a moderate supernaturalist, for there are places in his writings where he defends Divine Command Theory, which naturally supports the extreme version[4]; if only God could ground universal moral obligations, the living up to which were necessary for meaning in life, then God would be necessary for meaning. However, there are other arguments of Craig's the logic of which does support moderate supernaturalism, even if he does not accept this position. One of them appeals to the idea that a great meaning requires making an ultimate difference, something possible only if God and a soul exist.

Consider the following quotations:

> '(I)f theism is true, we have a sound basis for moral accountability....Evil and wrong will be punished; righteousness will be vindicated....(T)he moral choices we make in this life are infused with an eternal significance'. (Craig, 2009a, p. 31)

[4]   For instance, see Craig (2013, pp. 161–69).

'In the absence of moral accountability, our choices become trivialized because they make no ultimate contribution to either the
betterment of the universe or to the moral good in general
because everyone ends up the same. Death is the great leveler'.
(Craig, 2009a, p. 38)

'One of the reasons that moral accountability is important is that
we want our moral choices to make a difference....(I)t is precisely
because our moral choices do make a lasting difference that
attempts to improve this finite world are not futile'. (Craig,
2009b, p. 174)

'On naturalism our destiny, both as individuals and as a species,
is ultimately unrelated to moral behavior....(O)bjective values
and duties do not finally matter, since everything winds up the
same'. (Craig, 2009b, p. 183)

'(T)o believe that God does not exist and that there is thus no
moral accountability is quite literally de-moralizing, for then
we should have to believe that our moral choices are ultimately
insignificant, since both our fate and that of the universe will
be the same regardless of what we do'. (Craig, 2009b, p. 184)

Notice the recurrent qualifications. Speaking of 'eternal' significance
invites comparison with a less than eternal significance. Talk of an
'ultimate' contribution or of something being 'ultimately' meaningless or insignificant suggests a less than ultimate meaning or significance. Making a 'lasting' difference implies making a difference that
does not last. Hence, this argument is sensibly read as supporting a
moderate supernaturalism, according to which meaning is possible
in the world as known particularly well by science, but an eternal, ultimate, or lasting one is not and requires a God who rewards good and
punishes bad in the course of judging one's soul. In any event, that is
how I shall interpret the above quotations, regardless of Craig's own
intentions.[5]

In some ways, this reasoning harks back more than 2000 years to
some passages in Ecclesiastes.[6] The worry that all our lives end up
the same, regardless of the nature of our moral choices, is one factor

[5]   Despite the presence of spots when expounding this rationale where
Craig does go extreme, e.g., when he says that 'in light of the universe's
inevitable fate our children's lives are, indeed, utterly pointless' (Craig,
2009b, p. 184). 'Utterly' seems stronger than 'ultimately'.
[6]   For other, more recent (but briefer) advocates, see Mawson (2013,
pp. 1441–42) and Swinburne (2016, pp. 157–59).

that led Koheleth (the presumed author of the book) to proclaim that 'all is vanity' and that life is akin 'to the pursuit of wind'. He remarks of death: '(T)he same fate is in store for all: for the righteous, and for the wicked; for the good and pure, and for the impure....That is the sad thing about all that goes on under the sun: that the same fate is in store for all' (9.2–9.3; see also 2.14–2.16, 3.17).

Craig is not explicit when advancing this reasoning about how it is that God would hold us morally accountable and respond to our choices (nor is Koheleth about how he wishes God would do so). However, the picture seems to be a common one amongst Christian and Muslim theists, according to which God sends the souls of those who have exhibited moral virtue (whether in the form of faith or works) to Heaven, where they will enjoy eternal life with God, and God sends the souls those who have exhibited vice to eternal damnation in Hell. If, and only if, there is such judgement can one's moral decisions make an eternal, ultimate, or lasting difference and exhibit a corresponding meaning, so the argument goes.

Contra Craig, in the following section I maintain that it is not so much death, but more clearly immortality, that would be the great leveller. If we all had souls that could not perish, and if God determined the quality of life of those souls in response to their moral choices, then it would in fact be the case that everyone ends up the same and our moral choices do not make any real difference to the course of our lives or those of others.

3. Immortality as the Great Leveller

In this section I make the case that if we have immortal souls that God looks after, then our moral choices do not make a lasting difference and confer an eternal significance, whereas if we are mortal and on our own, then some difference remains possible, even if not a lasting one. I first show how the lives of others as moral patients would not be differentially affected by our ethical decisions if an Abrahamic spiritual realm exists (3.1) and then how our own lives as moral agents also would not be so affected (3.2).

3.1. No Difference to Others' Lives

Aspects of the first point have perhaps become familiar to the field. More than 30 years ago Martha Nussbaum recognized that, if we were immortal, then no virtue or justice could come from saving anyone's life (Nussbaum, 1989, pp. 338–39). Our moral choices could never make the important difference of rescuing anyone from death. Neither feeding children, nor stopping an axe-murderer, nor providing healthcare saves a life. Such actions could of course protect a body, but we persons are not identical to our bodies and can outlive them, according to the present form of supernaturalism.

Relatedly, our moral choices could never make the important difference of killing anyone. Just as one's actions could not matter for having saved a life, so one's actions could not 'anti-matter', i.e., reduce the meaningfulness of one's life (Metz, 2013, pp. 63–64, 71–72, 234–35), for having taken a life. If lives are indestructible for being housed in souls, then nothing one chooses can ever be so wrongful as to involve murder.

Now, these considerations extend beyond eliminating life to reducing the quality of life. If we had souls that God compensated for any undeserved or otherwise inappropriate harm, then it would also follow that our moral choices could never make the difference of preventing anyone from suffering a net loss of well-being. This point, too, has been made by others recently.[7] If X interferes with Y's life by stomping on Y's foot for no good reason, perhaps maliciously, then, supposing X did not compensate Y, God would do so in an afterlife. X could not impose a net harm on Y, given theism, meaning that our moral choices could not make a negative difference in respect of another person's life. By the same token, if one of us, Z, were to prevent X from stomping on Y's foot, Z would not be preventing Y from undergoing any net harm, since, were Z not to do so, God would step in and make up for the loss (if not in this life, then in the next). Hence, our moral choices could not make an important kind of positive difference, either.

Return to Craig's complaint that, without a spiritual realm, 'our choices become trivialized because they make no ultimate contribution to either the betterment of the universe or to the moral good in general because everyone ends up the same' (Craig, 2009a, p. 38). That complaint appears, in contrast, true of a world with a spiritual realm, since everyone remains alive by virtue of having a soul and God ensures that all lives are bettered (at least insofar as that is morally appropriate). Insofar as we could not rescue anyone from death or from a poor quality of life, it appears apt to describe our choices as 'trivialized because they make no ultimate contribution to the betterment of the universe'.

In reply, one sympathetic to Craig's view might point out that, even if one could not make a difference to others by preventing

---

[7]   See Wielenberg (2005, pp. 91–94), Hubin (2009), and Maitzen (2009).

death or harm to them, one could make a difference to them by conferring 'pure' benefits on them, by which I mean goods that do not consist of the removal of a bad.[8] One could direct someone's gaze to a beautiful moon, offer her chocolates, or give her a backrub. Or, supposing these actions would not give one moral credit, consider that one could just write a cheque to those who do not need the money to avoid harm. Supporting others' projects, whether it is playing chess, building a religious institution, or discovering facts about nature, plausibly confers moral credit.

The big problem with this tempting reply is that the moral credit could not be of the sort Craig maintains is essential for an ultimate significance, when the person being benefited has a soul destined for Heaven. If someone would spend eternal life in a supremely good state, then nothing one can do in a finite period would make any difference to the quality of that person's life. An infinity of bliss plus any finite amount of pure benefit would remain infinity.[9]

It is true that an eternal life would not form an 'actual' infinity in the mathematical sense of being complete or realized. It would be more aligned to the mathematical notion of a 'potential' infinity, one in which a series will never end. I do not think this distinction has much of a bearing on whether a finite contribution to a person's well-being could make a difference to his quality of life. After all, if the person's well-being would indeed go on forever, then any finite addition to it would make literally no difference to the life considered as a whole (even if not as ever completed), that is, as something that will continue forever.[10]

Just as God would remove the finite harm done to a person, meaning that one's removing it would make no difference to how

8   For the concept, see Shiffrin (1999).
9   Although this is the standard mathematical approach to infinite quantities, its logic does entail that any infinity of bliss plus a finite amount of harm would remain infinitely positive and so no worse than any infinity of bliss plus no finite amount of harm. We might prefer the latter to the former, on which see Jackson and Rogers (2019). It is open to theists here to develop some novel way of measuring infinite values.
10   On the other hand, if one elects to take the person's life at a certain point in time, noting that it remains finite despite its infinite trajectory, the billions of billions of years of bliss that it would at some point contain would render, say, cutting a cheque for 50 pounds to be negligible by comparison. I accept that, from the perspective of considering a potentially infinite life at a given moment, one's contribution would make some difference to her quality of life, but an arbitrarily small one, a difference that approaches zero as her life continues.

well her life goes, so God would confer infinite pure benefits on a person, or, more carefully, would do so forever, meaning that one's adding some would make no difference to how well her life goes. It is not death that is the great leveller, but rather God and a soul, when it comes to the effects of our actions on other people's well-being. We cannot influence their lives for better or worse considered as a net sum, and hence cannot, in one of Craig's central senses, make an ultimate difference with our moral choices.

3.2. No Difference to Our Own Lives

Even if we cannot make a difference in the sense of changing the quality of other people's lives, Craig could maintain that we could make a difference in some other senses. Specifically, he can point out that, even if, given theism, we could not make a positive or negative difference to others in the world, we could still make one to ourselves. We could make choices that have long-term consequences for our own lives, where these consequences are furthermore not the same for everybody. Recall that Craig remarks of theism: 'Evil and wrong will be punished; righteousness will be vindicated....(T)he moral choices we make in this life are infused with an eternal significance' (Craig, 2009a, p. 31). If we exhibited vice, God would punish us forever, and if we instead exhibited virtue, God would reward us for an eternity.

Set aside what counts as vice, but notice that, even if one could not commit the grave wrong of murder if we had souls, one could plausibly exhibit serious vice. One would surely count as a bad person if one incorrectly believed it were possible to kill others and intentionally sought to do so without justification. Hence, it appears that our moral choices would make a lasting difference in respect of our own lives if, say, people who try to kill those made in the image of God went to Hell and people who do not went to Heaven.

It does seem true, on this picture, that one's moral choices would have infinite ramifications and that not everyone would experience the same ones, hence making a 'lasting difference' and having 'eternal significance'. However, that is contingent on the premise of Hell, which is largely out of fashion these days[11] and for good reason. Philosophers of religion have come to doubt that God would send anyone to Hell, when that is understood as damnation that does not end.

[11]   But cf. the Doctrinal Statement of one of Craig's institutions: http://media1.biola.edu/bold/downloads/doctrinal_statement.pdf.

Comparing the Meaningfulness of Finite and Infinite Lives

For the considerations that will be familiar to many readers, recall that it is unlikely that a loving God would treat anyone that way.[12] A compassionate, caring God might well impose penalties, but they would be ones that would be lifted upon having done some good, such as reform of the wayward individual and reconciliation between him and others, including God. Such a God would not impose suffering merely for the sake of suffering because one had made others suffer (merely in the short term!).

Furthermore, even an angry, vengeful God would not judge that anyone of us should go to Hell, since nothing we can be or do would deserve such a penalty. Humans would deserve an eternal punishment only if they did or were something infinitely bad, and we may reasonably doubt that infinite disvalues are possible in an earthly life.

Still more, even if infinite disvalues were possible in an earthly life, it would not follow that eternity is needed to give people what they deserve; for supposing that one could do or be something infinitely disvaluable in one's 80 or so years here, then a response proportionate to this deed or state would require merely a finite amount of time.

Lastly, even if infinite disvalues were possible during an earthly life and even if only an infinite punishment would be proportionate to them, it is implausible to think that God would create such horrible beings in the first place. Of course free will has some final value, but it is hard to think that the specific kind producing the sort of vice or wrongness that warrants eternal damnation would be worth such a cost.

We must suppose, then, that universal salvation would be on the cards, if God and a soul existed. If so, then it appears, yet again, that 'our choices become trivialized because they make no ultimate contribution to either the betterment of the universe or to the moral good in general because everyone ends up the same' (Craig, 2009a, p. 38). Of course, some would surely take a detour on the route to Heaven; some bad people would require time away from God, perhaps even in the form of punishment, in order to become the sort of people to whom God would bestow the gift of eternal bliss. However, such a finite amount of time would not detract from the overall supreme quality of life that would come to everyone; for a life of never-ending happiness would be, if not literally an infinity of bliss, then so enormous as to make the punitive detour amount

---

[12]   For just a few references to the large literature over the past 30 years, see McCord Adams (1993); Kershnar (2005); Buckareff and Plug (2017); and Mawson (2019).

to nothing by comparison. And hence all lives would end up the same, regardless of the moral choices we make.[13]

One might be inclined to think that, just as there would be circles of Hell, there would also be circles of Heaven, with some concentric circles coming to closer to God than others (cf. Jeremiah 17:10, Matthew 16:27, 19:28–9; 1 Corinthians 3:7–15; 2 Corinthians 5:10; Qur'an 30:38–9; 56:1–11; 83:18–28). Some people's faith has been stronger, some of their virtue higher, some of their works better.

Even if that were true, it would not make any difference to people's quality of life, on what I take to be the standard understanding of this sort of infinity amongst mathematicians since Cantor. Two lives of infinite happiness would both be 'countable' infinities and hence the same, in the sense that for any quantity of value in an eternal life, it could be put into a one-to-one correspondence with the natural numbers.[14] The amount of goodness in two infinite lives would be the same.

In sum, *contra* Craig, theism is unable to ground a world in which our moral choices would make an ultimate difference. When it comes to preventing harm or conferring benefits on others, there is nothing we can do to change their quality of life relative to what God would do for them. When it comes to our own quality of life, given universal salvation, there is nothing we can do to make it the case that our quality of life would differ from that of others. When Craig complains that, in an atheist world, 'we should have to believe that our moral choices are ultimately insignificant, since both our fate and that of the universe will be the same regardless of what we do' (Craig, 2009b, p. 184), his complaint applies with comparable force to a theist world.

Craig's complaint might even apply with greater force to a theist world, insofar as in an atheist one it is at least possible for a moral agent to affect the net quality of other people's lives for better or worse. Of course, it does not follow that atheism would make it possible for our moral choices to make an *ultimate* difference in Craig's

---

[13]   I have argued above that all being destined for Heaven means that all would have the same quantity of quality of life, but a further argument to consider is whether we would also have the same quality of quality of life, so to speak. A standard picture of Heaven is that we would become impeccable, i.e., unable to exhibit vice, and that central to our lives would be the contemplation of God's nature. (For just two examples, see Henderson (2017) and Swinburne (2016, p. 160)). Would we all be destined to perform the same activities and have the same mental states? Could we be unique persons in Heaven?

[14]   For one clear exposition, see Barrow (2005).

senses. However, they could at least make a *real* difference. If neither God nor a soul exists, then it is possible to prevent other people from undergoing net harm and to improve their quality of life with pure benefits compared to what they would have had otherwise. In addition, it would still be possible (even if unlikely in our actual world) to apportion deserved penalties so that the wicked would face harms; as I and others have pointed out, an impersonal Karmic force could allocate burdens justly in the absence of a personal judge (Metz, 2013, pp. 83, 108–9, 125n2, 238–9; Kahane, 2018). In short, without God or a soul, we could in principle change the overall quality of people's lives, including our own.

One might object that, regardless of what would happen in an afterlife, we could still affect people's lives for better or worse here and now. That is true in one sense – there is no denying that, in the short term, our actions can have good or bad consequences. However, the argument I am presenting for thinking that atheism would uniquely enable our choices to make a difference turns on the concept of *net well-being over the course of a life*. The argument is that only if God and a soul do not exist would it be possible for us either to impose harm that would never be compensated in the future or to confer an amount of benefit that would not otherwise have come then.

Although I would be content to conclude that immortality in a God-ruled universe is *just as much* a great leveller as death, I submit that there is also reason to conclude that it would be *more* of a great leveller than death, making the overall quality of all our lives wind up the same. In contrast, without God or a soul, our moral choices can have differential effects on the net well-being of both others and ourselves, even if they are admittedly short-lived compared to what we can imagine. One might be inclined to suggest that God would recognize the problem I have raised and do something about it, finding a way to enable us to reap what we sow. However, if the above argumentation is sound, the only way God could do so would be by denying us immortality, removing one of the major legs of theism.

4. Immortality as the Great Overshadower

Suppose that, despite my argumentation in the previous section, somehow Craig were able to reach his conclusion. Perhaps he would suggest that the sense of 'making a lasting difference' sufficient for an eternal significance is making certain choices and then going to

Heaven, even if these choices could not change the overall quality of anyone else's life and even if one's own overall quality of life would end up the same as everyone else's. I submit that this sense of the phrase does not in fact seem to be the one pertinent to what would make one's life matter; after all, making a difference in respect of meaningfulness is intuitively understood to involve one's improving others' net quality of life and then not seeing the wicked and lazy end up doing as well as oneself, neither of which is possible on the assumption of theism, or so I argued in the previous section. However, let us grant Craig that he can reach his conclusion, that an eternal significance for one's life is possible with God and a soul and only with them.

In that case, I submit that the logic of Craig's position would render him unable to capture the intuition that life in an atheist world could be meaningful. Recall the difference between extreme and moderate supernaturalism. The former is the view that God or a soul is necessary for one's life to be meaningful, while the latter is the view that, although these spiritual conditions are not necessary for that, they are necessary for one's life to have a great or ultimate meaning. Reading Craig as providing an argument for the moderate variety, my claim is that, if he understands a great/ultimate meaning to be one that is eternal or infinite, then it is 'too big': for then a life of approximately 80 years amounts to nothing by comparison and Craig cannot make sense of the moderate claim that a meaningful life is possible without God or a soul.[15]

I note that the comparative aspect of this point has been made by others recently. For example, T. J. Mawson recognizes that 'given that the afterlife is potentially infinite, so any finite dollop will diminish in relative size, tending to nothing over time' (Mawson, 2016, p. 144), and Ingmar Persson and Julian Savulescu note that 'whatever value we bring to our lives or the lives of others will fade gradually to nothing in the course of eternity' (Persson and Savulescu, 2019, p. 234). What has not been acknowledged is that these plausible claims render moderate supernaturalism unstable. If a great meaning is an eternal one, then no life of 80 or so years can be

---

[15]   I made this point earlier in Metz (2019, pp. 30–33), from which some of the following phrasing is borrowed. However, I did not there apply the point to Craig's position, and, more deeply, I had there supposed the point applies to moderate supernaturalism as such, not particular versions invoking eternal or infinite meaning. I now recognize that a form of moderate supernaturalism can probably avoid the criticism, which I address below in the concluding section.

meaningful by comparison, undercutting moderate supernaturalism and returning us to an extreme form.

More carefully, there are two ways to make the objection, depending on whether the great/ultimate meaning is construed in temporal or quantitative terms. In terms of time, if God and a soul would afford eternal significance, then no earthly life of about 80 years can compare and hence the supernaturalist cannot account for the intuition that a such a life could be significant. If a life of eternal significance would bring an infinite amount of meaning in its wake,[16] then consider that no life with a finite amount of meaning can compare and hence the supernaturalist cannot account for the intuition that such a life could be meaningful.

To be sure, by the present position, although an 80 year life would 'tend to nothing', it need not be a 'flat zero' (Mawson, 2016, p. 5) in terms of the amount of meaning in it. However, it would, compared to infinity (or eternity), come as close to zero as is mathematically possible for a positive number, which, I maintain, fails to capture the judgement that a life can be meaningful absent God and a soul.

The moderate supernaturalist who invokes eternal life in Heaven needs to explain how we can avoid thinking that its value would ridiculously outweigh that of an earthly lifespan, reducing it to next to nothing by comparison, thereby leaving us unable to capture the intuition that an earthly life, such as that of Gandhi, Einstein, or Mandela, could ever count as meaningful on balance. Note that she cannot coherently suggest that judgements of whether someone's life is meaningful are not in some way comparative or relative, for the *defining point* of her view is precisely a particular comparative or relative judgement, viz., that a spiritual dimension would alone make possible a *greater* sort of meaning in life than what is on offer in the physical universe.

Prior to advancing this argument against Craig's appeal to eternal significance, I had done so in respect of Mawson's appeal to infinite significance, and Mawson has recently authored a substantial reply to it (Mawson, 2020). He makes two major criticisms that are relevant here, which I now aim to rebut.

Mawson's initial criticism is that the life in Heaven would be a merely potential infinity, not an actual one, and so the relevant comparison is not between a life that in fact has lasted for an infinite amount of time and a life that has not. '(T)he amount of meaningfulness our lives will ever contain is always going to be a potential

---

[16]   Which at least one scholar believes is true, viz., Mawson (2020, p. 2).

infinity, not an actual infinity, i.e., it will always be finite' (Mawson, 2020, p. 4).

However, the two points made above in the context of potential infinity apply here, too. On the one hand, if the life will indeed never end, then it is reasonable to compare a life that will have an unending amount of value with one that will have a finite amount. On the other hand, if one elects to consider the life at a given point in time, the logic of my point remains: for a life of billions of billions of years would also overshadow a life of approximately 80 years. An actual infinitude would be sufficient to overshadow, making any one of our earthly lives 'tend to nothing', but it is not necessary; a merely potential infinity will suffice.

Mawson's second criticism involves supposing that I believe that judgements of meaning are *solely* comparative, when they in fact are not. In the way judgements of whether something is big do seem to be merely comparative, Mawson says, 'Metz is, I suggest, naturally read as supposing that "meaningful" functions in a similar way. "Meaningful" means relatively meaningful, relative to some suitable comparison class and its relative meaning is the only meaning it has' (Mawson, 2020, p. 7). Mawson then reasonably contends that not all appraisals of whether someone's actual life is meaningful are relative to someone else's actual life or to that person's possible life. For Mawson, one can make an absolute judgement of meaning. Simply looking at one actual person's life, without knowledge of how anyone else is faring or how that person could have fared, one can determine whether her life has some meaning in it or not. In addition, 'No matter how much meaningfulness it's our destiny to receive, that future cannot diminish the absolute amount of meaningfulness we have at any time received' (Mawson, 2020, p. 15).

However, I do not deny that one can make absolute judgements of meaning in the ways that Mawson believes. And I do not need to hold that judgements of meaning are *only* comparative in order to make the point about overshadowing. I think all I need to note is that essential to Mawson's (and others') moderate supernaturalism is a comparative claim, namely, the judgement that a meaningful life is possible without spiritual conditions, but that they would alone make possible a *greater* meaning and specifically a (potentially) eternal or infinite one. When it is said that 'a meaningful life is possible without spiritual conditions', I take that to say more than just that a life could have *some meaning in it* without them. Instead, it is plausibly read as the claim that a life could have enough meaning in it to make it sensible to describe the whole life as *meaningful*, which is much more difficult to establish when an earthly life is put into comparison with eternal life in Heaven.

Recall that a key motivation for moderate supernaturalism has been the attempt to capture the widely shared intuition that the lives of Gandhi, Einstein, and Mandela were meaningful even supposing there is only a physical universe. That involves the claim that these lives warranted reactions such as pride from a first-person perspective and admiration and awe from a third-person perspective. It is difficult to see how that claim can be sustained if we are comparing these lives with those that have an eternal or infinite meaning, even a merely potential one. They simply are not that impressive by comparison. Central to moderate supernaturalism is the claim that, although a meaningful life is possible without God or a soul, these spiritual conditions would alone make a much *greater* meaning available, where that, for Mawson (and probably implicitly Craig) is a potential infinity. And so we are back to Mawson's own point that 'given that the afterlife is potentially infinite, so any finite dollop will diminish in relative size, tending to nothing over time' (Mawson, 2016, p. 144), where tending to nothing is not enough for a life to count as meaningful by comparison.

Notice the title of Mawson's essay: 'Why Heaven Doesn't Make Earth Absolutely Meaningless, Just Relatively'. My claim is that if supernaturalism entails that an earthly life is meaningless relative to Heaven, then it is no longer moderate, that is, no longer able to capture the intuition that an earthly life can be meaningful, even if a Heavenly life would have a greater meaning. Hence, I am not committed to holding that all judgements of meaning are comparative. Instead, the moderate supernaturalist is the one inviting us to compare degrees of meaning, indeed to compare (what I accept are) absolute amounts of it, in the present case between finite and infinite lives. When Mawson claims that eternal life in Heaven would give us a potential eternity or infinity of meaning, which is much more desirable compared to the dollop available on earth, we are to consider whether we would judge our dollop to afford us a life aptly described as 'meaningful' compared to a potential infinity and so warranting reactions of pride and awe. The answer, I submit, is 'No', which means that extreme supernaturalism is what is really being offered.[17]

---

[17] Another way to object to my position would be to maintain that judgements of meaningfulness are never relative and are solely absolute. That is not Mawson's view (on which see Mawson, 2020, p. 20n35), but my teenage son in discussion has suggested that judgements of whether a life is meaningful are similar to judgements of whether a piece of paper is red. He holds that, given enough redness as a percentage of a piece of paper, it

Thaddeus Metz

5. Concluding Thoughts about the Way Forward for Moderate Supernaturalism

William Lane Craig is usefully read as arguing that God and a soul are necessary for an eternal significance in one's life, although not a significant life as such, because only with them can one's moral decisions make a lasting difference to others and ourselves. I have advanced two major objections to this argument. On the one hand, I contended that theism would not enable us to make a lasting difference of the sort most clearly relevant to meaning. We could not affect how well off anyone else is over the course of their life since God would compensate for harm done to them and bestow endless benefit on them, and we also could not influence the quality of our own lives relative to that of others, on the reasonable supposition that Hell would not be on the cards for anyone and universal salvation would instead be expected from God. On the other hand, I maintained that, if the logic of Craig's argument is successful, it entails a conclusion that, upon reflection, is difficult to square with a genuinely moderate supernaturalism. If an eternal significance would come with the presence of God and a soul, then such a life would be so much more significant than one of our earthly lives as to render the latter insignificant by comparison.

Now, Craig's appeal to moral accountability is not the only rationale for moderate supernaturalism, and his appeal to eternal significance is not the only way to interpret moderate supernaturalism. If it is true, given theism, that our moral choices do not make a difference to the net quality of others' lives or our own and that an appeal to eternal significance is in effect extreme, then the moderate supernaturalist has reason to give up theism. However, that need not mean giving up the entire picture that philosophers working within the

---

would count as red, regardless of how big or small its area is, where, by analogy, given enough meaning as a percentage of a life, it would count as meaningful, regardless of how long the life lasted. While I am now inclined to suspect that happiness might function in that way, as Mawson would accept (see citation *supra*), we both find it harder to think that meaningfulness does, for one implication would be that an eight day old life with a high percentage of meaning would count as no less meaningful than an 80 year or 80,000 year one with the same high percentage. Furthermore, dialectically speaking, the present moderate supernaturalist cannot coherently avail herself of this purely noncomparative approach, since her view is by definition a comparative one, viz., that an eternal life would offer a greater meaning than an earthly life.

monotheist tradition have advanced. For one option to consider, it would be worth reflecting on whether God should be conceived as putting an expiration date on our souls, as it were. That is, imagine that we were able to survive the death of our body, with the virtuous receiving reward for a long while and the wicked receiving something negative, but that none of our selves would continue forever. Then, the significance of the afterlife would be greater than what an earthly life could afford, while not necessarily overshadowing it. In addition, then it would be the case that our moral decisions could in fact make a difference to the net quality of others' lives and also our own, for no eternal life would serve as a great leveller. Although this would be an unusual position for adherents to the Abrahamic faiths, I note that something broadly like it is the standard position for Traditional African Religion,[18] a globally under-recognized form of monotheism. It will be interesting to see how moderate supernaturalism continues to be articulated and defended as debate continues.[19]

University of Pretoria (South Africa)
th.metz@up.ac.za

References

John Barrow, *The Infinite Book* (London: Jonathan Cape, 2005) 55–74.
Andrei Buckareff and Allen Plug, 'Divine Love and Hell'. In Yujin Nagasawa and Benjamin Matheson (eds), *The Palgrave Handbook of the Afterlife* (London: Palgrave Macmillan, 2017) 197–214.

---

[18] As I point out in Metz and Molefe (2021).
[19] I am grateful to Mika'il Metz for discussion, Michael Hauskeller, Daniel Hill, Liz Jackson, Antti Kauppinen, Kirk Lougheed, Stephen Maitzen, T. J. Mawson, and Erik Wielenberg for written comments on a prior draft, and participants in the Royal Institute of Philosophy Annual Conference 2021 on Meaning in Life and the Knowledge of Death, organized by Michael Hauskeller at the University of Liverpool, and in the Mini-Conference on the Axiology of Theism, organized by Klaas Kraay at Ryerson University. I have not been able to answer in this draft all the important queries I received from these colleagues, but look forward to continuing the debate in future work.

Thaddeus Metz

John Cottingham, 'Meaningfulness, Eternity, and Theism'. In Joshua Seachris and Stewart Goetz (eds), *God and Meaning* (New York: Bloomsbury Academic, 2016) 123–36.

William Lane Craig, 'The Kurtz/Craig Debate'. In Robert Garcia and Nathan King (eds), *Is Goodness without God Good Enough?* (Lanham, MD: Rowman and Littlefield, 2009a) 23–46.

William Lane Craig, 'This Most Gruesome of Guests'. In Robert Garcia and Nathan King (eds), *Is Goodness without God Good Enough?* (Lanham, MD: Rowman and Littlefield, 2009b) 167–88.

William Lane Craig, 'The Absurdity of Life without God'. Repr. in Joshua Seachris (ed.), *Exploring the Meaning of Life: An Anthology and Guide* (Malden, MA: Wiley-Blackwell, 2013) 153–72 at 158–61, 166–7 (first published in 1994).

Luke Henderson, 'Heaven'. In Yujin Nagasawa and Benjamin Matheson (eds) *The Palgrave Handbook of the Afterlife* (London: Palgrave Macmillan, 2017) 177–96.

Donald Hubin, 'Empty and Ultimately Meaningless Gestures?' In Robert Garcia and Nathan King (eds), *Is Goodness without God Good Enough?* (Lanham, MD: Rowman and Littlefield, 2009) 133–50.

Guy Kahane, 'If There Is a Hole, It Is Not God-Shaped'. In Klaas Kraay (ed.), *Does God Matter? Essays on the Axiological Consequences of Theism* (New York: Routledge, 2018) 95–131

Stephen Kershnar, 'The Injustice of Hell'. *International Journal for Philosophy of Religion* 58 (2005), 103–23.

Elizabeth Jackson and Andrew Rogers, 'Salvaging Pascal's Wager', *Philosophia Christi* 21 (2019), 59–84.

Stephen Maitzen, 'Ordinary Morality Implies Atheism', *European Journal for Philosophy of Religion* 2 (2009), 107–26.

T. J. Mawson, 'Recent Work on the Meaning of Life and Philosophy of Religion', *Philosophy Compass* 8 (2013), 1138–46

T. J. Mawson, *God and the Meanings of Life: What God Could and Couldn't Do to Make Our Lives More Meaningful* (London: Bloomsbury Publishing, 2016).

T. J. Mawson, *Monotheism and the Meaning of Life* (Cambridge: Cambridge University Press, 2019).

T. J. Mawson, 'Why Heaven Doesn't Make Earth Absolutely Meaningless, Just Relatively', *Religious Studies* (2020), https://doi.org/10.1017/S0034412520000062.

Marilyn McCord Adams, 'The Problem of Hell: A Problem of Evil for Christians'. In Eleonore Stump (ed.), *Reasoned Faith* (Ithaca: Cornell University Press, 1993) 301–27.

Comparing the Meaningfulness of Finite and Infinite Lives

Thaddeus Metz, *Meaning in Life: An Analytic Study* (Oxford: Oxford University Press, 2013).

Thaddeus Metz, *God, Soul and the Meaning of Life* (Cambridge: Cambridge University Press, 2019).

Thaddeus Metz and Motsamai Molefe, 'Traditional African Religion as a Neglected Form of Monotheism', *The Monist* 104 (2021), 393–409.

Martha Nussbaum, 'Mortal Immortals: Lucretius on Death and the Voice of Nature', *Philosophy and Phenomenological Research* 50 (1989), 303–51.

Ingmar Persson and Julian Savulescu, 'The Meaning Life, Equality and Eternity', *The Journal of Ethics* 23 (2019), 223–38 at 234.

Philip Quinn, 'How Christianity Secures Life's Meanings'. In Joseph Runzo and Nancy Martin (eds), *The Meaning of Life in the World Religions* (Oxford: Oneworld Publications, 2000) 53–68.

Seanna Shiffrin, 'Wrongful Life, Procreative Responsibility, and the Significance of Harm', *Legal Theory* 5 (1999), 117–48.

Richard Swinburne, 'How God Makes Life a Lot More Meaningful'. In Joshua Seachris and Stewart Goetz (eds), *God and Meaning* (New York: Bloomsbury Academic, 2016) 149–64.

Erik Wielenberg, *Value and Virtue in a Godless Universe* (Cambridge: Cambridge University Press, 2005).

Clifford Williams, *Religion and the Meaning of Life* (Cambridge: Cambridge University Press, 2020).

God, The Meaning of Life, and Meaningful Lives

DANIEL J HILL

Abstract

In my 2002 piece 'The Meaning of Life' I argued that Life, meaning the sum of the lives of all living things, had a meaning if and only if it had been purposefully brought about by a designer or creator. Michael Hauskeller has recently criticized this argument, responding that this sense of 'meaning' is not the one in view when we are discussing 'the meaning of life'. In this piece I respond to Hauskeller's argument, and, while I stand by my 2002 argument in terms of one meaning of 'meaning', I admit that it does not apply to the different question of what makes a life meaningful. I assert that glorifying God is the activity that contributes the most meaningfulness to a life, though I deny that this is the only activity that can contribute meaningfulness to a life. This makes me, in terms due to Thaddeus Metz, a moderate supernaturalist rather than an extreme supernaturalist. Despite this distinction, Metz has argued in this volume that moderate supernaturalism is vulnerable to the same objection as in his view defeats extreme supernaturalism, and I close by responding to this argument.

1. The Meaning of 'The Meaning of Life'

Peter van Inwagen writes:

> If we have a purpose, then our existence 'has a meaning' in the only sense these words can be given. It must be admitted that it is not at all clear what these words do mean. The term 'meaning' has various senses, but none of them lends any sense to the question, What is the meaning of our existence? other than this sense: Explain why we exist in terms of the purposes we serve. (If Alice surprises a trusted employee who has broken into her office and is going through her files and asks that person, 'What is the meaning of this?,' she is requesting an explanation of a certain state of affairs in terms of the purposes of her employee or those whose agent the employee is.)[1]

---

[1]   Van Inwagen (2014, p. 303). Van Inwagen writes of 'existence' rather than 'life', but I don't think that this difference is relevant for our purposes.

doi:10.1017/S1358246121000266   © The Royal Institute of Philosophy and the contributors 2021

Daniel J Hill

Van Inwagen mentions that there are 'various senses' of the term 'meaning'. Robert Nozick distinguishes eight such senses in his *Philosophical Explanations*. The first is 'meaning as external causal relationship'. Nozick gives three examples in a row: 'those spots mean measles, smoke means fire, red sky at night means fair weather' (Nozick, 1981, p. 574). This sense of 'meaning' seems to be similar to H P Grice's 'non-natural meaning', and Nozick's first example is in fact taken from Grice (Grice, 1957, p. 213). Nozick's third sense is the one that van Inwagen has in mind, 'Meaning as intention or purpose'. Nozick's examples include 'what is the meaning of this outburst?', 'did you mean to do that?', 'this play is meant to catch the conscience of the king', and 'by that gesture he meant to insult us' (Nozick, 1981, p. 574). In what follows I restrict myself to this third sense of 'meaning'. I do not deny that the other senses may be relevant to the meaning of life, and so, while I gratefully adopt the rest of the passage from van Inwagen as my own, I don't adopt his 'none of them lends any sense [...] other than this sense'.[2]

Perhaps the primary use of 'meaning' in the sense outlined above, meaning as intention or purpose, is (or should be) in connection with actions, or even the agents themselves, rather than in connection with states of affairs. On this understanding, the primary use of the word 'meaning' in the sense of intention or purpose would be to refer to something that agents had in their minds, and the secondary use would be to refer to something that actions had in virtue of their being performed by agents with purposes in their minds. Nevertheless, just as the word 'meaning' in the linguistic case may be extended from language speakers to linguistic acts and then to some of the intended products of those acts, e. g. a written inscription or text,[3] so the word 'meaning' in the present context may be extended from the agents to the acts performed and then to the events or states of affairs produced by those acts.

Imagine, then, to vary the example slightly, that Alice discovered the state of affairs of her papers' being in a mess on the floor of the office, and asked 'what is the meaning of this?'. An answer to her question would consist in telling her that the state of affairs was the result of a purposeful action, and what the purpose behind that action was: for example, that someone wanted to upset her. The

---

[2]   I thank each of T J Mawson, Frances Kamm, and James Stacey Taylor for (separately) trying to get me to see this.
[3]   Note that not every intended product of the linguistic act has linguistic meaning: in speaking I may intend that you smell my breath, and the murderer might intend to write the will in the handwriting style of the deceased.

mess, however, would have no meaning in the sense of intention or purpose if it were the result of a purely natural process – if it had been caused by the wind, perhaps.[4] It would also have no meaning in this sense if it had been caused aimlessly by a conscious agent's accidentally knocking the papers onto the floor, or by a drunken or entranced agent's throwing them on the floor without any ulterior motive.[5] A more difficult case would be if a preoccupied agent randomly hurled them over their shoulder without having any intention concerning where or how they should land: in this case the mess would have been produced by a purposeful action, but the production of the mess would not have been a purpose of the action, so the mess would have no meaning in the sense of intention or purpose. Similarly, if an agent purposefully initiates a truly random process, then the fact that the process has a result will have a meaning in the sense of intention or purpose, since the agent intended that the process have a result, but there will be no meaning in this sense to the process's having the particular result that it does, since that particular result was not part of the agent's purpose. And, typically, if the agent intends to create a mess there will be no meaning in this sense to the existence of the precise arrangement of the mess that does result – there will be no meaning in this sense why this paper is on top of that one, rather than the other way around.

A tricky application of this link between an action's being done with a purpose or meaning and the having of a meaning in the sense of intention or purpose by the state of affairs or event produced concerns the ongoing existence of the state of affairs or event after the fulfilment of the purpose of the action that produced it. Suppose that the papers were left in a mess in order to upset Alice, is it still the case that there is a meaning in the sense of intention or purpose to the continuing existence of the mess if, after getting upset, Alice makes a full recovery, or even if she never gets upset at all? One thing we can do here is to distinguish between the bare existence of the mess, on the one hand, and, on the other, the continued existence of the mess after a certain time: it may be that the continued existence of the mess has no meaning in the sense of intention or purpose even if the fact of its bare existence does have a meaning. It seems to me that if Alice asks on her return 'what is

---

[4]   A theist might say here that the wind's blowing was the result of a purposeful action of God's, of course.

[5]   Again, a theist might say here that the agent's precise bodily movements were the result of a purposeful action of God's.

the meaning of this?' having forgotten about the incident then the correct response is to say 'the meaning is that it was put there in order to upset you'. But if Alice asks 'what is the meaning of this mess's still being here?' it is clear that she is asking what the purpose of her staff was in failing to clean it up. We have to distinguish between, for example, asking at 11pm 'what is the meaning of this?', on the one hand, and, on the other, asking (whether at 11pm or not) 'what is the meaning of this at 11pm?'. These two questions may have quite different correct answers.

In 2002 I drew as a corollary of this that if the existence of the World, by which I meant the sum of contingent states and events, had a meaning, then that meaning had to be a purpose that it gained in virtue of being an intended product of the purposeful action of a necessary being (Hill, 2002). This was because, for one thing, no contingent being would have existed beforehand to have endowed the World from its very first moment with meaning in the sense of intention or purpose,[6] and, for another, no contingent being as a matter of fact creates itself or even everything else, or even most other things. It could be argued in response that, if the World had no beginning, then it would be possible for each moment of the World to be endowed with meaning in this sense by an agent existing in a previous moment. Imagine, for example, a World consisting just of an endless backwards-infinite sequence of agents, each producing a successor, intending that the successor accomplish a certain purpose with their existence. (Note that it is not sufficient that an agent engage in reproduction for its own sake with no purpose for the successor's life, even if the agent knows full well that the existence of a successor will be the by-product of the reproduction.) Still, it seems to me that it does not follow from the existence of each moment of an infinite World's having a meaning in the sense of intention or purpose that the infinite World as a whole has a meaning in this sense – after all, the infinite World as a whole is not the intended product of any purposeful action. (Compare also here Leibniz's argument,[7] contested by

---

[6] I assumed that simultaneous and retroactive meaning-giving were impossible. Robert Nozick countenances retroactive meaning-giving in Nozick (1981, p. 589).

[7] Gottfried Wilhelm Leibniz, 'On the Ultimate Origination of Things', on-line at http://www.leibniz-translations.com/ultimateorigination.htm, accessed 3 April 2021.

God, The Meaning of Life, and Meaningful Lives

David Hume,[8] that an explanation for each member of an infinite sequence would not in and of itself suffice to explain the sequence as a whole. What would be the meaning in our example of the existence of *this* World, *this* endless backwards-infinite sequence of agents, rather than another one?)

What went for the World seemed to me to go for Life, by which I meant the sum of the lives of living things. If Life has meaning in the sense of intention or purpose, then it must have gained this meaning from being an intended product of the purposeful action of some non-living thing. This is because no living being would have existed beforehand to have intentionally produced Life from its very first moment,[9] and, as a matter of fact, no living being does intentionally produce all living beings, or even all other living beings, or even most other living beings.[10] Again, it would not seem to suffice, if Life had no beginning, for each individual life to have its meaning in the sense of intention or purpose given to it by an antecedent living thing in a backwards-infinite sequence, as Life as a whole would still not be the intentional product of a purposeful action. Also, what would be the meaning in this sense in our example of *this* Life, *this* endless backwards-infinite sequence of lives, rather than another one?

What about individual lives, especially human lives? It is possible that an individual's life could be endowed with meaning in the sense of intention or purpose by their parents. For example, it may be that the parents brought the child into existence in order to have someone to look after them in their old age. This example shows that a life can have more than one meaning in this sense, since a life can be the product of a joint action undertaken with different intentions. It is possible that the parents had different purposes in bringing the child into the world. Indeed, it is possible that a life could have two meanings or purposes that could not both be fulfilled: perhaps one parent decided to bring the child into the world to provide someone that would go away and earn money to keep them well off, whereas the other parent decided to bring the child into the world

---

[8]   Cleanthes, in David Hume, *Dialogues Concerning Natural Religion*, on-line at https://gutenberg.org/files/4583/4583-h/4583-h.htm, accessed 3 April 2021.

[9]   Again, I was here assuming that simultaneous and retroactive meaning-giving were impossible.

[10]   Note that God is not correctly described as 'living' or 'alive' in the literal sense of those terms (the sense being employed here). In my 2002 paper I missed this point.

Daniel J Hill

to provide someone that would stay at home as a full-time carer for them.

Also, while (given the assumptions above that retrospective and simultaneous donation of meaning are impossible) one cannot give meaning in the sense of intention or purpose to one's own life as a whole, one can give a large part of it meaning in this sense. Imagine someone tempted to commit suicide deciding at the last moment 'no, I shall live – and devote the rest of my life to the relief of suffering'. In this case, the person has, in a way, brought about the existence of the rest of their life by refraining from suicide, and brought it about with a specific purpose, the relief of suffering. This suffices, in my view, to give meaning in this sense to the rest of their life. (Perhaps more disturbingly, if my would-be murderer changes their mind and decides to spare my life in order that I may cook and clean for them for the rest of my days, that would also give meaning in this sense to the rest of my life, albeit a meaning that I might want to reject.) It is not necessary that one explicitly consider and reject suicide. If one thinks simply 'I shall devote the rest of my life to the relief of suffering' then one has repurposed the rest of one's life, just as one might repurpose a book as a paperweight or doorstop. Nor need this decision be conscious or explicit.

Drawing an inference from all the above, I wrote in 2002 that someone that believed that Life had no creator or designer was rationally compelled to believe that Life had no meaning in the sense of intention or purpose.

I should draw attention to the limitations of the thesis that I put forward. Not only does it not follow from Life's having a meaning in the sense of intention or purpose that each individual life has a meaning in that sense, but it also does not follow from an individual life's having a meaning in that sense that every moment or period of that life has a meaning in that sense. Indeed, it is possible that most of the life will have no meaning in that sense if, for example, the purpose for which the being was brought into existence was fulfilled pretty much immediately, and the being did not repurpose the rest of its life. On the other hand, it does not follow from a life's lacking meaning overall in the sense of intention or purpose that every significant period of it will lack meaning in that sense. Further, it does not follow from one's whole life's having a meaning in that sense that one is able to make it one's own meaning, that one is able to adopt it as one's own purpose for one's life – perhaps my parents intended that I be an Olympic athlete, but this dream is sadly impossible for me. Or perhaps my parents brought me into the world simply to show that they were capable of bringing a child into the world, leaving me nothing left to do to achieve this goal. Nor does it follow that if one is able to adopt it as one's own purpose that one should – perhaps my parents brought me into the world intending that I pursue a long-standing vendetta, but it would be wrong for me to do so. I should also stress that the argument concerns just states of affairs and events, such as lives. It does not concern individual substances, such as human beings, considered in themselves apart from their existence or lives.

Finally, I should emphasize again that the argument applies to only one sense of the word 'meaning': Nozick's third sense, viz. 'intention or purpose'. By contrast, in Nozick's first sense of 'meaning', viz. 'external causal relationship', while I insist that if someone denies the existence of a necessary being then they cannot consistently affirm that the World (i. e. the sum of contingent states and events) has a meaning, I do concede that if someone denies the existence of a necessary being and even of any creator or designer, they could nevertheless consistently affirm that Life (i. e. the sum of the lives of living things) had a meaning. This meaning would be a naturalistic explanation of the origin of life in terms of non-living things.[11]

2. Michael Hauskeller's Critique

Michael Hauskeller has criticized this account of mine in some on-line Reading Notes not only with respect to Nozick's 'meaning as intention or purpose' but also with respect to Nozick's first sense, 'meaning as external causal relationship':

> The problem is that when we ask about meaning in life we are not really asking for an explanation at all. Instead, in many cases what we are asking for is a *justification*. […] If life has a purpose, that purpose does not answer our question about life's meaning, or if it does, then not because it is life's *purpose*, but because it gives *us* a reason to live and to find our life worth living. The question we want answered is why we should live, or why we should go on living. It is not impossible that what gives us a reason to live and what makes our life worth living is in fact also the purpose of our life. But even if it were *not* the purpose of our life, whatever it is that gives us a reason to live and makes our life worth living would still continue to do so. (Hauskeller, manuscript)

---

[11] I thank Frances Kamm for bringing me to see this.

Daniel J Hill

It should be noted that Hauskeller's focus here is on the individual's life, not, as mine was, on Life as a whole.

Hauskeller also deploys three counter-examples to my account, including the famous example of Sisyphus, who was punished for tricking Death by being forced to roll a rock up a hill only for it to roll down when it got to the top, forcing him to go down to the bottom and repeat the process.

> If, for instance, God had created life because he thought he might enjoy the spectacle of our suffering, then *that* would be the meaning of our life. Or if my role in God's plan were to amass the largest collection of bottle caps, then this would be the meaning of my life however trivial collecting bottle caps may appear to me and to everyone else. If God had created us to forever roll rocks up a hill only to see them roll down again shortly before we get to the top, then this would be the meaning of our life, even though such a life, the life of a Sisyphus, is widely seen as a paradigmatic case of a life entirely devoid of meaning. Of course God, being God, would not think of creating life for such reasons. But that is beside the point. (Hauskeller, manuscript)

It should be noted that these counter-examples are against the assertion that purpose is *sufficient* for meaning in the sense relevant to 'the meaning of life'. They are not against the assertion that purpose is *necessary* for meaning in that sense, though Hauskeller disputes that too.

3. Response to Michael Hauskeller

I agree with Michael Hauskeller that there is a difference in meaning between 'the meaning of life', on the one hand, and 'meaning in life' or a life's being 'meaningful' on the other.[12] In particular, the meaning of the adjective 'meaningful' seems somewhat stronger than the meaning of the noun 'meaning'. We normally reserve the adjective 'meaningful' for valuable things or actions done from a valuable purpose. It does not normally suffice for an event to be called 'meaningful' that someone brought it about for a purpose. When we read in *Women in Love* that Gudrun 'paddled softly, lingeringly,

[12] I do not assume that 'meaning in life' and 'meaningfulness of life' are synonymous, though I do think that they are similar in meaning. In what follows I concentrate on meaningfulness. I thank Frances Kamm for getting me to see this.

longing for him [Gerald] to say something meaningful to her' (Lawrence, 2002, p. 163) we know that she would not have been satisfied by just any utterance that Gerald uttered with some purpose or other; she wants him to say something with a valuable purpose, such as telling her how he feels about her, or giving her happiness. (The version with the noun, 'longing for him to say something with meaning to her', would not seem as strong.)

I still believe that one meaning of 'meaning' in 'what is the meaning of life?' relates to the notion of purpose, just as it did in the example from van Inwagen of 'what is the meaning of this?' asked about the reading of private files or the making of a mess in Alice's office. In each case, one is looking for the purpose of the phenomenon (life, the existence of the mess or its being made) in terms of the intentions of agents in the purposeful action that had the phenomenon as its intended product. Nevertheless, I accept that Hauskeller is right that when people talk about the meaning of life it is often in fact the case that what they really want is an answer to what seems to me to be a different question, about what would make their lives meaningful.

Here is the connection I see between the two notions. In the case of 'the meaning of', we look at the purpose with which the thing in question, be it the World as a whole, or an individual constituent element of it, such as a human being, was brought into being. In fact, when people ask 'what is the meaning of life?' they often really mean 'is there a purpose that I should make my own for the rest of my life?'. I agree with Hauskeller that knowing the purpose for which one was brought into existence, if there was one, does not in and of itself tell one whether one should make that purpose one's own for the rest of one's life.

Consider this example to see more clearly the relation between the notions of meaning as purpose and of meaningfulness. Suppose two humans bring a child into the world to provide genetic material to save an older sibling.[13] Suppose further that the sibling sadly dies before the child is born, and that the parents lose interest in the child, who grows up to become a drifter with no set projects or purpose and accomplishing little of value. In this case, even though there was a meaning to the bringing into existence of the drifter it does not seem right to call the drifter's life 'meaningful', absent further information. And that is because neither the purpose with which the drifter was brought into the world nor any other purpose

---

[13]   I also suppose in this example that neither God nor anybody else has a different purpose for the child's life.

actually governed the drifter's life. For someone's life to be meaningful it has to be that the living of at least a significant portion of their life actually fulfils a purpose. In other words, a purpose actually has to direct at least a significant number of their major decisions, priorities, and plans. (Even a perfectly happy existence would be meaningless, it seems to me, if one's happiness were not the result of any purposeful actions, if one just sat there serenely doing absolutely nothing).[14]

This issue is also raised by Hauskeller's counter-examples. On my account, Sisyphus's existence would have a meaning in the sense of intention or purpose if his parents brought him into the world for a purpose. What is more, if his parents did bring him into the world for a purpose, then even the fact that he ended up being punished as he did in Tartarus would not bring it about that his existence overall lacked a meaning in the sense of intention or purpose. Furthermore, if the gods could have annihilated Sisyphus, but purposefully allowed him to continue to exist, then, on my account, Sisyphus's *continued existence in Tartarus* would also have meaning in the sense of intention or purpose, and it would also give meaning in this sense to his *activity* in Tartarus: the gods purposed or meant to punish him by it. Nevertheless, I acknowledge that the object of his activity, the *task* that occupies Sisyphus's post-mortem life, is meaningless in and of itself, and that is precisely why that task was chosen for him: it is of no value in and of itself, and, in and of itself, does no good to anyone.[15] Further, the intuition is that even if Sisyphus devoted his life to the rock-rolling, so that he literally lived to roll rocks, his life in Tartarus would still not be meaningful despite his giving himself this purpose,[16] at least, if he did not do it for an ulterior valuable purpose, such as punishing himself for his crimes by doing it.

This last point provides material for a response to Hauskeller's other two examples, featuring a trivial purpose and an evil purpose. What if my parents brought me into existence with the purpose of

---

[14]   It is worth noting in this connection that the Bible suggests that there will be work to be done in the next life: Daniel 7:18, Isaiah 65:21–23, and Revelation 22:3. Luke 19:17, although in a parable, may also be relevant.

[15]   Of course it could be argued that it does good in the sense of restoring the balance of justice by punishment, but it does not do good in that sense *in and of itself*.

[16]   Cf. Taylor (1970). It might be that William James would disagree: cf. 'Believe that life *is* worth living, and your belief will help create the fact' in James (1897, p. 62). I am grateful to Mawson (2016, p. 183) for this reference.

bringing into existence a bottle-top collector, and that for its own sake, not for any further purpose? Or what if my parents brought me into the world for sadistic reasons, to see me suffer? There would be no moral obligation on me to make those purposes my own, but what if in fact I did dedicate my life to one of those purposes? Would my life be meaningful in those conditions? On my account it would have meaning in the sense of intention or purpose, but I accept that it would not be meaningful. This is because these purposes are not valuable (even if they are mistakenly valued). Hauskeller is correct that a life's having a meaning in the sense of intention or purpose is not sufficient for it to be meaningful; the intention or purpose needs to be a valuable one.

Is it necessary, however, for a life to be meaningful that it be lived for a meaning or purpose for at least a significant proportion of it? Yes. Suppose that there were someone for whose life neither they nor anyone else, including God, had a purpose. Suppose further that, as it happened, this person aimlessly did things that, by accident, turned out to promote goodness or happiness: for example, in blundering about they accidentally broke a gun, thus preventing a murder from taking place, they accidentally dropped food that saved the life of someone starving etc. Would such a person have a meaningful life? No. They may have had a *lucky* life, or their life may have been lucky for others, but it was not meaningful if there was no purpose to it or any significant part of it.[17] What is more, this would apply, I think, even if they were brought into existence for a definite purpose, as long as that purpose did not control their actions.

I have been adding 'or any significant part of it' because it would be pedantic to insist that if someone dedicated their life from childhood to helping others they still did not have a meaningful life on the ground that they did not dedicate their life as a baby to helping others. When we ask whether someone had a meaningful life we do not insist that they must have had a purpose governing every second of it right from its beginning.

What, however, if someone, perhaps like Zorba in *Zorba the Greek*, had no long-term goals at all, and drifted from situation to situation, but, nevertheless, in each situation fulfilled a short-term intention of doing something worthwhile in that situation?[18] It is not a

[17] Here I disagree with Smuts (2013).
[18] In Nikos Kazantzakis's novel the narrator quotes Zorba as follows:

'I've stopped thinking all the time of what happened yesterday. And stopped asking myself what's going to happen tomorrow. What's

requirement of a life's being meaningful that it be lived with just one purpose. It seems obvious that a life can be meaningful even if a third of it is spent in a state (sleep) for which one might have no purpose at all.[19] It also seems obvious that a life lived half in pursuit of one purpose and then half in pursuit of a different purpose would not on that account be meaningless. So, it seems that a life composed of short-term purposeful episodes interspersed with purposeless episodes and with no overall long-term purpose would not on that account be meaningless.

It seems, intuitively, however, that a life would not be meaningful if one had a purpose for it, but one couldn't implement one's purpose.[20]

In short, it seems that it is necessary for a life to be meaningful that it be freely lived, at least in significant part, for a valuable (important and morally good) purpose, and that, to a significant degree, the life achieve that purpose. Is this condition also sufficient for a life's being meaningful? I am of the cautious view that it is, but I do not need this assumption in what follows. I deny that it is necessary that the life be enjoyed, or enjoyable, or satisfying, or varied, or interesting, or spectacular, or out of the ordinary, or allow for 'self-creative autonomy',[21] or that it be recognized in any particular way by others. Nevertheless, I do not deny that any of these features might increase the meaningfulness of a life, since it is possible for one life to be more meaningful than another not only in the degree to which it is devoted to a given purpose and the degree to which it achieves that purpose, but also in virtue of the degree of value embodied in the purpose. Meaningfulness is, thus, I think, like a recipe with some necessary

---

happening today, this minute, that's what I care about. I say: "What are you doing at this moment, Zorba?" "I'm sleeping." "Well, sleep well." "What are you doing at this moment, Zorba?" "I'm working." "Well, work well." "What are you doing at this moment, Zorba?" "I'm kissing a woman." "Well, kiss her well, Zorba! And forget all the rest while you're doing it; there's nothing else on earth, only you and her!"' (Kazantzakis, 2000, pp. 293–94). Not every intention of Zorba's is worthwhile, it should be said, and he has more long-term goals than he lets on.

[19] Of course, many people, perhaps most, do go to sleep, or make themselves ready to go to sleep, with a purpose, viz. to get refreshed.

[20] Cf. Mawson (2016, p. 9).

[21] *Pace* T J Mawson, who insists that, in one sense of 'meaningful', it is true that a life that does not allow for self-creative autonomy is meaningless: (Mawson, 2016, p. 41).

ingredients and some optional ingredients, which, despite being optional, might nevertheless improve the whole.

4. Glorifying God and meaningfulness

Back in 2002 I was writing about Life in general rather than individual lives when I said that the proposition that there was no creator or
designer implied that there was no meaning to Life. How would what
I wrote then apply to Michael Hauskeller's question about the meaningfulness of individual (human) lives?

In 2002 I wrote more generally about a 'creator or designer'. Now,
for the sake of convenience, I write more specifically about God. I
assert that God created the World as a whole, Life as a whole, humanity as a whole, and each individual human being in order that the
World, Life, humanity, and the individual human being might
glorify him.[22]

What is meant by 'glorifying God'? The most obvious way of glorifying or giving glory to someone is to praise them,[23] and that is the
way we use the term when we say things like 'all the glory in this
matter should go to the director', meaning that all the praise and
credit should be afforded to the director. But it is possible to

---

[22]   See Isaiah 43:7, which refers to 'everyone who is called by my name,
whom I created for my glory, whom I formed and made' (English Standard
Version), and Isaiah 60:21b, 'They are the shoot that I planted, the work of
my hands, so that I might be glorified' (New Revised Standard Version). I
should clarify that each of these texts is concerned only with God's people,
not with humanity at large. Each text could be read either as saying that God
created his people so that in so doing he could glorify himself, or as saying
that God created his people so that they might glorify him. It does not
matter for present purposes which is the intended reading because for
each reading there is supporting evidence for the proposition in that
reading in other parts of the Christian Scriptures. Evidence for the proposition of the first reading can be found in Ephesians 1:11–12, 'In him we were
also chosen [...] in order that we [...] might be for the praise of his glory'
(New International Version). Evidence for the proposition of the second
reading can be found in 1 Corinthians 6:20 'you were bought with a price.
So glorify God in your body' (ESV), where the 'so' is particularly instruct-
ive. For a detailed treatise, see Edwards (1765).
[23]   Compare the equation of glorification and praise in Romans 15:8–9,
'Christ became a servant to the circumcised [...] in order that the Gentiles
might glorify God for his mercy. As it is written, "Therefore I will praise
you among the Gentiles, and sing to your name"' (ESV).

Daniel J Hill

glorify other than by uttering words of praise. One can glorify someone by doing something for them, or in honour of them, or making them the supreme object of our thoughts or affections, or just by doing what they ask us to do to the best of our ability.[24]

I accept, as Hauskeller has pointed out, that it does not follow logically from someone's having brought us into existence in order that we might fulfil a particular purpose that we should make that purpose our own or that such a purpose would make a life meaningful (Hauskeller, manuscript). For one thing, the purpose might be immoral or impossible. This worry does not apply in this case, however: although it is impossible for us, at least in this life, thanks to our sin, to glorify God *fully*, it is certainly possible for us (though only with God's help) to glorify God *partially*, even in this life.[25] Secondly, I assert that, not only is glorifying God a morally good and meaningful activity,[26] but in fact there is no more valuable and meaningful activity that one can do in any possible world than glorifying God.[27] I assert further that it is in fact morally obligatory on every agent to try to glorify God as far as possible.[28] This might make it seem as though the fact that God created us in order that we should fulfil this purpose is irrelevant. To quote from Metz:

the mere fact that God is the source of a purpose is not what makes it meaningful; it is rather what the purpose would have us do, making the fact that it has come from God irrelevant. (Metz, 2019, p. 10)

In point of fact, though, God is our benefactor, having brought us into what is, for most of us, most of the time, a pleasant life, so we owe him a duty to use the gift of life as he asks us to use it. And, I assert, he does indeed ask us to glorify him.[29] Once more, I accept

---

[24]   1 Corinthians 10:31, 'So, whether you eat or drink, or whatever you do, do all to the glory of God' (ESV), would be an example of one or more of these.
[25]   See, e. g. Psalm 34:3, 63:3, 69:30, 86:9, 86:12, Daniel 4:37, Matthew 5:16, Luke 2:20, John 21:19, Romans 15:6, 15:19, and 1 Peter 2:12.
[26]   Compare Revelation 4:11, 'You are worthy, our Lord and God, to receive glory' (NIV).
[27]   The glorification of God is famously held out as 'the chief end' of humanity in the Westminster Shorter Catechism (1647).
[28]   Compare the command in Psalm 34:3 and that in 1 Corinthians 10:31, 'So, whether you eat or drink, or whatever you do, do all to the glory of God' (ESV).
[29]   See, as quoted above, 1 Corinthians 6:20, 'you were bought with a price. So glorify God in your body' (ESV).

that it does not logically follow from the fact that one's benefactor asks one to do something that one ought to try to do it, but, again, our benefactor is not asking us to try to do anything immoral or impossible for us. So, my view is that we should glorify God (a) because it is morally obligatory, (b) because our creator and benefactor asks us to, and (c) because it will make our lives more meaningful. Glorifying God is, thus, overdetermined as something we should do.

My view on the meaning of Life had the consequence that atheism implied that there was no meaning in the sense of intention or purpose of Life. Does my view here on what makes a life meaningful have the similar consequence that atheism implies that no life is meaningful? No. I do not assert that glorifying God is the only valuable or meaningful activity, or the only activity that can make life meaningful. Consider Micah 6:8, which states:

He has shown you, O mortal, what is good.
And what does the Lord require of you?
To act justly and to love mercy
and to walk humbly with your God. (New International Version)

Now, I hold that acting justly, loving mercy, and walking humbly can (and should), in fact, be ways of glorifying God, if undertaken for that end, but the point here is that the atheist might disagree and assert that, since there is no God, these activities cannot glorify God, but, nevertheless, can make life meaningful.[30] This assertion is quite compatible with my position on what makes a life meaningful.

5. Extreme Supernaturalism and Moderate Supernaturalism

Thaddeus Metz in many of his works provides an extremely helpful taxonomy of the possible views on the meaning of life. To begin with, he distinguishes supernaturalist theories, which are 'views according to which a spiritual realm is central to meaning in life' from naturalist ones, which are 'views that the physical world as known particularly well by the scientific method is central to life's meaning' (Metz, 2021a). Then he distinguishes 'extreme supernaturalism', which is 'the view that God or a soul is necessary for one's life to be meaningful' from 'moderate supernaturalism', which is 'the view that,

---

[30] Of course, the text says 'walk humbly *with your God*', but I do not deny that walking humbly is itself a virtue. Compare 1 Peter 5:5, 'Clothe yourselves, all of you, with humility towards one another, for "God opposes the proud but gives grace to the humble"' (ESV).

Daniel J Hill

although these spiritual conditions are not necessary for that, they are necessary for one's life to have a great or ultimate meaning' (Metz, 2021b, p. 116). Metz offers an important clarification for his definition of 'extreme supernaturalism':

> When it is claimed that God, for instance, is 'necessary' for life's meaning, this is shorthand for 'identical to' it (in part). The claim is not merely that there would be no meaning without God, but rather that there would be no meaning without God because meaningfulness essentially consists of human life relating to God in a certain way. (Metz, 2019, p. 9)

This is a very important clarification, since theists will typically insist that God is necessary for us even to exist as living beings.[31]

For my part, I prefer to define 'extreme supernaturalism' as the thesis that the only activity that can make a life meaningful is relating to God in a certain way, and 'moderate supernaturalism' as the thesis that, while many different activities can make a life meaningful, relating to God in a certain way makes a life more meaningful than does any other activity. I think Micah 6:8, quoted earlier, teaches that acting justly and loving mercy are meaningful activities in and of themselves, though I admit that the word 'meaningful' does not, in fact, occur in that text. Since I think that each of these activities is distinct from glorifying God, even though each should be undertaken as means of glorifying God, I reject extreme supernaturalism. Since I further hold that each of them, and every other activity distinct from glorifying God, is in and of itself less meaningful than glorifying God, I hold moderate supernaturalism.

Metz also argues against extreme supernaturalism, writing that it is:

> vulnerable to the charge that it counterintuitively entails that a life spent in an experience machine [on the one hand] and [on the other hand] a life spent making revealing discoveries à la Einstein, helping lots of people in the ways Mandela did and creating great artworks on the level of van Gogh would be equally meaningless. (Metz, 2018, p. 185)

I agree that the making of discoveries, the helping of others, and the creating of great artworks are meaningful activities, in and of themselves, even though they can be done in order to glorify God, and, indeed, should not be done apart from this aim.

---

[31] Compare the words the apostle Paul is recorded as quoting in Acts 17:28, 'In him we live and move and have our being' (ESV).

God, The Meaning of Life, and Meaningful Lives

Now, Metz in his piece in this volume seeks to build on this to argue that on this basis moderate supernaturalism must also be rejected:

> If a life of eternal significance would bring an infinite amount of meaning in its wake, then consider that no life with a finite amount of meaning can compare and hence the supernaturalist cannot account for the intuition that such a life could be meaningful (Metz, 2021b, p. 117).

It seems to me that there is an important difference between saying that life not lived in relation to God must be totally meaningless, on the one hand, and, on the other, saying that life not lived in relation to God can be meaningful, but is always far less meaningful than, and even paltry in comparison with, life with God. Metz argues, however, that there is no real difference, saying that the meaning of a life not lived in relation to God

> would not be a 'flat zero', but it would, compared to infinity, come about as close to zero as is mathematically possible for a non-zero number, and that arguably fails to capture the judgement that [a life not lived in relation to God could be] meaningful on balance absent God and a soul. Just as we would not describe someone's life as 'happy' if it had only a smidge of happiness compared to what is frequently on offer, so we cannot plausibly describe some-one's mortal life as 'meaningful' if it has only a small dollop of meaning compared to infinity. (Metz, 2019, p. 31)

I agree with Metz that we normally use words such as 'happy' and 'meaningful' in a comparative way, such that it would seem wrong to call someone's life 'happy' or 'meaningful' if its level of happiness or meaningfulness were very low 'compared to what is frequently on offer'. But the problem is that there are at least three different possible classes in relation to which we could be making the comparison:

(i) The class of all logically possible lives (or activities (which would be my preference)), including lives spent in, for example, Nozick's experience machine;
(ii) The class of all actual lives (or activities), including those after death;
(iii) The class of all actual lives (or activities) in the here and now, before death.[32]

---

[32] T J Mawson's discussion is clearly informed by an awareness of this distinction (Mawson, 2016, p. 6).

Daniel J Hill

The most natural comparison class is (iii). It would seem wrong to describe, in Metz's words, 'someone's life as "happy" if it had only a smidge of happiness compared to what is frequently on offer', i. e. frequently on offer in this life. If I asked someone whether they were happy, they would not normally reply 'I cannot say that I am, when one thinks about how much happiness is on offer in the next life', any more than if I asked whether they were healthy they would normally reply 'I cannot say that I am, when one thinks about how much health is on offer in the next life', or if I asked whether they were old they would normally reply 'I cannot say that I am, when one thinks about the longevity on offer in the next life'. Similarly, to revert to my earlier example from D H Lawrence, when Gudrun longs for Gerald to say something 'meaningful' to her, she is longing for something meaningful compared to what is frequently on offer in this world. So, the intuitive judgement to which Metz refers that a life not lived in relation to God could be 'meaningful on balance' is similarly based on a comparison with other lives in the here and now, not in the hereafter, and is accommodated by moderate supernaturalism. What is more, it is based on a comparison with the publicly accessible appearance of people's lives or activities, rather than on the secret state of their souls.

Now, it is true that in one of the passages quoted above Metz drew a comparison between certain lives in this world on the one hand, and life in the experience machine on the other. This would direct us to the first comparison class that I suggested, the class of all logically possible lives or activities, (i). But it is extremely difficult to work out an average over the whole class of logically possible lives or activities, and, for *any* possible life you choose of finite meaningfulness, there exists, it is plausible to think, a logically possible life (even one lived without reference to God) containing a life so meaningful (while still being finitely meaningful) as to make the one in question paltry in comparison, even if the life in question consisted of delirious happiness in millions of years of productive work in eliminating suffering. What is more, it is plausible that this point goes not only for lives measured extensively, but also for activities measured intensively, i. e. for any activity you choose of finite meaningfulness there is a logically possible activity whose intrinsic meaningfulness makes the one in question paltry in comparison. So, Metz's argument cannot be applied in connection with (i), for it would forbid one from calling *any* possible finite life or activity 'meaningful'.

I agree that if we adopt (ii) then Metz can compare lives or activities now with lives or activities in the hereafter, and say that all those in the here and now are meaningless by comparison with lives in the hereafter or the activity of sinlessly praising God in the hereafter, and I agree that here moderate supernaturalism gives us a verdict similar to that given by extreme supernaturalism.[33] But I deny that this is a problem. I simply do not have the intuition that a life in the here and now spent in alleviating suffering, say, must be meaningful *in comparison with a life of infinite meaningfulness in the hereafter.* What is more, even what I have said is the most meaningful activity possible in the here and now, glorifying God, will look meaningless when we compare it in our current sinful states with how the activity will be in the sinless state in the hereafter. I simply don't think that anybody routinely uses the word 'meaningful' in comparison with lives in the hereafter, any more than they routinely use the word 'happy' or the word 'old' in comparison with lives in the hereafter.

In sum, I insist that moderate supernaturalism does not fall prey to Metz's argument, and can accommodate the intuitions about which he worries. And I say this despite the fact that I assert that our lives in the hereafter, if lived in sinless union with God, will be, at every moment, actually infinitely meaningful, and more meaningful than any life, no matter how long, lived in the here and now. I have included the word 'actually' to show that my position is stronger than that of T J Mawson, who holds that our lives will only ever be *potentially* infinitely meaningful, and never become *actually* infinitely meaningful (Mawson, 2018, p. 202). So, my particular version of moderate supernaturalism is almost as close to extreme supernaturalism as it is possible for moderate supernaturalism to be.[34]

6. Conclusion

To sum up, I agree with Michael Hauskeller that my argument from 2002 that the meaning of Life is the purpose with which living things were created does not answer the question that most people mean to ask when they ask about 'the meaning of life'. Nevertheless, as it happens, I believe that we are commanded, and it is in any case right, to make our own purpose the purpose that God created us to fulfil, the purpose of glorifying him, and that this is an important and morally good purpose, indeed I believe that there is none more important or better. So, it seems to me that, if God exists, then glorifying him is not only the meaning of Life and of each life, but also can make each life

[33] The verdict is not identical, because extreme supernaturalism would, and moderate supernaturalism would not, give any life not lived in relation to God in the here and now 'a flat zero', to use T J Mawson's phrase.
[34] 'Almost' because a closer version would be my theory except with actually infinitely meaningful lives before death.

meaningful, indeed infinitely meaningful (if lived in sinless union with him after death).

I do not assert that God created each of us with only one purpose for that person to fulfil, and I do not assert that the glorifying of God is literally the only possible activity of value. Consequently, while I stand by my assertion from 2002 that the proposition that there is no creator or designer does imply that Life does not have meaning in the sense of intention or purpose, I do not assert that that proposition, or its close relative, naturalism, implies that individual lives or activities cannot be meaningful in the sense of being valuable and worth living or doing. That said, if God does exist, glorifying God is so far and away the most meaningful activity that any life not aimed at fulfilling that purpose is missing out on being as meaningful as it could be and looks paltry in comparison with the promise of sinless union with God after death.[35]

University of Liverpool
djhill@liverpool.ac.uk

References

Jonathan Edwards, *The End for Which God Created the World* (1765).
H P Grice, 'Meaning', *The Philosophical Review* 66 (1957), 377–88, reprinted in H P Grice, *Studies in the Ways of Words* (Cambridge, MA: Harvard University Press, 1991).
Michael Hauskeller, 'Daniel Hill on God, Purpose, and the Meaning of Life', on-line at https://www.academia.edu/37237245/Daniel_Hill_on_God_Purpose_and_the_Meaning_of_Life, (manuscript) accessed 3 April 2021, italics original.
Daniel Hill, 'The Meaning of Life', *Philosophy Now* 35 (March/April 2002), on-line at https://philosophynow.org/issues/35/The_Meaning_of_Life, accessed 3 April 2021.

[35] My thanks go first and foremost to Michael Hauskeller for detailed and helpful comments on several drafts of this piece. Secondly, I thank Frances Kamm, Antti M Kauppinen, T J Mawson, Thaddeus Metz, James Stacey Taylor, and Nicholas Waghorn, for their helpful comments at the conference 'Meaning in Life and the Knowledge of Death' held in 2021 under the auspices of the University of Liverpool and the sponsorship of the Royal Institute of Philosophy, and for correspondence afterwards. I thank Michael Hauskeller for inviting me to speak at this conference and to contribute to this volume. I thank Thaddeus Metz for permission to quote from his essay in this volume. Obviously, none of those just mentioned should be taken to agree with what I say.

God, The Meaning of Life, and Meaningful Lives

David Hume, *Dialogues Concerning Natural Religion*, on-line at https://gutenberg.org/files/4583/4583-h/4583-h.htm, accessed 3 April 2021.

William James, 'Is Life Worth Living?' in William James, *The Will to Believe and Other Essays* (London: Longmans, 1897), 32–62.

Nikos Kazantzakis, *Zorba the Greek*, tr. Carl Wildman (London: Faber and Faber, 1961, 2000).

D H Lawrence, *The First 'Women in Love'*, eds John Worthen and Lindeth Vasey (Cambridge: Cambridge University Press, revised edition, 2002).

Gottfried Wilhelm Leibniz, 'On the Ultimate Origination of Things', on-line at http://www.leibniz-translations.com/ultimateorigination.htm, accessed 3 April 2021.

T J Mawson, *God and the Meanings of Life* (London: Bloomsbury, 2016).

T J Mawson, 'What God Could (and Couldn't) Do to Make Life Meaningful' in Joshua W. Seachris and Stewart Goetz, *God and Meaning: New Essays* (New York: Bloomsbury, 2016), 37–58.

T J Mawson, 'God's Possible Roles in the Meanings of Life: Reply to Metz'. *European Journal for Philosophy of Religion* 10 (2018) 193–203.

Thaddeus Metz, 'God's Role in a Meaningful Life' *European Journal for Philosophy of Religion* 10:3 (2018).

Thaddeus Metz, *God, Soul and the Meaning of Life* (Cambridge: Cambridge University Press, 2019).

Thaddeus Metz, 'The Meaning of Life', *The Stanford Encyclopedia of Philosophy* (Spring 2021 Edition), Edward N. Zalta (ed), (2021a) on-line at https://plato.stanford.edu/archives/spr2021/entries/life-meaning/, accessed 19 July 2021.

Thaddeus Metz, 'Comparing the Meaningfulness of Finite and Infinite Lives: Can We Reap What We Sow if We Are Immortal?', *Death and Meaning: Royal Institute of Philosophy Supplementary Volume 90*, (ed) Michael Hauskeller (Cambridge University Press, 2021b).

Robert Nozick, *Philosophical Explanations* (Oxford: Oxford University Press, 1981).

Aaron Smuts, 'The Good Cause Account of the Meaning of Life', *Southern Journal of Philosophy* 51 (2013), 536–562.

Richard Taylor, *Good and Evil* (New York: Macmillan, 1970).

Peter van Inwagen, *Metaphysics* (Boulder, CO: Westview, 2015, 4th edition).

When Death Comes Too Late: Radical Life Extension and the Makropulos Case

MICHAEL HAUSKELLER

Abstract

Famously, Bernard Williams has argued that although death is an evil if it occurs when we still have something to live for, we have no good reason to desire that our lives be radically extended because any such life would at some point reach a stage when we become indifferent to the world and ourselves. This is supposed to be so bad for us that it would be better if we died before that happens. Most critics have rejected Williams' arguments on the grounds that it is far from certain that we will run out of things to live for, and I don't contest these objections. Instead, I am trying to show that they do not affect the persuasiveness of Williams' argument, which in my reading does not rely on the claim that we will inevitably run out of things to live for, but on the far less contentious claim that it is *not unthinkable* we will do so and the largely ignored claim that *if* that happens, we will have *died too late*.

In this paper I will provide a new interpretation of Bernard Williams' well-known argument for the undesirability of immortality (Williams, 1973). I will do this by focusing on Williams' claim that if we extended our life span indefinitely and, in consequence, would in due course reach a stage of terminal 'boredom' in which we would be left with nothing to live for, *we would have 'died too late'*. My guiding question will be why and in what sense we can be said to have died too late if and when that happens.

1. Dying Too Early

It is commonly thought that people can, and often do, die too early. Death is rarely welcome, but we tend to think that if it has to come someday, it should not come before a person's life has run its normal, natural course. The death of a child or a young adult is generally felt to be worse than the death of an old person. We mourn the death of the old we know and love, but we have also resigned ourselves to it and accept it as a necessity, while the death of the young is considered a tragedy because there was still so much life to be lived, so

doi:10.1017/S1358246121000278   © The Royal Institute of Philosophy and the contributors 2021

Michael Hauskeller

many good experiences to be had, so much potential to be realised. There is a certain fittingness to the death of the old that is absent from the death of the young, which is why if we die young, people will say that we died *too* young.

However, what is considered too young can change over time. In modern wealthy societies the average life expectancy today is roughly twice as high as it was a hundred years ago, which means that if we die in our sixties today, our death will still be thought to have occurred too early by many because a majority of people live longer than that. Consequently, even though with sixty we may no longer be exactly young, we are still considered to be too young to die, largely because at that age there is *still* quite a lot of life to be lived. In this way, the average life expectancy in our social environment clearly has a certain normative significance for us.

Yet there are also other, less conventional ways to determine whether a life has been long enough that do not rely on what is normal or natural. Geoffrey Scarre for instance has argued that no matter whether we die early or late, our lives will in any case have been too short because even if we lived to a ripe old age, we would still not have had the time to explore all the opportunities that life offers us (Scarre, 1997). There is just so much to do and so little time to do it, so that as long as we are confined to the current human life span, we will always be frustrated in our most basic life project, which is that of 'living a valuable and fulfilling human life' (Scarre, 1997, p. 279). According to this view, not only are those with shorter lives worse off than those with longer lives, because their 'lives are like narratives without a proper middle or ending' (Scarre, 1997, p. 274), but we in fact *all* die too early because presently there is simply not time enough to pursue all the interesting and worthwhile projects that we may want to pursue: 'Should we become a philosopher or a footballer, a concert pianist or a world-traveller? If we had an extra century, we could be them all' (Scarre, 1997, p. 278).

That certainly sounds appealing, although living a lot longer than we currently do would not by itself be sufficient to make the dream of being able to pursue, consecutively, multiple careers come true. A lot else would have to change too. For starters, we would have to stay fully adaptable and at the height of our powers for much longer. It is, after all, for most of us *already* far too late to become a concert pianist or a (professional) footballer, and another century added to our current life span would not change that. So, if we really want to do all those things, it seems that what prevents us from doing them is not so much that we die too early, but that we *age* too early. That

148

being said, I am happy to concede the point. Although I personally think that the average human life span is long enough to allow the vast majority of people to do all the things they really want to do[1] and to live a 'valuable and fulfilling human life', there are clearly more things we could do and might want to do if we had more time, and in that sense we can be said to have died too early if we died before we were able to do them.

In any case, it is widely accepted that one can indeed die too early, and for the purpose of this paper I shall assume that this is correct. Now, when we say about someone that they have died too early, we are implying that it would have been better, in some way, if they had lived longer. Very often we mean that it would have been better *for them*, though this is not always the case. Sometimes we say that somebody died too early when we think that their continued existence would have been good for *others* – for instance when it is claimed that, say, the American president John F. Kennedy or the rock musician Jimi Hendrix died too early, not only because they were still comparatively young (Hendrix in his late twenties and Kennedy in his mid forties) when they died, but also, and perhaps primarily, because it was expected that they would have done more good, world-enriching things if they had lived longer: 'Sadly', one commentator writes, 'Hendrix died ... far too early to see his musical vision fully realized' (Fricke, 1992).

We may even say that someone died too early when living longer would not have been good for them at all, for instance when their death has allowed them to escape what we consider a just punishment for their actions. In this way, Pol Pot, the leader of the Khmer Rouge responsible for the death of almost two million Cambodians in the 1970s, who died from heart failure before he could face trial, 'died too early for justice to be served' (Bartrop, 2015, p. 533). We don't like war criminals to die of natural causes before they have paid for their crimes.

2. Dying Too Late

Yet dying too early is not what this paper is about. The question that interests me and that I want to focus on in the remainder of this

---

[1] Clearly, we often do *not* get around to doing all the things we would like to do or fancy ourselves doing, but this is not usually because our lives are too short, but because we lack the opportunity or the necessary resources to do them.

Michael Hauskeller

discussion is this one: if we can die too early, *can we also die too late*, in the sense that it would have been *good for us* if we had died earlier than we in fact did? Let us first gather some preliminary evidence. There are certainly situations in which the claim that someone has died too late would appear not entirely implausible. For instance, if somebody has lived a happy, fulfilled life until, one day, disaster strikes and something terrible happens that makes their life from then on utterly miserable (say, their family is killed in a car crash) or if they descend into dementia and forget who they were and what used to be important for them (as it happened to Iris Murdoch, who towards the end of her life became increasingly childlike and had all but forgotten that she was actually a famous novelist) (Conradi, 2001, p. 591), then we may well feel that it would have been better for them if they had died before that happened. Even John F. Kennedy, whom I mentioned above as someone who was widely thought to have died too *early* (not counting, obviously, those who disliked his politics and what he stood for and for whom his death couldn't come soon enough) may have died just in time to avoid being revealed as just another politician unable to live up to the hopes invested in him by his admirers. From that perspective, as an editorial in *The Independent* has it, JFK 'died too early to disappoint, leaving only a legend',[2] implying that he would have died *too late* if he had lived longer and thus been given the chance to spoil his legacy. So, what is being suggested here is that it was actually *good* for him that he died when he did. Compare the case of Rudy Giuliani, the former mayor of New York, who in the aftermath of 9/11 was hailed as a hero for his leadership, lauded as 'America's Mayor' by Oprah Winfrey, and named 'person of the year' by *Time Magazine*, and who might now always be remembered for (or perhaps not remembered at all because of) his crazy antics as one of Trump's worst stooges, dabbling in conspiracy theories and generally making a fool of himself. Would it be wrong to say that he has lived too long for his own good and that it would have been better for him if he had died shortly after 9/11?

It may seem, though, that these are all exceptional cases and that most of us do not die too late. If anything, we die too early. But perhaps we are wrong about that. One who strongly suggested we

---

[2] 'The real John F. Kennedy has been obscured by legend, while America's respect for politicians has dwindled away', *The Independent*, 20 November 2013. Accesssed 27 June 2021. https://www.independent.co.uk/voices/editorials/real-john-f-kennedy-has-been-obscured-legend-while-america-s-respect-politicians-has-dwindled-away-8952603.html

might be is Friedrich Nietzsche. In *Thus Spoke Zarathustra*, he rather enigmatically proclaimed that 'many die too late, and some die too early. Strange is still the doctrine "Die when the time is right"'[3]. The doctrine is still strange today, perhaps stranger than ever. The speed of technological progress in the past three decades or so has fuelled hopes that we will soon be able to extend the average human life span by potentially hundreds of years,[4] and with that prospect constantly dangled before our collective imagination, we have become more reluctant to accept that our life must end and will end within the time frame alloted to us by nature and more inclined to believe, like Geoffrey Scarre, that almost *everyone* currently dies too early. Nietzsche, however, suggested that it is not only quite *possible* for us to die too late, but that far from being the exception, dying too late is actually the rule: *some* die too early, he wrote, but *many* die too late. Unfortunately, Nietzsche was not entirely clear about why he thought that. Following his proclamation, he talks about those who are 'not needed', about the glory of dying as a victor or, even better, in battle, 'throwing away a great soul'. He talks about the ageing of the heart and the ageing of the spirit and suggests that we might become too old 'even for our truths and victories'. Lasting fame, he says, requires that one 'leave at the right time' (Nietzsche, 1966, p. 334). Make your death a feast, he recommends, welcome it, seize it, own it; don't cling to life. According to him, it is best to die when life is at its very peak and we are still in full possession of our powers.

This is indeed a strange doctrine because it flies in the face of our conventional understanding of when we should die, and it flatly contradicts what we said earlier about when one's death can reasonably be said to have occurred too early. What Nietzsche sees as the best time to die is precisely what almost everyone else would see as too early: the common view is that we should definitely not die when life is still good; it would be best if we didn't have to die at all, but if we must die sometime, then we should die only when life is good no longer, when we are way past our peak, when there is not much left to look forward to and to keep us going. For Nietzsche, this would be too late.

In a similar vein, the British novelist Julian Barnes, reflecting on his own fear of death in his memoir *Nothing to Be Frightened of*, cites Somerset Maugham who once remarked that the 'great tragedy of life is not that men perish, but that they cease to love',

---

[3] Nietzsche (1966, p. 333), my translation.
[4] See for instance Kurzweil and Grossman (2005).

Michael Hauskeller

which, regrettably and rather ironically, seems to be exactly what happened towards the end of his life to Maugham himself. 'For all his practical wisdom and knowledge of the world,' writes Barnes, '– and for all his fame and his money – Maugham failed to hold on to the spirit of humorous resignation. His old age contained little serenity: all was vindictiveness, monkey glands[5], and hostile will-making. His body was kept going in vigour and lust while his heart grew harder and his mind began to slip, he declined into an empty rich man. Had he wished to write a codicil to his own (wintry, unwarming) advice, it might have been: the additional tragedy of life is that we do not perish at the right time' (Barnes, 2009, p. 84).

Barnes goes on to recall the way he reacted to Maugham's apercu when, as a young man, he first came across it. Not much to it, he thought. When love ends, you can, after all, always love again. Lose your old lover, find a new one, no harm done. But that is of course not what Maugham meant at all. He was not talking about the love that comes and goes, that you feel for one object or person and then for another. Rather, as the older Barnes realised (who was then, at the age of 63, approaching old age himself), Maugham's words should be understood as 'a lament for the loss of the ability to feel, first about your friends, then about yourself, and finally about even your own extinction. ... As your ears get bigger, and your fingernails split, your heart shrinks. So here's another would-you-rather. Would you rather die in the pain of being wrenched away from those you have long loved, or would you rather die when your emotional life has run its course, when you gaze at the world with indifference, both towards others and towards yourself?' (Barnes, 2009, p. 174).

This is not an easy choice to make. It is hard to die when life is good and we are still able to love and lucky enough to be loved. But might this not still be better than waiting until it is all gone and all that is left is indifference so that not even death and the spectre of annihilation is feared anymore?

3. Bernard Williams' Reflections on the Tedium of Immortality

This question takes us to Bernard Williams and the argument he presents in 'The Makropulos Case'. A lot has been written about it since

---

[5]   The grafting of monkey testicle tissue ('monkey glands') on to the testicles of ageing men to maintain and restore youthfulness was all the rage in the 1920s and 30s. See Rémy (2014).

the paper was published almost fifty years ago. However, much of it has failed to address what strikes me as the essential crux of his argument, which is that the title-giving Elina Makropulos, whose fictional case Williams uses to question the desirability of radical life extension, has reached a stage in her life when her death would inevitably *come too late*. It is this particular claim that I will focus on.

Let us briefly revisit the case, which Williams borrows from a play by Karel Čapek about a woman who as a young girl took an elixir of life that has allowed her to live for more than 300 years without getting any older physically. After all this time, Elina has become tired of living and is now stuck in a 'state of boredom, indifference and coldness' (Williams, 1973, p. 82), because she has done everything she ever wanted to do and there is now nothing left for her to do and want. After analysing the case, Williams concludes that even though death, or more precisely premature death, is indeed an evil, 'it can be a good thing not to live too long' (Williams, 1973, p. 83).

Now why exactly is that? The usual interpretation of Williams' argument goes like this: if we extend our lives indefinitely, we will most likely – no matter what kind of person we are and what kind of environment we find ourselves in – reach a point in time when we will have run out of 'categorical desires' – which is what supposedly happened to Elina Makropulos. Categorical desires are desires that provide us with reasons to go on living (for instance when we do not want to die because we wish to see our children grow up or finish the book that is meant to be our crowning achievement). The only way to prevent this from happening is by changing so drastically that we are no longer the person we used to be. Yet if we will not be the same person that we are today, so that the person that will exist will, for all intents and purposes, not be *us*, then we have no good reason to bring about that person's existence. Therefore, since we need categorical desires for life to be worth continuing and, if our life span were radically extended, we would (most likely or perhaps even inevitably) run out of such desires unless we changed beyond recognition, immortality is not desirable, and we should not pursue it. Doing so would only make sense for us if we could be certain that we would never reach that stage of terminal boredom, and we can never be certain of that. So long as we remain the particular person that we are, Williams claims, even radical changes in our environment won't be sufficient to prevent us from ending up with no reasons left to live, which puts us in a difficult position because even though we may not want to reach that stage, we don't want to die too early either: 'I will eventually have had altogether too much of myself. There are good reasons, surely, for dying before that happens. But equally, at times earlier than that moment, there is reason for not dying. Necessarily, it tends to be either too early or too late'. According to Williams, the only way to avoid this fate is by 'dying shortly before the horrors of not doing so become evident' (Williams, 1973, p. 109).

4. Williams' Critics

Williams' argument has been much criticized in the literature. Wholehearted support is rare.[6] The alleged dilemma – that radical life extension will either lead to terminal boredom, which makes it undesirable, or requires us to change who we are to avoid it, which also makes it undesirable – is deemed unconvincing by most critics. Some attack the first leg of the dilemma, arguing that either categorical desires are not needed for life to be worth living or that it is far from certain that we will run out of them, some attack the second leg, arguing that even radical changes of our personality don't have to undermine personal identity, and some attack both.

Let us briefly look at a few examples. Fischer (2013) insists that not all pleasures are self-exhausting. Some are repeatable and can be enjoyed over and over again, indefinitely, for instance simple pleasures such as sex or eating, or more refined ones such as our enjoyment of art and music, or of philosophising, suggesting that those who fear that an immortal life might quickly become boring (like Williams), should just 'chill out a bit and allow themselves to be receptive to the magic and beauty of life as it unfolds' (Fischer, 2013, p. 352). In a similar vein, Rosati claims that categorical desires are neither necessary nor sufficient to make life meaningful and worth living (Rosati, 2013). We don't need them, and we need in any case more than them. Boredom is an unlikely outcome because being what we are, we are likely to continue 'creating and securing value in our lives' (Rosati, 2013, p. 378), which is all that is needed. Buben suggests that we could sustain categorical desires indefinitely through a commitment to a project of perpetual self-cultivation (Buben, 2016), and Wisnewski concludes that while it is quite *possible* that we might eventually get bored of life, it is by no means *necessary* because new possibilities are likely to continue to arise, providing new material to previous categorical desires (Wisnewski, 2005).

---

[6] For some exceptions, see Althuser (2016); Scheffler (2013, pp. 88–95); Shiffrin (2013, pp. 146–47).

Bortolotti and Nagasawa (2009) use research findings from psychology to tie the likelihood of reaching a state of habitual or chronic boredom – which seems to be caused not by the repetition of experiences and the satisfaction of categorical desires, but by their absence – to the presence of certain character traits, such as a lack of imagination. They argue that people who have those traits are likely to experience chronic boredom no matter how long or short their life is, while those who do not will probably continue to be fine even if their life goes on indefinitely (Bortolotti and Nagasawa, 2009, p. 269). Similarly, John Harris is confident that ongoing scientific and technological progress will ensure that there will always be plenty of new things to excite and engage us, so that 'only the terminally boring are in danger of being terminally bored', adding, rather scornfully, 'and perhaps they do not deserve indefinite life' (Harris, 2007, p. 64).

Smuts (2016, p. 183) attacks the second leg of Williams' dilemma, insisting that even a radical change of categorical desires would not necessarily undermine personal identity, and Chappell (2007, 30–44) attacks both legs, arguing that radical change is compatible with the preservation of personal identity so long as there is some continuity, and that there is also no good reason to think that we will ever run out of worthwhile projects. Overlapping projects might see some categorical desires expiring and new ones arising, but that change is unproblematic if there is, as there is likely to be, an unbroken narrative thread that connects them. Like Fischer, Chappell thinks that there may well be inexhaustible goods and that we need in any case more time to do all the (indefinitely many) things we want to do.

Even those who share some of Williams's concerns about the alleged desirability of immortality don't find his argument particularly compelling. Temkin (2008), while conceding that it is quite possible that we will all eventually get tired of living, agrees with Smuts and Chappell that radical changes of one's values and priorities are compatible with identity and do not make the pursuit of life extension irrational. Some, like Burley (2009) and partially Gorman (2017), support the idea that boredom *might* be unavoidable, but point out, quite sensibly, that we cannot be sure either way. Gorman, defending Williams against Smuts and Fischer, argues that while we can indeed conceive of inexhaustible categorical desires, we cannot know whether or not we will actually have such desires.

To sum up, while Williams' critics focus on different aspects of his argument and while some are more sympathetic to his concerns than others, they all agree that while some might indeed experience the kind of boredom that Williams describes if their life were indefinitely

Michael Hauskeller

extended, such an outcome is by no means *necessary*, certainly not for everyone. Immortality, therefore, need not be bad, and no good reason has been identified (at least not by Williams) why we should not desire and pursue it.

5. The Unthinkability Condition

The objections we just looked at are all based on the assumption that the persuasiveness of Williams' argument depends on the claim that terminal boredom would be *unavoidable* in any radically extended life. Fischer calls this the 'Necessary Boredom Thesis' (Fischer, 2014). If we make that assumption, refutation is quite easy and straightforward. We simply have to show that, for all we know, terminal boredom is *not* necessary and that it is in fact entirely *conceivable* that we could go on living indefinitely without ever reaching a stage of complete indifference. And if it turns out that we have no good reason to think that terminal boredom is inevitable, then Williams' argument has failed. But what if that assumption were wrong? What if for Williams' argument to work it were sufficient that terminal boredom was simply *possible*? Williams himself indicates as much when he asserts that boredom must be 'unthinkable' for eternity to be worth pursuing (Williams, 1973, p. 95). Unthinkable means impossible, something that we are very sure *cannot* happen, which is very different from merely 'not necessary'. And yet, to my knowledge, no critic has claimed that the state of utter indifference to life that Williams imagines will sooner or later engulf us could *not possibly* occur. It is generally deemed far from certain, perhaps even unlikely, but its possibility has not been seriously questioned by anyone. No argument has been put forward to show that it would be *unthinkable* that we would ever reach a state of terminal boredom if our life were radically extended. Might that not be enough to make it unwise to pursue it?

That it doesn't really matter whether terminal boredom is a necessary feature of an immortal life because the mere possibility of it is enough to make it undesirable has recently been argued by David Beglin. If it turns out that one does indeed get terminally bored, then by relinquishing mortality, he claims, 'one has damned oneself to a very bleak existence. Immortal boredom would mean forever living in a world in which nothing seems meaningful – an endless existence of alienation from one's life and environment' (Beglin, 2017). This interpretation of Williams' argument has the advantage of allowing us to make sense of Williams' unthinkability

156

claim because if that is what *could* happen, then the risk would be considerable and each of us would have to think very carefully about whether we are really willing to take our chances in the hope that it won't happen to us. If one of the possible outcomes of our decision to become immortal is truly horrifying, we certainly do have a good (though not necessarily compelling) reason to reject that option.

However, the problem with Beglin's argument is that immortality in a strict sense is not really on the table and never was. Whatever happens, we are not going to be like Douglas Adams's Wowbagger, the Infinitely Prolonged, who simply cannot die and therefore cannot escape what Adams calls 'the Long Dark Teatime of the Soul' (Adams, 1982, p. 9). The best (or worst) we can hope for is radical life extension, which, if it is indefinite, leads to what I call *postmortality*,[7] which is a state where we still *can* die, but no longer *need* to die because of our biological constitution. If it is postmortality rather than immortality we are talking about, then by achieving it we have not at all condemned ourselves to an endless existence of alienation, simply because we can always decide to end our existence once it has become so alienated and if we find this intolerable. There is, in other words, an escape route from that grim fate Beglin envisions, should it indeed materialise. And we all have an interest in keeping that escape route open, which is why it is rather obvious why strict immortality (meaning you *cannot* die) is not something worth having: there are clearly situations in life when ceasing to exist seems to be far more attractive than continuing to exist. If your life is hell, you certainly don't want it to last forever. That is precisely why the Christian hell is envisaged as eternal: it makes it a lot worse than any finite punishment could ever by. Accordingly, nobody seriously wishes to be no longer *able* to die. The ability to die is an important freedom that few of us would be willing to give up in exchange for an eternal life.

Now Williams certainly uses the term 'immortality', yet what he is actually talking about is postmortality. As Connie Rosati has pointed out, correctly, Elina Makropulos, whose case Williams uses to develop his argument, is *not* immortal (Rosati, 2013, p. 359). She can die, and indeed she eventually does die when she feels that her radically extended life is no longer worth living because it has run its course many times over and no longer offers anything worth having, or more precisely nothing that *she* cares to have. Her life had been extended for 300 years, and she now decides that this is enough and declines to take another dose of the elixir that would

---

[7] See Hauskeller (2015).

grant her a further extension. This, then, is the situation Williams is talking about, not one in which we are condemned to eternal misery. And yet he still insists that terminal boredom must be unthinkable to make a radically extended life worth pursuing. If we want to fully understand Williams' argument, we need to figure out why he makes that rather astonishing claim.

6. Opting Out

According to Williams, when Elina Makropulos dies, she dies too late. Too late in what sense, though? Too late for what? Since we are dealing with radical life extension and postmortality rather than immortality, it is obviously not too late for her to die, and that makes it hard to understand what the problem is. Say we decide to have our life indefinitely extended once that becomes possible (if it ever does), we then keep on living until we get tired of it. We enjoy our extended life as best we can and as long as we can, and should it turn out one day that we are really running out of categorical desires and other reasons to carry on, we can, as John Harris put it, still decide to 'opt out' (Harris, 2007), which we can do anytime. It seems that in that case we haven't lost anything. We have not lived too long but just long enough. So why not try it out and see what happens? The worst that can happen is that one day we will no longer want to live, but we don't know for sure that will ever happen, and even if it does, suicide will always be possible, so there is plenty to gain and nothing to lose when we extend our lives to the greatest possible extent. We simply live for as long as we find it worth our while and quit when it ceases to be so. As long as we have the freedom to quit, this looks like a win-win situation, and that is so even if eventually entering a stage of terminal boredom is in fact unavoidable so that at some point in our radically extended life we definitely *will* fall prey to it. Whether it is necessary or merely possible, makes no difference at all.

This seems like a rather obvious objection, so why has Williams not thought of it? It is hard to believe that it simply didn't occur to him. It is more likely that he didn't think it was relevant. But how could it not be? Why would killing myself or 'opting to die' not solve the problem of my having lived past the point up to which life still appeared worth living to me? Before I try to answer that question (which I believe is crucial for our understanding of Williams' argument), let us have another look at the possible cases of 'dying too late' I introduced and briefly discussed earlier on. The examples I gave were 1) someone who has lived a happy and fulfilled life until something terrible happens to them and they suddenly lose everything they ever cared about or cared about the most, 2) the gifted writer and thinker who develops dementia, becomes dependent and fearful, and all but forgets who she is and what she has achieved (Murdoch), and 3) the once revered statesman who lives long enough to disappoint, become irrelevant, and perhaps even a figure of widespread contempt and ridicule (Giuliani). I suppose we can make sense of the claim that all three died or will have died too late by using some sort of hedonic calculus where we try to measure the overall quality or 'actual value' of a life by adding up all the goods someone has had in their life and subtracting from it all the bad,[8] in which case the net sum of happiness or utility would be higher for anyone who died before their life would have taken a turn for the worse. But is that really the reason why we think that it might have been better for them to have died earlier? When a story ends badly, it is not just the ending that is bad, because the bad ending affects the way we understand the story as a whole. A tragedy is not any less a tragedy just because things looked so good for much of the time before it all went downhill. A sad ending always makes for a sad story, and a happy ending for a happy story. As Josuah Seachris once put it, 'the ending relevantly frames the entire story' (Seachris, 2011).

Life may not be a story, but it still seems as if in the cases we have looked at the bad things that happened in those people's lives cast a shadow back on their *whole* life, making the *good* parts less good than they would otherwise have been. And it seems to me that once the damage is done, it would be woefully inadequate to suggest that if they don't like the situation they suddenly find themselves in, they can just 'opt out' anytime by taking their own life. They can, of course, but it wouldn't make things any better. It would be too late to do anything about the harm that has been inflicted on them (or, in some cases, that they have inflicted on themselves) because the real harm does not consist in what is happening in those people's lives *after* their situation has taken a turn for the worse, but in what *did* happen. The real harm has already been done and that harm is not only considerable, but also irreparable.

7. Retroactive Harm

That it is possible for an event that occurs while we are still alive to affect the value of our life as a whole is certainly not less plausible

---

[8]   See for instance Gardner and Weinberg (2013).

Michael Hauskeller

than that the value of our lives can be affected by what happens to us (or our plans and interests) after our death, which has frequently been argued.[9] If for instance we think that how well our life is going depends among other things on the extent to which we manage to achieve our goals and ambitions – some of which may only come to fruition or be thwarted after we have died – it seems reasonable to conclude that it must be possible for our life to be made worse by events that occur after our death. 'If someone destroys your life's work, that is bad for you, even if it happens far from you. Whether it happens just before or just after your death would not seem to make the difference' (Keller, 2014, p. 187). It has also been argued that, more specifically, the *meaningfulness* of our life can be affected by what happens after our death. 'Since the narrative significance of an event can change even after one's death', writes Antti Kauppinen, 'the meaningfulness of a life may be influenced posthumously. What if Martin Luther King's campaigns eventually turn out to have led to catastrophic consequences for African-Americans? Shall we think of his life as having been as meaningful, or to have been as good for him as we do now?' (Kauppinen, 2021, p. 374, fn.). If retroactive harms exist and my life can even be rendered meaningless by an event that occurs *after* my death, then surely it can also be rendered thus by an event that occurs *before* my death.

Consider the following case that I borrow from Simon Keller: 'Suppose that you think of yourself as living a wonderful life, featuring professional success, good friends, and a healthy marriage. Suppose also that your colleagues do not really respect you, your apparent friends do not really like you, and your spouse does not really love you. Suppose that they all make fun of you behind your back, suppose that your own beliefs about your life are utterly misguided. But suppose also that the pretense carried out by your colleagues, friends, and spouse is immaculate, never making any difference to your subjective experience. Your life so imagined does not look like a life that goes well for you. It does not look like a life high in welfare – not because you have bad subjective experiences, but because your life, though you do not know it, is based on a lie' (Keller, 2014, p. 186).

Obviously, this little tale is not an example of posthumous harm, but of circumstances in a person's life that they are completely unaware of and that do not in any way impact on their subjective

---

[9]   See for instance Pitcher (1984); Nagel (2012, pp. 1–10); Nussbaum (2013, pp. 33–34); Luper (2013). For an opposing view, see Taylor (2005).

well-being, but which we tend to feel are still *bad* for them (Feinberg, 2013). We would probably pity such a person if we knew what was going on, and why would we pity them if it did not do them any harm? Personally, however, I am not convinced that, in the rather unlikely event that all the deception that is going on here remains completely unnoticed by the one who is thus deceived and that their life is in no way different from what it would be if they were not deceived, that person actually suffers a *harm*. They are certainly being *wronged* because they are being lied to, but you can be wronged without being harmed (as well as harmed without being wronged). But there is no need to argue the point here. Instead, let us imagine that the person to whom all this is happening *discovers* at some point that they have been lied to practically all their life. They now do know that their whole life was based on a lie. They must face the fact that what they thought was real was not and that what they valued was actually entirely worthless. Can we doubt that this would be a world-shattering and utterly devastating discovery?

We may of course wonder whether it would also have been *better* for them if they had never learned the truth (and, more importantly for our purposes, better if they had *died* before learning the truth). That depends on what we think is more important, that our beliefs align with reality or that they make us feel good. We may, after all, prefer a devastating truth to a reassuring lie. But now imagine another twist to the story. Suppose that what that person believes they have discovered is not actually the truth about their life. They have had this wonderful life with a loving spouse, good friends, and a successful career, and then, at some point, they become convinced that none of this has been real, that it has all been a lie (even though in fact it has not). Clearly, the effect on them would be just as devastating and their life, if they remained convinced that it was all a lie, would be just as ruined as it would be if they were right, and it would not make things any better if they now ended their life. It would be too late.

This is what I am suggesting would happen if we ever entered the state of terminal boredom that Williams was so worried about.

8. The Horrors of Terminal Boredom

However, this follows only if, for one thing, it is indeed possible for an event in our life to change, as it were retroactively, what went on before and especially the *value* or *worth* of what went on before, and for another, if the transition to terminal boredom that Williams

Michael Hauskeller

believes will very likely occur at some point in an indefinitely extended life is indeed such an event. But is it? It may seem that the situation Williams is talking about is very different from the situations we looked at before because nothing terrible will have happened in our life if one day we discover that we have run out of categorical desires and things don't really matter to us anymore. Boredom, even chronic or terminal boredom, is certainly an unpleasant state of mind, but it is hardly a catastrophic event that changes everything for us. Except that, for Williams, that is precisely what it is. The only way, he says, we can avoid dying either too early or too late is by 'dying shortly before the horrors of not doing so become evident' (Williams, 1973, p. 100). Is boredom a 'horror' then? It seems to me that we can only make sense of this claim (and the corresponding claim that we would have died too late if we ever reached that stage) if we understand what is happening here as just such a catastrophic event that causes irreparable harm to whoever experiences it. That event is not the state of boredom itself, but the transition from a normal mortal life – which is often right to the very end rich with, and only rarely entirely devoid of, things to live for – to the state of complete indifference that Williams, perhaps for lack of a better word, calls 'boredom' – but which he also describes as 'distance from life', the 'death of desire', a 'cold' and 'stony' existence (Williams, 1973, p. 91). How so?

Williams starts his paper by declaring his intention to show that 'immortality, or a state without death, would be meaningless', so that 'in a sense, death gives the meaning to life' (Williams, 1973, p. 82). In light of the discussion that follows this declaration, the state of boredom that Williams thinks we would eventually reach if we became immortal (which in practice means: if our life were indefinitely extended) must be understood as a state of utter meaninglessness: nothing would make sense anymore; nothing would mean anything, it would all be the same to us. If it is at that stage 'too late to die', this can only mean – since it is obviously still *possible* to die – that the loss of meaning that we will then experience will not only affect the life that we could still have if we chose to go on living, but also the life that we will then have lived already. All the meaning that our life may have had up to this point would be cancelled and irretrievably lost. Our *entire* life will suddenly have become meaningless because we do not merely stop caring, but also wonder why we ever did. If our life had value before, it has now lost it, or more precisely, it has *revealed* itself as being without value. We used to think that things mattered, but now we know (or think we know) that they don't. We were wrong about life. The things we valued weren't really valuable. It was all a lie or an illusion. Or so it appears to us. Would entering such a state of mind not be horrible?

Such a complete loss of meaning may well be unavoidable because the ageing process does not merely affect the body, but also the mind. There is such a thing as mental ageing, caused by the sheer accumulation of past in a person's life, which goes along with a loss of (a subjective sense of) meaning (Hauskeller, 2011). It is not the environment that is the problem; it is the agent and the disappearance of all substantive commitments (Beglin, 2017, pp. 2015–16). Worthwhile things may be inexhaustible, as Fischer and others have argued, but that doesn't mean that we will still be able to relate to them in such a way that they make our life (both the life that might still lie ahead of us *and* the life that lies already behind us) appear worth living (Beglin, 2017, p. 2025). 'Consider,' writes Julian Barnes (without reference to Williams), 'how boring that "me" would become, to both me and others, if we went on and on and on' (Barnes, 2009, p. 87).

It is true, of course, that we don't know whether this is actually going to happen and if so when, since nobody has tried it out yet, but even if it is not unavoidable, unless we can be fairly certain that it won't happen to us (which I don't think we can), we may not want to risk retroactively making our whole life meaningless by living too long, not necessarily because it is very likely that this is going to happen, but because the stakes are simply too high. Terminal boredom is a state that can engulf us even in a mortal life and when that happens it is indeed terrible, and we have every reason to avoid it. We don't usually call that state boredom, but major depression, but that is what Williams is talking about. In major depression 'activities and projects that used to be pleasurable lose all significance, future events are stripped of their emotional resonance, and the motivation to move forward and engage with the world breaks down' (Aho, 2016, p. 59) which sounds very much like the state that Elina Makropulos is in. Major depression, can be understood as 'a nonterminal world-collapse, in which one experiences the possibility of the impossibility of every way of existing, and traumatically endures their own death' (Hughes, 2020, p. 207), thus leading to a 'radical transformation of the meaning and significance of one's life' and, because that state appears unlimited, an 'immortalization' of one's suffering and despair (Hughes, 2020, p. 208).

If radical life extension considerably increases the risk that something like this happens to us, which is certainly not *unthinkable* if

Michael Hauskeller

we go 'on and on and on', we may well have good reason not to strive
for it.

University of Liverpool
m.hauskeller@liverpool.ac.uk

References

Douglas Adams, *Life, the Universe, and Everything* (London: Pan,
1982).

Kevin A. Aho, 'Heidegger, Ontological Death, and the Healing
Professions', *Medicine, Health Care and Philosophy* 19 (2016),
55–63.

Roman Altshuler, 'Immortality, Identity, and Desirabiliy', in
Immortality and the Philosophy of Death, edited by
Michael Cholbi (London and New York: Rowman and
Littlefield, 2016), 191–203.

Julian Barnes, *Nothing to Be Frightened of* (London: Vintage Books,
2009).

Paul R. Bartrop, 'Pol Pot' in *Modern Genocide. The Definitive Resource
and Document Collection*, Volume 1, edited by Paul R. Bartrop and
Steven Leonard, (Santa Barbara: ABC-CLIO 2015).

David Beglin, 'Should I choose to never die? Williams, boredom, and
the significance of mortality', *Philosophical Studies* 174/8 (2017),
2009–2028.

Lisa Bortolotti and Y. Nagasawa, 'Immortality without Boredom',
Ratio 22/3 (2009), 261–77.

Adam Buben, 'Resources for Overcoming the Boredom of
Immortality in Fischer and Kierkegaard', in *Immortality and the
Philosophy of Death*, edited by Michael Cholbi (London and
New York: Rowman and Littlefield, 2016), 205–219.

Mikel Burley, Immortality and Boredom: A Response to Wisnewski,
International Journal for Philosophy of Religion 65/2 (2009), 77–85.

Timothy Chappell, 'Infinity Goes Up on Trial: Must Immortality
Be Meaningless?', *European Journal of Philosophy* 17/1 (2007),
30–44.

Peter J. Conradi, *Iris Murdoch. A Life* (London: HarperCollins,
2001).

Joel Feinberg, 'Harm to Others', in *The Metaphysics and Ethics of
Death*, ed. James Stacey Taylor (Oxford: Oxford University
Press, 2013), 171–90.

John Martin Fischer, 'Immortality', in *The Oxford Handbook of Philosophy of Death*, edited by Ben Bradley, Fred Feldman, and Jens Johansson (Oxford: Oxford University Press, 2013), 336–54.

John Martin Fischer, 'Immortality and Boredom', *The Journal of Ethics* 18 (2014), 353–72.

David Fricke, 'Jimi Hendrix: The Man and the Music', *Rolling Stone* (6 February 1992). Accessed 27 June 2021. https://www.rollingstone.com/music/music-features/jimi-hendrix-the-man-and-the-music-197412/

Molly Gardner and Justin Weinberg, 'How Lives Measure Up', *Acta Analytica* 28 (2013), 31–48.

A.G. Gorman, 'Williams and the Desirability of Body-bound Immortality Revisited', *European Journal of Philosophy* 25/4 (2017), 1062–1083.

John Harris, *Enhancing Evolution: The Ethical Case for Making Better People* (Princeton: Princeton University Press, 2007).

Michael Hauskeller, 'Forever Young? Life Extension and the Ageing Mind', *Ethical Perspectives* 18/3 (2011), 385–405.

Michael Hauskeller, '"Life's a bitch, and then you don't die". Postmortality in Film and Television', in *The Palgrave Handbook of Posthumanism in Film and Television*, edited by Michael Hauskeller, Thomas D. Philbeck, and Curt Carbonell (Basingstoke: Palgrave Macmillan, 2015), 205–213.

Emily Hughes, 'Melancholia, Temporal Disruption, and the Torment of Being Both Unable to Live and Unable to Die', *Philosophy, Psychiatry, & Psychology* 27/3 (2020), 203–213.

Antti Kauppinen, 'Meaningfulness and Time', *Philosophy and Phenomenological Research* 84/2 (2021), 345–77.

Simon Keller, 'Posthumous Harm', in *Life and Death*, edited by Steven Luper (Cambridge: Cambridge University Press, 2014), 181–97.

Ray Kurzweil and Terry Grossman, *Fantastic Voyage. Live Long Enough to Live Forever* (Emmaus, PA: Rodale, 2005).

Steven Luper, 'Retroactive Harms and Wrongs', in *The Oxford Handbook of Philosophy of Death*, edited by Ben Bradley, Fred Feldman, and Jens Johansson (Oxford: Oxford University Press, 2013).

Thomas Nagel, *Mortal Questions* (Cambridge: Cambridge University Press, 2012).

Friedrich Nietzsche, *Werke in drei Bänden*, Vol. II (Munich: Carl Hanser Verlag 1966).

Michael Hauskeller

Martha Nussbaum, 'The Damage of Death', in *The Metaphysics and Ethics of Death*, ed. James Stacey Taylor (Oxford: Oxford University Press 2013).

George Pitcher, 'The Misfortunes of the Dead', *American Philosophical Quarterly* 21 (1984), 183–88.

Catherine Rémy, '"Men seeking monkey-glands": the controversial xenotransplantations of Doctor Voronoff, 1910–1930', *French History* 28/2 (2014), 226–40.

Connie S. Rosati, 'The Makropulos Case Revisited. Reflections on Immortality and Agency', in *The Oxford Handbook of Philosophy of Death*, edited by Ben Bradley, Fred Feldman, and Jens Johansson (Oxford: Oxford University Press, 2013), 355–90.

Geoffrey Scarre, 'Should We Fear Death?', *European Journal of Philosophy* 5/3 (1997), 269–82.

Samuel Scheffler, *Death and the Afterlife* (Oxford: Oxford University Press 2013).

Joshua W. Seachris, 'Death, Futility, and the Proleptic Power of Narrative Ending', *Religious Studies* 47 (2011), 141–63.

Seana Valentine Shiffrin, 'Preserving the Valued or Preserving Valuing?', in Samuel Scheffler, *Death and the Afterlife*, 143–58.

Aaron Smuts, 'Love and Death. The Problem of Resilience', in *Immortality and the Philosophy of Death,* edited by Michael Cholbi (London and New York: Rowman and Littlefield, 2016), 173–88.

James Stacey Taylor, 'The Myth of Posthumous Harm', *American Philosophical Quarterly* 42/4 (2005), 311–22.

Larry S. Temkin, 'Is Living Longer Living Better?', *Journal of Applied Philosophy* 25/3 (2008), 193–210.

Bernard Williams, 'The Makropulos Case: Reflections on the Tedium of Immortality', in Bernard Williams, *Problems of the Self* (Cambridge: Cambridge University Press 1973), 82–100.

J. Jeremy Wisnewski, 'Is the Immortal Life Worth Living?', *International Journal for Philosophy of Religion* 58/1 (2005), 27–36.

Desirability without Desire: Life Extension, Boredom and Spiritual Experience

DREW CHASTAIN

Abstract

In response to Bernard Williams' suspicion that we would inevitably become bored with immortal life, John Martin Fischer has argued that we could continue to enjoy repeatable pleasures such as fine wine, beautiful music, and spiritual experiences. In more recent work on near-death experiences, Fischer has also explored the non-religious meaning of spiritual experiences in more depth. I join this deeper exploration of spiritual experience, and I also join Williams' critics who question his view that character and desire are needed to explain the desirability of life, while providing additional reason for concern that Williams' way of valuing life may itself actually be a cause of boredom with life. With an eye to spiritual experience, I indicate how we can distance ourselves even further from Williams' view, and I suggest how the attitude that *life is good but death is not bad* emerges from spiritual experience, as expressed in numerous religious and secular spiritual traditions. This lends support to the conclusion that radically extended life is desirable even if not actively desired.

> 'Be little self-regarding and make your desires few'.
> ~ *Daodejing* 19

> 'He who studies is daily enlarged; he who follows the Dao is daily diminished. Diminished and then diminished yet more, at last attaining non-action (*wu-wei*)'.
> ~ *Daodejing* 48[1]

Since the 1970s, a debate on the desirability of unending life has circled relentlessly around Bernard Williams' concept of categorical desire, the kind of desire that gives one reason to live, propelling oneself forward in life. Williams' pessimistic stance is that our categorical desires are likely to be depleted in a life that continues longer than the normal human lifespan, and then we will end up terminally bored. Therefore, radically extended life is not desirable.[2]

---

[1]   Translated by Robert Eno (2010). I'll make some observations about Daoism and other spiritual traditions in the concluding section of the paper.
[2]   See Williams (1993).

doi:10.1017/S135824612100028X   © The Royal Institute of Philosophy and the contributors 2021
Royal Institute of Philosophy Supplement **90** 2021   167

Drew Chastain

John Martin Fischer has responded by accepting Williams' talk of categorical desires, at least for the sake of argument, but denying Williams' conclusion. Sure, categorical desires might be needed to keep us going, but it shouldn't be expected that we will run out of activities that give us a reason to live. Among the endless activities Fischer says an immortal being could repeatably find pleasurable are fine dining, good music, sexual enjoyments and spiritual experiences.

Williams' basic stance on the supposed tedium of immortality has attracted much support and also much skepticism over the years, with Fischer standing out as a primary foil.[3] Here I'd like to explore how special attention to the spiritual experiences mentioned by Fischer affects the overall inquiry into immortality. After I have set up a non-religious account of spiritual experience, I want to develop and deepen a challenge to the idea that our interest in life, or our motivation to live, is fundamentally propelled by categorical desires. Criticism of Williams' appeal to categorical desire has been launched already, and in different ways, but I think attention to spiritual experience can provide additional compelling reason for doubting Williams' view. This will more decisively distance us from any philosophical orientation that insists so fervently on the idea that the value of life crucially depends on some sort of goal orientation. Additionally, the way of understanding spiritual experiences presented here provides a diagnosis of the sort of chronic boredom Williams thinks is inevitable if we live too long, so it will be important to understand the varieties of boredom and their causes as well as we can.

It will be interesting to first explore Fischer's own more recent investigation of near-death experiences (NDEs), since they are a kind of spiritual experience. I think that what Fischer says about NDEs is insightful, but I also think that a fuller account of spiritual experiences can say a bit more. Regardless of the details, a main takeaway is that spiritual experiences reaffirm the value of life while taking the focus off of self. As for the relevance of spiritual experience to the question of immortality, I believe that spiritual experience leads to a kind of ambivalence. While a radically extended life involving spiritual experiences can be quite livable, the *demand* that I myself live is at the same time lessened. This helps to explain how a deeply insightful spiritual tradition such as Buddhism can affirm both compassion

---

[3]   Later in the paper I'll be referencing critics of Williams, but those who support Williams' position against immortality, though not always for the same reasons, include Beglin (2017), Cholbi (2016), Hauskeller (2013, Ch. 6), Kagan (2012, Ch. 11) and Scheffler (2013, Lecture 3).

and self-negation. An appreciation of vitality and connection in life is maintained, but that the life be mine is not as important, a kind of ambivalence that will be explored further at the end of this discussion. We will see that, against Williams' view, spiritual experience supports a sort of passive desirability of immortality, a desirability without desire.

1. Near-Death Experiences and Spiritual Experiences

Fischer calls himself an 'NDE realist' (Fischer, 2020, pp. 148, 181), meaning only that he believes that, in brushes with death, people do indeed subjectively or psychologically experience themselves to be outside of their bodies, traveling toward a light, crossing over a river, or passing over into another realm (Fischer, 2020, p. 144), not that he believes anything supernatural actually happens. Still, Fischer argues at length that NDEs can be profoundly meaningful even if we live in a physicalistic reality that bars the possibility of our souls leaving our bodies to join our friends, relatives, and divinities to live out our everlasting lives in a wondrous transcendent dimension. NDEs are meaningful primarily because of their narrative nature, and Fischer identifies the common story that unfolds as 'a voyage from a known (or familiar) place to a relatively unknown (or unfamiliar) situation or status, guided by a benevolent parental (or authority) figure (or figures)' (Fischer, 2020, p. 174).

Fischer explains that this narrative journey counts as a spiritual experience because 'the self is not the focus of the experience' and 'the content [of the experience] is present as objectively true – ultra-real'.[4] Additionally, NDEs inspire awe and wonder, even if we deny that they serve as evidence of divinity or supernatural survival. Fischer developed this line of argument with co-author Benjamin Mitchell-Yellin, noting that we can experience awe with natural grandeur (such as the night sky) or with human grandeur (such as great achievements in art or science) or with the birth of one's children (Fischer and Mitchell-Yellin, 2016, p. 159), yet the presence of the supernatural is not needed to elicit awe in these cases. Also, one can find wondrous narrative spiritual meaning in an LSD experience without thinking there to be anything but natural causes for such an experience (Fischer and Mitchell-Yellin, 2016, pp. 161–63). So, physicalist explanations don't undermine the meaning of NDEs.

---

[4]   Fischer (2020, p. 169). Also see Fischer (2020, pp. 134, 177). Fischer draws this analysis from Pollan (2018, p. 390).

Though we can't reasonably hope for an eternal afterlife if soul/body dualism is false, the stories of solidarity and guidance that unfold in NDEs do offer us a different kind of hope because they 'resonate with us, comfort us, and transform us' (Fischer, 2020, p. 180).

I think that Fischer has gotten a lot right, and that the significance of spiritual experience does not depend on our settling the debate between physicalists and dualists or between naturalists and supernaturalists, because the significance has centrally to do with how the experience transforms us. But I also think that, if we are pursuing a general account of spiritual experience (which is not Fischer's main goal), a focus on NDEs could lead us to overstate the role that narrative plays. Some spiritual experiences are journeys, but not all. Still, Fischer's discussion of spiritual experience in the context of NDEs is a welcome advancement over his appeal to spiritual experiences in the context of his response to Bernard Williams. In objecting to Williams, Fischer is focused mainly on examples such as prayer, meditation, and yoga, which are more like activities intentionally performed.[5] Alternately referring to them as 'experiences' and 'activities', Fischer includes spiritual experiences on a list of repeatable pleasures that 'seem capable of providing the basis for positive categorical desires, even in an immortal life'.[6]

By contrast, in his exploration of NDEs, which presumably aren't the sort of experience one would typically seek out on purpose, Fischer is instead analyzing what are clearly unintentional spiritual experiences and getting to the heart of their significance. It is important to clarify the ways in which spiritual experiences 'help to propel one forward' in life (Fischer, 2020, p. 126), but not in the form of a desire or an activity that one desires to perform, keeping in mind that spiritual experiences aren't always intentional or easily repeatable activities. On the emotional end of things, Fischer places much emphasis on awe and wonder, which is a fairly common move in the analysis of spiritual or religious experience,[7] but Fischer also discusses love and social solidarity in his account of NDEs (Fischer, 2020,

---

[5]   See Fischer (2011, p. 89) and Fischer (2015, p. 351), where he calls the 'repeatable pleasures' of 'prayer and meditation' 'activities'; Fischer (2020, pp. 125–26).

[6]   See Fischer (2011, p. 89).

[7]   Religious theorists, such as Rudolf Otto a century ago (Otto, 1923), or John Cottingham today (Cottingham, 2019, p. 25), relate this awe to an encounter with the numinous or with God. Non-religious theorists, such as Ronald Dworkin, can find wondrous beauty in the natural order of the cosmos (Dworkin, 2013, Ch. 2).

p. 177, p. 180). I think that this element of love – which I am inclined to call the element of connection – should be made more central to an analysis of spiritual experience, though it shouldn't be focused exclusively on the human social, or even the social.[8]

We can feel connected to other people, but also to other animals, and also to the world, and also to oneself. This metaphor of connection is one we commonly use, though it doesn't show that we are literally connected to anything. I think it just means that we are returning to an experience of our spirit or vitality – our *joie de vivre* – after having felt disconnected from self, world and others. Although it may at first seem paradoxical, I think that the self is a main reason why we come to feel disconnected, or at least there are aspects of oneself that become excessive and stifle and strangle spirit, a set of dispositions relating to identity that can be marked out as 'ego'.[9] Iris Murdoch has identified the 'fat, relentless ego' as a problem common to both religion and morality.[10] Bypassing the term 'religion', I take the primary spiritual concern to be that the ego disconnects us from a more spontaneous, lived self, while also disconnecting us from others and the world, making us feel separate, alienated, empty, fake, and also bored; in which case, it is no surprise that spiritual experiences are notably absent of ego. I am not appealing here to any particular psychoanalytic idea of ego or any theory of personal identity over time. I am just pursuing the common sense observation that human beings are very self-absorbed, for social reasons and for existential reasons, and also for the reason that we're highly self-aware and, well, no matter where you go, there you are.

I think that spiritual experience can come to us at different times in different ways in varying degrees of wonder, vitality, and connection, and not just in rare, special experiences set far apart from everyday life. Rather, spiritual experiences sit on a spectrum with ordinary experiences, not found only in NDEs, meditation and prayer, but in times with family and friends, or walks alone in nature or in the

[8] Affirming the importance of connection/love, another theorist of spirituality without religion, Robert Solomon, says that the three main spiritual emotions are 'love (predictably), reverence, and trust' (Solomon, 2002, p. 29).

[9] To provide a more specific idea, our egoic tendencies can lead us to be excessively concerned with matters such as self-image, recognition, status, winning, self-interest, activity, goals, outcomes, agency, control, responsibility, autonomy, uniqueness, security, etc., none of which is inherently wrong, but which in excess can serve to cage us in a state of disconnection.

[10] Murdoch (1971, p. 52). I thank Michael Hauskeller for bringing my attention to Murdoch's focus on this theme.

neighborhood, or in religious services or at festivals, or at art galleries or while making art or making dinner, or when you are just listening to music on your headphones on the subway. Many associate spiritual experience with transcendent or supernatural realities, and I am not here to argue that such ontologies are untrue, only that the metaphysics doesn't determine the core experiential and normative significance of spirituality.[11]

2. Varieties of Immortality

When it comes to the question of how spiritual experience affects the desirability of immortality, a physicalist naturalist could only be talking about some enduring embodied form of extended life, while someone open to transcendent metaphysics could be thinking of a soul leaving the body for a better place, perhaps finding a more perfect body, or perhaps returning to life in another body, and so on. Now, if we are talking about some far out transhumanist possibilities, like cryopreservation, digital mind-uploading, and body switching, then it may turn out that we can achieve a kind of resurrection or reincarnation without souls, so it behooves us to keep in mind that extended life for the individual could, in theory, be achieved in numerous ways, and it is also worth noting that which options are available affects how desirable each of the other options are. In particular, I think that the perceived availability of a more perfect eternal life in communion with one's soul mates in the oceanic loving light of the divine tends to cast any pursuit of earthbound physical immortal into shadow, since clinging to this life could be perceived as just foolishly, greedily putting off the big reward.[12]

However, Bernard Williams believes that visions of supernatural immortality fail to explain how we wouldn't get bored with bliss, that is, if we took with us to the afterlife the intellectual faculties that he believes give our present life worth. He thinks that those imagining forever in heaven have to assume that we'd lose our reflective

[11]   I haven't provided a full analysis of spiritual experience here, which receives fuller treatment in Chastain (forthcoming). There I emphasize that the form of spirituality I believe to be most important is normatively oriented (normative spirituality), which can be distinguished from metaphysical spirituality, or belief in the paranormal or supernatural, even if the two can helpfully combine.

[12]   As Diogenes Allen (2004, p. 394) explains: 'This life is not sufficient to satisfy our aspirations, at least once we are aware of perfect love'.

consciousness, becoming something like lobotomized lotus eaters (Williams, 1993, pp. 86–87). I don't think this is right, and I think that people get chronically or existentially bored for reasons other than just continued life, one danger actually being too much egoic emphasis on our supposedly higher intellectual functions, to be explored more in what follows. But I do want to say something here about how belief in this transcendent option influences spirituality. For instance, if there is a God, then it would be rather odd for God to create us and then just let us die while God lives on, which appears to be part of the historical reason that the Judaic tradition gradually developed a belief in an eternal afterlife, though there is negligible Biblical support for this view (Gillman, 2004, 94–108). Such anti-abandonment logic likely influences a theist's interest in immortality, so that the desirability question is not entirely about the goodness of prolonged life in itself. Someone who is spiritual but not supernaturalist presumably must reject the heaven idea, but can still have desirability concerns extrinsic to extended life's basic goodness, such as overpopulation, intergenerational fairness, equality of access to life extension technology, etc. In this case, extrinsic concerns may tend to count against the option of radical life extension, since the pursuit of life extension would likely create so many extrinsic problems in earthly society, no matter how desirable longer life is in itself.

As I unpack the desirability question here, I will be focused on the intrinsic question of the desirability of radically extended lifespans, and to my mind, the intrinsic question is clarified if we bracket the possibility of a more perfect transcendent immortality. I believe this supernatural option guarantees a bit too much on faith while producing a comparative bias against physical life, which has influenced religious and secular minds alike to neglect a deeper, more sacred appreciation of our immanent earthbound existence. I'd also like to keep it as real as possible, though I'll push at the bounds a bit to keep the thought experiment interesting. Current conservative medical science cautions us not to get our hopes up too high if we have them, pointing to a biological law of mortality governing human lifespans. Age 85 seems to be the average for humans on one estimate, with 115 being the upper limit that only a tiny minority will ever breach, barring genetic modification (Olshansky and Carnes, 2019, S7–S12). Of course, for transhumanists, genetic modification is just par for the course, and Aubrey de Grey and others continue to pursue numerous other strategies for considerably prolonged life.[13]

---

[13]   de Grey (2004, pp. 249–67). As for genetic modification, Chinese researchers made a breakthrough in early 2021, extending the lifespan of mice

Drew Chastain

I suspect that humans lifespans will increase, but even then, the question of desirability I want to ask is not whether it is sensible to *actively* desire to increase the human lifespan.

If I were to imagine being offered a fantastical immortality potion or a free spot in a cryopreservation clinic, personally, I am not sure I would choose more life if it weren't already in the genetic cards, so to speak, unless I had some strong reason for the extra time, like if it is the only way to save the planet, or something like that. When I opt for health, it is more for the purpose of experiencing life as healthy, not so that I will experience more life. To put some personal cards on the table, I feel like I have experienced plenty of life, and I feel like I 'get the idea', which is a somewhat bored thing to say, I'll admit. I will also confess my own view (though I am not trying to convince anyone of it) that there is no God or cosmic purpose or immaterial soul or eternal afterlife or deep metaphysical free will. Though many think such conditions are needed for there to be meaning to life, I don't think so, and so I tend not to angle my emotions toward transcendent hope. But if I – even with a personality and character that might come off as bored and pessimistic in a way – were born in a future generation that lived longer in healthy bodies because of developments in medical science, and a radically extended life of 200 or 300 years or more were in the genetic cards for me, could that be desirable? Sure, I think so, and I feel that my overall attitude is informed by, or is at least consistent with, spiritual experience or spiritual wisdom, as I will explain. I will also say more about the distinction between an active and passive sense of desirability as we get closer to the end, but first we've got to do the work of discharging Williams' boredom thesis, with an eye to what boredom really is.

3. Boredom and Ego

Is it possible to get bored with life itself? I mean, would that really be boredom per se, rather than some more complex disaffection? Peter Toohey disagrees with Lars Svendsen on the matter, both of whom have recently written books on the subject of boredom.[14] Toohey

---

by 25%: 'Chinese scientists develop gene therapy which could delay ageing', https://www.reuters.com/article/us-china-genes-ageing/chinese-scientists-develop-gene-therapy-which-could-delay-ageing-idUSKBN29P02V (accessed June 2021).
   [14]   Toohey (2011); Svensden (2005). Svendsen also provides further reflections, partly in response to Toohey, in Svendsen (2017). Wendell

distinguishes between simple boredom (also called situational boredom), chronic boredom (also called habitual boredom), and existential boredom. Simple or situational boredom is being bored by something or someone or by a circumstance because of some features of whatever it is that is boring – and also, it should be conceded, because of one's inability to be engaged by the boring thing. Perhaps one person would be bored in a given situation but not another, but regardless, once one has been relieved of the boring thing, one can return to one's capacity for engagement. Chronic boredom is more persistent and doesn't go away when the typically boring things do, correlating with chemical imbalance, risk-taking and sensation seeking. Existential boredom is supposed to be something more profound than a psychological or behavioral disorder, but Toohey suspects that the term more likely designates a hybrid of simple boredom, chronic boredom and depression that's just been overintellectualized, especially by moderns hung up on their self-importance (Toohey, 2011, Ch 2. for chronic boredom, pp. 141–42 for a key statement about existential boredom).

Although Svendsen is more interested than Toohey in earnestly exploring the phenomenon of existential boredom and does seem to think that existential boredom is in some sense warranted, there is a way in which the two writers' diagnoses of existential boredom align. Svendsen's diagnosis for existential boredom is basically Romanticism: 'The problem for the Romantic is precisely that he does not recognize his own size; he has to be bigger than everything else, transgress all boundaries and devour the whole world' (Svendsen, 2005, p. 142). Also from this modern European tradition, Svendsen says we get the idea of needing a personal meaning in the form of a 'unique meaning for me, as something that alone can give my life meaning' (Svendsen, 2005, p. 153). In his 2005 book, Svendsen gains much inspiration and guidance from Heidegger's account of boredom, adding that 'according to Heidegger, the emptiness that crops up in this more profound form of boredom is the emptiness left by "our proper self"' (Svendsen, 2005, p. 120).[15]

I say that Toohey and Svendsen have a similar diagnosis for existential boredom, because they both think it results from a sense of self-

---

O'Brien provides a very helpful overview of the history of ideas on boredom and related psychological states here: https://iep.utm.edu/boredom/ (accessed June 2021).

[15] Heidegger's discussion of boredom can be found in William McNeill and Nicholas Walker (1995, Part One).

importance, an explanation that isn't necessary to explain simple boredom. One sees oneself on a grand scale, and then on that grand scale, one sees something fundamentally lacking with the world as a whole. This kind of boredom seems to be driven more by an egoically inspired evaluation than by mere loss of stimulation. I think that the question whether existential boredom is a legitimate category, emotion, or attitude isn't really about whether humans can be said to get worn out with life psychologically, as if we were only wired to handle a certain quantity of life or repetition. I think it comes down to the question whether the judgment that life itself is boring is valid (and this is a judgment, not just an emotion), and by 'life itself' I don't mean life under such and such circumstances, but life understood with respect to its most general features – life in general, or life as such. There is an anthropocentric attitude, which I will be critiquing further in what follows, that tends to produce a negative assessment of life itself, life apart from human activity, that looks down upon animal life and nature, and this, I suggest, plants the toxic seeds of existential boredom. Svendsen, for instance, reinforces the problem by glorifying humans over other animals for having the exalted ability to experience meaning and its lack, declaring that, for this reason, animals can't really feel boredom, at least not what he takes to be the more important kind.[16] This is a source of irritation for Toohey, who thinks the more important kinds of boredom are situational or chronic, which other animals certainly do experience, for instance, when they are locked in cages as pets, or in zoos or in animal experimentation labs.[17]

In his 2005 book, Svendsen seems to have no solution for overcoming boredom, rejecting Heidegger's own optimistic stance as just more problematic Romantic overreach (Svendsen, 2005, p. 132). But in a 2017 article, he responds to Toohey, and accesses the theories of meaning in life provided by Harry Frankfurt and Susan Wolf to give more shape to his talk of meaning. Svendsen admits that existential boredom bears a resemblance to depression, but argues that this is no reason for dismissing it, since existential boredom can be set apart from depression as a kind of lack of meaning, rather than just psychological dysfunction. But what is it to regain meaning? Following

[16] Ibid., p. 32, where Svendsen says, 'Animals can be understimulated, but hardly bored'.

[17] Toohey expounds: 'Existential boredom, for so many thinkers, has come to be seen as one of the costs, or even the badges, of modernity or civilization, both conditions to which non-human animals do not have access' (2011, p. 88).

Wolf, Svendsen agrees that there is a subjective side and an objective side to meaning, in that having meaning in life involves combining subjective attraction and objective attractiveness, or as Wolf also puts it, meaning in life comes from active engagement in projects of worth.[18] Svendsen observes that the problem of existential boredom puts a lot of weight on the subjective condition, but still follows Wolf in affirming the idea that 'in order to have a meaningful life, a person must care about what he fills his life with. You must be committed to something, because commitment gives life substantial meaning' (Svendsen, 2017, p. 211).

What I would like to note about this kind of suggestion is that it solves what looks like a problem caused by ego in some way or other by building up that ego, making it more 'substantial', by giving yourself goals that are as important as you can make them, and then taking strenuous control over your life so that you are continually committed to them. I wonder if this kind of life strain is really a good long-term remedy, or can it become the problem by caging the spirit? One could put the point in terms of freedom, as Brian O'Connor has in his interrogation of an array of modern and contemporary European criticisms of idleness. O'Connor identifies a 'worthiness myth' which he finds in philosophers as diverse as Kant, Sartre, Frankfurt, and Christine Korsgaard: 'It is essentially a thesis of the Enlightenment, and it continues to sustain the remarkable idea that we must build and perfect the self as an autonomous moral entity if we are to become properly human'.[19] It is a myth, because it hasn't been proven that humans naturally desire a higher or more substantial self or that we should meet this normative demand or that substantial commitments are required for meaning in life. For instance, in Kant's well-known illustration of the categorical imperative in the *Groundwork of the Metaphysics of Morals*, Kant does not explain what would motivate a wanton idler to consider whether it is his moral duty to cultivate his talents to make himself useful: 'This would seem like too much effort for someone who had already lived well and in his own way' (O'Connor, 2018, p. 46).

[18] Svendsen (2017, pp. 209–210). Wolf's view is laid out in Wolf (2010). I present critiques of Wolf's view in Chastain, (2019, section 3); and Chastain (2021, sections 3, 4.1).
[19] O'Connor, (2018, p. 28). In a similar manner, Elijah Millgram critiques Frankfurt's explanation of boredom as a failure to be properly oriented to final ends, tracing this way of thinking back to Aristotle, and implicates Williams and Korsgaard in this way of thinking as well (Millgram, 2004, pp. 178–80 inc. fn. 23).

Drew Chastain

O'Connor suggests that freedom can mean being who you already are rather than working yourself up to be something more, and I'm suggesting a corollary about freedom from boredom – that existential boredom becomes more of a threat for those who are in pursuit of the self-inflation enterprise.[20] In summary, to stay connected with self, others, and the world – while preventing existential boredom – it is wise (i) not to pursue the project of self so fervently, and (ii) to also remain sensitive to what makes life itself worthwhile and meaningful, apart from one's own desires, activities, and projects. I'll be bringing this perspective into a discussion of Williams and his critics.

4. Categorical Desire and Desirability without Desire

Williams' case for our eventual justified boredom with a very long life appears to access the mood of existential boredom. His point is that death is made bad by our having categorical desires that get thwarted by death, but if we live life too long, we'll run out of the desires that make death bad. To exemplify his point, Williams uses Elina Makropulos, or EM, from Karel Čapek's play *The Makropulos Case*.[21] At the end of the play, EM confesses that she is 337, though she appears only 37, because it was at that age that she was forced by her father to test out an elixir of immortality, and she wound up being the only one to consume it, therefore enduring her uniquely prolonged life alone. After her confession, EM explains to the men in the room the feelings she has had for the last two hundred years:

> Boredom. Melancholy. Emptiness. [...] Everything's so stupid. Empty, pointless. [...] It makes no difference. To die or disappear behind doors, it's all the same. [...] It's not right to live

[20]   Millgram likewise suggests that 'the life of rational agency ... is a life you won't be able to stand' and 'that the lives that boredom doesn't veto are somewhat *dis*integrated, and maybe a bit frayed around the edges to boot' (Millgram, 2004, p. 183, emphasis in original). Though disagreeing somewhat with Millgram's understanding of boredom, Cheshire Calhoun agrees with Millgram's basic diagnosis that 'the effort to live meaningfully may itself be the source of boredom' (Calhoun, 2018, p. 118).

[21]   As Fischer and Mitchell-Yellin (2016, p. 354, fn. 1) note, Williams mistakenly describes EM's age to be 342 rather than 337. She gets the nickname EM because she has also had other names fitting those initials over her very long life, such as Elsa Miller and Ekaterina Myshkina (Čapek, 1999, Act 3).

so long! [...] We weren't meant to. A hundred, a hundred and thirty years, maybe. Then ... then you realise, and your soul dies inside you.[22]

Williams believes that EM's feelings would be our own after a similar stretch of existence, though it should be acknowledged that, in this scene, EM was also 'very' drunk on whisky, sniffed what was said to be cocaine 'or something', and was also poisoned by one of the men. Still, *in vino veritas,* and I take it as plausible that someone could develop such negative attitudes toward life in EM's position, but should we expect that every long-lived person would be so distraught?

Entertaining the idea that this question gets settled by categorical desires, let us more closely define that concept. Williams specifically defines it as a desire that decides whether you continue living, which he clarifies with the case of someone rationally contemplating suicide, that is, someone who is not under undue influence of emotions or a psychiatric condition, but simply trying to sort out whether there is sufficient reason for believing it is worth it to keep going. In this context, the sort of desire that would serve as a genuine reason to keep living would be a categorical desire, though you don't have to be contemplating suicide to have them.[23] Now, will any desire do? Not according to Williams' intuition, because he excludes '*just* the desire to remain alive',[24] though he doesn't here explain why it must be something more than that. But let's hold that thought and next think about how these desires relate to getting bored.

According to Lisa Bortolotti and Yujin Nagasawa, who are keen on the distinction between situational (or simple) boredom and habitual (or chronic) boredom, EM strikes them as someone affected with the condition of chronic boredom (which gets characterized here as boredom with life), afflicting those having normal lifespans as well: 'the subject is not bored with something specific, but with life in general. Among the phenomena correlated with habitual boredom or directly stemming from it, we find inactivity, withdrawal, anxiety, alienation, anti-social behavior, alcohol and drug abuse,

[22] Čapek, (1999, Transformation).
[23] Williams, (1993, p. 77).
[24] Williams, (1993, p. 78, emphasis in original). He says the desire to live must 'be sustained or filled out by something else', but without clear explanation as to why. Indicating a sort of deprecatory view of the desirability of life in itself that I will push back on below, Williams describes the desire to live as a 'sheer reactive drive to self-preservation', as if valuing life itself could have no reflective foundation.

and even depression and suicide' (Bortolotti and Nagasawa, 2009, pp. 268–69). As these critics of Williams observe, even those living normal lifespans can lose their categorical desires because of their complex and unfortunate disaffection, and one begins to suspect that Čapek and Williams are unjustifiably projecting this disorder onto immortals by simply selecting an imagined case who would be especially prone to an extremely aggravated death wish.

Connie Rosati also emphasizes this point, concluding that 'it is hard to separate Emilia's fate from the peculiarities of her situation', forced by her father as she was into her immortal journey alone, 'leaving her to drift through time,' adding: 'Without the capacity to love – to connect – nothing our lives might hold out will seem to us to matter' (Rosati, 2012, pp. 377–38). Rosati also critiques Williams' appeal to categorical desires. She believes that, even if EM could not, we could imagine many other individuals who could 'derive happiness just from the things that she desires given that she is alive', what Williams calls 'conditional desires'.[25] The idea is that not all desires are of the caliber of categorical desires to propel one forward into hard nothingness. Quite a lot of our desires seem to merely fill in the blank for the statement, 'well, since I'm here, I guess I might as well _____'. But why shouldn't that be enough reason to live, or to be happy with life? Why should boredom follow just because all of one's desires are of the conditional rather than the categorical sort?[26] Is boredom really the result of having no answer for the question of the larger direction I am taking my life because I have no sizable projects or commitments? Or is that just a fantasy of the intellect?

Thankfully, Rosati goes even deeper in her analysis, bringing to our attention that we live in 'a world that we do not experience simply in terms of desire – bare, conditional, or categorical' (Rosati, 2012, p. 368). And when she speaks of desirability, she doesn't mean only an active desire for something, as in a 'genuine longing'

[25]   Rosati (2012, p. 361). See Williams (1993, p. 77). Rosati is not alone in sensing the power of conditional desires to sustain life. See, for instance, Rosenbaum (1989, pp. 88–89).

[26]   If one thinks too hard about this, it might turn out that the two kinds of desires might just be distinguished by their strength. Ben Bradley and Kris McDaniel provide a thorough examination of Williams' concept of categorical desire that seems to leave it no functional footing whatsoever, psychological, normative or axiological. Interestingly, on one of Bradley and McDaniel's readings of categorical desires, even other animals can have them: 'As long as an animal lacks a desire to die and has just one other desire, that desire will be categorical' (Bradley and McDaniel, 2013, p. 131).

but also allows for a 'mere standing readiness to continue living, other things equal, for as long as one can'.[27] Rosati goes on to distinguish between the desirability of living and the desirability of being.[28] The felt desirability of living pertains to the aesthetic, pleasurable experiential qualities of life, such as feeling a blanket against one's skin, or hiking in the woods, or simply breathing in air and letting it fill your lungs (ibid.). The desirability of being pertains more specifically to the being of our distinctive human agency: 'capacities to reason and assess, to explore and discover, to create and appreciate beauty of form and sound, to will and to love' (Rosati, 2012, p. 371). Rosati indicates that the desirability of our agential capacities is really what explains the desirability of immortality, rather than the desirability of living, since living contains not only pleasures but also pains. Rosati also claims, 'The object of seeming worth cannot be life or being alive, but *your* (or *my*) being alive, *your* (or *my*) existing as [an] individual agent with a distinctive vantage point' (Rosati, 2012, p. 370, emphasis in the original). But I think this is untrue, even if a rational being with a vantage point is needed to make the judgment of worth. While Rosati denies Williams' view that categorical desires are needed to make it meaningful enough to go forward in life, she still maintains what I take to be a neighboring view that human agential capacity explains the desirability of life, expressing a common intuition that you have to add something to life, probably in the form of a rational human characteristic, in order for life to gain some sort of meaning.

Against this view, I think that in spiritual experience, the meaningfulness of life itself becomes manifest, a view that I think should be taken more seriously. And by meaningfulness, I mean *objective* meaningfulness, a qualification I use in the way that Susan Wolf emphasizes, following David Wiggins, indicating that it is not just some one person's idiosyncratic, dim-witted or perverted point of view.[29] When these philosophers speak of meaning, they are on the

[27] Rostai (2012, p. 379, fn. 11). Michael Cholbi (2016, p. 225) makes a point about the undesirability of pain in a way that could be flipped to explain the desirability of pleasure or other positive subjective states without reference to desire. 'But its undesirability may not be best explained by the fact that we do not desire it. Pain feels bad. That is what renders it undesirable and why we do not desire it'.

[28] Rosati (2012, p. 369). Rosati applies this analysis to a quote from Unamuno's *Tragic Sense of Life* (originally published in 1912), also used by Williams.

[29] David Wiggins (1976); Wolf indicates Wiggins' influence in Wolf (1997, p. 209).

hunt for something that gives an individual human life meaningful direction, but what I am pointing to is something that gives all direction (or even lack of direction) meaningful grounding. When one experiences wonder, vitality and connection in spiritual experience, one comes to see that life isn't meaningful just because of me, or because I just happen to experience it or value it. In spiritual experience, we come to appreciate the deep value that life itself has – not just my life, but the vastly wondrous, spontaneous, creative, vivacious, interconnected, awe-inspiring phenomenon of life and reality itself.[30] One is also readily inclined toward gratitude because life wouldn't be meaningful if it weren't for something beyond my agency that enables me to experience this life and my agency.[31] Further contributing to a sense of objective meaningfulness, one readily concludes that life was meaningful before I and other rational creatures and our kin got here, and life will be meaningful even when I and all of humanity are gone. Life's basic meaningfulness has nothing to do with me and my aims. Life is the basic creative potentiality that is able to breathe the play of spirit into my agency and its preoccupations, without which all of my endless aimfulness would become empty vanity.[32]

This inadequacy of human vanity emerges in what has come to be known as the 'midlife crisis', which has been helpfully explored by Kieran Setiya. Also harboring a critique of Bernard Williams, Setiya identifies a problematic sort of goal orientation in life as a central explanation for the emptiness of a midlife crisis. Interestingly, he does not believe that immortality in itself would alleviate the underlying problem that supposedly occurs at 'midlife' (Setiya, 2014, p. 3), even though awareness of mortality seems to be among the triggers, because mortality inspires you to quantify the number of completed projects you will achieve in life, leading to the question of what it all adds up to (Setiya, 2014, p. 10). Yet, Setiya suggests that we could find a radically extended life worth living if we can overcome the key problem that generates the crisis, which is precisely the idea of completing projects, or what he more concisely terms 'telic activities'. Setiya observes that many recent philosophers have difficulty seeing

---

[30] This is my way of putting it in 'Faith, Meaning, and Spirituality without Religion'.

[31] For clarification of how gratitude as a spiritual attitude makes sense in secular context, see Chastain (2017); Lacewing (2016); Solomon (2002, pp. 103–106).

[32] Stan Godlovitch makes this point: 'we shouldn't perhaps forget that the world "out there" came up with us' (1999, p. 23).

the value of life as anything but telic, and he calls out Williams in particular for defining persons in terms of desires and projects. 'Williams is wrong. You are not what you plan to get done. And the activities you love need not be projects. Atelic activities, ones that do not aim at terminal states, have value, too. There is pleasure in going for a walk, just wandering or hiking, not to get anywhere, but for the sake of walking itself' (Setiya, 2017, p. 140).

Given the problem with telic activities, Setiya concludes that 'the best life, the ideal life, would be one in which we could, without evaluative error, treat telic activities purely as means' (Setiya, 2014, p. 16). To put it another way: 'The way out is to find sufficient value in atelic activities, activities that have no point of conclusion or limit, ones whose fulfillment lies in the moment of action itself. To draw meaning from such activities is to live in the present – at least in one sense of that loaded phrase – and so to free oneself from the tyranny of projects that plateaus around midlife' (Setiya, 2017, p. 144). I think Setiya provides a much needed balance to the problematic orientation we have been discussing, but I think we can take the analysis even further away from telic activity, because, as I have indicated, we don't even have to understand the desirability of life in terms of human activities or ends at all, telic or atelic, which still traps meaning in the sphere of the human ego. Sure, everything we experience can be placed under the description of an activity, but that doesn't mean that its value is entirely or most basically captured by that description.

What is really needed is the experience of connection that gives being in the moment or mindfulness its depth, a component which Brian Treanor includes in his description of 'vital action':

> In vital action we experience a loss of self, which is the result of being completely engaged or absorbed in the activity. But the 'self' that is lost here is the conscious, egoistic, monadic self, the self that makes efforts in order to accomplish things and be productive. What remains when the conscious self, concerned with acting on the world and the achieving results, gives way? ... A self more engaged and participatory, one that acts in and with the world rather than on it, one that delights in the process, the activity itself. The self of vital activity reveals that we are, at some fundamental existential level, a part of this world. It is not merely that we have a home here, but that we belong here in the deepest ontological sense. (Treanor, 2021, pp. 70–71)[33]

---

[33]   In the ellipsis, Treanor cites Laozi, Michel Serres, and Annie Dillard as writers he is appealing to for this insight.

In my analysis of spiritual experience, I gloss what Treanor describes here simply as an experience of vitality and connection that balances ego for the benefit of self. No boredom here. Treanor claims there is a loss of self, or at least an egoic kind of self, which can allow for reconnection with one's deeper lived self, which those favoring the ego would probably view as the animal. Now, for Williams this was the whole problem with visions of an eternal afterlife in heaven, or even with just losing oneself in intense intellectual inquiry, because Williams felt 'the desire for freedom can, and should, be seen as the desire to be free in the exercise and development of character, not as the desire to be free of it'.[34] What we need to resist, then, is the idea that there is some kind of either/or that we must choose between, when in reality there are times when we must develop character and discipline and other times when we must affirm connection with the world and with others and with a deeper, more amorphous self that does not align with some idea of character that we are overweeningly aiming for. To not allow ourselves freedom from a too demanding and limiting ego can produce alienation and boredom and a negative assessment of life itself.

5. Concluding Remarks on Spiritual Ambivalence about Life

On the way toward affirming the desirability of radically extended life, I have really just been promoting a view of the desirability of life that doesn't depend on desires or even on any special qualities of human existence. Spiritual experiences of wonder, vitality, and connection bring out what is most deeply positive about living. I am not asking anyone to imagine a life that is free of activities, or a life dominated by spiritual experiences, but only to imagine an evaluation of the desirability of life focused by spiritual experience rather than by ego. It is important not to place too much emphasis on the value of human goals, because an imbalanced view about the value of life can impact the way we live and life's resulting desirability. Talk of appropriate commitments and such may carry an important moral or ethical message for wayward or lost humans, and the

[34] Williams (1993, p. 90). As some readers will have noticed, I have sidestepped Williams' argument that an immortal being's identity must be maintained by way of maintaining the same desires. It is not clear that this is, indeed, how one's character remains more or less the same, or how we are justified in counting a person the same over time, but in any case I think that Fischer has sufficiently responded to this aspect of Williams' argument. See, for instance, Fischer (2020, pp. 117–20).

moral and spiritual are also natural allies in many ways. However, the spiritual should be allowed to speak for itself sometimes, and the silencing of an often overly self-absorbed ego is a condition for hearing the spiritual wisdom.

I think this desirability of life achieved by way of balancing or diminishing ego also allows for the view that death is not bad, though death is often viewed as life's enemy. For this reason, I call this pairing of attitudes about life and death coming out of spiritual experience 'spiritual ambivalence'. To think more about this phenomenon, and to see how spiritual ambivalence can get expressed in different ways, I will close by considering a brief sampling of different spiritual traditions, including Daoism, Buddhism, and Epicureanism.

Daoism celebrates action without action, which is one way to translate *wu-wei*. In that ancient Chinese mystical tradition, there is a way of having everything you need, but not because you were trying hard to get it. Perhaps this isn't good advice for youngsters who need to learn from a more formative morality about how to become mature adults, but then spirituality is more like advice to disciplined adults who need to learn how to be more childlike and less controlling. Daoists do not recommend a life of inactivity, but instead encourage us to be more *ziran*, or self-so, like the other animals, who are what they are in what they are doing. The idea is to not reach so strenuously beyond oneself in what one does, distending oneself out of harmony with oneself and one's surroundings.

Judging from references to death in the *Zhuangzi*, a primary text in the Daoist canon, acceptance and affirmation of death is recommended, alongside the affirmation of life: 'Life and death are matters of fate. ... [The Sage] takes death in youth to be good; he takes old age to be good. He takes life's beginning to be good; he takes life's end to be good'.[35] I am not advocating for any particular spiritual tradition, and I find myself immediately wanting to reframe the startling assertion that death in youth is good.[36] But notice the cultivated ambivalence toward life on display here, a spiritual ambivalence explained by balancing of the ego and its fear of death and need for control. Life is good, yes, and lived better with ego tamed – and Daoist tradition certainly has its alchemical

---

[35] Eno (2019, 6.2).

[36] We can of course acknowledge that premature death deprives the young of much potential, but perhaps also consider Schlick's view (1979, p. 123): 'The more youth is realized in life, the more valuable it is, and if a person dies young, however long he may have lived, his life has had meaning. In the concept of youth, so viewed, there is an infinite abundance'.

seekers of immortality[37] – but also, death is not bad, because it is all part of the Way of Nature, and it is not about you.

It is known that Buddhism's core doctrine of non-self resonates well with what is being confirmed by empirical cognitive science today.[38] Our experience of a unity of consciousness and personhood and of agential control is mostly an illusory, constructed experience emerging from the brain. When we are having an experience of loss of ego in spiritual experience, this really does seem to be getting us closer to the truth, though the focus of my point here has only been that we get the meaning of connection out of a spiritual experience, and that this diminishes the strength of our egoic impulses. Belief in a controlling agent and hope for an enduring self after the body dies are among the causes of dissatisfaction with life, and so the Buddha advises us to relinquish these dispositions in order to lessen our suffering. But the aim of *nibbāna*, or extinguishing the craving for existence as if blowing out the flame of a candle, is not the same as actively desiring to die (or *vibhavataṇhā*), which is instead taken to be a perverse inversion of the craving for immortality. Also, not all desire is discouraged as craving, as some simplistic interpretations of Buddhism have it, so love and compassion can be encouraged, enabling a kind of love of life. Thus, we see that yet another spiritual tradition affirms the idea that life is good and that death is not bad.[39]

The Epicureans also have this basic view, which has been much maligned by analytic philosophers of death in recent years. Well known for the view that death is not bad (because when dead, there is no experiencing subject for whom death can be bad), Epicurus also affirms the desirability of life: 'The wise man does not deprecate life nor does he fear the cessation of life. The thought of life is no offence to him, nor is the cessation of life regarded as an evil. And even as men choose of food not merely and simply the larger portion, but the more pleasant, so the wise seek to enjoy the time which is most pleasant and not merely that which is longest'.[40] Samuel Scheffler has less of an issue with the Epicurean view that

---

[37] See Olson (2003).

[38] See Robert Wright, (2017, chs. 5–9).

[39] Abraham Velez provides a helpful overview of the historical Buddha's philosophy based on the Sutta Piṭaka of the Pali Canon: https://iep.utm.edu/buddha (accessed June 2021). See esp. 3b–f for Buddhism's view of non-self.

[40] Diogenes Laertius, (1975, Chapter X, pp. 651–53). Also quoted in Rosenbaum (1989, p. 83).

death is not bad than with the similar but separable Epicurean assertion that we should not fear death. For Scheffler, this fear is not just a
fear of the loss of future opportunities of which I will be deprived by
death, but more basically a fear of the annihilation of me:

> In some people at least, there is a distinctive kind of terror that is
> produced by the strange and sui generis character of the thought
> that I myself – the thinker of my thoughts, the perceiver of what I
> perceive – will simply stop being. ... The egocentric subject –
> which is what has provided the fixed background for all my pre-
> vious endings – is itself to end. ... And this induces, or can
> induce, *panic*. (Scheffler, 2013, pp. 85–86)

Scheffler suggests that the Epicurean attempt to fight fear with philosophical arguments is inadequate (Scheffler, 2013, p. 87), and also
finds arguments à la Buddhism that there is no self in the first
place similarly inadequate (Scheffler, 2013, p. 103), choosing
instead to address the appropriateness of the panic response. I
mention Scheffler's point, not to engage or oppose Scheffler's argument for the appropriateness of death panic, but only to add that,
even if a case can be made that fear of death is appropriate, I think
it is also true that loss of fear of death is desirable, which would
seem to be a better fit for Scheffler's overall view that eventual
death is good. As for how to achieve that loss of fear, philosophical
argument may help on some level, but I think spiritual experience
and spiritual wisdom can play a bigger role, and there are certainly
other methods.

Again, I am not advocating for any one particular way of housing
spirituality, only noting an underlying pattern. The spiritual ambivalence I am highlighting does not produce the view that life is both
good and bad, but rather the view that life is good and death is not
bad, a kind of soft ambivalence that sides with life, yet does not
side against what is often viewed as life's opposite. This ambivalence
pivots on the diminution of the ego, tending to reduce the role that
ego plays in evaluating life or death, and there can be many variations
on that theme, given the metaphysical or philosophical principles
housing the spirituality, though I don't think any elaborate structure
is needed – the humblest hermit shack will do.

Many secular theorists today think it can't make sense to care about
life but not be troubled by death, because they think caring about life
must be entirely egoic[41], based entirely in commitments to one's own
life in some way, caring about projects or ideals or the people you are

---

[41] Not 'egoistic', so this is consistent with 'altruistic'.

attached to, or in concern for pleasures or opportunities that one is deprived of because of death. Williams asserted an egoic ambivalence, an ambivalence conditioned on ego's rise and fall, declaring life good when ego is buzzing along with categorical desires, and not so good when ego peters out, implying that this makes death good.[42] I think this is too dark a picture of life, and it is a more complex ambivalence, a harder ambivalence, one that flips its evaluation of both life and death when ego dries up, while the softer spiritual ambivalence doesn't flip – it always loves life. Spiritual ambivalence can even love life if euthanasia is chosen on the reasonable conclusion that my life is no longer livable, because this love of life is not based only on the conditions of one's own life. An enduring love of life without fear of death is a possibility with spiritual ambivalence, and spirituality is a possibility for secularists that I think is desirable, because it makes life overall more desirable, no matter how long one lives it.[43]

Loyola University New Orleans
chastain@loyno.edu

References

Diogenes Allen, 'Epilogue: Extended Life, Eternal Life: A Christian Perspective' in Stephen G. Post and Robert H. Binstock, *Fountain of Youth: Cultural, Scientific, and Ethical Perspectives on a Biomedical Goal* (Oxford: Oxford University Press, 2004), 387–96.

David Beglin, 'Should I Choose to Never Die?: Williams, Boredom, and the Significance of Mortality', *Philosophical Studies* 174 (2017), 2009–28.

Lisa Bortolotti and Yujin Nagasawa, 'Immortality without Boredom', *Ratio*, 22 (2009), pp. 261-77.

---

[42] I thank Michael Hauskeller for bringing to my attention that Williams doesn't explicitly say that death is made good by too long a life, but Williams' closing statement in 'The Makropulos Case' does seem to imply it – that it is possible to be 'lucky in having the chance to die' (Williams, 1993, p. 92).

[43] For helpful feedback, I am grateful to Michael Hauskeller, Bryon K. Ehlmann, and Eric Wilson, and to those present at the Meaning in Life and the Knowledge of Death conference held at the University of Liverpool, July 2021.

Ben Bradley and Kris McDaniel, 'Death and Desire', in James Stacey Taylor (ed.), *The Metaphysics and Ethics of Death* (Oxford: Oxford University Press, 2013), 118–33.

Cheshire Calhoun, 'Living with Boredom' in Calhoun, *Doing Valuable Time: The Present, the Future, and Meaningful Living* (Oxford: Oxford University Press, 2018), 117–44.

Karel Čapek, 'The Makropulos Case', in Peter Majer and Cathy Porter (trans.), *Four Plays* (London: Metheun World Classics, 1999 [1925]).

Drew Chastain, 'Gifts without Givers: Secular Spirituality and Metaphorical Cognition', *Sophia* 56 (2017), 631–47.

Drew Chastain, 'Can Life Be Meaningful without Free Will?', *Philosophia* 47.4 (2019), 1069–1086.

Drew Chastain, 'Deep Personal Meaning', A Subjective Approach to Meaning in Life', *Journal of Philosophy of Life* 11 (2021), 1–23.

Drew Chastain, 'Faith, Meaning, and Spirituality without Religion', in Roderick Nicholls and Heather Salazar (eds.), *Mind Over Matter* (Leiden: Brill | Rodopi, forthcoming).

Michael Cholbi, 'Immortality and the Exhaustibility of Value', in Cholbi (ed.), *Immortality and the Philosophy of Death* (London: Rowman & Littlefield, 2016), 221–36.

John Cottingham, 'Philosophy, Religion, and Spirituality', in David McPherson (ed.), *Spirituality and the Good Life: Philosophical Approaches* (Cambridge: Cambridge University Press, 2019), 11–28.

Laozi, Daodejing, trans. by Robert Eno (2010): http://hdl.handle.net/2022/23426 (accessed June 2021).

Aubrey de Grey, 'An Engineer's Approach to Developing Real Anti-Aging Medicine', in Stephen G. Post and Robert H. Binstock, *Fountain of Youth: Cultural, Scientific, and Ethical Perspectives on a Biomedical Goal* (Oxford: Oxford University Press, 2004), 249–68.

Ronald Dworkin, *Religion without God* (Cambridge: Harvard University Press, 2013).

John Martin Fischer, 'Why Immortality is Not So Bad', *Our Stories: Essays on Life, Death, and Free Will* (Oxford: Oxford University Press, 2011), 79–92.

John Martin Fischer, 'Immortality', in Ben Bradley, Fred Feldman, and Jens Johansson (eds.), *The Oxford Handbook of Philosophy of Death* (Oxford: Oxford University Press, 2015), 336–54.

John Martin Fischer, *Death, Immortality, and Meaning in Life* (Oxford: Oxford University Press, 2020).

John Martin Fischer and Benjamin Mitchell-Yellin, *Near-Death Experiences: Understanding Visions of the Afterlife* (Oxford: Oxford, University Press, 2016).

Neil Gillman, 'A Jewish Theology of Death and the Afterlife' in Stephen G. Post and Robert H. Binstock, *Fountain of Youth: Cultural, Scientific, and Ethical Perspectives on a Biomedical Goal* (Oxford: Oxford University Press, 2004), 94–108.

Stan Godlovitch, 'Creativity in Nature', *The Journal of Aesthetic Education* 33.3 (1999), 17–26.

Michael Hauskeller, *Better Humans?: Understanding the Enhancement Project* (Durham: Acumen Publishing Ltd, 2013).

Martin Heidegger, *The Fundamental Concepts of Metaphysics: World, Finitude, Solitude*, trans. by William McNeill and Nicholas Walker, (Bloomington: Indiana University Press, 1995).

Shelly Kagan, *Death* (New Haven: Yale University, 2012).

Michael Lacewing, 'Can non-theists appropriately feel existential gratitude?', *Religious Studies* 52 (2016): 145–65.

Diogenes Laertius, 'Epicurus', *Lives of Eminent Philosophers*, vol. 2 (Cambridge: Harvard University Press, 1975), 528–678.

Elijah Millgram, 'On Being Bored Out of Your Mind', *Proceedings of the Aristotelian Society* 104 (2004): 163–84.

Iris Murdoch, *The Sovereignty of Good* (New York: Schocken Books, 1971).

S. Jay Olshansky and Bruce A. Carnes, 'Inconvenient Truths About Human Longevity', *Journals of Gerontology: Medical Sciences* 74.S1 (2019): S7–S12.

Stuart Alve Olson, *The Jade Emperor's Mind Seal Classic: The Taoist Guide to Health, Longevity, and Immortality* (Rochester, VT: Inner Traditions, 2003).

Rudolf Otto, *The Idea of the Holy*, trans. by John W. Harvey (London: Oxford University Press, 1923).

Wendell O'Brien, 'Boredom: A History of Western Philosophical Perspectives', *Internet Encyclopedia of Philosophy* https://iep.utm.edu/boredom/ (accessed June 2021).

Brian O'Connor, *Idleness: A Philosophical Essay* (Princeton: Princeton University Press, 2018).

Michael Pollan, *How to Change Your Mind* (New York: Penguin Press, 2018).

Connie Rosati, 'The Makropulos Case Revisited: Reflections on Immortality and Agency', *The Oxford Handbook of Philosophy of Death*, (ed.) Ben Bradley, Fred Feldman, and Jens Johansson, (Oxford: Oxford University Press, 2012), 355–90.

Stephen Rosenbaum, 'Epicurus and Annihilation', *The Philosophical Quarterly* 39.154 (1989).

Samuel Scheffler, *Death and the Afterlife* (Oxford: Oxford University Press, 2013).

Moritz Schlick, 'On the Meaning of Life', in Henk L. Mulder and Barbara F. B. Van de Velde-Schlick (eds.), Peter Heath (trans.), *Philosophical Papers: Volume II (1925–1936)* (Dordrecht: D. Reidel Publishing Co., 1979), 112–29.

Kieran Setiya, 'The Midlife Crisis', *Philosophers' Imprint* 14.31 (2014): 1–18.

Kieran Setiya, *Midlife* (Princeton: Princeton University Press, 2017).

Robert Solomon, *Spirituality for the Skeptic: The Thoughtful Love of Life* (Oxford: Oxford University Press, 2002).

Lars Svendsen, *A Philosophy of Boredom*, trans. by John Irons, (London: Reaktion Books, 2005).

Lars Svendsen, 'Boredom and the Meaning of Life', in Michael E. Gardiner and Julian Jason Haladyn (eds.), *Boredom Studies Reader: Frameworks and Perspectives* (London: Routledge, 2017), 205–215.

Peter Toohey, *Boredom: A Lively History* (New Haven: Yale University Press, 2011).

Brian Treanor, *Melancholic Joy: On Life Worth Living* (London: Bloomsbury Academic, 2021).

Abraham Velez, 'Buddha', *Internet Encyclopedia of Philosophy* https://iep.utm.edu/buddha/ (accessed June 2021).

David Wiggins, 'Truth, Invention, and Meaning in Life', *Proceedings of the British Academy* 62 (1976), 331–78.

Bernard Williams, 'The Makropulos Case: Reflections on the Tedium of Immortality', in John Martin Fischer (ed.), *The Metaphysics of Death* (Stanford: Stanford University Press, 1993), 73–92.

Susan Wolf, 'Happiness and Meaning: Two Aspects of the Good Life', *Social Philosophy and Policy* 14 (1997) 207–225.

Susan Wolf, *Meaning in Life and Why It Matters* (Princeton, NJ: Princeton University Press, 2010).

Robert Wright, *Why Buddhism is True: The Science and Philosophy of Meditation and Enlightenment* (New York: Simon & Schuster, 2017).

Zhuangzi, 'Death and the Dao' in Robert Eno (trans.), *Zhuangzi: The Inner Chapters* (2019): http://hdl.handle.net/2022/23427 (accessed June 2021).

'Creatures of a Day': Contingency, Mortality, and Human Limits

HAVI CAREL

Abstract

This paper offers a nexus of terms – mortality, limits, contingency and vulnerability – painting a picture of human life as marked by limitation and finitude. I suggest that limitations of possibility, capacity, and resource are deep features of human life, but not only restrict it. Limits are also the conditions of possibility for human life and as such have productive, normative, and creative powers that not only delimit life but also scaffold growth and transformation within it. The paper takes a less known interpretation of the term '*ephēmeros*', to mean 'of the day', rather than 'short-lived' and suggests that as ephemeral, human life is contingent and mutable, subject to events beyond our control. However, virtue can still be exercised – indeed, can be exuberantly displayed – when we respond to contingent events marked by adversity.

1. Introduction

Death is not the only worrisome limit that plagues human life and demands reflective coping. There are, as philosophers have suggested, different kinds of finitude that characterise human existence. Heidegger (1962) points out how we can die not only biologically (an event he calls 'demise', *ableben*) but also die existentially, by becoming 'unable to be' (Carel, 2007a). Benatar (2017) has pointed out the futility and limitations of both life *and* death – death because it annihilates us and deprives us of pleasure; life because it is inherently bad. MacIntyre (1999) has laid out the 'facts of life' as vulnerability to affliction, dependence on others, and subjection to powerful external forces (cf. Carel and Kidd, forthcoming).

Limitation – of possibility, of capacity, of resource – marks human life in deep and unsettling ways. And yet, although these limits have been tackled as a practical challenge, insofar as they have been addressed they have been seen as a negative feature of human life to be rejected, revolted against, or got rid of.[1] The reason for this may be our positive stance: embracing technological advances, hopes for

---

[1]   There are, of course, notable exceptions to this, such as the philosophy of illness and the philosophy of disability, some existentialist work and feminist philosophy, but these are notable for being viewed as specialised areas

doi:10.1017/S1358246121000369   © The Royal Institute of Philosophy and the contributors 2021

Havi Carel

a transhumanist future, or the view of humanity's trajectory as that of potentially unlimited progress, that drives us to overlook or reject limitations. Psychological reactions – denial, idealisation, wishful thinking – also cause our 'sensitive minds', as Freud puts it in *On Transience*, to 'recoil from anything that is painful' (1957). Psychic pain interferes with our possibility of enjoyment, says Freud, so we push thoughts about transience aside, in favour of a more palatable focus on progress, achievement, and success.

That we are transient, fleeting visitors to this world – that we are *temporally* finite – has been a time-honoured philosophical theme for millennia, from Epicurus to Heidegger. As part of this engagement, Michael Hauskeller offers the ancient Greek term for humans: *ephēmeroi* which he translates as 'the short-lived ones', or 'those who live only for a day (*epi hemera*)' (2019, pp. 11–12).

The term 'ephemeral' can also be understood in another way. We are also ephemeral in that we are subject to the ever-changing days, to the variable, mutable world we inhabit. We are *ephēmeros* – *day creatures*, to use Pindar's elegant term, in our phenomenal world.[2] We are subject to change: change can engulf us, swallow us whole and spit us onto a raft crossing the channel, into the midst of a civil war, subject to social and political upheaval, pandemics, wars, coups, and other events over which we have little control. We can express this sense of *ephēmeros* – our vulnerability to external events and the changes of the phenomenal world in which we exist – by stating that we are temporally finite but also existentially finite, with finite abilities and possibilities (Carel, 2007a). These kinds of limit – not finitude of time but finitude of choice and possibility – are no less philosophically rich than temporal finitude.

This essay resists the recoiling of our 'sensitive minds' against transience, death, and what is painful, suggesting instead that what we have taken to be our limits is simply our way of being. The essay examines in what ways limits are philosophically pertinent and suggests that limits and boundaries are transcendental conditions of human life as we know it. Death is a major, but by no means the primary, limit of human life. We are limited in other ways too, that are important and profoundly shape human existence.

I propose a dual understanding of finitude, seeing it both as temporal finitude and as existential finitude. By existential finitude I

---

of philosophical work (see Carel and Kidd (forthcoming) for further discussion of this).

[2] An alternative translation is 'creatures of a day'. See Lefkowitz (1977).

mean that we have finite possibilities, are subject to the contingencies of life, and have finite capabilities. This broad view, emphasizing our mortality, also often includes the claim that not only is life finite, it is also short (Nagel, 1970).[3] However, following Fränkel's (1946) philological analysis, I want to suggest that life is ephemeral not because it is short, but rather because it is long, and as such susceptible to the effects of contingency and limitation which shape and delimit our existence in ways analogous to, but importantly different from, death. We are both mortal and existentially finite.

2. Being towards death: Heidegger on temporal finitude

In the 1929–1930 lecture course *The Fundamental Concepts of Metaphysics* Heidegger writes: 'Finitude is not some property that is merely attached to us, but is *our fundamental way of being*' (1996, p. 6). Death defines and shapes Dasein's existence as its limit. It is 'the limit-situation that defines the limits of Dasein's ability-to-be' (Blattner, 1994, p. 67).[4] This limit becomes existentially significant because of Dasein's unique capacity to anticipate it, a capacity that structures human life as 'being-towards-death'. Death limits life not only as an end point towards which we progress each day, but also as imbuing our actions and decisions with singularity and unidirectionality (Carel, 2006a). We live each moment once only because of our temporal finitude. Therefore, Heidegger's analysis focuses on how Dasein's existence is shaped by mortality and how life is a process of dying (*sterben*). Finitude shapes the projects and plans we make and is therefore implicit in our self-conception. As Stephen Mulhall writes, 'Phenomenologically speaking, then, life is death's representative, the proxy through which death's resistance to Dasein's grasp is at once acknowledged and overcome' (2005, p. 305).

Being towards death is therefore an active and practical stance: 'Death is a way to be, which Dasein takes over as soon as it is'

---

[3]   Although not all philosophical traditions lament life's shortness. Against the contemporary consensus that life is short, other views can be found in ancient Greek and Roman philosophy, some emphasising phenomenal life's insignificance relative to the permanent world of the forms (Plato) to a view of life as being long enough 'if you know how to use it' (Seneca).

[4]   In this section I will use Heidegger's term, Dasein, to denote the human being.

(Heidegger, 1962, p. 288).[5] Dasein's way of being towards death reveals itself in its choices of possibilities towards which it projects itself, which constitute Dasein's movement towards its future. When Dasein *anticipates* death it frees itself, because death illuminates all other possibilities as part of a finite structure. Seeing itself as a finite structure enables Dasein to see itself as a whole. This understanding is not theoretical but enacted. Therefore Dasein not only understands itself as a finite whole but *exists* as one.

There are two ways for Dasein to respond to its mortality: authentically and inauthentically. Dasein can choose to respond authentically to death by resolutely anticipating it. This opens the possibility for Dasein to authentically engage with its existence, since it has now grasped it as finite. Dasein can also flee from death by dismissing it as irrelevant to the present. Heidegger calls this attitude 'inauthentic'. The two attitudes to death underlie everyday practical concerns and engagement with the world because our actions are performed within a temporally finite horizon. As a result, no one is exempt from having some sort of attitude towards death. Whether Dasein assumes an authentic attitude towards death or flees from its mortality, it is always death-bound. Death determines Dasein's relationship to its future and its conception of itself as finite and temporal.

Returning to the theme of limits, Heidegger defines Dasein's death as a possibility [*Möglichkeit*] which can occur at any time, and hence death is an ever-present condition of every one of Dasein's possibilities. Every possibility one considers is shadowed by the possibility of death: of not having any more possibilities, or as Heidegger puts it: 'Death is the possibility of the absolute impossibility of Dasein' (1962, p. 294).

Both the possibility of being unable to be (or what Blattner calls 'existential death') and temporal finitude are conditions for the meaningfulness of all other possibilities, and both are limit cases that define the boundaries of meaningful experience. In this sense there is an affinity between the two types of finitude (Carel, 2007a). Existential death is a state of being unable to press into any possibilities – existential paralysis, if you like, in which one's very ability to exist is put in abeyance, in a clear parallel to death, in which one's ability to exist is permanently annihilated.

But in what sense is death a possibility? Being-towards-the-end defines Dasein as finite temporality, as a constant movement

---

[5]   Hans Jonas, too, defines life through its constant struggle against falling back into nothingness. So in a way, for Jonas, Dasein is not towards death, but away from it. I thank Michael Hauskeller for drawing this contrast.

towards its annihilation. Beyond all possible projections into the future lies the ultimate anticipation [*Vorgriff*] of shutting down Dasein's temporal trajectory. Consequently, Dasein's end is something that is only ever impending, but can never be made actual, that is, be experienced by Dasein, because death is simply its annihilation. Moreover, whereas other things are possible only at certain times, Dasein's end is possible at any moment. Our end is 'always and only a possibility' (Mulhall, 2005, p. 303). But as such a possibility, it foregrounds every possibility, choice, and action we take.

We can now see how finitude of possibility and temporal finitude are conceptually related. Both define the end or limitation of life, and as limit concepts they assign significance to life by delineating its confines. Being-towards-the-end expresses temporal finitude; death is the finitude of possibilities, in both senses: temporally and existentially. The concepts are further linked through the concept of *Angst*, or anxiety. Anxiety is the state of being existentially dead because one is too anxious to be able to act. One is effectively paralysed by anxiety and thus in a state of existential death (Blattner, 1996). *Angst* is also the affective state that discloses Dasein to itself as temporally finite, as being-towards-the-end, so both kinds of 'inability to be' are experienced through anxiety.

The question that emerges with respect to these two types of finitude is not how one ought to die, but how one ought to live knowing that one will die, taking into account both mortality and existential finitude. Our relation to our death is not something that is realized when we die, but something we either realize or fail to realize in our life (Mulhall, 2005). Confronting life as Dasein's ownmost possibility requires Dasein to acknowledge that its being is always an issue for it, that 'its life is something for which it is responsible, that it is its own to live (or to disown)' (ibid., p. 306). Because death could come at any moment, the radical contingency of each individual life becomes apparent, and to acknowledge this is to acknowledge finitude, 'the fact that our existence has conditions or limits, that it is neither self-originating nor self-grounding nor self-sufficient, that it is contingent from top to bottom' (ibid.; see also Hatab, 1995, p. 411). I now turn to these limits and contingencies, to continue building the picture of what Ian Kidd and I call the 'facts of life'.

3. Finite possibilities and the 'facts of life'

Grounded in Heidegger's analysis of being towards death, we have secured the understanding of life as temporally finite and also

Havi Carel

begun to see how existential death foreshadows and formally mirrors death. The previous section has articulated the duality of finitude for Heidegger: it is both temporal finitude *and* existential death, i.e., being paralysed by anxiety and unable to press into any possibilities, and hence unable to *exist* in Heidegger's sense. There are other forms of finitude we now turn to: finitude of possibility, contingency, and finitude of our capacities.

Our limits are the ways in which we are restricted. We may be restricted in our freedom, our possibilities for action, our choices, or constrained by what Heidegger called our 'thrownness' [*Geworfenheit*]: the historical, social and existential context into which we are 'thrown', or in which we find ourselves when we come into existence. These limits restrict us but are also what enables us to live as human within a world that both affords possibilities and threatens their closure. Our limits can therefore be interpreted as positive – as opening vistas of possibility and experience – or as negative: as restricting or delimiting our being in the world. One way of reconciling the two is by stating, like Freud, Hauskeller, and others, that the risk and possibility of injury and disappointment are a necessary price – indeed, one worth paying – to have beauty, value and love. As Hauskeller asks: 'And what kind of adventure would [life] be if we couldn't be hurt, if nothing could be lost?' (2019, p. 20).

It is because we invest libidinally in others (and more generally in external objects and values) – or love them, more simply – that we make ourselves vulnerable, says Freud. With love comes the threat of disappointment, rejection, desertion, and betrayal; the possibility of loss. With joy comes the fear of finding ourselves empty or sad again. With value – Freud mentions patriotism – comes the threat of what we cherish being harmed, destroyed, or taken away.

On this view, life is premised upon trade-offs: life's positives are fragile, precious, and hence difficult to non-ambivalently embrace. We are psychologically prone to experience ambivalence, to a certain extent, about many of our endeavours: from relationship and connection making to creative efforts, to throwing ourselves into various projects, to the making of our world: love and loss are intertwined. When we press into possibilities, or pursue projects, we propel ourselves into our future. We make our future and make ourselves through this projection [*entwerfen*], to use Heidegger's term (1962) (see also Inwood 1999, pp. 176–78). Projection implies both doing and investing, as well as accepting the risks and limitations such doing and investing entail. But we are never just projection – we are always also thrown, hence Heidegger's compact definition of the human being as 'thrown projection', encompassing both our freedom and our limitations (Heidegger, 1962; Inwood, 1999).

Freud's view could be called the 'trade-off' view: it sees life as this kind of risk taking: the risk of losing is what makes the game fun, one might say. Or, more poetically: 'Tis better to have loved and lost/ Than never to have loved at all'.[6] The view is neither black and white nor a simple cost-benefit calculus. Freud is at great pains to explain why attaching to things outside ourselves is crucial to our psychic life and why not doing so is existentially and psychologically pathological, if not impossible. Hauskeller (2019) poses the view as a challenge to a certain transhumanist view, arguing that immortality and invulnerability are not ideals to aspire to and that the risk involved is life's driver and provides it with variation and intensity.

Here is another way of understanding the same phenomenon. The dark side of life − loss, pain, rejection, despair − are not a necessary evil we need to put up with in order to obtain the more pleasurable aspects of life. Rather they are the conditions of possibility enabling human life to contain the variety it does. Without them, we would not be who we are and although we are primed to forever want more, we are, at the same time, aware of the futility of our avarice. For wanting more can lead to further philosophical dismay. Take death, for example. As Bernard Williams argues, death is undeniably bad, but so is immortality. That it is better always to live on does not mean that it is better to live always, as he (1973) argues. *Contra* Nagel (1970), life is not a linear accumulation of pleasures so that more is always better than less. Life has a more complex structure. Going on to live indefinitely is not necessarily the happily (for)ever after that we may fantasise about, and there is a clear disconnect between such fantasies and the complexity and deeply ambivalent nature of life.

What would understanding our limits, contingency, and vulnerability as conditions of human life look like? I'd like to start developing this view in relation to what Ian James Kidd and I have called the 'facts of life'. In a recent paper we suggested that the facts of life arise from three aspects of human life (Carel and Kidd, 2019). First, we are embodied and hence subject to injury and illness. Second, we are social and hence vulnerable to exploitation, abuse, and oppression by others. Third, we initiate meaningful projects, and these can fail, or go wrong, or be thwarted by others.

---

[6] *In Memoriam A. H. H. OBIIT MDCCCXXXIII: 27,* by Alfred, Lord Tennyson. https://www.poetryfoundation.org/poems/45336/in-memoriam-a-h-h-obiit-mdcccxxxiii-27 (accessed 20 August 2021).

Havi Carel

The meaning and value of our lives and that we find in our lives can be subverted in any of these ways. As MacIntyre puts it:

> We human beings are vulnerable to many kinds of affliction and most of us are at some time afflicted by serious ills. How we cope is only in small part up to us. It is most often to others that we owe our survival, let alone our flourishing, as we encounter bodily illness and injury, inadequate nutrition, mental defect and disturbance, and human aggression and neglect (1999, p.1).

MacIntyre captures the fragility and tenuousness of human life, which is vulnerable to accident, affliction and subjection in the three ways mentioned above. On this view illness and disability play a much more central role in our understanding of human life. Our bodies are vulnerable not only contingently, but also fundamentally open to external forces, in ways that make us extremely vulnerable (as we've seen in the current pandemic). We live in social groups and political systems and are dependent on their continued support. So our own agency, wellbeing and autonomy are also deeply contingent on the continued stability and freedoms afforded by such systems when they operate positively. Finally, we invest time and energy and much emotion in the projects that matter to us. But that investment, as we have seen in Freud's *On Transience*, is, again, contingent on our efforts being well received and supported by others, rather than thwarted by external forces, deliberately or not.

With MacIntyre and Kidd, I propose we see limits, contingency and vulnerability as fundamental modes of human life, not just a necessary evil. This affects our self-understanding as autonomous agents, because our epistemic and practical agency operates against a 'facts of life' background, meaning that our scope for choice is less extensive, our freedom less unbounded, than we might suppose. Human agency is deeply conditioned by complex sets of circumstances, which makes our concrete situation much more of a determinative feature of our life than we may think and makes our control, decision-making and choice less obvious. I suggest we see such limits as enablers of life experiences. In the same way that immortality would, as Williams (1973) argues, make life meaningless and intolerably tedious, removing other limits or barriers can similarly devalue and obliterate meaning from life.

We can reconfigure these limits so as to see their transcendental and meaning-giving nature by mapping them on to the three 'facts of life'. First, we said that there are limits to our bodily capacities. We cannot fly or breathe under water, for example. But not being able to fly or breathe under water are not seen as bodily failures but as ways of defining what human bodies are. In contrast to, say, not being able to breathe air, which would be a bodily failure, not being able to breathe under water is a feature of our mammalian land existence: we are creatures who breathe air. Bodily limits are also enablers in an additional way. Fighting against those limits can be creative and fun; coming close to or testing our bodily limits is an enjoyable challenge and human endeavour. For example, extreme sports, strength training, marathon running, and so on, are an engagement with those limits 'from the inside' as it were, but still attempting to push the boundaries of what our bodies are capable of.

Second, our way of being with others is inherently social (Szanto and Moran, 2016). This is expressed by Heidegger in his notion of being-with [*Mitsein*]: whether in a fulfilled or privative mode, we are always and inherently being with others. We seek human companionship and need others for almost every aspect of life. This makes us deeply dependent on others, as MacIntyre (1999) emphasises, and requires trust in others for everything we do (Bernstein, 2011). That dependence and trust make us vulnerable, as MacIntyre claims, but they also make us into persons who are nurtured by connection and relationships. We care deeply about others and about what others think of us. That makes us vulnerable, but it also opens up certain life forms and fundamental concepts such as friendship, love, family, care, and respect.

To appreciate how deep our sociality runs and the extent to which it is an organising principle for human life, we can look to how our social interactions have been profoundly disrupted and restricted during the lockdowns and social distancing measures we recently experienced in the pandemic. The social deprivations and restrictions have made ever more salient that we need other people in a deep way, both practically and psychologically. Our need for social connection and meaningful embodied friendships has been revealed in the marked increase in mental ill health and reported loneliness, sadness, grief, and isolation caused by the pandemic and social distancing (Froese et al., 2021).

Our dependence on others is not some weakness or accidental feature of our big brains and infantile needs. Rather, this dependence is a central and fundamental feature of human life. That dependence, again, can be a source of vulnerability but also an elemental feature of our embodied being. We are grown inside another human, we are nursed and looked after intensively during our infancy and early years and remain dependent on others in ways that are profoundly important to philosophy (Stone, 2019). That dependence is a source of creativity, shared intimacy and joy. It has also been radically underappreciated by mainstream philosophy with the notable exception of feminist authors such as Carol Gilligan (1989), Sarah Blaffer

Havi Carel

Hrdy (1999), Sarah Ruddick (1989), and Alison Stone (2019), to name a few.

Third, our projects are limited by our cognitive abilities, energy, time, enthusiasm, and of course external constraints such as financial and political limits and other people's support or thwarting of these projects. When we invest time and energy in a goal or project, to use Heidegger's term, that investment is limited by our resources and capacities and the willingness of others to support our efforts. These limits delineate what is possible to achieve and what requires more help or a collective effort; what projects we ultimately choose to pursue has a generative function, in that it shapes and defines who we become (Heidegger, 1962).

These three types of limits – our limited embodied nature, our dependence on others, and our limited capacity to project – enable human life and should be seen as akin to Heideggerian possibilities: choosing to press into one possibility closes off other possibilities but it is existence; we press into possibilities in ways that define us, and each choice excludes other possibilities but at the same time also opens other, new possibilities to us (ibid.). Similarly, having limits to bodily capacities, limits (and norms) for social interactions, and having limited capacities to carry out our projects not only limits but also proscribes and defines what is possible.

To conclude this section, let us describe the general features of the three types of limitations. First, they provide boundaries to measure ourselves and push against. These limits define and frame human action: without them our ability to judge and assess our actions and success or its absence would be highly compromised. How can we say whether a bodily performance is successful or not – say, athletic – if we don't have a sense of what our general human limits are and a personal capacity to measure our performance against?

Second, limits combine with the 'life cycle' view to provide a framing that helps with the creation of meaning and meaning-making processes. By 'life cycle' I mean the form of a human life – where significant stages of that life are ones in which we are helpless and depend on others' care: before and at birth and during infancy, as well as during periods where our physical and mental capacities diminish, and we become dependent once again. When we view someone as being in a particular life stage – infancy, say – we can view their actions in that context and then judge whether they have met or exceeded their limits. This is an important way to contextualise and understand how humans change over time, how they develop, and what limits characterise each life stage.

Finally, limits also provide us with a normative basis because they set our expectations. We understand our actions against a backdrop of a set of norms (these could be norms of health, norms of moral conduct, norms of success) and without limits that would be impossible. In short, limits do not just restrict us, but set out what is possible; in that sense limits are enablers.

4. Contingency: 'man is all accident'

Another significant element of the 'facts of life' is contingency. We cannot control what the day brings or shape our lives independently of that fact. Our decisions are only ever attempts, often futile, to bring about certain states of affairs. But, as the Stoics tell us, at most we can control our attempts and our responses to what unfolds; we cannot control what unfolds (Epictetus, 1891). Epictetus reminds us that we are actors in a drama, not its authors (*Enchiridion* XVII). How our desires and goals encounter the forces of our day's reality can never be entirely planned. Our choices are often confounded by material and other facts about our abilities and bodily constraints (Carel and Kidd, 2019; Carel, 2016a).

We can never fully anticipate the outcome of our choices or dictate the neat unfolding of our future, despite our best efforts. This is a central theme in Greek tragedy: Oedipus chose not to kill his father or sleep with his mother, but in his attempts to avoid these events he ended up doing exactly what he feared. Oedipus' story is often taken to be an illustration of the ancient Greek focus on the clash of human free will with 'fate'. However, the contested and often misunderstood concept of 'fate' lacks nuance on this reading and takes the notion of free will to be more developed than it was at the time of Sophocles' (1984) rendition of the story in *Oedipus Rex*. This view also posits free will in strong juxtaposition to 'fate' in misleading ways that require a rigid understanding of these concepts (see Carel, 2006b for a full discussion). Gould agrees with this view: 'the Greeks before the Stoics had not yet conceived of the will as we do and so did not see fate and free will as exclusive alternatives' (Gould, 1988, p. 51).

Rather than seeing the story of Oedipus as that of a conflict between free will and fate, it provides us with a morally nuanced lesson about how people can be destroyed by 'circumstances whose origin does not lie with them,' and 'things that they do not control,' due to the 'ungoverned contingency [of] social life' (Nussbaum, 2001, pp. 25, 89). As H.D.F. Kitto (1958, p. 1) comments on Greek tragedy, '"the gods" [are] simply those aspects and conditions of life which we have to accept because we cannot change them'. On this interpretation, the monolithic and explanatorily opaque notion of 'fate' becomes a more nuanced and hermeneutically productive force of contingency.

Seen this way, Oedipus' story illustrates a general truth about human life: any decision-making is always done in the thick of life. Any such decisions could be thwarted, twisted, or otherwise frustrated by a variety of factors and forces, many of them beyond our knowledge, understanding, and control. In the words of Robert Burns, in a 1785 poem to a mouse whose nest he accidentally overturned with his plough: 'The best laid schemes o' Mice an' Men/Gang aft a-gley'– often go awry.

Returning to our earlier discussion of *ephēmeros*, this view of contingency is supported by a less familiar meaning of the term. Contingency is a foundational aspect of being *ephēmeros*, 'of the day', which can also mean 'belonging to the day' or 'subject to the day' (Fränkel, 1946). Rather than understanding 'of the day' as meaning 'short lived', being 'of the day' means humans are owned by the flux and continual mutability of the days, to which we must adapt to the best of our ability. We are subject to contingent factors imposed on us by the norms and structures of the day and these are both out of our control and changeable, because what is 'of the day' must change as the days change: mutability marks human life which is lived within ever changing conditions.

As Fränkel writes, 'the term implies that man is moulded and remoulded by changing events and circumstance' (1946, p. 133). Life is ephemeral not in the familiar sense that it is short and passing, but rather because it is too long to retain any sense of stability within it (Fränkel, 1946, p. 134 fn. 13). Thus, *ephēmeros* also denotes what is unstable or precarious: there is no certainty of permanence over the many days of our lives. Even if things are stable, that stability is not guaranteed because life is 'of the day', and hence characterised by this mutability – political, social, personal, existential. Change is also a constant feature of physical bodies, with growth, development, illness, and ageing; this sits well with the 'life cycle' view offered in the previous section.

We also change mentally, with changes in our beliefs, attitudes, values and desires; L. A. Paul's notion of transformative experience provides a framework for understanding how our experiences can give rise to such changes (Paul, 2014; Carel and Kidd, 2019). Such changes, suggests Paul, are characterised by being epistemically transformative (giving us new information we would not otherwise have) and personally transformative (changing our beliefs, values, preferences, etc.). Experiences that are both epistemically and personally transformative are what Paul calls 'transformative experiences', and they are the ones that change us. I argue (2019) that such change need not only be seen as momentous, dramatic change, but that we can also be transformed by the cumulative effects of mundane experiences – perhaps the more familiar way of gradually modifying our beliefs and acquiring modest amounts of new knowledge.

And of course, there is continuous social change, with political events and the updating of societal norms, values, and institutions. Taken together, these three main ways in which we change physically, mentally and societally, articulate human openness – some may say vulnerability – to change. We do not have absolute control over any of these types of changes. Change is an existential feature of human life which is therefore ephemeral in its mutability and openness to contingency. In the words of Solon: 'man is all accident' (cited in Fränkel 1946, p. 135). An alternative translation by Joshua Anthony reads: 'man is entirely of circumstance' and A. D. Godley translates: 'man is entirely chance' (Herodotus, 1920).[7] We are made up of our contingent circumstances.

From this, second, meaning of *ephēmeros* as being 'of the day' or 'subject to the day' and hence subject to an unexpected flux of events which cannot be controlled by any individual, Fränkel draws a 'doctrine of personal variability'. This is a negative doctrine which Fränkel attributes to a certain strand of ancient Greek thinking during the epic and lyric eras: we adapt to our circumstances in ways that can be deceitful, dishonest, or opportunistic. We 'seize the day' in order to exploit, fit in, and utilise versatile identities. We need to do all that because we are subservient to the present day, atmosphere, and people we are surrounded with. The doctrine of personal variability sees the self as 'pliable and passive', contributing to a sense of helplessness and inadequacy of man (Fränkel, 1946, p. 136).

But personal variability can also be seen as a positive trait, so change in oneself in accordance with life's events can also indicate openness and flexibility. Our ability to change and adapt, to respond to life's events and circumstances, is surely a crucial feature of one's resilience, flexibility, and creativity. Adjustment, says Fränkel, 'makes the vicissitudes of life easier to bear' (ibid. p. 138).

---

[7] https://classicalanthology.theclassicslibrary.com/2019/08/11/histories-1-30-1-1-33-solon-at-the-court-of-croesus-part-2-cleobis-and-biton/ (accessed 7 September 2021).

Havi Carel

I would like to go further and suggest that in being *ephēmeros* humans are also *open* to life's events, rather than vulnerable to events and hostage to fortune, because we are able to creatively respond to life's challenges. Adaptability isn't merely a passive responsive mode. Adaptability also implies a creative dimension: when we respond by adapting to a new condition or circumstance, that response is often creative. We adapt to new situations by deploying new strategies, changing our behaviour, adjusting our goals, updating our beliefs, and so on. These responses include a generative element in virtue of the creation of new modes of interaction and action within the new day.

Take the example of falling ill or becoming disabled: when we respond to limitations brought about by illness or accident, we adapt by inventing new ways to achieve our goals or, if required, we can modify our goals and look for new ones that are compatible with our illness. These could be new modes of motility, for example, or new ways of envisaging our future. New sources of enjoyment, or a new way of thinking about our situation. This is not an attempt to assert a 'bright-siding', to borrow Barbara Ehrenreich's (2010) useful term, or a Pollyanna-like minimising of the negative aspects of illness. Of course there is much sadness, loss and negativity in this process, but it is not monolithically bad, as many assume (Carel, 2016a, ch. 6). It is a much more diverse, nuanced, complex, changing and – indeed – *creative* process than is often appreciated (Carel, 2007b; 2016b). This creativity emerging in response to adversity is important to document, witness, and celebrate because illness plays a large role in almost every human life and seeing it as purely negative carries significant costs. Articulating the richness and diversity of illness can bring into view the active agency that is still possible even in severe illness and to therefore contribute to the sense that agency, dignity, and personal growth are not impossible in serious illness. Taken more broadly, this offers a different way to that discussed by Fränkel of understanding how one may respond to the events of the day: not by being hostage to circumstance, but by actively and creatively responding to contingent events.

What are the consequences of being 'day creatures', *ephēmeros*? First, our vision is limited to what is known and accepted by the present day. Our perspectives, beliefs, and values, and hence our choices and actions, are coloured by our contingent position in a particular point in time and place. Second, our opinions and beliefs may not be grounded in permanent, timeless principles. They are 'of the day', so may be anchored in the phenomenal world rather than in timeless truths. Third, our beliefs may change quickly and

continuously because circumstances change (Fränkel, 1946). We
need to constantly update our beliefs and our understanding of the
world around us in tandem with new evidence and facts as they
emerge and in response to new information and new experiences.
Being *ephēmeros* means that epistemically we are perhaps less robust
than we hope. But it also means that we can be edified and changed
by new knowledge, and that events and circumstances can transform
us, again, seeing our openness and responsiveness as positive features
of our ephemeral existence (cf. Paul, 2014; Kidd, 2012; Carel and
Kidd, 2019). The acknowledgement of our impermanence and the
epistemic limits this entails need not be an acknowledgement of a
weakness; it can also be seen as an openness to contingency, an embracing of creativity.

5. Conclusion: vulnerability and virtue

I have so far discussed three themes of human life: it is temporally
finite, existentially limited, and subject to contingency; I based
those features on a 'facts of life' framework, articulating vulnerability
and dependence on others. Here I return to the notion of vulnerability, which will allow us to connect the three themes and offer concluding remarks.

The first feature of vulnerability is its universal nature. We are all
vulnerable, to a degree, and share important vulnerabilities (e.g. to
illness, pain and death), although some people are more vulnerable
than others in important ways, as I discuss below (Carel, 2016a;
Carel and Kidd, forthcoming). Vulnerability is present as a constant
possibility (a 'fact of life'), but it is also uniquely enacted in each
person's case. Social, economic, legal, and political conditions will
make some persons more vulnerable than others and therefore
subject to the vulnerabilising effects of e.g. illness, disability,
sexism, ageism, racism, ableism and other forms of social injustice
and discrimination (Carel and Kidd, forthcoming; for an in-depth
case study see Tremain, 2021).

A second feature of vulnerability is that it is never elected: no one
chooses to become vulnerable to disease, natural disaster, accident, or
violence. But nonetheless becoming vulnerabilised has the power to
profoundly transform us – for example, through the edifying
powers of illness (Kidd, 2012), the reflective coping that adversity
demands (Carel, 2018), or the posttraumatic growth afforded by
trauma (Haidt, 2006; Carel, 2016a, ch. 6).

Despite the sharedness of vulnerability and it being a 'fact of life', it
is often unevenly distributed, giving rise to social and other kinds of

injustice. In other words, vulnerability is both shared as a feature of human existence, and lived in highly specific ways by each person. The term 'vulnerability' has become common in these pandemic times because of the labelling of some groups and people as 'vulnerable' to covid-19.

However, as Shelley Tremain (2021) points out, the term can mask, rather than reveal, what it denotes. I therefore proposed, with Ian Kidd, to use Tremain's term 'vulnerabilisation' to articulate the important claim that one *becomes vulnerabilised* by the actions of others, institutional failings, and broad political processes and life events (Carel and Kidd, forthcoming). We use the term 'vulnerabilised persons' to pick out a large and diverse group of people who suffer situational vulnerabilities, those which were 'caused or exacerbated by the personal, social, political, economic, or environmental situations of individuals or social groups' (Mackenzie et al., 2014, p. 7). Such situations may be brief or prolonged and episodic or continuous right up to the level of institutionalisation. These could be, for example, persons with chronic ill health (somatic or mental), those deprived of proper education, those with learning disabilities, people who have suffered adverse early childhood events, such as abuse, neglect, or frequent placement moves, neurodiverse persons, persons living in poverty and deprivation, those who are elderly and frail, and those traumatised by political or economic circumstances, in ways that affect their life opportunities and conduct.

This is not an exhaustive list, but an indication of the diversity of this group. This partial list demonstrates that vulnerabilisation is complex, its sources varied and diverse, and its effects on one's life far-ranging. Moreover, since the causes and forms of vulnerabilisation are many and complicated, we need a nuanced taxonomy. Consider, for instance, that vulnerablisation can take many different forms, like creating, intensifying, exploiting, threatening, or making salient one's vulnerabilities.

We call members of this group 'vulnerabilised' rather than 'vulnerable' because – following Tremain's (2021) important observation, these individuals are *made vulnerable* by circumstances – political, economic, medical, educational, legal, and so on – that are beyond their control, but which impact on their lives in profound and sustained ways. Tremain sees vulnerability as neither natural nor intrinsic to certain individuals. She writes: 'rather than a prediscursive inherent human trait, vulnerability is a contextually specific social phenomenon whose politically potent and artifactual character could be recognized and acknowledged if feminist philosophers (among others) were to take up Foucault's idea of "eventalization"' (Tremain, 2021).

One is not born vulnerabilised, but rather becomes vulnerabilised through social, legal, and personal processes. All humans are susceptible to such vulnerabilisation and therefore vulnerability is a general feature of human existence. Given that we may each at any point become vulnerable, we need to incorporate this vulnerability as a deeply embedded feature of our life, including it in any discussion of the good life or of the meaning of life. The 'facts of life' ought not to exclude the possibility of flourishing, because flourishing can, and often does, happen against a backdrop that is non-ideal. Flourishing should be possible even to imperfect, limited human forms of life (Carel, 2016b). This is not an attempt to cover up or minimise the powerful effects and profound damage that can be inflicted by vulnerabilisation, for example, by falling ill. Rather, it illuminates the possibility that moral excellence and perhaps other kinds of flourishing are possible even under conditions that are far from ideal and even with limited resources and personal capacities.

All lives are imperfect but some are more so; this fact entails crucial social and political commitments, as has been spelled out in detail in the social justice literature (for a discussion see Carel and Kidd forthcoming). We shouldn't overlook the possibility of flourishing despite diminished capacities and vulnerabilities. We ought to ameliorate and reduce vulnerabilisation and vulnerability, whilst avoiding unnecessarily narrowing the space of flourishing (ibid.; Carel, 2016b).

This paper offered a framework that takes seriously the facts of life, respects contingency, understands limits, and attends to vulnerability. I presented the life cycle view which enables pluralism within a life to reveal the different capacities and characteristics of the different stages of life. Rather than looking to the vulnerabilities or deficiencies of infancy or old age, I suggest that each developmental stage has corresponding virtues and these ought to be studied and recognised in any discussion of the value, meaning or structure of life (Carel, 2016b).

The life cycle view fits neatly into the 'facts of life' framework, that takes our vulnerability to affliction and accident and our dependence on others to be key features of life. That dependence, central also to the life cycle view, is not a weakness or negativity but an articulation of the deep social bonds inherent in human life. The limits spelled out by the 'facts of life' are perhaps mostly acutely reflected in human mortality, or temporal finitude. Human mortality structures human life by seeing us as 'being towards death'. This offers us the helpful contrast between 'being able to be' (life) and 'being unable to be' (death or anxiety) but also the parallels between the inability to be within life (*Angst*) and death. Finally, I articulated the role of contingency in human life and how individual decision-making and choices encounter contingency, going beyond a rigid view of contingency as 'fate' or what one stands helplessly before. I enlisted a second meaning of *ephēmeros* to examine what it means to be 'day creatures' who are subject to the changing conditions of a mutable present, providing an account of contingency's central role in human life, endeavours, and wellbeing.

Vulnerability, finitude, contingency, limitations, and incapacity are constitutive of the human condition. They are conditions of possibility for human life as we know it. All humans are vulnerable at the start and end of life, and many were, or will be, vulnerable or vulnerabilised at some point in their life. Such vulnerability both requires and tests virtues such as fortitude, creativity, patience, resilience, and acceptance and often requires us to be adaptive and creative in responding to life's contingencies. When we face our own vulnerability, or that of others (e.g. by caring for someone who is ill or dying) we are provided with an exuberant opportunity to exhibit excellence by responding well to adversity. Being vulnerable is a challenge, and can be a disruption or crisis; illness is a paradigmatic and near-universal case of such disruption. It is also morally demanding: it requires us to attend to bodily failure and death, to acknowledge our limits and finitude, to recognise our inability to control external events and to fully reveal our dependence on others.

Such moral, existential, and personal labour is not only a cost but also an opportunity: moral and other kinds of excellence surely must include excellence displayed in one's response to adversity. So points of vulnerability such as ageing and illness are not just practical problems but challenges that require moral, existential, and personal resources, in order to reflectively cope with our finitude, contingency, vulnerability and dependence. The absence of what we take to be essential components of a human life form does not preclude the possibility of moral excellence, as we can see in Primo Levi's (1979) account in *The Truce*, of a fellow inmate at Auschwitz, attending to a sick man:

> [Charles] lifted Lakmaker from the ground with the tenderness of a mother, cleaned him as best as possible with straw taken from the mattress and lifted him into the remade bed in the only position in which the unfortunate fellow could lie. He scraped the floor with a scrap of tin-plate, diluted a little chloramine and finally spread disinfectant over everything, including himself. I judged his self-sacrifice by the tiredness which I would have had to overcome in myself to do what he had done.

The absence of resources and capacities can result in deep and signifi-cant instantiations of virtue, so it is not merely those who are cogni-tively and emotionally well-equipped, those who have much, who can act virtuously, as we can see in Levi's description. Illness and other deprivations do not preclude moral virtue. Adversity can be edifying and such edification through hardship is a significant transformative feature of human life. So the final calculus is not one that prefers a long life, a life without adversity, or a life free of suffering and limits, but that sees a life which includes some adversity as one that seizes opportunities for transformation, change, personal growth, posttraumatic growth, and reflective coping.

Pindar's eighth Pythian, in which the term '*ephēmeros*' appears, is an ode to victory strangely permeated with descriptions of loss, falling, and the intermittent nature of success (Lefkowitz, 1977). After descriptions of combat, wrestling, and other conflict, the ode moves to the famous line: 'Day-creatures [*ephēmeros*]! What is any one, and what is any one not? Man is a shadow in a dream' (Fränkel's (1946) translation).[8] While Matthew Cosgrove (2014, p. 12) takes the line to be an early articulation of Platonic ontology, the line can also be read as an acknowledgement of human fallibility and vulnerability to contingency. We are vulnerable, and perhaps 'all accident', but our accidental, vulnerable lives open a space for possibility, transformation, and growth.[9]

References

David Benatar, *The Human Predicament. A Candid Guide to Life's Biggest Questions* (Oxford: Oxford University Press, 2017).
Jay Bernstein, 'Trust: on the real but almost always unnoticed, ever-changing foundation of ethical life', *Metaphilosophy* 42 (2011), 395–416.
W. Blattner, 'The concept of death in *Being and Time*', *Man and World* 27 (1994) 49–70.
Havi Carel, *Life and death in Freud and Heidegger* (New York: Rodopi, 2006a).
Havi Carel, 'Moral and epistemic ambiguity in *Oedipus Rex*', *Janus Head* 9 (2006b), 91–109.

[8]   Or: 'Creatures of a day. What is someone? What is no one? A shadow's dream is a human being' (Lefkowitz (1977) working translation).
[9]   I thank Michael Hauskeller for inviting me to the 'Meaning in Life and the Knowledge of Death' conference which took place online in July 2021, and for his helpful comments on this paper. I also thank Ian James Kidd who offered his thoughts in response to a draft.

Havi Carel

Havi Carel, 'Temporal finitude and finitude of possibility: the double meaning of death in *Being and Time*', *International Journal of Philosophical Studies*, 15 (2007a), 541–56.

Havi Carel, 'Can I be ill and happy?', *Philosophia* 35 (2007b), 95–110.

Havi Carel, *Phenomenology of illness*, (Oxford: Oxford University Press, 2016a).

Havi Carel, 'Virtue without excellence, excellence without health', *Proceedings of the Aristotelian Society Supplementary Volume* 90 (2016b), 237–53.

Havi Carel, *Illness: the cry of the flesh* (3rd edition) (London: Routledge, 2018).

Havi Carel and Ian James Kidd, 'Expanding transformative experience', *European Journal of Philosophy* 28 (2019), 199–213.

Havi Carel, and Ian James Kidd, 'Vulnerabilised persons in illness and disability', *Journal of Philosophy of disability* (Forthcoming).

Matthew Cosgrove, What are 'true' *doxai* worth to Parmenides? Essaying a fresh look at his cosmology, *Oxford Studies in Ancient Philosophy*, 46 (2014) 1–32.

Barbara Ehrenreich, *Smile or die: how positive thinking fooled America and the world*, (London: Granta Books, 2010).

Epictetus, *The works of Epictetus.*, Trans. T. W. Higginson (Boston: Little, Brown and co, 1891).

Hermann Fränkel, 'Man's "ephēmeros" nature according to Pindar and others', *Transactions and Proceedings of the American Philological Association*, 77 (1946) 131–45.

Tom Froese, Matthew Broome, Havi Carel, Clara Humpston, Alice Malpass, Tomoari Mori, Matthew Ratcliffe, Jamila Rodrigues and Federico Sangati, 'The Pandemic Experience: A Corpus of Subjective Reports on Life During the First Wave of COVID-19 in the UK, Japan, and Mexico', *Frontiers in Public Health* (2021) https://doi.org/10.3389/fpubh.2021.725506.

Carol Gilligan, *Mapping the moral domain: a contribution of women's thinking to psychological theory and education*, (Cambridge, Massachusetts: Harvard University Press, 1989).

Thomas Gould, 'The Innocence of Oedipus: the Philosophers on *Oedipus the King*'. In *Sophocles' Oedipus Rex*, Bloom Harold (ed.), (New York: Chelsea House, 1988) 49–63.

Jonathan Haidt, *The happiness hypothesis,* (London: William Heinemann, 2006).

Lawrence Hatab, 'Ethics and finitude: Heideggerian contributions to moral philosophy', *International Philosophical Quarterly* 35(4) (1995), 403–417.

Michael Hauskeller, 'Ephemeroi – Human Vulnerability, Transhumanism, and the Meaning of Life', *Scientia et Fides* 7 (2019), 9–21.

Martin Heidegger, *Being and time*, (London: Blackwell, 1962 [1927]).

Martin Heidegger, *The Fundamental Concepts of Metaphysics: World, Finitude, Solitude*, (Bloomington IA: Indiana University Press, 1996 [1983]).

Herodotus, *The Histories*, Trans. A. D. Godley, (Cambridge MA: Harvard University Press, 1920).

Sarah Blaffer Hrdy, *Mother nature*, (New York: Pantheon Books, 1999).

Michael Inwood, *A Heidegger Dictionary* (Oxford: Blackwell, 1999).

Ian James Kidd, 'Can illness be edifying?', *Inquiry* 55 (2012), 496–520.

H.D.F. Kitto, *Sophocles, Dramatist and Philosopher*, (Oxford: Oxford University Press, 1958).

Mary Lefkowitz, 'Pindar's Pythian 8', *The Classical Journal* 72 (1977), 209–221.

Primo Levi, *If this is a man & the truce*, (London: Abacus, 1979).

Alasdair MacIntyre, *Dependent, Rational Animals: Why Human Beings Need the Virtues* (London: Duckworth, 1999).

Catriona Mackenzie, Wendy Rogers, and Susan Dodds, *Vulnerability: new essays in ethics and feminist philosophy*, (Oxford: Oxford University Press, 2014).

S. Mulhall, 'Human mortality: Heidegger on how to portray the impossible possibility of Dasein', in H. Dreyfus & M. Wrathall, *The Blackwell companion to Heidegger*, (London: Blackwell, 2005) 297–310.

Thomas Nagel, 'Death', *Noûs* 4 (1970), 73–80.

Martha Nussbaum, *The fragility of goodness: Luck and ethics in Greek tragedy and philosophy*, (Cambridge: Cambridge University Press, 2001).

L. A. Paul, *Transformative experience*, (Oxford: Oxford University Press, 2014).

Sarah Ruddick, *Maternal thinking*, (New York: Ballantine Books, 1989).

Sophocles, *The Three Theban Plays*. trans. Robert Fagles with an introduction by Bernard Knox, (New York & London: Penguin Books, 1984).

Alison Stone, *Being born*, (Oxford: Oxford University Press, 2019).

Thomas Szanto and Dermot Moran, *Phenomenology of Sociality: Discovering the 'We'*, (London: Routledge, 2016).

Havi Carel

Shelley Tremain, 'Philosophy of Disability, Conceptual Engineering, and the Nursing-Home Industrial Complex in Canada', *International Journal of Critical Diversity Studies* (in press, 2021).

Bernard Williams, 'The Makropulos case: reflections on the tedium of immortality', In *Problems of the Self*, (Cambridge: Cambridge University Press, 1973) 82–100.

The Meaning of Pain and the Pain of Meaning: A Bio-Hermeneutical Inquiry

TEODORA MANEA

Abstract
My main interest here is to look at pain as a sign of the body that something is wrong. I will argue that there is a meaning of pain before and after an illness is diagnosed. An illness contains its own semantic paradigm, but the pain before the diagnosis affects the pace of life, not only by limiting our interactions, but also as a struggle with its meaning and a reminder of mortality.

My main approach is what I call bio-hermeneutics, an extension of medical hermeneutics branching out from the Continental hermeneutical tradition. As such, I will explore the connection between pain and language, temporality, dialectics, and ontology. Given the centrality of language in constructing the meaning of pain, my analysis is informed by the semantics (looking at pain metaphors), syntax (pain as incoherence), and pragmatics (pain as companion) of expressing pain.

The last section explores the meaning of pain in connection with death, as *memento mori*. Revisiting an old definition of philosophy as *melete thanatou*, or 're-hearsal of death', I will reflect on the difficulty of finding meaning not only for pain, but also for death as cessation of all existential possibilities.

> To learn about value and proportion we need to honour illness, and ultimately to honour death. (Frank, 2002, p. 120)

1. Methodological clarifications

The symmetry of the title was inspired by an ontological connection between *pain* and *meaning* that I noticed during my work in medical settings. As a medical interpreter, I had to lend a voice to people in pain and to witness how pain was transferred into stories, where both patients and physicians added elements of meaning and negotiated semantic possibilities.

I will not talk here about 'spiritual' pain, given the complexity of this area and the different approaches needed for its comprehension. Also, for the purposes of this text, I need to launch a *via negativa*[1]

---

[1] I understand *via negativa* in this context as a way of thinking focusing on what something is *not*, in order to keep as much as possible from the

doi:10.1017/S1358246121000291   © The Royal Institute of Philosophy and the contributors 2021
Royal Institute of Philosophy Supplement **90** 2021

Teodora Manea

attempt of sorting out my topic, to not get lost in the richness of cultural representations around the concept of pain. I will not consider self-inflicted or anticipated pain, like the pain that we know we will experience after a new physical activity, or after an operation. The reason is that in these cases, there is a direct causal correlation between activity/fact and pain that carries a certain semantic or at least an explanatory platform. I will also exclude child-birth pain, given that it is 'expected' or anticipated to a certain extent, and also it abounds in cultural significations. Without diminishing the excluded types of pain, my interest here is in exploring how we describe, assess, and associate the meaning of pain that signals some problems or malfunctions of the body before we know what exactly causes it.

From this perspective – regrading a pain-signal as a semantic problem that starts a heuristic process – I am interested in constructions of meaning ranging from 'worrying pain' to extreme experiences of pain. I would like to keep previous philosophical thoughts on this topic as a safety net and adventure into the world of medicine, where the immediate presence of pain opens new possibilities of reflection. For this reason, I will use medical narratives on pain as the main source of reflection. The testimonies of pain I use stem mainly from two sources: Arthur Frank's book *At the Will of the Body*, in which he describes his experience with cancer, and Peter Dorward's collection of stories inspired by his work as a general practitioner, *The Human Kind*.

2. Bio-hermeneutics

My main intention is to look at pain as a sign of the body that something is wrong. I will argue that there is a meaning of pain before and after an illness[2] is diagnosed. The diagnosis gives pain a certain meaning: an organ is damaged; a nerve is firing in a weird way, a certain disease takes over the body, a tumour is growing and pressing on other organs etc. An illness contains its own semantic paradigm. But the pain before the illness, before the diagnosis, brings the

---

content of an unexplored topic before fixing it in certain definition or determination.

[2] Disease is normally understood as a pathological process, deviation from a biological norm (see Boyd, 2000). Illness is the subjective experience of a disease. Sickness is the role negotiated with society (see the concept of sick role in Parsons (1951)).

The Meaning of Pain and the Pain of Meaning

possibility of 'something wrong' into the pace of life. My interest here is in examining how people cope with it, how they construct their lives around unexplained pain.

The complex semantics of pain and the efforts to integrate it into discourse requires introducing what I call *bio-hermeneutics*. In contrast with *medical* hermeneutics[3], bio-hermeneutics is not how science or medicine make sense of biological processes. It is how people make sense of inaccessible biological facts that manifest themselves as symptoms, and primarily here, as pain. More than that, bio-hermeneutics should include our interpretation of pain and illness of other living creatures from our environment: a suffering pet or an injured wild animal will require our attention and assessment and influence our actions. John Nessa, writing about medical hermeneutics, excludes veterinary medicine: 'human medicine is, unlike veterinary medicine, an enterprise where the object is an individual, a person, not a biological being only. To understand a man is to understand a being who understands himself' (Nessa, 1996, p. 372). While the second part of the quote is accurate, non-human animals are not usually mere 'biological beings' either. In veterinary practices, veterinarians have to deal with pet owners who care a lot about their pets, present their worries, expectations and their own interpretations of their animals' illness or suffering. Even farm animals are not beyond farmers' intentions and interpretations. It can be true that certain animals are not strongly included in the web-of-significance for a certain human life, but bio-hermeneutics should apply to those who are in our proximity: a pet, a horse, animals in zoos or conservation areas, many other species enacted as 'pests' etc. When someone takes the 'sad' houseplant to a garden centre to be 'diagnosed', this opens a hermeneutic chain of interpretation. Bio-hermeneutics opens a wider perspective for the understanding of our relationship with our *living* environment and how we make sense of it and interpret its problems, from pets and houseplants to forests and ultimately to the pressing and present understanding of our planet in the light of climate change.

Bio-hermeneutics deals with the *symptomatic reading*[4] of pain as a sign. Medicine tries to reveal 'biological *facts*', but ultimately all it can

---

[3] See Svenaeus (2001).

[4] 'Symptomatic reading' is a concept coined by Friedrich Nietzsche in *Twilight of the Idols* (1889) and used in the Continental tradition of hermeneutics (e.g. Louis Althusser). It focuses on underlying presuppositions, especially the ones that are hidden for different reasons (from cultural taboos to ideological constraints).

offer is an *interpretation* of these. However, there are incongruences between medical and personal interpretations of illnesses and also of pain. John Nessa, from the perspective of medical semiotics (inspired by Peirce and Saussure) agrees that 'diagnoses depend heavily on the doctors' interpretations, since diagnosing is naming, structuring of reality. None of the diagnoses are in essence *facts* belonging to the external world, but linguistic and cognitive structuring of reality, ways of interpreting experiences and perceptions' (Nessa, 1996, p. 371). Nessa distinguishes between a *scientific* and a *hermeneutic* mode of understanding, where the latter includes personal and interpersonal dimensions of meaning and values that are imbedded in the communication process (Nessa, 1996, p. 373).

From its origin, medicine had to interpret signs and symptoms of the body. Therefore, as an art, medicine has always been a hermeneutic process. However, modernity and the Cartesian representation of the body-machine led medicine towards a scientific paradigm of explanation (Gadamer, 1996, pp. 6-8) while hermeneutic aspects became marginal. Hermeneutics as a discipline was designed for the interpretation of religious and literary texts. It was only the existential analytic of Heidegger and Gadamer's late work that re-established the centrality of hermeneutics for the process of understanding how things *are*, therefore for *ontology*. Although Heidegger wrote about *care* and *angst*, about the centrality of experience, *authenticity*, and *being-towards-death*, he did not attempt to develop a *medical* hermeneutics. Gadamer first reconnected hermeneutics and medicine in order to understand the 'enigma of health'. Contemporary attempts to recognise hermeneutical aspects of medicine include Donna Orange's hermeneutics of clinical practice (Orange, 2011), Fredrik Svenaeus's hermeneutics of medicine (Svenaeus, 2018), and Havi Carel's phenomenology of health (Carel, 2016). Even if hermeneutics of medicine can restore the centrality of meaning and interpretation in the bio-sciences, the widening of hermeneutics towards other interpretative processes within our living environment needs some basic interpretation scaffolding. Analysing the interpretation theories of Schleiermacher, Dilthey, Heidegger, and Gadamer, Richard Palmer (1969, pp. 242-53) proposed thirty theses on interpretation. Many of them are appliable only to literary texts. The main points presented in these theses and useful for my project of a bio-hermeneutics are:

1.   The hermeneutical experience is intrinsically *historical* and *linguistic*. Language articulates meaning, and temporality cannot be eluded from interpretation.

The Meaning of Pain and the Pain of Meaning

2.   The hermeneutical experience is *ontological*, as it discloses a specific way of being of things/people/animals.

3.   The hermeneutical experience is a *disclosure of truth* and is *dialectical*.

'The emergence of truth in hermeneutical experience comes in that encounter with negativity which is intrinsic to experience; in this case the experience comes as "aesthetic moment" or "language event". Truth is not *conceptual*, not *fact* – it *happens*' (Palmer, 1969, p. 245). For Palmer, the encounter with negativity broadens and illuminates self-understanding. Pain and illness can be regarded as experiences of negativity. The 'disclosure of truth' is for the case of pain, the diagnosis. Many medical tests function as *exclusion* of certain hypotheses. Patient's *symptoms* and even medical *signs*[5] are for the vast majority of cases not univocal. Thus, a *differential diagnosis* becomes necessary as the process of differentiating between two or more conditions which share similar signs or symptoms. A disease is normally identified after excluding other possible maladies. It requires a delicate dialectic process, where the negation of one possibility – usually done by a test result or by an imaging process – opens space for the exploration of a new hypothesis and so on.

The dialectic movement of interpretation is generated by the fact that the vast majority of medical signs and symptoms are not *pathognomonic*[6], meaning they are not characteristic of a particular disease, or not beyond any doubt. When a sign or symptom is specific to a disease, it can be used to make a quick diagnosis. A univocal connection between a sign and a disease is for example the presence and location of 'Koplik spots' in the mouth as a pathognomonic sign of measles (Markel, 2015). But many other symptoms, and even medical signs are not specific. An abdominal pain a patient complains about can be anything from appendicitis to cancer. Similarly, a cough or high temperature can be considered medical signs, but again they can be present in a wide array of diseases from viral to bacterial infections. The occurrence of more signs and symptoms together make the process of diagnosis easier because they can add to the picture of a certain disease. The medical hermeneutic process of diagnosis is the subsumption of a particular case under the generalities of a disease (Gadamer, 1996, p. 19). The patient's personal and subjective

---

[5]   Medical language differentiates between *signs* and *symptoms*: *symptoms* are normally *reported* by the patient and not measured, and *signs* are observed by the physician at the bedside (Nessa, 1996).

[6]   From the Greek πάθος pathos (disease) and γνώμων gnomon (indicator).

Teodora Manea

experience of illness is confronted with the anonymity of the clinical apparatus (Gadamer, 1996, p. 20) designed to identify what is 'out of place' (Gadamer, 1996, p. 129). However, there is an essential difference Gadamer missed between what is 'out of place' in terms of medical semiotics (e.g.: a higher or lower value of a blood test, the presence of a tumour) and how this 'out of place' interferes with subjective, personal, historical experience and interpretation of a disease.

The Hippocratic tradition of medicine recognised the *temporal* dimension of a symptom, articulating past (*anamnesis*), present (*diagnosis*) and future (*prognosis*) (Honkasalo, 1991). The insertion of temporality in the hermeneutic analysis of symptoms accentuates the confluence of personal history as *curriculum vitae* with the history of something else, an alien state or entity (virus, bacteria, abnormal growth) that inhabits the body. An *anamnesis* (medical history or case history) regards only the history of this alien state of the body. As an example, the present-day pandemic statistics register patients who have died within 28 days of a positive Covid test. In this case, the history of the disease takes precedence – as public interest – over the personal history of the people who have died. At the beginning of the Covid pandemic, especially when Italy was ravished by the virus, the age of patients was highlighted in the news, somehow leading people to believe that especially old people are at risk. The point here is that although it relates to the same body and person, a patient's medical and personal history (other than 'age' as a further medical criterion) is rarely considered in their existentially relevant conjunction.

Coming back to the connection between pain and the experience of the world, Honkasalo's ethnographic study analysed the spatial experience of the body in chronic pain and how pain as a way of being in the world (referring to Merleau-Ponty) limits the spatial experience and interaction, by shrinking, distorting, and circumscribing the world of those affected (Honkasalo, 1998). Even if chronic pain is normally different (not always diagnosed) from the unexplained pain I focus on, it is relevant for the understanding of pain as an experience that limits our world and with it our existential possibilities.

In the following sections, I will talk about how this alienation – focusing on pain – is metaphorically reflected in language and how the different rhythms of body-engulfed-by-illness and body-as-used-to-be creates existential incoherence.

3. Pain and meaning

The case of undiagnosed pain outside of the diagnosis-paradigm remains the most fascinating type of pain from a hermeneutical perspective. Without diagnosis, pain remains a symptom outside comprehension, and somehow its ontological status cannot be disclosed. Peter Dorward, a general practitioner, recalled one of his patients, Moira, and her confusion about undiagnosed pain: '"What I don't understand", she says, angry with me, as she often is, 'is what's actually wrong with me? Is it arthritis like the scan says? Or is this fibromyalgia, like the achey joint specialist says? Or is it chronic pain like the pain person says? Or is it all in my head? Like you seem to be saying? Or do you all just not have an effing clue?"' (Dorward, 2018, p. 317). The failure of a consistent diagnosis to explain what is 'out of place' somehow cannot articulate pain's temporal existence either, and with this ontological non-situationality, the very existence of a symptom is questionable. Without diagnosis there is no *present* and no prognosis for the *future*, so that Moira wonders if someone really believes that her pain exists. This example shows the importance of spatio-temporal situatedness and understanding of a symptom.

To contrast unexplained with 'situated' pain, childbirth offers a good example. In this case pain has a meaning, it is expected and connected with labour and birth. It has a location and a duration, and nobody is contesting its ontological status, or its 'objective' nature. Yet, even with expected pain, the intensity of it during childbirth brings many women to a 'regression', to an 'animal' stage, which comes with the incapacity to keep rational, or keep control over one's body. In this extreme case, pain and reason reveal themselves as incompatible. Intense pain can become a state where meaning dissolves.

To counter the aporia of pain, and to re-install a kind of order or criteria, pain-scales were invented. Their use is based on the assumption that there are *degrees* of pain, and people can assess and describe the *quantity* or *quality* of pain (e.g. the McGill pain questionnaire as one of the most complex pain assessment tools (Melzack, 1975)). Most certainly, everybody who has ever complained about pain to a physician has heard the question: 'On a scale from 1 to 10, how would you rate your pain?' This is an attempt to situate pain, even if only on a numerical, imaginary scale. While pain in different scalar stages opens the possibility of meaning, absolute pain dissolves meaning. Physicians search for the quantity of pain mainly for the medical triage. Urgency and gravity are established by the quantification and qualification of pain as a symptom. And yet, the use of traditional Aristotelian categories to assess such a complex human experience – as being in pain – might be inadequate from the point of view of an

Teodora Manea

existential analytic[7]. Categories can reify pain, transpose it from the private experience to an *object* of medical intervention. Following an existential analytic, pain as human experience should be examined using existentials as *fear, care, meaning* and *being-towards-death*. Under such a frame, pain might reveal its power to absorb the whole human being, or to distort every other experience.

The algorithm of tests and interventions based on pain-scales evokes another actor: the *painkiller*. The concept of the painkiller is highly metaphorical and specific to the English language. In German, medicines against pain are called *Schmerzmittel*, *analgésiques* in French, *antidolorifici* in Italian. In these examples, the concepts describe something *against* pain, a negation of *algos/dolor* (pain in Old Greek/Latin), but none of them has the power of *killing* the pain. Now, it is questionable if painkillers really *kill* pain (in the sense of completely extinguishing it), or if they just diminish or mask it. Paracetamol, for example, blocks chemical messengers in the brain that tell us we have pain. Ibuprofen reduces hormones that cause pain and swelling in the body. But they will of course work only for specific types of pain caused by inflammation. In many cases, over-the-counter painkillers do not work. Medicine has constantly refined substances that can alleviate pain. An interesting example are *opiates*. 'This is how opiates work: They don't take away the pain, they render you *indifferent* to it. Which tells you something important: in this context at least, the nature of pain lies not in sensation, but in the anguish that it brings' (Dorward, 2018, p. 294). The interpretation of how opiates work reveals the centrality of meaning associated with pain. *Indifference* points not towards quantity and quality of pain, but towards existential aspects like angst and meaning.

The difficulty to assess, understand and address pain in its diffuse nature makes it hard to comprehend pain through a phenomenological approach. Pain is in many respects (or at least certain types of pain) *aphanological*, faceless, hard to define and locate. Arthur Frank, while describing his pain before he was diagnosed with cancer, emphasises the *facelessness* of pain: 'pain has no face because it is not *alien*. It is from myself. Pain is my body signalling that something is wrong. It is the body talking to itself, not the rumblings of an external god' (Frank, 2002, p. 13). The internal dialogue of the body with itself is felt, but not comprehensible in the way rational

[7]   See Martin Heidegger's distinction between *categories* and *existentials* in Heidegger (2010, pp. 44-45).

discourse is. The pain signals are not univocal, they are polyphonic and cacophonic, leading to the greatest incoherence between body and mind. The body's internal talk can only be approximated by language, and not totally expressed. For Frank, the strong sedatives he took to be able to sleep made pain gain a *form* and a *face* as nightmares (Frank, 2002, p. 32). But even the image provided by his nightmares seemed to be preferable to an aphanological experience. The ultimate act of giving pain a *face* transforms it into something else, into a kind of *companion* one has to accept in one's life.

In order to surpass these difficulties in addressing pain in a phenomenological way, I am adopting a different perspective, focusing on pain's linguistic manifestation. Elaine Scarry, in her book *The Body in Pain* (Scarry, 1985), argues that the concept of pain is something that resists language or, even more, it destroys language by transforming speech into grunts, moans and cries. Although Scarry is right in noticing the capacity of extreme pain to dissolve language, people use a wide range of metaphors to describe pain. I will examine the language of pain according to the triad of *semantics* (enquiring metaphors of pain), *syntax* (looking at the incoherence generated by pain) and *pragmatics* (how people deal with chronic pain).

3.1. Semantics: Metaphors of pain

Dorward noticed that people 'become artists, masters of self-expression when it comes to the communication of this urgent thing: *I am in pain*' (Dorward, 2018, p. 312). He talks about the negotiation of pain metaphors between doctors and patients. Pain is sometimes expressed in terms of electricity: it feels like an *electric shock*. Older representations of neuropathic pain described it as *scalding* or *lancinating*: 'at a time when a person might understand what that was, how it felt to be lanced' (Dorward, 2018, p. 312). In the 19th century, pain was described as 'fury'. Joanna Burke, in *The Story of Pain* (Burke, 2014), advances the hypothesis that the metaphors used to describe pain have a profound impact on the way we *feel* pain. In other words, *language* influences the *experience* of pain. The metaphors she selected and analysed show *historical* and cultural changes in the sensation of pain (Burke, 2014, p. 53). Burke classified pain metaphors and situated them historically (Burke, 2014, pp. 60-65): pain as something moving inside the body (1770s), something that ruptures, shatters or rips apart the body (1960s), weapons breaching the integrity of the body (1890s), pain as a weight or a colour (1930s) etc. Burke explains the changes in metaphorical representation as being mainly influenced by three factors: changes in how we understand the physiological body, developments in the external environment, and ideological shifts (Burke, 2014, p. 66). The configurations of the social world contribute to shape not only in the way we communicate internal experiences, but also in the way we feel them.

Even before diagnosis, patients make efforts to integrate the expression of pain into a shared paradigm of understanding and to make the fuzzy, inchoate internal experience more concrete. Metaphors of pain have their phylogeny, which goes hand in hand with the science of the time and with social practices. For example, the word 'gout' comes from French *gouttelette*, which means droplet. 'It alludes to drops of molten lead splashing on the skin: the metaphor communicating vividly the common understanding shared then by the doctor and his patient, *but not shared now*, of how a drop of molten lead splashed on the last joint of the big toe would *feel*. "Gout" is a word and a metaphor that has lost its ground' (Dorward, 2018, p. 313).

To be able to communicate pain, to mitigate the subjective experience of it, people need to share language and cultural assumptions, and to find a common emotional connection. Pain is enacted through metaphors, gestures, grunts, and noises, and this display made Dorward call it the *theatrics of pain*. Physicians have to interpret it and face the difficulty of being situated between the 'evidence-based medicine' and the theatre of human expressions. The theatrics of pain and its metaphors constantly pendle between the individual *part* and the *whole*. To understand this complex picture and movement, Dorward (2018, p. 323) noticed that we are always *social beings* in pain. How we experience and understand pain depends on our history, beliefs and culture. The *theatrics* of pain is actually the need to put a face, a mask,[8] to something that is aphanological by its very nature.

3.2. Syntax: Pain as incoherence

I use the term syntax here to refer to the idea of order, rhythm and coherence that we feel not only in the use of language – impossible without its grammar – but also in the use of a healthy body that integrates seamlessly into our routine or generally into our rhythm of life.

---

[8]   In the Ancient Greek theatre, *prosopon* had the meaning 'face' and actor's 'mask'. From *prosopon*, the term *persona* was derived.

The Meaning of Pain and the Pain of Meaning

A healthy body has its internal 'invisible harmony' mentioned by Gadamer. Pain is capable not only of breaking this harmony and incapacitating the body, but also of spreading incoherence and engulfing our entire experience of being-in-the-world.

Burke noticed that 'by using metaphors to bring the interior sensation into a knowable, external world, sufferers attempt to impose (and communicate) some kind of order onto their experiences' (Burke, 2014, p. 55). Without communication, the attempt to restore coherence seems to be impossible: Frank experienced the silence and with it the isolation generated by pain, and for him this isolation that actually even increases pain is the beginning of incoherence.

A first aspect of incoherence depicts pain as a *disruption* of life as rhythm. The routine that keeps us anchored in our daily living becomes less and less possible. It also becomes a reminder of death as the final disruption. In the chapter 'Seeing through pain', Frank states that his pain was experienced most at the beginning of the illness, *before* physicians understood what was happening, and 'at the *end*, when the body becomes *unpredictable*' (Frank, 2002, p. 29). Stories of illness are attempts to restore order and coherence, very similar to the process of diagnosis as a way of making sense of pain, of transposing the incoherence of the body into the coherence of a disease description and *prognosis* (as an attempt to *predict* what happens with the body).

In the previous section, I talked about the multitude of words describing pain, from piercing to lancinating. Pain can be *burning* or *stubbing*, but while these words describe how a certain type of pain feels like, they do not describe the *experience* of pain, its debilitating effects. Franks agrees that 'we lack terms to express what it means to live 'in' such pain. Unable to express pain, we come to believe there is nothing to say' (Frank, 2002, pp. 29-30).

A healthy body can be read as a coherent body, with parts working in harmony, sustaining the pace of normal activities that insert us into a certain environment. A body in pain loses its natural rhythm, and with it our future plans or expectations are shadowed. 'Order breaks down and incoherence takes its place' (Frank, 2002, p. 30). Frank, like many other cancer patients experienced pain especially during the night. 'As the tumours took over my body, pain took over my mind. Darkness compounds the isolation and loneliness of pain (...). In darkness the world of those in pain becomes unglued, incoherent' (Frank, 2002, p. 30). For him, as mentioned before, *isolation* is the beginning of *incoherence*. When confronted with something incoherent that escapes understanding, we start to create a mythology of what threatens us, we start putting theatrical masks

Teodora Manea

on a faceless actor who is probably nobody else than an unknown version of the self. The stories we try to create about inexplicable pain are nothing but an attempt to gain coherence. Much has been written about the therapeutic effect of narratives (Charon, 2006). The order of words replaces – or at least tries to mend – the disorder of a body in pain. The narrative efforts here do not concern only what people depict about their pain, but also covers what doctors normally propose as a diagnosis hypothesis. Many times, a diagnosis not supported by bio-medical 'hard evidence' is actually a negotiated story between patients and physicians, as the dialogue between Peter and Moira illustrated above. Not having an answer about the source of pain spreads the incoherence of the body towards the entire world of an individual. World is no longer a possibility of expression and action, but something to bear and to 'cope' with.

Fredrik Svenaeus analysed health as *homelikeness* and illness as *un-homelikeness* (Svenaeus, 2011) touching on Heidegger's idea of being or not being at *home* in the world. As *Dasein*, we are thrown into the world, constantly trying to find an attunement to the world. In this sense, 'world' refers to what we share with the other human beings as our living space. But there is another meaning of 'world' I will use here, as *my world*, meaning my representation, understanding and experiences of the 'big world'. This is close to what Heidegger referred to as *poetic living*. The 'big world' can never be entirely *my* world, because it includes people and places that I will never meet, visit or experience, while my world is a unique form of *cosmos* created by my experiences, interactions and representations. We constantly make efforts to define and redefine ourselves in order to maintain and fuel the harmony of our micro-world. What we care about – from the 'presentation of self' to our house, garden, and relations with others – depends upon the invisible harmony of the body 'at home'. 'At the moment when the incoherence of illness and pain makes it seem that all you have lived for has been taken away or is about to be lost, you can find another coherence in which to live' (Frank, 2002, p. 35). To do this is to create another *cosmos*. From Frank's experience, and not only his, the encounter with beauty[9], the creation of a new order, and a restored coherence of expression are some of the poetic ways of returning to living in our micro-world.

[9] Frank describes what he encountered during one of his sleepless nights: the image of a tree projecting the shadows of its branches against a window as a moment of beauty that changed his experience with illness.

226

The Meaning of Pain and the Pain of Meaning

3.3. Pragmatics: Nietzsche's Dog: Pain as a Companion

In many cases, chronic pain becomes an existential *companion*. Even if the micro-world can be redefined or at least repaired by a fragile sense of order and harmony, pain has to be integrated rather than expelled from one's world.

Nietzsche's personal struggles of dealing with pain brought him to a similar situation: the need to give a face to pain, to move from the aphanological and incoherence towards a degree of visibility or representability. Nietzsche called his pain *dog*, a faithful companion: 'I have given a name to my pain and call it "dog": it is just as faithful, just as obtrusive and shameless, just as entertaining, just as clever as any other dog' (Nietzche, 1910, p. 244). With this act, pain is transformed into a constant life companion, into an *existential companion*. Other representations of pain as a *feminine* companion were mentioned by Burke citing Thomas Smyth, an influential Presbyterian minister (1850s) who 'described how "we walked arm in arm, dwelt in the same house, been fellow lodgers in the same body and occupants of the same bed"' (Burke, 2014, p. 60).

More than giving pain a face, we always try to connect a meaning to it, a meaning that can range from punishment[10] to a heroic view. Nietzsche's reflections on pain transforms it into the *ultimate emancipator of the spirit*, which is not something that necessarily makes us better as a human being, but rather something that makes us look deeper into what our humanity is about. 'It is great pain only, the long slow pain which takes time, by which we are burned as it were with green wood, that compels us philosophers to descend into our ultimate depths, and divest ourselves of all trust, all good-nature, veiling, gentleness, and averageness, wherein we have perhaps formerly installed our humanity. I doubt whether such pain "improves" us; but I know that it *deepens* us' (Nietzche, 1910, p. 7). Pain that deepens us can be regarded as an experience that makes us reflect on the limits and structure of our world, and on new possibilities of finding meaning in activities or things we might have ignored before.

Another meaning of pain for Nietzsche relates to self-preservation. The hurtful essence of pain contains a *message* that Nietzsche put in a

---

[10] It is worth noticing that 'pain' derives – via the Old French *peine* – from the Latin word *poena* meaning 'penalty'. In Middle English pain had the meaning of 'suffering inflicted as punishment for an offence'. See Merriam-Webster Dictionary: https://www.merriam-webster.com/dictionary/pain. Accessed 29 Jul. 2021.

metaphoric way: 'In pain I hear the commanding call of the ship's captain: "Take in sail!" "Man," the bold seafarer, must have learned to set his sails in a thousand different ways, otherwise he could not have sailed long, for the ocean would soon have swallowed him up. We must also know how to live with reduced energy: as soon as pain gives its precautionary signal, it is time to reduce the speed – some great danger, some storm, is approaching, and we do well to "catch" as little wind as possible' (Nietzche, 1910, p. 247). He continues with the glorification of people who do not sail away from pain, but confront it in a courageous way, and even celebrate it. In the contemporary context of a Scottish GP practice, Dorward observed that both patients and their doctors value stoicism. 'People don't want to be a burden, they don't want to seem to be *weak*, or *moaning*, or *dull*' (Dorward, 2018, p. 324). Of course, a stoic presentation of self (Goffman, 1956) might have its advantages in terms of social interactions or even into consolidating a type of narrative people need for themselves. But it remains questionable if the stoic version (where meaning is only *internally* negotiated, not shared with others) has the same healing value as the narrative alternative, which expresses pain through stories. In a similar way to how Moira negotiated with her GP, we often negotiate the meaning of pain with ourselves: 'I fantasized that pain was "just for tonight", that it was *muscular stress* and would be gone tomorrow. This fantasy was fuelled by my fear of what might truly be wrong with me, but it was also supported by what my doctor was telling me' (Frank, 2002, p. 32).

Once pain is identified and understood, it can be regarded as an *ally*, as a warning about body malfunction or the need to change. Even with the discovery of a fatal illness, re-establishing a sense of coherence seems to be the paramount task for regaining meaning in life. The connection between meaning, coherence and beauty reinforces the Pythagorean idea of *cosmos*. Probably the turning point is when a person manages to restore a world ravished by pain to a *cosmos*, a world with a sense of beauty and order. For Frank, this point came with seeing a tree projecting an intricate pattern of light and shadows on his window. The beauty he found was also the possibility of expression: 'Where we see the face of beauty, we are in our proper place, and all becomes coherent' (Frank, 2002, p. 33).

4. Between *memento mori* and μελέτη θανάτου

Pain is incoherence, but an even greater incoherence is death, which is the total disruption of all we know: how can all of this continue to

The Meaning of Pain and the Pain of Meaning

exist if/when I am gone? And yet, while death – as an event – *limits* life, positioning ourselves into its horizon can bring structure and meaning to life. By identifying the limits of an object, we can create its shape. I like to explain it by adding a twist to the famous Aristotelian example of the statue contained in its block of marble: if we imagine death as what sculpts the statue out of an amorphous, banal lump of marble, every cut and blow contributes to the definition of a new shape. By thinking about our finitude, most of us are able to remove the existential debris that covers an authentic self. We think about death as the cessation of all existential possibilities, and in this sense issuing an imperative to develop what is *still* important for us. For that purpose, death paradoxically appears as a *causa efficiens,* an agent that actually contributes to not only the deeper knowledge but also to the *actualisation* of the world. This view contrasts with other ways of thinking about death, for example as an 'experiential black' (Carel, 2016, p. 151), something hard to comprehend from a phenomenological point of view, therefore not in accord with our existential rhythm. The incoherence of illness, pain and death makes it seem that all one has lived for is about to be lost, our *cosmos* faces its irreversible destruction.

Is pain a *memento mori*, a slow burning green wood that brings us to our depths? Is pain, along with death, what we fear most? But while death has its inexorable mystery, pain is the dance of limits, the source of chaos and incoherence, the ultimate crisis of meaning. Pain is a constant reminder of death, but at the same time a link between life and death. Pain makes us fear that we might 'die too early'. And yet pain engrains itself into the way we signify our existence and our finitude. For Carel (2016, p. 150), death is part of the illness experience, it is positioned on its existential horizon, therefore illness is a *memento mori.*

After a serious climbing accident, Dorward remembered moments of extreme pain, where death seemed to be very near: 'Hunched like a beast behind the darkening crags is pain, with his claws and unblinking red eyes, waiting, and beyond him, silent, something quite unknowable, but to you none of that matters now. You are half detached from the world already, huddled and indifferent, chasing after that last remnant of warmth in your core, focused on stillness, not moving, journeying deeper and deeper within' (Dorward, 2018, pp. 287-88). When pain disconnects us from the world we shared with the others, somehow it brings us back to the 'warm core' where we tend to search for something beyond sensation, colour or shape. We don't problematise what happened when we entered the world as much as we talk about death as its symmetrical exit.

Teodora Manea

Romain Rolland in a letter to Freud (written in 1927)[11] coined the term 'oceanic feeling', in which the ego is not separated from the world. Freud interpreted it as a hypothesis about our beginning in early infancy when every perception, colour, and sound reveals and constructs the external world and, through this, separates us from it as 'exteriority'. For Freud, an 'incentive' for separating ourselves from the external world is the feeling of pain and the accompanying desire to avoid it. Without wandering further into the psychoanalytic discourse, we should ask what happens when pain is unavoidable, when it becomes our uninvited companion? Is our personal *cosmos* somewhere between the *oceanic feeling* and the 'external world'? Maybe we should regard birth and death as symmetrical not merely as the beginning and the cessation of an individual life, but as the *unfolding* and *relapsing* of a uniquely articulated *cosmos*.

In my first year of studying philosophy, many years ago, I learned, while reading about Plato's *melete thanatou*[12], that philosophy *prepares* you for death. And yet I had my doubts that the devaluation of the body, or any other wise exercise of distancing us from life can prepare people for death. According to the *Greek-English Lexicon* (Liddell et al., 1996), μελέτη has different meanings including: *care* (for), paying *attention* to something, *practice*, *exercise* and even *rehearsal* (of a discourse). My attention was drawn towards the medical meanings of μελέτη, which include the *threatening symptom* of a disease: "μελέτη καὶ προοίμιον ἐπιληψίας" (symptom and sign of epilepsy).

How can we connect and put together these multiple meanings[13]? Probably all are linked to death as something we need to pay attention

[11] Sigmund Freud discusses the *oceanic feeling* at the beginning of Freud (2002, pp. 4–6).

[12] Plato, *Phaedo*: (80e – 81a) '(...) ἐὰν μὲν καθαρὰ ἀπαλλάττηται, μηδὲν τοῦ σώματος συνεφέλκουσα, ἅτε οὐδὲν κοινωνοῦσα αὐτῷ ἐν τῷ βίῳ ἑκοῦσα εἶναι, ἀλλὰ φεύγουσα αὐτὸ καὶ συνηθροισμένη αὐτὴ εἰς ἑαυτήν, ἅτε μελετῶσα ἀεὶ τοῦτο— τὸ δὲ οὐδὲν ἄλλο ἐστὶν ἢ ὀρθῶς φιλοσοφοῦσα καὶ τῷ ὄντι τεθνάναι μελετῶσα ῥᾳδίως: ἢ οὐ τοῦτ' ἂν εἴη μελέτη θανάτου'

'if it (the soul) departs pure, dragging with it nothing of the body, because it never willingly associated with the body in life, but avoided it and gathered itself into itself alone, since this has always been its constant study—but this means nothing else than that it pursued philosophy rightly and *practiced being in a state of death*: or is not this the *practice of death*?' (Plato, 1903).

[13] Some other meanings of *melete* selected from the same Lexicon: 'I. *care*, *attention*, Hes.Op.412, Epich. [284]: pl., Emp.110.2: c. gen. objecti,

The Meaning of Pain and the Pain of Meaning

to, something that should not be ignored, but rather cared about, and this is the task of philosophy. In its existential form, philosophy must deal with the *symptom* of death, with the fact that as human beings, our existence is *towards-death* (Heidegger, 2010, pp. 241, 232), and as such death imbues all our semantic exercises. What role does pain play in this scenario? Heidegger did not refer to the role of pain, nor did he grasp the existential dimension of it. While *angst* and *care* have rich existential meanings, pain was probably ignored due to its 'empirical' nature. And yet, the experience of pain and its connection with an incoherent way of inhabiting the world opens the space for redrafting the *chaos-cosmos* dialectic in a new bio-hermeneutical way. 'The ultimate value of illness is that it teaches us the value of being alive. (...) illness and, ultimately, death remind us of living' (Frank, 2002, p. 120). In this sense, death ceases to be the enemy of life, transforming into an axiological restorer of living. Restoring living means to restore our sense of proportion and beauty. Seen from the terminal point of death as 'the end of the road' – one of death's representations discussed by Heidegger – our lives appear as attempts to make sense, to find the meaning of what we are living through. For Frank, like for many other people writing narratives of their illnesses, illness is a unique possibility of self-reflection, the creation of a new personal *cosmos*.

But how can we *rehearse* death? Is it enough to think of and examine our *relatedness to death* (Dastur, 1996) as something that makes us human? Understandably, we project death as an event of the future, and this is covered under Heidegger's concept of 'being-towards-death'. We want to cast it so far away into the fogginess of the future that we can forget about it for most of the time. However, there may be a trap of meaning here, an existential

---

μ. πλεόνων care for many things, Hes.Op.380; μελέτην τινὸς ἐχέμεν, = μελετᾶν, ἐπιμελεῖσθαι, ib.457; ἔργων ἐκ πολλοῦ μ. long-continued attention to action, Th.5.69: c. gen. subjecti, care taken by one, 'θεῶν μελέτη' S.Ph.196 (anap.); of a trainer, B.12.191: abs., 'μελέτη κατατρύχεσθαι' E.Med.1099 (anap.): pl., Emp.131.2. 2. Medic., treatment, Hp.Fract.31, 35 (pl.), Art.50. II. *practice, exercise,* 'ὀξεῖα μ.' Pi.O.6.37; 'ἔχων μ.' Id.N.6.54; ἡ δι' ὀλίγου μ. their short practice, Th.2.85; πόνων μ. painful exercises, of the Spartan discipline, ib.39; 'μάθησις καὶ μ.' Pl.Tht.153b; 'μ. θανάτου' Id.Phd.81a; 'ἡ ἐγκύκλιος τῶν προπαιδευμάτων μ.' Ph.1.157. III. *practice, usage,* 'ἃς οἱ πατέρες ἡμῖν παρέδοσαν μ.' Th.1.85. IV. *threatening symptom or condition, of disease,* 'μελέτη καὶ προοίμιον ἐπιληψίας' Posidon. ap. Aët. 6.12; 'ὀδύνη .. μ. λύσεως' Aët.5.100, cf. Steph. in Hp.1.191 D.

Teodora Manea

mistake, that we think about death by relating the present-self to a future-self (either dying or dead). We fear the pain of approaching death and the closure of all our *existential possibilities*. But what happens if we change the perspective and examine the meaning of death by relating the present-self to the past-self (or selves)? The past-self has also closed most of its existential possibilities except one, which is the present self. When I was a teenager, I dreamed of being a doctor, a film director, an opera singer. I still remember, and we all do so, the effervescence of life in our 20s, the wonders of early childhood. Going through life is a constant reduction and denial of many, many possibilities of being. Is our fear of dying constructed around our self-reflection around lost possibilities? And should philosophy here help us understand, dialectically, that only by losing possibilities we can actualise a few of them? This will reinforce the idea of death as *causa efficiens* of our present *cosmos*, rather than as a total closure of some imaginary world we might live in while approaching our extinction.

Faced with his terminal patients' question of what happens when we die, Peter Dorward gives them this medical-metaphorical speculation: 'you disappear gradually into yourself. At first you will be aware of the world around you, and the people around you, but it all becomes progressively less vivid, and it all comes to matter less, or matter less immediately. Their presence might be a comfort, especially at first, but they are a long way off, and diminishing, and your own world starts to shrink down too. Any discomfort you might have will diminish too, and you will stop feeling hungry or thirsty, and you will become more sleepy, so that you are hardly awake at all. It's like you disappear to a pinpoint, and then you disappear altogether' (Dorward, 2018, p. 288). Dorward's intuition – and it is only intuitions that we can really have about the event of death – reinforces the change of perspective I mentioned above: maybe we disappear into ourselves, into our self-made cosmos. Maybe what the brain will play to us in our last moments is nothing but the beauty and memories that we have created along the way. If we don't 'pass away' into a pink transcendence, 'better world', and some such, *melete thanatou* should be understood as our concern for a poetic way of living, one that can generate enough beauty for the ultimate trip into oneself.

University of Liverpool
teodora@liverpool.ac.uk

References

K.M. Boyd 'Disease, illness, sickness, health, healing and wholeness: exploring some elusive concepts', *Medical Humanities* 26 (2000), 9–17.

Joanna Burke, *The Story of Pain. From Prayers to Painkillers* (Oxford: Oxford University Press, 2014).

Havi Carel, *Phenomenology of Illness* (Oxford: Oxford University Press, 2016).

Rita Charon, *Narrative Medicine. Honoring the Stories of Illness* (Oxford: Oxford University Press, 2006).

Francoise Dastur, *Death. An Essay on Finitude*, translated by J. Llewelyn (London: The Athlone Press, 1996).

Peter Dorward, *The Human Kind: A Doctor's Stories from the Heart of Medicine*, (London: Green Tree, 2018).

Arthur W. Frank, *At the will of the body: Reflections on illness*, (Houghton Mifflin Harcourt, 2002).

Sigmund Freud, *Civilisation and its Discontempts*, translated by D. McLintock (London: Penguin Books, 2002).

H.G. Gadamer, *The Enigma of Health. The Art of Healing in a Scientific Age*, translated by J. Gaiger and N. Walker (Cambridge: Polity Press, 1996).

Erving Goffman, *The Presentation of Self in Everyday Life* (Edinburgh: University of Edinburgh, 1956).

Martin Heidegger, *Being and Time*, translated by J. Stamburg (Albany: State University of New York Press, 1953/2010).

Marja-Liisa Honkasalo, 'Medical symptoms: A challenge for semiotic research', *Semiotica* 87 (1991), 251–68.

Marja-Liisa Honkasalo, 'Space and Embodied Experience: Rethinking the Body in Pain', *Body & Society*, 4 (1998).

Henry George Liddell, Robert Scott, Henry Stuart Jones, Roderick McKenzie, *The Greek-English Lexicon*, 9th Edition (Oxford: Clarendon Press, 1996).

Howard Markel. 'Koplik's Spots: The Harbinger of a Measles Epidemic', *The Milbank Quarterly* 93/2 (2015), 223–29.

R. Melzack, 'The McGill Pain Questionnaire: Major properties and scoring methods', *Pain* 1 (1975), 277–99.

John Nessa, 'About signs and symptoms: can semiotics expand the view of clinical medicine?', *Theoretical Medicine and Bioethics* 17/4 (1996), 363–73.

Friedrich Nietzsche, *Twilight of the Idols* (1889).

Friedrich Nietzsche *Gaia Scientia / The Joyful Wisdom*. Complete Works, Volume Six, translated by T. Common, P.V. Cohn,

M.D. Petre, edited by O. Levy (Edinburgh and London: T.N. Foulis, 1910).

Donna Orange, *The Suffering Stranger. Hermeneutics for Everyday Clinical Practice* (New York: Routledge, 2011).

Richard Palmer, *Hermeneutics: Interpretation Theory in Schleiermacher, Dilthey, Heidegger, and Gadamer* (Evanston: Northwestern University Press, 1969).

Talcott Parsons, *The Social System.* (1951), Glencoe, IL: The Free Press.

Plato, *Platonis Opera*, ed. John Burnet, (Oxford University Press. 1903).

Elaine Scarry, *The Body in Pain. Making and Unmaking of the World* (Oxford: Oxford University Press, 1985).

Fredrik Svenaeus, *The Hermeneutics of Medicine and the Phenomenology of Health* (Linköping: Springer, 2001).

Fredrik Svenaeus, 'Illness as unhomelike being-in-the-world: Heidegger and the phenomenology of medicine', *Med Health Care Philos.* 14 (2011), 334–36.

Fredrik Svenaeus, *The Hermeneutics of Medicine,* and *Phenomenological Bioethics. Medical Technologies, Human Suffering, and the Meaning of Being Alive* (London: Routledge, 2018).

Grieving Our Way Back to Meaningfulness

MICHAEL CHOLBI

Abstract
The deaths of those on whom our practical identities rely generate a sense of disorientation or alienation from the world seemingly at odds with life being meaningful. In the terms put forth in Cheshire Calhoun's recent account of meaningfulness in life, because their existence serves as a metaphysical presupposition of our practical identities, their deaths threaten to upend a background frame of agency against which much of our choice and deliberation takes place. Here I argue for a dual role for grief in addressing this threat to life's meaningfulness. Inasmuch as grief's object is the loss of our relationship with the deceased as it was prior to their death, grief serves to alert us to the threat to our practical identities that their deaths pose to us and motivates us to defuse this threat by revising our practical identities to reflect the modification in our relationship necessitated by their deaths. Simultaneously, the emotional complexity and richness of grief episodes provides an abundance of normative evidence regarding our relationship with the deceased and our practical identities, evidence that can enable us to re-establish our practical identities and thereby recover a sense of our lives as meaningful.

Albert Camus' novella *The Stranger* (1946) is one of the literary centrepieces of the existentialist movement. Except for the novella's final pages, in which his impending execution sparks anxiety and examination of his life, the protagonist Meursault is an existentialist anti-hero, a picture of alienation from wider society. He lives emotionally detached from others, with no apparent investment in them or their fates. He willingly cooperates in his friend Raymond's plan to exact cruel vengeance on the latter's girlfriend and can give no accounting of his motivations for shooting an Arab man on the beach. Indeed, aside from the transient pleasures of sex, movies, and *café au lait*, Meursault hardly seems motivated by anything at all.

Curiously, Camus uses grief, including grief's *absence*, to illustrate Meursault's alienated condition. The novella opens with Meursault attending the funeral of *maman*. He gives no evidence of the psychological turmoil associated with grief though. At most, Meursault goes through the motions of mourning, passively participating in its rituals but without the death of *maman* occupying his attention in the slightest. Later, at his murder trial, his prosecutors introduce

doi:10.1017/S1358246121000308   © The Royal Institute of Philosophy and the contributors 2021

no material evidence concerning his crime. Instead, their strategy, which of course proved successful, focuses on how Meursault not only failed to grieve but quickly resumed his hedonistic lifestyle after *maman*'s death. As the novella concludes, a condemned Meursault notices parallels between his own predicament and *maman*'s. He sits alone in his cell with death creeping ever nearer, much as *maman* might have as she slowly declined in the retirement home. For Meursault, this insight does not seem to provoke grief for *maman* exactly; but he finds comfort all the same in this newly discovered solidarity with her. At the very least, he undergoes some of the tender feelings that a less alienated person would likely have undergone in response to their mother's death.

Camus clearly intended *The Stranger* as an interrogation of the morality of grief. He later wrote that the novella could be summarized with the observation that 'In our society any man who does not weep at his mother's funeral runs the risk of being sentenced to death'. Merusault is convicted, Camus said, because he 'does not play the game' of grieving in accordance with societal expectations (Carroll, 1955, p. 27). But *The Stranger* also represents an *ethical* arc connecting grief and meaningfulness in life. At the novella's outset, Meursault does not grieve *maman,* and experiences his life in terms that (I expect most would agree) are meaningless; he is not connected to anything greater or larger than himself, has no enduring concerns or commitments, and takes satisfaction only in transient pursuits. Ironically, his condemnation awakens in Meursault an awareness of the finitude of mortal human lives and, in turn, a recognition of the central role that our relationships with other finite creatures plays in making our lives meaningful. We see in his reflections on the parallels between his fate and that of his *maman* an inkling of how isolation from others corrodes meaningfulness in our lives, and in observing that although he will die in front of a hostile crowd, his death will at least not be a lonely one, Meursault glimpses how meaningfulness is out of reach in a life impoverished of any significant emotional entanglement with others.

Fortunately, few of us are as alienated from others, and from the world as a whole, as Meursault was. Nevertheless, I wish to highlight how Camus' tale gestures at a philosophically significant relationship between the grief we undergo in response to the deaths of particular others and the meaningfulness of our lives. Meursault's initial inability to grieve is evidence of the meaninglessness of his life, whereas the sorrows and worry he faces as his life concludes (though they do not quite rise to the level of grief) suggest his growing susceptibility to grief and a correlative growth in both the meaningfulness of his life and his recognition of the centrality that our relations with others play in rendering our lives meaningful. The case of Meursault thus illustrates how grief serves as a barometer of the possibility of meaningfulness in life (or at least of one important contributor to it). Grief reflects a susceptibility to losses in meaningfulness in life since it tracks events that represent a threat to life's meaningfulness. Simultaneously though, grieving can enable us to recover or even amplify the overall meaningfulness of our lives. Hence, for those of us not handicapped by Meursault-like alienation, grief can be recommended on the grounds that it can both diagnose threats to life's meaningfulness, but thanks to certain distinctive affective features it has, grief also has the potential to resolve these threats.

Vindicating these claims will require exploration of the nature of grief as well as of life's meaningfulness. In section 1, I defend positions regarding the scope, object, and the temporal structure of grief.[1] Section 2 situates these positions vis-à-vis a prominent contemporary account of meaningfulness in life (that of Cheshire Calhoun) that explains how grief enables the recognition that the deaths of others can threaten the meaningfulness of our lives. I turn in section 3 to an elaboration of how grief nevertheless contains the seeds of a solution to this threat.

1. The nature of grief

Others' deaths prompt many emotional responses in us. But not all of those responses are grief responses. We may feel distress or anger when we learn of large numbers of individuals killed by severe weather events, transport accidents, or war and terrorism. Likewise, in reading obituaries of strangers, we may have a pang of sadness for them or for their families and loved ones. But such responses, while genuine, are not instances of grief. Grief is selective and particularized, a response specifically to the deaths of those with whom we stood in an antecedent personal relationship. But what kind of relationship is requisite to prompt grief? Our paradigmatic cases of grief are those in which the relationships in question involve love, intimacy, or attachment – grief resulting from the deaths of spouses, family members, or close friends. But not all cases of grief involve these attributes. We also grieve the deaths of those that we admire

---

[1]   Space considerations prevent a thorough defense of the claims advanced in section 1, but I hope to make these claims at least plausible. For fuller defenses, see my (2017), (2019) and (2021, chapters 1–3).

but do not love, such as professional role models, inspiring political leaders, or innovative artists. Nor are we intimate with or emotionally attached to these individuals. We sometimes grieve individuals with whom we had a relationship that was cut short in its very earliest stages, such as parents who grieve the death of a miscarried child or the lover who grieves the death of the beloved whom she had only met days before. In these cases, grief occurs despite the relationships lacking the rich histories found in the paradigmatic cases of grief.

The *scope* of grief – who we do and can grieve for – is thus more puzzling than it appears at first consideration. We grieve not only for close relationships, but also for more distant but nevertheless significant relationships, as well as for relationships whose basis was grounded almost exclusively in future hopes concerning the relationship rather than being deeply rooted in the past. What unites the relationships for which we grieve, I suggest, is that we grieve in response to the deaths of those in whom we have invested our *practical identities*. As articulated by Christine Korsgaard, a practical identity is not a 'theoretical' fact about oneself or an 'inescapable scientific fact' about who one is. Rather, a practical identity 'is better understood as a description under which you value yourself, a description under which you find your life to be worth living and your actions to be worth undertaking'. Korsgaard observes that practical identities will typically have many levels or elements.

> Practical identity is a complex matter and for the average person there will be a jumble of such conceptions. You are a human being, a woman or a man, an adherent of a certain religion, a member of an ethnic group, a member of a certain profession, someone's lover or friend, and so on. (Korsgaard, 1996, p. 101)

Each of these elements of a person's practical identity is a source of practical reasons, according to Korsgaard. That you are Muslim may give you a reason to undertake pilgrimages; that you are a psychiatrist a reason to adhere to norms of patient confidentiality; that you are Ella's friend reasons to celebrate her achievements; and so on.

Crucially, the vast majority of the elements of our practical identities assume, both ethically and metaphysically, other individuals. The goals, concerns, and commitments that comprise a practical identity provide us reasons that make certain actions 'worth undertaking'. But the justifiability of many such actions – indeed, the very possibility or intelligibility of performing them – requires the existence of others. A marriage, a friendship, parenthood, participation in a profession or a religious faith, belonging to a fan club, contributing to a political movement; none of these are enterprises one can undertake alone. Hence, to the extent that these relationships are sources of one's practical identity, one's practical identity normatively implicates others. And when that is the case, our practical identities are *invested* in those others.

Grief occurs, on my view, when a person in whom we have invested our practical identity dies. The wide range of individuals whose deaths we grieve reflect the wide range of ways in which our practical identities are invested in others. We are invested in our spouses or close family members by virtue of love or affection; in mentors, by virtue of emulation; in public figures, by virtue of admiration; in our future children or lovers, by virtue of hope. In each of these cases, we had come to *count on* the other as critical to certain of our goals, concerns, and commitments. This will not be the case with respect to the deaths of others that do not or should not prompt grief. Those deaths may rightfully result in impartial moral reactions such as indignation or generic instances of emotions such as sympathy. But those deaths do not have the practical and agent-relative gravity of the deaths we grieve. At heart then, grief is an ego-centred reaction, a response to the deaths of persons that are incorporated into our self-conceptions or self-understanding in non-trivial ways.

Grief is thus a response to a particular kind of threat to our interests. This self-interested role does not entail, though, that grief is objectionably *selfish*. Grieving seems likely to be among those activities in which we permissibly pursue our interests. Nor does it entail that grieving itself is unduly *self-centred*. One might infer from my claim that we grieve those in whom we have invested our practical identities that the psychological focus of grieving falls largely or exclusively on oneself – that the various emotions, memories, and so on that constitute a grief episode are directed at, or focused upon, oneself. If so, then grief may seem like an act of emotional vanity, in which others' deaths lead us to linger Narcissus-like over our own emotional condition. But this inference is incorrect. From the fact that we grieve those who matter to us insofar as we have invested our practical identities in them it does not follow that grief must be solely self-concerned. There is an aspect of grief that is self-concerning, I shall argue later. But what instead dictates the content of our grief experience are the particularities of the relationship in question. Many of the relationships in which we have invested our practical identities (and hence, we have reason to grieve when the other member of the relationship dies) are ones in which the investment involves love of one kind or another. And part of loving another is that their fate or their well-being matters to us in a distinctive and disproportionate way. We revel in the happiness of those we love, as we despair in

Michael Cholbi

their sufferings. For loving them entails that what matters to them comes to matter to us. Thus, when we grieve in connection with loving relationships, a proportion of our grieving will be directed at what has happened to the other, such as what they may have gained or lost by dying, the quality of their dying process, etc. But our own investment in them as a constituent in our practical identities frames this attention to their well-being or their fate. We do not reflect in the same way or with the same intensity on the fates of those who have died in whom our practical identities have *not* been invested or in whom our investment does not take the form of love (grieving a revered political activist, say). Our practical identities thus serve to bring into relief the practical identities (the well-being, concerns, commitments, etc.) of those in whom our identities are invested. Therefore, there is no contradiction between the claim that we grieve those who matter to us because we have invested our practical identities in them and the observation that grief itself, particularly in connection with loving relationships, often focuses emotionally on the deceased rather than on the bereaved. Indeed, the former claim explains both why grief focuses on the deceased when it does and why it does not focus on the deceased when it is not focused on them.

That we grieve those in whom we have invested our practical identities sheds little light, however, on grief's emotional texture. The central emotion within grief tends to be sadness or sorrow, but other emotions are not uncommon: anxiety, guilt, anger, disorientation, puzzlement, a sense of alienation from oneself and one's environment. The diversity and complexity of the emotions raises questions about how we should understand the *loss* to which grief is a response. Here again certain tempting answers prove implausible. For instance, we might suppose that grief responds to the loss suffered *by the deceased* by dying. But this is clearly inadequate. For one, as we just observed, not all grief relationships involve practical identity investment of the kinds that result in a focus on the losses suffered by the deceased. In grieving (say) a political leader such as Nelson Mandela, most people are not grieving whatever he (Mandela) personally lost by dying. Furthermore, some deaths are arguably not bad for the deceased. The voluntary death (by euthanasia, say) of a person who had lived a long and complete life but faces a painful or undignified process of dying prompts grief in those whose practical identities are invested in that person, and justifiably so. But the deceased did not seem to lose much by dying. Indeed, dying at that time may have been beneficial to the deceased. Similarly, believers in the possibility of salvation in the afterlife

may sometimes believe that their deceased loved ones are now enjoying heavenly bliss. And yet grief seems intelligible in such cases
despite the loved one's death being the greatest conceivable benefit
they could attain.

Another possibility is that grief responds to the loss suffered *by the
bereaved* due to the others' death. This seems more promising since it
more readily explains why grief hurts. But this too proves vulnerable
to counterexamples. We may grieve those who, despite our practical
identity investment in them, did not augment our well-being and
were, on balance, harmful to us. Individuals may grieve the deaths
of abusive spouses or neglectful parents. A caregiver may grieve a
person's death even though their death relives them of caregiving
burdens that made their lives miserable. Furthermore, that grief responds to the loss suffered by the bereaved is difficult to square
with the intuition that grief is highly particular, grounded in the *irre-
placeability* of the deceased. Seneca once argued that just as a person
who loses his cloak should immediately find a replacement, so too
should someone grieving a dead friend immediately strike up new
friendship with others. Seneca's reasoning seems wrongheaded if intended to imply that we can replace those for whom we grieve.
Indeed, the particularity of a friend is among the factors that distinguishes friends from cloaks. While we can replace a cloak by acquiring
another cloak that provides the goods cloaks provide, efforts to
replace a dead friend with a new friend leave a crucial remainder,
even if the new friend is as good as the old in all the relevant ways.
We thus seem to grieve persons, not the goods we derive from them.

This last observation seems to suggest another candidate for the
loss behind grief: that we grieve the loss *of the relationship* with the
deceased. This proposition has several advantages: It does not
require either that the deceased or the bereaved are harmed by the
former's death, and the loss of a relationship could well cause not
only sadness, but other emotions common in the course of grief
(again, anxiety, guilt, disorientation, etc.) that could vary depending
on the specific relationship in question. However, this proposition
needs refinement. For it incorrectly implies that the deaths of those
in whom our practical identities are invested results in the end of
said relationship. In reality, many individuals continue their relationships with the dead, albeit on very modified terms.[2] They continue to
acknowledge the influence of the deceased on their lives, they com-
memorate their deaths, and engage in imagined conversation with

---

[2]   Shuchter and Zisook (1993); Klass, Silverman and Nickman (eds.,
1996).

the deceased. (This is especially likely if the bereaved believe in the afterlife, since they presumably relate to the dead as if they literally continue to exist.) Our bonds with the deceased often continue, but their deaths necessitate a *transition* in those bonds. The terms of those bonds can no longer include, for example, reciprocity, thus precluding planning, negotiation, or mutual promises. Morally significant interactions such as apologies, forgiveness, or gratitude become elusive or impossible. And whatever our obligations to the deceased, they diverge from our obligations to the living in key ways.

Matthew Ratcliffe has observed that because the death of others can topple a 'system of possibilities' in which we are practically immersed, grief can feel like a loss not only of the other but a forced divorce from the world in which one has lived (Ratcliffe, 2019). A world previously suffused with meaning may appear as a world of normatively disenchanted things. This aspect of grief thereby underscores how grief discloses to us shifts in the possibilities for our practical identities. As mentioned earlier, the deaths of those in whom our practical identities are invested *foreclose* some possibilities for our relationships. But their deaths also *open* new possibilities for how we relate to them. Their deaths may shift our attention from promoting their happiness to securing their legacies. In the case of the death of a spouse, the question of remarriage emerges, a question which implicates us in our relationship with the deceased.

Hence, the loss for which we grieve is not the loss (i.e., the cessation) of the relationship but the loss *of the relationship as it was*. In many cases, the relationship will continue in a new guise, adapted to the strange new circumstance that one of its members is dead.

Curiously though, even though the relationship is not destroyed, our response to that loss – grief itself – is nevertheless emotionally taxing because the relationship at issue has been disrupted. Recall that we grieve those in whom our practical identities are invested. The disruptions in our relationships with them wrought by their deaths thus represent a disruption to our practical identities as well. Some of the practical reasons we formerly operated under are no longer applicable to our choices. Their deaths thus spark an emotional condition, grief, that is often disorienting to one's self-conception. Many grieving people find themselves interrogating a world in which they previously felt more at home, and some find themselves not entirely at home in their own bodies. As I see it, these emotions represent how the other's death threatens or undermine our practical identities. Whatever clarity or confidence one's practical identity previously had — to whatever degree one affirmed a description under which one was valuable, one's life was worth was worth living, and

Grieving Our Way Back to Meaningfulness

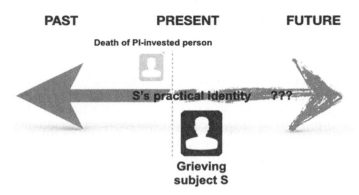

Figure 1. How Grief Responds to Threats to Practical Identity Posed by Others' Deaths

one's actions were justifiable in light of that description – is shaken by the death of someone who formed part of the foundation of that identity. It is thus understandable that the losses encountered in grief are often described not simply as losses to the self but as losses *of* self. For the grieving person is in the midst of an identity crisis rooted in the concurrent crisis in their suddenly evolving relationship with the deceased.

This practical identity crisis has a cross-temporal autobiographical character. On the one hand, the death of the person for whom one grieves is the death of someone whose normative significance originates in the past. For the bereaved have *already* invested their practical identity in that person. But on the other hand, this prior investment was also an investment in one's future, a future in which that person's continued existence was assumed. Grief is thus often a complex interplay of attempting to make sense of one's past with an eye to crafting the future. The bereaved individual is attempting to navigate a transition from a past practical identity to one more reflective both of the fact of the death of the other and of the goals, commitments, and concerns it would be rational to her to adopt in light of that fact. As represented in Figure 1, the grieving subject has been unmoored from the practical identity under which she operated prior to the other's death, but has yet to develop and settle upon a new practical identity, and so her future practical orientation may well feel hazy or 'up in the air'. This ethical reality, in my estimation, accounts for why the emotions felt in grief episodes are not only backward-looking (sadness, most notably) but also forward-looking (such as anxiety or disorientation).

Michael Cholbi

2. Calhoun on meaningfulness in life: Grief and disruptions to frames in agency

Grief, then, tracks a disruption in our relationships with others and in our practical identities. But some of the emotional resonances of grief are isomorphic with how it feels for our lives to suffer diminished *meaningfulness*. The ingredients of a meaningful life are of course a matter of philosophical dispute, but many partisans in those disputes will recognize in grief – or more accurately, in the loss of our practical identity-constituting relationships as they were to which grief is a response – signs of a threat to meaningfulness in one's life. The grieving individual is likely to sense that the other's death has diminished the scope or significance of their own life, or that their connection to concerns larger than themselves has weakened. Similarly, the person in grief may intuit that the other's death has knocked their own life narrative off-kilter or that they have somehow lost their direction in the world.

Such thoughts are naturally at home in those subjectivist conceptions of life's meaningfulness according to which a person's life is meaningful because and to the extent that one has a certain evaluative pro-attitude toward one's life, such as caring about one's projects, endorsing one's values, or viewing one's life as embodying a coherent whole. One such conception, Cheshire Calhoun's, is particularly illuminating in explaining how grief corresponds to a threat to our lives' meaningfulness (Calhoun, 2018).

Calhoun's account of meaningfulness is distinctive in foregrounding how our relation to *time* is integral to meaningfulness. Calhoun does not speak in terms of practical identity, but her account can be restated in such terms without much residue or distortion. The past and the present shape our practical identities, but as Calhoun observes, our agency is oriented toward the future because it is the future where the goals, commitments, and concerns that constitute our practical identities will be pursued and realized. Fortunately, for most of us most of the time, we look forward to our futures, and in particular, we look forward to our futures as the timeframe in which to implement or act upon our practical identities. Typically, the future 'stretches out ahead' as a valued resource 'in which to do things' (Calhoun, 2018, p. 49). And it is this orientation toward the future that lends our lives their meaningfulness. For Calhoun, a person's life is meaningful to the extent that she has ends that she understands as justifying her expenditure of her future time. Transposed into the language of practical identity, a person's life is meaningful to the extent that her practical identity is one whose future pursuit or implementation she welcomes to a sufficient degree that expending her future on its pursuit or implementation is justifiable to her.

But Calhoun enumerates a number of ways in which our interest in expending our own futures, and hence our desire to choose and act in anticipation of those futures, can be weakened. We may come to doubt that our ends are attainable, and so find ourselves helpless in the face of the fast-arriving future. Or we may suffer such grotesque pain that our ability to attend to our ends (deliberating about them or about how to attain them, or even enjoying them once attained) is severely hampered. Such developments upend what Calhoun calls 'background frames' of agency, those beliefs and attitudes concerning our agency that are typically taken for granted as we exercise our agency and whose presence makes the exercise of agency in deliberating, choosing, and acting coherent to us. The erosion of such frames induces meaninglessness to the extent that it removes our grounds for wishing to continue into the future. At its worst, such erosion could make suicide rational.[3]

Our relationships to others, and in particular the relationships in which our practical identities are invested, are another central background frame of agency. The existence of such relationships, established in the past, nevertheless projects our agency into the future since many of our goals, commitments, and concerns implicate the continued existence of those relationships and, thereby, of the other participants in those relationships. Absent such relationships, or if such relationships come to lack the properties that make them normatively relevant to the pursuit of our goals, commitments, and concerns, then our agency will not have the same traction it would have otherwise. Our practical identities cannot serve so effectively as anchors for deliberation and choice. The deaths of those in whom we have invested our practical identities compels a reconfiguration of those relationships and so act to upend 'the future as we imagine, anticipate, predict, assume, or sense it will be' (Calhoun, 2018, p. 8). In terms of Calhoun's account of life's meaningfulness, their deaths pose a threat to our being intelligibly drawn into our own futures and so pose a threat to meaningfulness.

Because grief is a response to the disruption in our practical identities that results from the deaths of others, grief alerts us to this threat to meaningfulness in our lives. Grief thus resembles an emotion such

[3]   See my (2021).

as fear in signalling threats to ourselves or what matters to us. Grief is a sign of a potential or emerging threat to a background frame of agency and so invites our attention to the possibility of a crisis in the meaningfulness of our lives.

Crucially, grief itself will not generally be the source of meaninglessness. For grief gives *evidence* of the threat but will rarely constitute a threat to life's meaningfulness. It is not impossible for grief itself to threaten meaningfulness as it is understood in Calhoun's theory. A person whose grief persists at an intense level for years on end may be unable during that time to attend to any other concern besides the alleviation of her suffering, in which case the grief itself has wrecked a background frame of agency. But usually, grief's relation to meaningfulness is to track it, not embody it.

3. Grieving to recover meaningfulness

As I have presented it so far, grief's role is epistemic and *negative*: It alerts us to threats to the meaningfulness of our lives by giving evidence that the relationships in which we have invested our practical identities cannot continue just as they were. Of course, a person such as Camus' Meursault seems not to have invested his practical identity in relationships with others, and hence the death of his mother (a relationship in which many people invest their practical identity) does not elicit grief in him. Her death poses no threat to his practical identity and so grief has no epistemic part to play in notifying him of such a threat. To the degree that a profoundly alienated figure such as Meursault has background frames for his agency at all, his relationships with others are not among them.

The good news, however, is that grief also has a *positive* epistemic role to play vis-à-vis meaningfulness. It alerts us to threats to the meaningfulness of our lives but also makes available a robust trove of evidence concerning our own good, evidence we can draw upon to deflect the threat to meaningfulness that others' deaths can represent.

To the extent that the average person knows much about how psychologists and others have theorized about grief, they are aware of Elisabeth Kübler-Ross' five-stage account of grief, according to which individuals grieve by undergoing denial, anger, bargaining, depression, and acceptance (Kübler-Ross, 1969). Subsequent empirical research has shown that this account rarely holds true at the level of detail. Many bereaved people do not undergo one or more of those stages; or undergo other emotions in the course of grief; or do not undergo the stages in that order.[4] But Kübler-Ross' account captures something important about grief episodes, namely, that they are complex emotional processes involving many types of affect. As discussed earlier, grief nearly always includes sadness, but will often include disorientation as well as emotions such as guilt or anxiety. That grief is a complex emotional process is not at all surprising if (as I have argued here) grief's object is the loss of a practical identity-constituting relationship as it was in its pre-mortem incarnation. For human relationships are themselves emotionally complex, particularly our relationships with those in whom we invest our practical identities. Take a fairly standard case of grief, that felt by an adult in response to the death of a close sibling. We expect sadness in such a case, but it would not be surprising for such a grief episode to include other emotions rooted in the relationship between the siblings. The bereaved sibling who served as the deceased sibling's medical surrogate might feel anxiety or guilt about medical decisions she made on the deceased's behalf. Or the bereaved sibling might feel anger because the deceased sibling's lifestyle (for example, smoking tobacco) led to a premature death that deprived the bereaved sibling of further time with them. If grief marks not the cessation of a relationship with another but a necessary transition within it, then grief itself is an event within that relationship and so will bear the emotional marks of other attempts to understand, process, or reconfigure that relationship.[5] In coming to terms with the loss of the deceased and in attempting to craft a revised practical identity that fully reflects the significance that such a loss has on one's practical identity, a bereaved individual will be drawn to attend to the relationship in question in its totality. The emotional complexity of grief will therefore tend to mirror the normative complexity of the relationships whose disruptions are grief's object.

Bereaved individuals are engaged, I propose, in an effort to deflect the threat to their lives' meaningfulness caused by another's death (or if that meaningfulness has already been diminished, to recover lost meaningfulness). They are seeking, however unwittingly, to establish a revised practical identity in which the other's existence or availability is no longer assumed. And this undertaking has a significant epistemic dimension. For establishing this revised practical identity requires a metaphysical-cum-normative engagement with one's relationship with the deceased, and more indirectly, with oneself and

[4] Maciejewski, Zhang, Block and Prigerson (2007, popularly known as the 'Yale bereavement study'); Bonnano (2009) and Kongsberg (2011).
[5] See my 2019 (pp. 501–502).

one's practical identity in relation to the deceased. This is why grief often involves puzzlement or questioning. For a grieving person is in effect asking, 'who am I – or who *can* I be – without you?'

Fortunately though, the emotional richness of grief positions us well to answer this question. For grief is not simply a 'dumb' distress signal, merely alerting us to the threat without disclosing its nature to us or pointing us toward its neutralization. Grief is a kind of emotional 'data dump', revealing to us a wide array of information about the depth of our commitments, the nature of our goals, and the place of specific (now deceased) individuals in both of these (Cholbi, 2017, p. 102). This information, so salient to revealing our practical identities and enabling their revision, allows us to find our normative bearings again and puts us on track to 'recovery' from grief. Grieving well, on my account, consists in attaining a form of practical self-knowledge in which one's new practical identity is both recognized and recognized as worthy of endorsement.

For these reasons, talk of grief as a 'wound' or 'injury' is misleading. To do so is to confuse grief, which I have argued alerts us to the 'wound' or 'injury' that the death of others can imprint on the meaningfulness of our lives, with the wound or injury itself. Grief may hurt, but it enables our recognition of the wound or injury without being by its very nature a wound or injury in its own right.

We should therefore be grateful that grief, despite its emotional burdensomeness, affords us the chance to know ourselves better and be more firmly anchored in our practical identities. Yet grief, by being distressing, also has value to us by *motivating* us to know ourselves and to reconstruct our practical identities in the wake of a death that disrupts them. I have reservations about the claim that grief must be arduous labour, as suggested by the phrase 'grief work'. But grief is a happy phenomenon to the extent that it not only alerts us to a threat to our lives' meaningfulness, but is also a vital resource for undertaking the 'work' needed to defuse this threat.

So depicted, grief is not a passive emotional 'sensation' of hurt or loss. It is instead a robust species of activity and attention[6] in which we make evidence-responsive moves in an effort to normatively adapt to deaths that implicate our practical identities. This does not mean we necessarily make the right moves; some episodes of grief may conclude with individuals continue to adhere to practical identities that are essentially out of date. These individuals are, in a fairly literal way, living in the past. As such, they have missed a

---

[6]   For a defense of the thesis that emotions often take the form of attention to evaluatively significant facts, see Brady (2013).

critical opportunity to render their lives more meaningful. But when successful, grieving rejuvenates a vital frame of agency. In Calhoun's terms, we rebuild our practical identity-constituting relationships so that they can return to playing the reason-giving role they had prior to the death of a person in whom we had invested that practical identity. Our normative relation to our own future alters as a consequence: after their death but prior to grief (or in its midst or prior to its successful resolution), our futures are hazy, as we do not entirely know what goals, commitments, or concerns it makes sense for us to invest that future in. With the successful resolution of grief, this haze lifts. Grief helps make our futures meaningful to us once again.

4. Conclusion

Grief often feels bad. Yet I have argued elsewhere that it is often in fact beneficial to us insofar as it helps us to augment our well-being (Cholbi, 2021, chs. 2 and 3). So too in the case of grief and meaningfulness in life: Though grief includes sadness and other affective states we otherwise have reason to avoid, it enables us to sustain or augment the meaningfulness of our lives. Only at the end of Meursault's life did he seem to have invested himself in the fate of others in such a way that he became susceptible to grief. But for those of us less alienated from others, grief is a powerful tool for navigating threats to life's meaningfulness stemming from the precarity of the relationships in which we invest our practical identities.

In defending grief as a tool for enabling meaningfulness in life, I drew upon Calhoun's subjectivist account of meaningfulness in life. Does this imply, then, that objectivist accounts of meaningfulness in life, according to which meaningfulness in life depends not on our attitudes toward our life (such as that our futures are worth expending, as in Calhoun's account) but on facts independent of our attitudes, should be rejected? Not exactly. It seems possible to affirm that grief enables meaningfulness in the way that I have described while maintaining that objective facts contribute to life's meaningfulness. For instance, suppose that a particular friendship has been particularly useful in enabling someone to realize some good that putatively confers objective meaningfulness on one's life. The friendship could, for example, involve working with a friend at a charity that improves quality of life for poor or marginalized peoples. If that friend were to die, the bereaved individual might therefore find herself deprived of a relationship that enabled her to confer greater objective meaningfulness on her life. Grief might be seen as

Michael Cholbi

evidence of this deprivation and a motivational catalyst to finding new avenues for acquiring objective meaningfulness of this kind.

This is not an incoherent story. Nevertheless, the phenomena relating grief and life's meaningfulness I have outlined in this article exert pressure on *purely* objective accounts of life's meaningfulness. For this story seems not to explain certain aspects of grief experience. The surviving friend could understandably experience the other's death as a loss of meaningfulness, but it would be hard to see with the surviving friend should feel disoriented or puzzled in the way bereaved individuals often do. To return to Seneca's remarks about replacing a lost cloak: What the surviving friend has lost is not only the source of objective meaningfulness afforded by the friendship. She has lost the friendship itself (or is forced to adopt new terms of friendship), a friendship that is part of her own self-conception or practical identity. 'Replacing' that which the friend fostered by finding a new way to improve others' quality of life is possible, but it would not substitute for the relationship in which she had invested her practical identity. Nor ought the surviving friend feel a sense of puzzlement or bewilderment at the friend's death. For no difficult questions about the shape of one's future practical identity need arise if the relationship's significance was purely a conduit to objective meaningfulness. Grief registers a personal loss because it registers losses of what matters, as well as registering how those losses matter *to us*.

Hence, a purely objective account of meaningfulness in life, in my estimation, underestimates or misdescribes the losses to which grief responds. My arguments suggest that meaningfulness in life is at least a hybrid fact, one resting both on 'subjective attraction' to what one cares about and the 'objective attractiveness' of what one cares about (Wolf, 2015, p. 112).

University of Edinburgh
mcholbi@ed.ac.uk

References

George Bonnano, *The Other Side of Sadness: What the New Science of Bereavement Tells Us About Life After Loss* (New York: Basic Books, 2009).

Michael Brady, *Emotional Insight: The Epistemic Role of Emotional Experience* (Oxford: Oxford University Press, 2013).

Cheshire Calhoun, *Doing Valuable Time: The Present, the Future, and Meaningful Living* (Oxford: Oxford University Press, 2018).

Albert Camus, *The Stranger*, translated by S. Gilbert (New York: Vintage, 1946).

David Carroll, *Albert Camus the Algerian: Colonialism, Terrorism, Justice* (New York: Columbia University Press, 1955).

Michael Cholbi, 'Finding the good in grief: What Augustine knew but Meursault could not', *Journal of the American Philosophical Association* 3 (2017), 91–105.

Michael Cholbi, 'Regret, resilience, and the nature of grief', *Journal of Moral Philosophy* 16 (2019), 486–508.

Michael Cholbi, *Grief: A Philosophical Guide* (Princeton: Princeton University Press, 2021).

Michael Cholbi, 'The rationality of suicide and the meaningfulness of life', in I. Landau, ed., *Oxford Handbook of Meaning in Life* (Oxford University Press, 2021).

D. Klass, P.R. Silverman and S. Nickman (eds.), *Continuing Bonds: New Understandings of Grief*, (New York: Taylor and Francis, 1996).

Ruth Davis Konigsberg, *The Truth About Grief: The Myth of Its Five Stages and the New Science of Loss* (New York: Simon and Schuster, 2011).

Christine Korsgaard, *The Sources of Normativity* (Cambridge: Cambridge University Press, 1996).

Elizabeth Kübler-Ross, *On Death and Dying* (New York: Macmillan Co., 1969).

Paul K. Maciejewski, Baohui Zhang, Susan D. Block, and Holly G. Prigerson, 'An empirical examination of the stage theory of grief', *Journal of the American Medical Association* 297 (2007), 716–23.

Matthew Ratcliffe, 'The phenomenological clarification of grief and its relevance for psychiatry', in G. Stangheillni, M. Broome, A. Raballo, A.V. Fernandez, P. Fusar-Poli, and R. Rosfort, eds, *Oxford Handbook of Phenomenological Psychopathology* (Oxford: Oxford University Press, 2019) 538–51.

S.R. Shuchter and S. Zisook, 'The course of normal grief', in M. Stroebe, W. Stroebe, and R. Hansson, eds., *Handbook of Bereavement: Theory, Practice, and Intervention* (New York: Cambridge University Press, 1993).

Susan Wolf, *The Variety of Values: Essays on Morality, Meaning, and Love*, (New York: Oxford University Press, 2015).

Can We Measure the Badness of Death for the Person who Dies?

THOMAS SCHRAMME

Abstract

I aim to show that the common idea according to which we can assess how bad death is for the person who dies relies on numerous dubious premises. These premises are intuitive from the point of view of dominant views regarding the badness of death. However, unless these premises have been thoroughly justified, we cannot measure the badness of death for the person who dies. In this paper, I will make explicit assumptions that pertain to the alleged level of badness of death. The most important assumption I will address is the assignment of a quantitative value of zero to death, which leads to the conclusion that there are lives not worth living for the affected person. Such a view interprets the idea of a live worth living in quantitative terms. It is in conflict with actual evaluations of relevant people of their lives.

1. Introduction

If death is bad for people, as many philosophers believe,[1] then how bad is it? Many people believe that it is not the worst thing that can happen to people. Philosophers regularly assert that there might be conditions people find themselves in that are worse than death.[2] Hence, death might not be as bad as some conditions but worse than others. In other words, death is somewhere between extremely bad conditions and good conditions on a scale of qualities of life. This seems plausible enough, but I will show that the claim comes with contested assumptions which undermine its credibility.

If we ask how bad death is, we are relying on a comparative evaluation of different possible lives of a person. The values of these lives are usually generated in relation to a person's wellbeing or, more generally, what is good for them. I will accordingly ignore concerns of other types of values, such as aesthetic or moral values, which

---

[1]   See Nagel (1979, pp. 1–10); Feldman (1992, pp. 172ff.); Scarre (2007, pp. 85ff.); Belshaw (2009, pp. 64ff.); Bradley (2009, pp. 47ff.); Luper (2009, pp. 82ff.); Fischer (2014).
[2]   See McMahan (2002, pp. 121ff.); Malek (2016); Kamm (2020, pp. 1ff.).

doi:10.1017/S135824612100031X   © The Royal Institute of Philosophy and the contributors 2021
Royal Institute of Philosophy Supplement **90** 2021   253

Thomas Schramme

might very well also be important when considering the badness of death. But can we actually make sense of the idea that a condition can be worse than death, if death is nonexistence? There are numerous conceptual and logical puzzles involved here. Several of these have been addressed and, as far as I can see, resolved in the relevant literature. However, there is one specific idea that to my mind challenges attempts to include death and nonexistence in a theory of prudential value: That is the idea of death as a point on a scale. It is important to identify the premises leading to this specific idea.

My aim in this paper is therefore to make explicit and critically assess certain assumptions that are regularly made in the philosophical literature on the badness of death. These assumptions become pertinent when claims are made about the level of badness of death, for instance when it is asserted that death is worse for a child than for an old person. Some of these claims express ordinal judgements, that is, they refer to the comparative badness of instances of death without saying how much worse they are. Other judgements rely on cardinal measurement, for instance when it is said that two deaths are twice as bad as one death. Cardinal numbers are also often introduced to align different goods in life on a single scale. Without these cardinals, certain comparative claims remain unsupported.

It should be stressed that I do not doubt the meaningfulness of life comparisons as such, or of assuming values of lives, even numerical values. There are many relevant and helpful assessments of this kind, for instance in health care economics. However, the relevant discussion in the philosophy of death has other purposes and is concerned with the value of life or death *for the* affected *person*. I will show that once the problem of badness of death for the person who dies has been transferred into an abstract problem as to whether death is a bad event, the first step has been done in a string of assumptions. Based on these assumptions, it is but a small step to conclude that lives that contain less quantitative prudential value than death are lives not worth living. The individual steps in this thought process are not necessary, of course, but because they are intuitive, they are also hard to resist. Making the contested steps visible is hence a valuable form of critique, I believe, despite its destructive form.

The assumptions I will tease out are the expression of the locution 'bad-for' in terms of abstract or impersonal value, the summative nature of overall prudential value, the comparability of good (and bad) things, the allocation of negative quantitative values to bad things, the linearity of prudential values and, most importantly, the assignment of a quantitative value of zero to death. All these assumptions are questionable.

In the second section, I discuss ways in which things can be bad for human beings to sort out the feasible options of theories regarding the badness of death. A comparative account and a noncomparative account are the most promising options. They either claim that death is making a person worse off or that death is a noncomparatively bad thing. The third section then elaborates on these accounts of badness in relation to the badness of death and shows that the common explanation, which focuses on the privation of the good things in life by death, leads to an abstract perspective on prudential value. According to such a view, events that are not experienced or even merely counterfactual can have an impact on the value of a person's life. In the fourth section, I aim to show that, although not in itself a problematic claim, the abstract perspective results in additional assumptions in relation to the cardinal measurement of death. These assumptions are to do with the numerical or quantitative assessment of lives' values. In the fifth section, I show how they eventually lead to the notion of a life not worth living via the assumption of a zero level of prudential value.

I do not deny that we can reasonably attach values to human lives. What I deny is that we can measure these values in a personal way, that is, as a value for the person who dies. We can still assign values to lives, for instance if we assume social or economic values. But the value of a life for the person herself cannot be measured because it is not a quantifiable value.

Before I begin my examination, I need to add a terminological clarification: in the philosophical literature on death, it has become customary to distinguish between three different notions in relation to the phenomenon of death: the process of dying, death itself and being dead.[3] Hardly anyone would question that dying can be bad for the person who dies. It is often a painful and slow process, hence might be very bad indeed, even so bad that death itself may seem a good thing – although in truth the termination of existence is rather the required means to end an unbearable situation. Death is the termination of life. It is probably best to understand death as the end of the process of dying. What criteria exactly mark the occurrence of death is of course contested, but we do not need to be very precise. Many philosophers and medical personnel define death as the irreversible cessation of all vital functions of an organism (Lizza, 2021). There is a definite moment when someone has died – whenever exactly it

---

[3] See, for instance, Scarre (2007, p. 6f).

happens – and this person is then dead and transitions to a state of being dead. We will later see that there are some philosophical puzzles around the notion of nonexistence, which are also pertinent to the state of being dead. The main problem when discussing the badness of death for the person who dies is how to make sense of putting a value on a condition that lies outside a person's existence.

2. Bad things

In this section I discuss ways in which things can be bad for human beings. The badness of these things will be featured in terms of their impact on the wellbeing, welfare or, more abstractly, the good of the affected person. In terms of philosophical value theory, I therefore talk about prudential value, about things that are relevant from the perspective of self-interest (Griffin, 1986, pp. 30ff.; Sumner, 1996, pp. 20ff.).

The problem whether death is bad for the person who dies can be expressed in many different ways (cf. Bradley, 2009, pp. 47ff.). Death might indeed be simply bad, as I just said, without any further specification. Death can also be disadvantageous, not good (in contrast to being positively bad), or harmful; that is, it can have certain bad features and results that altogether make it bad. Death can itself be a harm or an evil, hence constitute a bad thing. Death can also be personally undesired or frightening – and accordingly be an object of negative evaluation. It seems that death is actually bad for human beings in all of these respects, albeit perhaps not always jointly.

Some philosophers have declared that death is actually not bad, because after death there is no person anymore for whom death could be bad. One of the first philosophers to, famously, make that claim was Epicurus in his *Letter to Menoeceus* (Epicurus, 1940). As many know, he built his argument on a specific theory of wellbeing, hedonism, according to which things that are bad for sentient beings need to be capable of being experienced. Assuming that we cannot experience anything bad when we are dead, it seems indeed, as Epicurus put it, that death is 'nothing to us'. However, this simply means that being dead cannot be bad for the dead person, which is altogether not so great news for those who worry about death, not about what happens after death. The fact that being dead is not bad for a person does not mean that death cannot be bad for the person before her death or when death occurs. Although I stay uncommitted regarding the value of afterlife, I still think we should not belittle Epicurus's insight. After all, for the Ancients it was apparently a constant worry what will happen to the person after death (Warren, 2004, pp. 3ff.). To be able to ease the fear about individual afterlife and its possible harm was certainly a philosophical accomplishment. Yet, it does not take the sting out of death itself.

In the following, I will refer to 'bad things' on numerous occasions. Importantly, this expression allows for experiences, events, resulting facts, and even counterfactual, fictional and hypothetical events to be able to bear the property of prudential badness. I do not regard this as suspicious or problematic. It is important to mention, though, because I will therefore include what Stephen Rosenbaum calls 'abstract' bads – events happening in the world – as well as 'concrete' bads – conditions of people – in my brief overview (Rosenbaum, 2000; 2013). The idea of abstractly bad things is not alien to language use, nor metaphysically dubious.[4] We can similarly use Matthew Hanser's terminology of state-(of-a-person-)based theories of harm as opposed to event-based theories of harm (Hanser, 2011).

I avoid the term *harm* in this paper as much as possible, because it is usually used in ethical contexts, including legal circumstances. These contexts consider acts of harming, which are again considered to be based on intentional or careless action, which might then exclude natural events. To be sure, natural events can put people in a harmed condition (Feinberg, 1984, p. 31), but death or being dead are difficult to be accounted for as a harmed condition of a person. A natural event can certainly be bad for us, even if it might not constitute harming action. Hence, I refer to bad things, not harmful things.

First, events such as death can make us worse off than before. Importantly, some events can be bad although the affected person does not suffer an impairment of wellbeing. This is unusual, because normally an event that makes a person worse off would have to reduce the level of wellbeing. People can be worse off, despite their wellbeing staying on the same level, if they are prevented from reaping a specific benefit. If a gust of wind blows my lottery ticket away and it would have won, even if the latter fact is unknown to me, then that event can make me worse off. Here, the comparison is between a possible future and the actual future of a person's life. After the lottery draw, I am worse off than I would have been, were it not for the gust of wind. This is the counterfactual sense of being made worse off. It is also called the counterfactual account of comparative harm.

---

[4]   Cf. Sider (2012).

Thomas Schramme

According to the common comparative interpretation, things can only be bad in the negative sense of preventing a good thing if the benefit is expectable, reasonably hoped for, normal or rightfully owed. Not to find Aladdin's lamp or not being able to jump to the moon, though potentially a huge benefit to a person, are not bad things, or harms for that matter (Draper, 1999). Hence not all things that would be good for someone and that are prevented from coming about are bad. We need a threshold of normal or expectable good things, which can be set for specific purposes, to distinguish between things that make us worse off and that merely fail to bestow a benefit.

It is usually relatively straightforward to distinguish between bad things and things that are simply not good, though admittedly there is a grey area in terms of the normative elements of being expectable, etc. In relation to the badness of death this specific aspect has led some philosophers to assume that death is only a bad thing for the person if the benefit of a longer life can still be expected or the event of death would be abnormal. In other words, death would not be bad if a longer life cannot reasonably be expected, especially at an advanced age, in terms of statistical probability or medical possibilities.

Second, things can be bad, not due to their results, but due to their inherent features; the way they are as such or directly present themselves in relation to us. The most straightforward example is pain. Pain is bad in itself for a person, due to its phenomenal features. Pain might actually make a person better off than she would have been, for instance when it causes children to turn their hand away from a hot surface. Still, the experience of pain is usually bad for the affected person. Other examples are being bullied, insulted or feeling nauseous. Death, because not being experienced (as we assume), does not easily align with this type of bad.

Events can also be bad for people, despite not being experienced, but still due to their inherent features (Shiffrin, 2012). If a person is betrayed by a friend, then this is bad for her, even if she does not know about it. The betrayal itself is a bad thing for her, not in the sense that she feels worse as a result or that the experience of being betrayed is bad, but in the sense that she is the object of a bad event, an instance of betrayal. It is, in a word, a noncomparatively bad thing. Such a bad thing can be due to a positively bad thing or a loss of something valuable (Hausman, 2015, p. 350). Betrayal, for instance, can accordingly be described as a loss of a trustful relationship. Admittedly, this specific type of things being bad is perhaps more contested than the comparative interpretation, because it relies on evaluative claims about certain events, including death, as allegedly constituting inherently bad events. We would need to hear more about the relevant theory of value. But at this point we are concerned with the types of bad things, not its most plausible content.

There are more ways in which things can be bad for people, for instance in the sense that they are opposed to the goods of a human life form. But the two important interpretations for our purposes are of the comparative and the noncomparative type. Death can make us worse off or it can be noncomparatively bad. Both these types of bads cannot be due to any phenomenal features, if we assume that death involves the end of all experience for the affected person. This is one of the reasons why much of the philosophical literature focuses on the event or fact of death – in other words, on abstract evaluations.

An abstract or impersonal perspective comes with a perhaps unwanted consequence. It allows to discuss badness in a sense that seems unrelated to the personal way we normally conceptualise bad things. If *events* – in addition to conditions that affect people – can be bad for someone, they might also be bad as such, without concretely affecting the relevant person. In an extreme version there might then be events that are bad for nobody but nevertheless bad things to happen (Tenenbaum, 2010). This can be an awkward consequence for our purposes, because when talking about the badness of death, we normally consider the problem as involving an assessment of the concrete badness of death for the person who dies; we usually do not consider the badness of death from an abstract or even impersonal perspective.

Death and life, at least in a first approximation, are not abstract values, but values for persons. 'Personal values accrue to objects in virtue of the fact that those objects have value-for, or are valuable to, someone – not in virtue of the fact that those objects have value simpliciter, or are valuable, period' (Rønnow-Rasmussen, 2011, p. xiii). We will see that the modern philosophical debate on the badness of death has led to perspectives that make death a value simpliciter – a zero value to be precise.

3. How death is bad

We have seen that two explanations of the badness of death seem most plausible: A comparative and a noncomparative account. The comparative account maintains that death is bad for the person who dies, insofar as it prevents valuable things to continue in her life or

Thomas Schramme

makes people worse off. The noncomparative account holds that death as such is a bad thing to happen to people. In this section we will look more closely at these two types of accounts.

The comparative account of the badness of death is usually linked to the privation (or deprivation) account because it focuses on what death takes away from us or deprives us of. Death involves the absence of the good things for the person who has died. In the modern analytical debate on the badness of death, this theory originated from Thomas Nagel and was further developed by Fred Feldman (Nagel, 1979; Feldman, 1991; 1992). Today it has numerous supporters.[5] Although the deprivation account is usually put forward in a comparative version, it does allow a noncomparative version as well. Here, the event of death involves a loss of inherently good things.

Now, there seems to be a problem for the comparative account because the relevant comparison seems to be between the life of a person and the condition of this person when being dead. Yet the person does not exist after death, of course, at least not in the relevant sense of allowing a meaningful comparison in terms of, say, quality of life, or other interpretations of prudential value. This can be called the no-wellbeing-without-being problem. There are two routes to answer this problem:[6] One is to claim that we do not need to compare a condition of life with a condition of death, but only two conditions of life. The other is to allow for counterfactual conditions of people to be added to the comparison.

Both these replies must retreat to more abstract aspects of the lives of people. To be plausible, they cannot rely on a comparison of real conditions of people but assume a comparison of events or 'social situations' (Fleurbaey and Voorhoeve, 2015). In other words, they move from a personal stance to an impersonal stance. In addition, comparative accounts must assume a summative theory of wellbeing or prudential value: Additional goods in life can only add to the value of a person's life if the temporal values can be added in some way (Horton, 2021). Otherwise no meaningful comparison between states of affairs would be possible.

The first response to the no-wellbeing-without-being problem has been put forward by Feldman and refined by other theorists (Feldman, 1992; 1992; McMahan, 2002, pp. 105ff.; Bradley, 2009, pp. 50ff.). Feldman suggests comparing the value of the life of person P at t1, the moment of death, with the value(s) of the life of

---

[5]   E.g. McMahan (2002); Bradley (2009); Kagan (2012, pp. 205ff.).
[6]   Cf. Bykvist (2015); Arrhenius and Rabinowicz (2015, p. 435).

the same person P at t2, which is a moment in the nearest possible world (Feldman, 1991, pp. 214ff.). The nearest possible world is the one which is different in only one respect: P has not died. We can assume, for instance, that in the nearest possible world P lives on for another 30 years and enjoys numerous goods. Whatever the quantitative value of this life in the possible world is, it is presumably higher than the value of P's life at the time of P's death in the real world. After all, her life was cut short by death and we can safely assume that living longer would have involved good things for her. That's why death is bad for her.

Note that this verdict cannot be generalised. Death is not always bad for the person who dies according to this theory. If the life of P in the nearest possible world would not have led to more good things, then death would not be bad for the person who dies. But be that as it may, what exactly happens in the nearest possible world is of course not known to us. This fact poses an epistemological problem in assessing the relevant values. This might not be a huge problem, because it seems a safe bet to claim that more life is normally better than less life, so we can at least make an ordinal comparison between life and death. Death is hence a comparative bad for the person who dies. But it will be very difficult, if not impossible, to determine cardinally how much worse the shorter life is compared to the longer life. This problem will become more relevant at a later stage of this paper, but it is worth mentioning here, because it naturally leads to the idea of putting a zero value on death.

The counterfactual theory of comparative harm similarly introduces possible alternative scenarios to the death of the person (Feinberg, 1986). If the person had not died, she would have very likely made more pleasurable experiences, achieved relevant goods or had some important desires fulfilled. So whatever theory of prudential value we assume, it is again relatively plausible to claim that death prevents an improvement in the value of life.

Altogether the comparative account – be it its possible world or its counterfactual variant – seems plausible and can straightforwardly explain the badness of death for the person who dies. However, it relies on two important assumptions that need to be scrutinised and that might lead to consequences that are not necessarily foreseen by the proponents of the comparative account.

First, because we do not have access to the actual value of people's lives in possible worlds or in counterfactual situations – that would, at least according to many theories of prudential value, require access to their subjective point of view – the comparative theories need to revert to states of the world, including persons for whom certain events are good or bad. Thus, Feldman says that his theory 'calculates the value of a *state of affairs* for a person by considering what would happen (whether as consequence or not) if the *state of affairs* were to occur, as compared to what would happen (whether as consequence or not) if it were to fail to occur'.[7]

Second, the comparative theory additionally needs to assume that the good things for a person can be accumulated in some way. Good things add up to a bigger value of a life and bad things reduce the value. But this assumption may well be controversial.[8] Simple accumulation is particularly controversial if a further assumption regarding the linearity of relevant values is added. We can reasonably deny that the good life for human beings is gradable along a scale and instead hold that it involves an absolute, nongradual achievement. Epicurus, for instance, thought that the best condition of a human being to achieve was *ataraxia*, which is usually interpreted as absence of all mental pain, a kind of calmness, free of fear, or tranquillity of the soul. If we have achieved this ideal state, there can be no improvement to our life. Whether this is plausible or not is not our concern, of course, but accumulative accounts of the good for human beings are certainly not the only reasonable option.

A noncomparative account of the badness of death claims that death involves the loss of something valuable for human beings. As we have seen, it is more difficult to find something positively bad in death, because it is not an event in our life. But death can be bad in the privative sense of taking noncomparatively good things from us. According to F. M. Kamm, for instance, it is 'the fact that death deprives us of goods of experience and action that makes death bad for us' (Kamm, 1998). Other noncomparative theories similarly allege agency, absence of pain etc. as intrinsic or basic goods for human being.[9] It is hence not a bad experience or a bad personal condition that makes death bad, but a fact about the loss of good things.

The noncomparative account can avoid the somewhat implausible consequence that the comparative account faces, according to which death at very old age is not bad for the person who dies. Death in old age still takes away the good things of life, so it is inherently

---

[7]   Feldman (1991, p. 218) emphasis added; see also Luper (2009, pp. 84ff.).
[8]   For a detailed scrutiny of the issues and additional conditions of intrapersonal wellbeing aggregation, see (Hirose, 2014, pp. 89ff.).
[9]   See Gert (2005, pp. 90ff.); Shiffrin (2012, p. 386); Burri (2019).

bad, although it might be accepted that it is comparatively not as bad as dying young. More generally, the noncomparative account can explain that under specific circumstances death might be the lesser evil, but still (noncomparatively) bad. This seems to be an important insight. 'When a person dies, her death thwarts all her ongoing plans and projects, thus rendering some of her past efforts futile. This makes a person's death absolutely bad for her, even when it is overall good, thereby potentially turning her death into a lesser of two evils' (Burri, 2019, p. 185).

The main problem for the noncomparative account is to make good the claim that some things, such as experience or agency are good things for human beings. Why not *ataraxia* or indeed even a life full of pain and danger instead? On what basis do we decide what is the correct account of a good life for human beings? Arguably the most plausible strategy is to simply leave the evaluation of the life of people to the relevant individuals themselves. In other words, it is not a fact about something being present or not that makes personal life good, but whether the person makes the life good, in the sense of infusing their life with things they find valuable. But then it is not clear anymore why death could be deemed bad for a person from an abstract perspective, without considering her individual assessment of her own life.

In this section, we have looked more closely at the most common theories of the badness of death for the person who dies. They come in two main types, a comparative and a noncomparative version. Although both theories are successful in explaining the badness of death, they need to revert to controversial assumptions. Comparative theories need to assume an accumulative nature of the good things for human beings. They also need to revert to an abstract account of bad things for persons, which refers to events, facts or states of the world. The latter assumption is often shared by noncomparative theories. Noncomparative accounts usually presume certain objective goods or bads, and they hence also retreat to an abstract perspective where the concrete evaluation of, or the meaning of things to, people does not count for establishing the value of things in life.

4. How bad is death?

Whether death is bad for the person who dies has been traditionally an important problem in philosophy. We have seen that there are reasonable arguments affirming death's badness. But there is a second problem that needs to be answered: How bad is death? This question

Thomas Schramme

goes over and above the ordinal problem posed before, at least in the comparative perspective, where the badness of death has been explained by an interpersonal ordinal comparison – death makes people worse off. In order to say how bad death is we need to expand our view to cardinal evaluations.

The idea of measuring the level of badness of death for the person who dies might seem ludicrous. If we ask, for instance, how bad death might be for ourselves, it will be very difficult to come up with an answer. We would not even know what kind of measure would be involved. Are we supposed to put a monetary value on our life, in the sense that we might say: death would for me be equivalent to, say, a loss of £500K? Or should we state that death is as bad as having to eat 300 marmite sandwiches in a day? The whole idea is obviously not easy to make sense of.[10]

But at least ordinal comparative evaluations of deaths seem to be feasible. Philosophers certainly think that they can achieve these. Christopher Belshaw, for instance, quite simply says: 'For someone in good health, hit by a bus, death at eighty-two is considerably worse than it is for someone who is already terminally ill. And this is true whether or not it is in some sense absolutely bad'.[11]

In addition, many researchers rightly insist that there are numerous occasions where we need to assess the relative value of death.[12] For instance, when allocating scarce resources in medicine, we want to know whether it would be better to invest into, say, treatment of extremely premature newborn babies or of dementia patients.[13] If we think that this kind of assessment should be made with the impact on affected people in sight and not based simply on external considerations, such as the impact of deaths on the nation's economy, we need some kind of comparison of death for different people. Perhaps we are then able to say that death for a newborn is worse than death for a demented patient.

Similarly, we might encounter ethical questions where different policies have an impact on future life and deaths.[14] For instance, if we do not prevent climate change, many people will die due to floods or droughts. But if we invest into alleviating climate change, we have less resources available to research into medical treatment.

[10] Cf. Nord (2019).
[11] See Belshaw (2009, p. 107); cf. McMahan, (2002, pp. 185ff).
[12] Cf. Broome (2008); Millum (2019, p. 62).
[13] Cf. McMahan (2002, pp. 162ff.); Millum (2019).
[14] See Parfit (1986, pp. 351ff.); Harman (2004); Greaves (2015).

264

Can We Measure the Badness of Death for the Person

Accordingly, more people will die from theoretically preventable or curable diseases. Which deaths are ethically more significant?

There are also occasions where we want to assess death within the context of an individual life. People who contemplate suicide or euthanasia on behalf of incapacitated patients seem to assess the death of an individual person in terms of comparing (perhaps vicariously) death to the current quality of life of the person. Occasionally, they might come to the assessment that death for this person or themselves is actually better than continuing life.[15] To make sense of such evaluations we need some idea about the comparative value of death.

So, there is some need for interpersonal and intrapersonal comparative assessment of death. It might be possible, in some contexts, to restrict the relevant evaluation to ordinal judgements, for instance when we come to the conclusion that death early in life is worse than death later in life, or that life for a particular individual is worse than continuing to live. However, it seems that at some point we also require cardinal judgements, because occasionally we will deal with different numbers of people. Is saving two babies from death better than treating fifty dementia patients and preventing their deaths for another year? Similarly, whether life for a specific individual is worse than death will depend on some considerations of their wellbeing or quality of life over time. This might also require some cardinal evaluation to make good the overall assessment.[16]

It is easy to see how there will be an incentive for putting a specific value on death, not just because we need to make the mentioned judgements but also because it will allow us to compare policies involving the death or nonexistence of people with alternatives that affect the prudential value of people. In other words, it is beneficial for the mentioned practical purposes to make death comparable in a wider sense. However, as we will see, such a move comes with problems that are often overlooked.

In the discussion so far, we have already achieved an abstract perspective on the value of death. This allows us to seamlessly aim at putting a value on death for a person that is not determined individually by the person herself, but by an assessment of the relevant events involving the deaths of people. We have also seen that the comparative account assumes the accumulative nature of the good things in life. Theorists can therefore be hopeful to make use of the comparative account and develop it for the practical purposes of measuring the

[15] See Brandt (1992); Feldman (1992, pp. 221f.); Kagan (2012, pp. 318ff.).
[16] Cf. Broome (2012, p. 228).

badness of types of deaths – for instance the deaths of infants in comparison to the deaths of old people – and perhaps even individual tokens of death – for instance whether the death of a specific person might be better for her than going on living.

Cardinal measurement requires numerical values. As we have seen, it will not do, for certain practical purposes, to restrict our assessment of death to ordinal measurement. For instance, is the event of the death of two healthy babies worse than the death of fifty demented patients? If the values of the individual deaths itself were equal, then the answer would be easy. The event of the death of fifty people is worse than the death of two. But the very idea of the comparative account of the harm of death was to say more than just that death is bad. It was supposed to allow an assessment of *how bad* death is. The answer of the comparative account is that death is bad relative to the loss of the value of possible life.[17] Accordingly, we cannot simply equalise the value of the death of a healthy baby with the value of the death of a demented person and then multiply with the numbers of affected individuals. Rather, we have now additional factors to include in our overall assessment. Similar considerations might be factored into individual lives. Whether a person, say, has important life plans can have an impact on how much of a loss death would be for her. Similarly, whether death spoils the story of a person's life – one's life's unity – might be included in the assessment of the badness of an individual death.[18]

Importantly, to determine the level of badness of a death requires a metric. A way of factoring in considerations such as length of life, narrative significance or mental restrictions can only be factored in if values are made comparable. This is often achieved by introducing numerical values. The most obvious metric is drawn from quality of life or wellbeing measures. There are numerous available in welfare and health care economics.[19] Philosophers who write on the value of death usually do not invest much time into this and make up their own values. This seems acceptable because they do not normally speak to real policy issues. But it requires certain assumptions that are worth being made explicit because they are certainly debatable.

---

[17] See Bigelow, Campbell and Pargetter (1990, p. 126); Feldman (1992); Belshaw (2009, p. 111); Bradley (2009); Fletcher (2016, pp. 145ff.); Broome (2012).

[18] See Velleman (2015, p. 173); see also McMahan, (2002, pp. 174ff.); Fletcher, (2016, pp.132ff.); Fischer (2009).

[19] Cf. Hausman (2012); Broome (2004).

Can We Measure the Badness of Death for the Person

The first assumption is that good and bad things in life can be made comparable. For instance, a possible life where a person moves to another city to take up a new job can be compared to a life where she stays, keeps her job and buys a puppy. In other words, different good and bad things in life need to be integrated into a single scale.[20] Yet it seems fairly difficult to make the relevant comparisons. Joseph Millum states that 'crucially, we do not know the relative weight that should be given to each of these characteristics. For example, how important is simple sentience as compared with self-awareness?' (Millum, 2019, p. 69). Perhaps we can isolate certain features of a life, for instance the length of the life or the health status of the person who lives the life. Accordingly, we might be able to maintain that a longer life is better than a shorter one, or that life in health is better than the same life where the person has a disease. Still, to make more complex comparisons, especially cardinal measurements, we need to assume comparability of fairly complex features of individual lives.[21]

The second assumption of the cardinal comparative account is that bad things have a negative value (Feldman, 1991, p. 209). This seems intuitive enough; after all, pain, harms and losses are negatively evaluated. So why not assign them negative values? Yet, there are already problems with the simple valence of affect.[22] Although pain is usually worse than pleasure, that does not seem to be true for all examples. Pain attended by significant others, or pain that is instrumental to achieve a thing of value, or desired pain, are all not necessarily negative, and they are most likely not worse than any conceivable pleasure, such as a warm bath.[23] Accordingly, even simple sensations such as pleasure and pain are not clearly distinguishable in terms of valence. For purposes of measurement, they would need to be translated into a publicly available and intersubjective scale. The problems which come with this task had already been appreciated by Bentham, despite his reputation of inventing a simplistic hedonistic calculus (Harrison, 1983, pp. 152ff.; Collard, 2006).

What is more, we should not forget that the metric for cardinal comparison is our own making. Less charitably put, it is arbitrary. In order to indicate the relatively lower value of pain as opposed to pleasure, we might as well assign lower values, not negative values.

---

[20] Cf. Feldman, (1992, pp. 153ff.); McMahan, (2002, p. 175).
[21] Cf. Chang (2015).
[22] De Boer (2014); see also Haybron (2008, pp. 199ff.).
[23] Cf. Shiffrin (2012, p. 383). Harrison (1983, pp. 152ff.); Collard (2006).

Thomas Schramme

For instance, we could say that a toothache is worth 5 units, whereas eating a piece of chocolate cake is worth 20 units. That would also allow to assign positive and even higher values for certain types of pain in comparison to pleasures, instead of the straightforward but controvertible allocation of negative values to bad things and positive values to good things. From the comparative account as such, in combination with assumptions about prudential value, we can merely infer that pain is normally worse than pleasure. Regarding more complex events, we can also legitimately assume, say, that winning the lottery is (other things being equal) better than losing a leg.

Still, to claim that bad things are of a negative numerical value seems to be justified by the assumption that there is a neutral level of wellbeing, relative to the good and bad things for us; some kind of indifference that is usually represented by the value of zero on a scale. This is sometimes illustrated by a state of unconsciousness (Kamm, 1998, p. 14) or by 'an empty life' (Broome, 1999, p. 169). Ben Bradley similarly states: 'When I am sitting in a chair and having no pleasant or painful experiences, I have a wellbeing level of zero' (Bradley, 2009, p. 106). Since pain and losing a leg is worse than the neutral level, it seems legitimate to assign them negative numbers, after all. But, again, the neutral level could alternatively be set on a scale as, for instance, a point of 100 units of the metric of wellbeing – whichever is chosen for the purpose of introducing cardinal comparisons. The comparative account as such does not require a value of zero for representing a neutral level of wellbeing.

The third assumption is linearity of assigned values. Here, the idea is that values that can be put into a scale form a steady gradient, so that, for instance, five instances of toothache are five times as bad as one. In other words, the increase or decrease between intervals of numeric values is supposed to be constant, similar to metrics such as the usual temperature scales or distance measures. Again, this seems acceptable, at least as regards simple experiences, such as toothache. To allow for known deviations from linearity, for instance marginal utility, we can incorporate additional factors into our function. But how plausible is the assumption of linearity, really?

Take pain for instance. As Daniel Wodak rightly points out: 'The spectrum from indifference to noticeable pain to agony is vast. To represent this by using numbers linearly would be a "cumbersome task"' (2019, p. 31). This is obviously an understatement, given the problem of identifying a single dimension of comparison for such diverse experiences. In addition, we might easily fall into the trap he calls the representational fallacy and consequently make false assumptions. We can easily forget that our values are fairly arbitrarily chosen numbers on a scale which we have assumed to be organised in a linear fashion. From these representational values we can then easily slide into unaccounted and potentially false assumptions, say, that 8 units of pain are twice as bad as 4 units, similarly to the false assumption that 30 degrees Celsius is twice as hot as 15 degrees Celsius (Wodak, 2019).

In this section, we have started from the practical requirements of being able to make cardinal evaluations of situations involving the deaths of persons. We have seen that there are numerous assumptions involved that could potentially lead to false conclusions. In the next section of the paper, I will focus on one specific assumption that – to my mind – has particularly harmful consequences that are normally not appreciated: the representation of death by a zero level of prudential value.

5. Zero level of prudential value

Consider the following example that Derek Parfit introduces in his book *Reasons and Persons*. It's a hypothetical case; he calls it 'the Wretched Child': 'Some woman knows that, if she has a child, he will be so multiply diseased that his life will be worse than nothing. He will never develop, will live for only a few years, and will suffer pain that cannot be wholly relieved' (Parfit, 1986, p. 391). For Parfit, this is an example of a life that he calls 'not worth living' (Malek, 2016; DeGrazia, 2012; 2016). Although he says that '[t]his description can be ignored by those who believe that there could not be lives that are not worth living',[24] it is indeed hard to avoid such a notion if we assume that certain situations come with persistent negative values for human beings and, importantly, if we also assume that above the negative, accumulated value there is a better situation for the person, namely death, which is represented by a zero level of whatever the exact metric of assessment is. In other words, the notion of a life not worth living is a conclusion that follows from certain assumptions, especially the alleged negative numerical value of bad things in life and the alleged zero value of death. It is then easy to see how philosophers come to the conclusion that there are real (or potential) lives of human beings that are comparatively worse than

---

[24] Parfit, (1986, p. 358). It makes no difference to my argument that the terminology can be changed to 'a life worth not living' or 'a life not worth starting'. My point is about the foundational assumptions of this perspective.

Thomas Schramme

death. With the relevant assumptions in place, it is but a small step to translate 'worse than death' to 'not worth living'. In this section, I want to scrutinise the premise according to which death can be represented by a zero value.

To represent the event of death as a zero value is actually fairly common in the philosophical debate.[25] Sometimes the assumption is made about the possible state of nonexistence, where this value is assigned during existence (to avoid assigning values to lives that will never come into existence). More importantly for our purposes, the zero value is also assigned to death. Christopher Belshaw expresses this idea most clearly: 'Death brings our level of wellbeing down to zero. This is surely, in part, what is bad about it'.[26] To assign a zero value of wellbeing (or another evaluative metric) to nonexistence allows additional comparative judgements that are not pertinent to our purposes, so I will ignore the difference between nonexistence and death.

One problem with the zero level is the possible confusion of a numerical value, zero, with the absence of anything that could be valued. Because there is nothing that could be valued in relation to death, it seems we cannot put death on our scale. David Heyd agrees: '[T]here is no way to compare the amount of suffering of states of actual people and the state of nonexistence of these people. We should resist the temptation of assigning a zero-value to nonexistence, thus making it quantitatively commensurable with either the positive or the negative net value of the lives of actual people' (Heyd, 2009, p. 13).

Still, it is important to appreciate that the problem we are facing here is not the same as the no-wellbeing-without-being problem discussed earlier. We have left the latter problem behind by introducing events or states of the world as the relevant features for comparison. The problem at this point is an axiological one. It concerns the specific value given to death, namely zero. The problem is that this is an unwarranted choice, based on the dubious assumption regarding negative and positive numerical levels of prudential value and the idea of identifying death with a level which is devoid of valuable events.

What is worse, it leads to ethically dubious conclusions, such as Parfit's wretched life case. Here, the impersonal perspective is easily confused with a personal one. In fact, there is a clash

---

[25] See Roberts (2003); Holtug (2001, p. 366; 2009, p. 79); Bradley, (2009, pp. 90ff.)

[26] Belshaw (2009, p. 97); see also Feit (2021, p. 91).

between the theoretical claim that a specific type of life is not worth living with the real assessment of people who are in the suggested states (Bernfort et al., 2018). People who live allegedly wretched lives are often in reality leading happy lives to their own standards. To assign to them a life not worth living is a form of usurping their wellbeing. Of course, many will quickly respond that the lives they use as examples are far worse than lives with relatively common disabilities. In other words, they will say that wretched lives are extremely rare and usually lead to a very early death. But my point is a different one. It is not about the referents of the concept of a wretched life or a life worse than death, but the very concept itself. It is an ethically unwanted concept that is only made possible by dubious theoretical assumptions.

Although there are numerous purposes for discussing the comparative values of lives and deaths, there is no additional purpose served by introducing the notion of a life not worth living,[27] or of 'being better off dead' (Conley, 2016). It seems better to 'eliminate' or put to death the notion of a life not worth living, as Roberto Fumagalli has recently argued (Fumagalli, 2018). I agree, although I would recommend restricting the elimination to the quantitative interpretation of the notion. It is indeed regrettable that the positive ideal of a life worth living, understood as an examined life, has been replaced by a reductionist conception focused on quantitative value. In this way, philosophy has replaced a traditional and valuable philosophical idea with a superfluous, contested and potentially harmful conception.

Conclusion

The problem whether death is bad for the person who dies has led to a considerable amount of philosophical debate. The most attractive position seems to be provided by a comparative version of the privation account. According to this view, death is bad because it deprives the dead person of the good things in life. The comparative account also allows for ordinal and cardinal evaluations of deaths, which can indeed be helpful in practical contexts, such as health care economics or population policies. Yet, such evaluations are helpful only if they are reliable and accurate, otherwise the help is illusory and may even lead to harm.

---

[27] But compare Grill (2016, p. 230).

Thomas Schramme

In order to determine *how bad* death is for a person, an abstract perspective is required, which does not sit well with the initial problem, because it leads to a perspective on death's badness that is disconnected from the badness for a person. It also leads to the assumption that for some people death is actually not bad, independent of their own assessment of their lives. As we have seen, the common explanation of the grade of badness of death rests on numerous contested claims. Especially the comparability of different prudential values, their linearity, the negative numerical values of bad things and the zero value of death are dubious assumptions.

We cannot measure the badness of death for the person who dies. Indeed, this type of badness of death does not pose a quantitative question. Common philosophical explanations lead to a conclusion that is untenable: the idea that there are lives that are not worth living for reasons of lacking a sufficient amount of positive value to make them better than death. This idea should be rejected, as long as no better justifications of the underlying assumptions are available.[28]

University of Liverpool
t.schramme@liverpool.ac.uk

References

Gustaf Arrhenius and Włodek Rabinowicz, 'The Value of Existence' in: Iwao Hirose and Jonas Olson (eds.), *The Oxford Handbook of Value Theory* (Oxford: Oxford University Press, 2015), 424–443.

Christopher Belshaw, *Annihilation: The Sense and Significance of Death* (Stocksfield: Acumen, 2009).

Lars Bernfort, Bjørn Gerdle, Magnus Husberg, Lars-Åke Levin, 'People in states worse than dead according to the EQ-5D UK value set: would they rather be dead?', *Quality of Life Research*, 27 (7) (2018), 1827–1833.

Ben Bradley, *Well-Being and Death* (Oxford: Oxford University Press, 2009).

[28] For helpful comments, I would like to thank audiences at the Royal Institute of Philosophy Conference 'Meaning in Life and the Knowledge of Death' and at the Summer School 'Exploring New Methods for Applied Ethics'. I am also very grateful to Roberto Fumagalli and Michael Hauskeller, for their detailed feedback.

Richard B. Brandt, 'The Morality and Rationality of Suicide', in: *Morality, Utilitarianism, and Rights* (Cambridge: Cambridge University Press, 1992), 315–335.

John Broome, *Ethics out of Economics* (Cambridge University Press, 1999).

John Broome, *Weighing Lives* (Oxford University Press, 2004).

John Broome, 'What Is Your Life Worth?' *Daedalus*, 137 (2008), 49–56.

John Broome, 'The Badness of Death and the Goodness of Life', in: Ben Bradley, Fred Feldman, and Jens Johansson (eds.), *The Oxford Handbook of Philosophy of Death* (Oxford: Oxford University Press, 2012), 218–32.

Susanne Burri, 'How Death Is Bad for Us as Agents', in: Espen Gamlund, Carl Tollef Solberg and Jeff McMahan (eds.), *Saving People from the Harm of Death* (New York: Oxford University Press, 2019), 175–86.

Krister Bykvist, 'Being and Wellbeing', in: Iwao Hirose and Andrew Reisner (eds.), *Weighing and Reasoning: Themes from the Philosophy of John Broome* (Oxford: Oxford University Press, 2015), 87–94.

Ruth Chang, 'Value Incomparability and Incommensurability'. in: Iwao Hirose and Jonas Olson (eds.), *The Oxford Handbook of Value Theory* (Oxford University Press, 2015), 205–224.

David Collard, 'Research on Well-Being. Some Advice from Jeremy Bentham', *Philosophy of the Social Sciences* 36, (2006), 330–354.

Sarah Conly, 'Better Off Dead: Paternalism and Persistent Unconsciousness', in: Glenn Cohen, Holly Fernandez Lynch, Christopher T. Robertson (eds.) *Nudging Health: Health Law and Behavioral Economics* (Baltimore: Johns Hopkins University Press, 2016), 287–96.

Jelle De Boer, 'Scaling happiness', *Philosophical Psychology*, 27 (2014), 703–718.

David DeGrazia, *Creation Ethics. Genetics, Reproduction, and Quality of Life* (Oxford: Oxford University Press, 2012).

David DeGrazia, 'Procreative Responsibility in View of What Parents Owe Their Children', in: Leslie Francis (ed.), *The Oxford Handbook of Reproductive Ethics* (Oxford: Oxford University Press, 2016), 641–55.

Kai Draper, 'Disappointment, sadness, and death', *Philosophical Review* 108 (1999), 387–414.

Epicurus, 'Letter to Menoeceus', in W. J. Oates (ed.) *The Stoic and Epicurean Philosophers* (New York: The Modern Library, 1940), 30–34.

Joel Feinberg, *Harm to Others* (Oxford: Oxford University Press, 1984).

Joel Feinberg, 'Wrongful Life and the Counterfactual Element in Harming', *Social Philosophy and Policy* 4 (1986), 145–77.

Neil Feit, 'Death Is Bad for Us When We're Dead', in Michael Cholbi and Travis Timmerman (eds.), *Exploring the Philosophy of Death and Dying: Classical and Contemporary Perspectives* (London: Routledge, 2021), 85–92.

Fred Feldman, 'Some Puzzles About the Evil of Death', *Philosophical Review* 100 (1991), 205–227.

Fred Feldman, *Confrontations with the Reaper: A Philosophical Study of the Nature and Value of Death* (Oxford: Oxford University Press, 1992).

John M. Fischer, J.M., *Our Stories: Essays on Life, Death, and Free Will* (Oxford: Oxford University Press, 2009).

John Martin Fischer, 'Mortal Harm', in: Steven Luper (ed.) *The Cambridge Companion to Life and Death* (Cambridge: Cambridge University Press, 2014), 132–148.

Guy Fletcher, *The Philosophy of Well-Being: An Introduction* (London: Routledge, 2016).

Marc Fleurbaey and Alex Voorhoeve, 'On the Social and Personal Value of Existence', in: Iwao Hirose and Andrew Reisner (eds.), *Weighing and Reasoning: Themes from the Philosophy of John Broome* (Oxford: Oxford University Press, 2015), 95–109.

Roberto Fumagalli, 'Eliminating "life worth living"', *Philosophical Studies*, 175 (3) (2018), 769–792.

Bernard Gert, *Morality: Its Nature and Justification* (Oxford: Oxford University Press, 2005).

Hilary Greaves, 'The Social Disvalue of Premature Deaths', in: Iwao Hirose and Andrew Reisner (eds.), *Weighing and Reasoning: Themes from the Philosophy of John Broome* (Oxford: Oxford University Press, 2015), 72–86.

Kalle Grill, 'Asymmetric population axiology: Deliberative neutrality delivered', *Philosophical Studies*, 174 (2016), 219–236.

James Griffin, *Well-Being: Its Meaning, Measurement, and Moral Importance* (Oxford: Clarendon Press, 1986).

Elizabeth Harman, 'Can We Harm and Benefit in Creating?' *Philosophical Perspectives*, 18 (2004), 89–113.

Matthew Hanser, 'Still More on the Metaphysics of Harm', *Philosophy and Phenomenological Research* LXXXII (2) (2011), 459–469.

Ross Harrison, *Bentham* (London: Routledge, 1983).

Can We Measure the Badness of Death for the Person

Daniel Hausman, *Preference, Value, Choice, and Welfare* (Cambridge: Cambridge University Press, 2012).

Daniel Hausman, 'The Value of Health', in: Iwao Hirose and Jonas Olson (eds.), *The Oxford Handbook of Value Theory* (Oxford: Oxford University Press, 2015).

Daniel M. Haybron, *The Pursuit of Unhappiness: The Elusive Psychology of Well-Being* (Oxford: Oxford University Press, 2008).

David Heyd, 'The Intractability of the Nonidentity Problem', in Melinda A. Roberts and David T. Wasserman (eds.), *Harming Future Persons: Ethics, Genetics and the Nonidentity Problem* (Dordrecht: Springer Netherlands, 2009), 3–25.

Iwao Hirose, *Moral Aggregation* (Oxford: Oxford University Press, 2014).

Nils Holtug, 'On the Value of Coming into Existence', *The Journal of Ethics*, 5 (2001), 361–384.

Nils Holtug, 'Who Cares About Identity?', in Melinda A. Roberts and David T. Wasserman (eds.), *Harming Future Persons: Ethics, Genetics and the Nonidentity Problem* (Dordrecht: Springer Netherlands, 2009), 71–92

Joe Horton, 'Partial aggregation in ethics', *Philosophy Compass* 16: e12719 (2021), 1–12.

Shelly Kagan, *Death* (New Haven: Yale University Press, 2012).

Frances M. Kamm, *Morality, Mortality. Volume I: Death and whom to save from it* (Oxford: Oxford University Press, 1998).

Frances Kamm, *Almost Over: Aging, Dying, Dead* (Oxford: Oxford University Press, 2020).

John P. Lizza, 'Defining Death in a Technological World. Why Brain Death is Death', in: Travis Timmerman and Michael Cholbi (eds.) *Exploring the Philosophy of Death and Dying: Classical and Contemporary Perspectives* (London: Routledge, 2021), 10–18.

Steven Luper, *The Philosophy of Death* (Cambridge: Cambridge University Press, 2009).

Janet Malek, 'The Possibility of Being Harmed by One's Own Conception', in: Leslie Francis (ed.) *The Oxford Handbook of Reproductive Ethics* (Oxford: Oxford University Press, 2016), 571–588.

Jeff McMahan, *The Ethics of Killing: Problems at the Margins of Life* (Oxford: Oxford University Press, 2002).

Joseph Millum, 'Putting a Number on the Harm of Death', in: Gamlund et al., *Saving People from the Harm of Death* (Oxford: Oxford University Press, 2019), 61–75.

Thomas Nagel, 'Death', in: *Mortal questions* (Cambridge: Cambridge University Press, 1979).

Thomas Schramme

Erik Nord, 'Quantifying the Harm of Death', in: Espen Gamlund, Carl Tollef Solberg and Jeff McMahan (eds.), *Saving People from the Harm of Death* (New York: Oxford University Press, 2019), 21–32.

Derek Parfit, *Reasons and Persons* (Oxford: Clarendon Press, 1986).

Melinda A. Roberts, 'Can it Ever Be Better Never to Have Existed at All? Person-Based Consequentialism and a New Repugnant Conclusion', *Journal of Applied Philosophy*, 20 (2), (2003), 159–185.

Toni Rønnow-Rasmussen, *Personal Value* (Oxford: Oxford University Press, 2011).

Stephen E. Rosenbaum, 'Appraising Death in Human Life: Two Modes of Valuation', *Midwest Studies In Philosophy* 24 (2000), 151–171.

Stephen E. Rosenbaum, 'Concepts of Value and Ideas about Death', in: James Stacey Taylor (ed.), *The Metaphysics and Ethics of Death: New Essays* (Oxford: Oxford University Press, 2013), 149–168.

Geoffrey Scarre, *Death* (Stocksfield: Acumen, 2007).

Seana V. Shiffrin, 'Harm and Its Moral Significance', *Legal Theory* 18 (2012), 357–398.

Theodore Sider, 'The Evil of Death: What Can Metaphysics Contribute?' In: Ben Bradley, Fred Feldman, and Jens Johansson (eds.), *The Oxford Handbook of Philosophy of Death* (Oxford: Oxford University Press, 2012) 155–166.

Lawrence Sumner, *Welfare, Happiness, and Ethics* (Oxford: Clarendon Press, 1996).

Sergio Tenenbaum, 'Good and Good For', in Sergio Tenenbaum (ed.), *Desire, Practical Reason, and the Good* (Oxford: Oxford University Press, 2010), 202–233.

J. David Velleman, 'Well-Being and Time', in *Beyond Price: Essays on Birth and Death* (Cambridge: Open Book Publishers, 2015), 141–174.

James Warren, *Facing Death: Epicurus and his Critics* (Oxford: Oxford University Press, 2004).

Daniel Wodak, 'What If Well-Being Measurements Are Non-Linear?' *Australasian Journal of Philosophy*, 97 (2019), 29–45.

Meaning in Lives Nearing Their End

F. M. KAMM

Abstract

In this paper, I consider the idea of meaning in life as I believe it has arisen in some discussions of ageing and death. I critically examine and compare the views of Atul Gawande and Ezekiel Emanuel, connecting their views to the idea of meaning in life. I further consider the relation of meaning in life to both the dignity of the person and the reasonableness of continuing or not continuing to live. In considering these issues, I evaluate and draw on Bernard Williams' distinction between categorical and conditional desires, Susan Wolf's work on meaning in life, and Jeremy Waldron's views on dignity in old age.

In this paper, I consider the idea of meaning in life as I believe it has arisen in some discussions of ageing and death. I consider the views of Atul Gawande and Ezekiel Emanuel, connecting them to ideas of meaning in life, reasons to continue or not continue living, and the dignity of the person. In considering these issues, I evaluate and draw on the work of philosophers Bernard Williams, Susan Wolf, and Jeremy Waldron among others.

1. Atul Gawande's Being Mortal

In Gawande's (2017) book *Being Mortal*[1] he emphasizes the importance of continuing to have aims that give life meaning as it is approaching its end. These aims may be characterized by 'narrowed focus' given that projects that require long-term survival are not feasible and there may be an overall focus on relationships rather than on projects. One particular role that Gawande thinks can give meaning to life as it ends is the 'dying role' in which one passes on truths about life or brings to closure relationships.

Aiming to retain meaning in life to the end of life goes beyond merely avoiding pain and suffering, the original aim of hospice and palliative care. However, Gawande supports hospice because he thinks that the dual aims of not suffering and retaining meaning

---

[1] For my earliest discussion of his book see Kamm (2017). It is the basis for Chapter 3 in *Almost Over*.

doi:10.1017/S1358246121000321

often imply that one should not pursue medical treatments that have only a small chance of success. This is not only because they may cause suffering but because pursuing them can interfere with remaining activities that give meaning to life and in particular with the dying role.

I find it useful to connect these views of Gawande's with the distinction that Bernard Williams drew between conditional desires and categorical desires.[2] (One might also speak of conditional and categorical goods that can be the objects of desires and of conditional and categorical reasons these goods can give one.) Avoiding pain and suffering are objects of conditional desires in that they are things one could reasonably want if one will continue to live.[3] However, they are not typically the objects of categorical desires as Williams understands these, since objects of categorical desires give one a reason to go on living in order to get them (even when a primal desire to remain alive, which Williams recognizes, is absent[4]). Desires for simple activities that one looks forward to can be categorical desires; they needn't be for what he calls 'ground projects.'[5] Avoiding pain and suffering is not typically something one wants to stay alive to get.[6]

[2] See Williams' (1973) and also his (1981). I make use of Williams' distinction in discussing various views in *Almost Over*.

[3] The things it would be reasonable to want if one goes on living need not be conditional in the sense that one will go on living only if (on condition that) they are present. This sense would make them like side constraints on going on and their absence decisive reasons for not going on living.

[4] He says 'I do not want to deny...a sheer reactive drive to self-preservation'. (However, he thinks 'this cannot be the minimal categorical desire' since when the question whether to go on gets asked, the reactive drive is already shown not to be enough by itself to sustain life (Williams, 1973, p. 86). I raise some objections to this view in *Almost Over*, Chapter 6.)

[5] He says 'propelling concerns may be of a relatively everyday kind such as certainly provide the ground of many sorts of happiness' (1981, p. 12). One of the benefits of speaking of categorical objects of desires or categorical reasons to desire certain things is that even if someone doesn't actually desire anything, there can be objects worthy of being desired and reasons to have these things. This makes it possible for someone's life to be worth continuing even if he desires nothing since things will actually occur in his life without his desiring them (they just occur) that are good in a way that makes it reasonable to continue on to get them (e.g., friendship that arises despite someone not ever thinking to desire it). To simplify matters, I will mostly speak of categorical and conditional desires but these other possible uses of the categorical/conditional distinction should be assumed to exist as well.

[6] At least this is so if one assumes that death involves nonexistence for if one is trying to avoid the pains of Hell, one might want to stay alive in order

Gawande's idea that pursuits and relationships that provide meaning in life should continue to life's end implies, I think, that even those who are near the end can have categorical desires which provide a reason to go on living even in the short term. Hence one might not resist death by pursuing unlikely-to-succeed medical treatments that interfere with satisfying the categorical desires. Yet one would not seek death (for example, by suicide or by refusing easy life-saving measures[7]) since one would not want to escape the life one was living. Instead, one would simply accept that death was coming shortly.

In the part of his book concerning those not terminally ill but aged, Gawande also emphasizes the importance of pursuits that continue to provide meaning in life. He claims that having these is more important than the safety and security that professionals who care for the aged typically emphasize. He says that without what gives meaning in life people are likely to lack the will to live and will omit to do even easy things that are needed to stay alive (e.g., take a flu shot).

Given his emphasis on retaining meaning in life, I hypothesize that (though he does not specifically say so) Gawande might believe that if one lacked meaning in life, it would not be prudentially senseless – putting aside moral objections – to seek or to not resist the end of one's life even though one was not physically suffering.[8] This would mean that absence of meaning was a sufficient if not a decisive reason to seek or to not resist the end of one's life. (By 'sufficient reason' I mean that it can justify an act by showing it to be reasonable; not merely that it can explain the act's occurrence causally as a matter

---

to avoid pain and suffering in one's afterlife. A scientist's project could be proving that a certain drug will prevent his pain and suffering. So he could go on to live because his life would lack pain and suffering. But this is only a means to living on to prove the drug works.

[7] To the extent that hospice care is inconsistent with such easy measures (e.g., flu shots or antibiotics), it too may pose a problem for satisfying short-term categorical desires.

[8] Some may think seeking death by suicide would be senseless because it is morally wrong. I argue against this view in various places, including Chapter 7 of *Almost Over*. Furthermore, in this discussion I am only concerned with the significance of the presence or absence of meaning in life for the person whose life or death is at stake rather than for others whom his life or death might affect. Notice that omitting easy resistance to death may occur even without seeking death. This is because one might merely seek not to be complicit in keeping oneself alive. I discuss this issue in Chapter 6 of *Almost Over*.

F. M. Kamm

of motivation.) Similarly, that one will have fun could be a sufficient reason for going to an amusement park but it needn't be decisive; one could have sufficient reason to do something else because it will instead be relaxing. Further, one person could be more attracted to the possibility of relaxation whereas someone else could be more attracted to the possibility of having fun without impugning the reasonableness of the other person's choice. (Even more strongly, as Thomas Scanlon says,[9] 'reasons can render an action rationally eligible without making it rationally required in the absence of some countervailing reasons...Reasons themselves are not optional: a consideration is a reason in a certain situation or it is not. What is optional is acting on certain reasons.' So one could have a sufficient reason that is not decisive even in the absence of a sufficient reason to do something else. As an example, Scanlon says that for the pleasure it would give me 'it makes sense for me to listen to some music, but even if I know this I do not have to have some countervailing reason for not turning on the radio in order not to be open to rational criticism for failing to do so'.)

Might it also be true that the absence of meaning in one's life is a decisive reason for not staying alive and for seeking or not resisting the end of one's life? Then the presence of meaning in life could be understood to be a necessary condition for the reasonableness of staying alive.

I think the interpretation of Gawande's view that makes having meaning in life a necessary condition for the reasonableness of staying alive is implausible. For he discusses a case in which a man says that he would go through quite a lot to keep living even if his life only involved watching football and eating chocolate ice cream. It is hard to believe that these things provide meaning in life rather than merely being types of pleasure that arise from actively enjoying certain things (as opposed to being pleasure caused by neural stimulation). Yet the man seemed to have enjoyment (e.g., of football and chocolate ice cream) as an object of categorical desire and Gawande thought the man's view could make sense, as do I. I conclude that while lack of meaning in life might be a sufficient reason for not going on in life (and Gawande may think this) it isn't a decisive reason for not going on (so that going on couldn't make sense); for example, there can be other sufficient reasons to stay alive and other grounds for categorical desires.

So far in discussing Gawande I have used the terms 'meaning in life' and 'giving meaning to life' but not said what Gawande thinks

[9] In his (2014, pp. 106–107).

the terms mean. In the section of the book discussing those who are dying, Gawande takes having meaning in life to involve having a particular type of pleasure felt at narrative high points in life, a little bit of which can outweigh many bads and whose absence can outweigh many goods. This strikes me as a Millian view, reducing all goods to pleasure but distinguishing pleasures by quality and not only quantity. Gawande supports his view with the example of a ball game. He says of watching the team that has performed beautifully and then loses: 'We feel that the ending ruins the whole experience. Yet there's a contradiction at the root of that judgment. The experiencing-self had whole hours of pleasure and just a moment of displeasure, but the remembering self sees no pleasure at all' (Gawande, 2017, p. 239).

I do not think this experientialist conception of meaning in life is correct. In the case of the ball game there is no contradiction. In focusing on the loss, the so-called remembering self need not forget all the prior experiential pleasure nor judge the moment of displeasure at the loss as qualitatively more important. Rather it does not forget that the point of the game is to win and this point gives meaning to most of what is done in the game. That point is more important than the pleasure (or displeasure) the game produced either during its course or even in its successful (or unsuccessful) end. I think that the merit of Gawande's example of the ball game is that it shows that the meaning represented by an achievement or relationship in life is not a matter of the amount of pleasure had in or in response to it. One can suffer greatly to achieve something meaningful without thinking that the amount or quality of pleasure had in, or in response to, the achievement outweighs the suffering that makes possible what is meaningful. This is because it is not in terms of pleasure that one evaluates meaningful events or things at all. (Elsewhere in his book Gawande offers a different account of meaning in life which I will consider below.)

I have other concerns about Gawande's views of meaning at the end of life. First, he attributes great significance to endings suggesting that having meaning in them is worth giving up on even many earlier goods. This is one reason he frowns on taking risks to extend one's life by medical means that will probably fail and leave one with a bad end of life. This is also why he uses the analogy of the ball game whose importance is in how it ends not in hours of pleasure or displeasure preceding the end. He also makes use of psychologist Daniel Kahneman's Peak-End Rule, according to which people remember episodes by their peak of good or bad and how the episode ends rather than by the total amount of time spent in good or bad states (Redelmeier and Kahneman, 1996). One of Kahneman's examples is colonoscopy: people remember the worst part and how it ends. So they are more likely to repeat the procedure on the basis of more favorable recollections of colonoscopies that involve overall more pain but whose final moments are not as painful as they would be if the procedure ended earlier. Whereas Kahneman's Peak-End Rule is an empirical report of retrospective evaluation and its effects on future choices, Gawande suggests that the Peak-End Rule could also apply to the 'anticipatory' (prospective) evaluation of events and experiences, and that deciding whether to apply it is a normative ('should') question. When the rule is used normatively, he thinks that it shows that in living and making choices, one should not merely be concerned with the average of good and bad in one's life but with the narrative structure of one's life that involves goals achieved and the character of endings. A prospective use of the rule seems to recommend doing what will still allow for meaningful (high) points and a good end. One way of achieving this would be to have one's life end on a high point. The fact that this is not Gawande's recommendation suggests that he is not opposed to living through (and ending on) some declines from a good peak. However, the rule might still recommend bringing about some very good peak, even if it can only be followed by a lengthy bad experiential period that is worse than nothing, so long as one will then rise to a minimally less bad ending. This does not seem like good advice (if the ending is not necessary to secure the goodness of the very good peak). And if someone were asked antecedent to a colonoscopy whether he would want to have it extended so that he will have overall more pain in order that it end with lesser pain, he should (and probably would) reject this if his concern were only about this colonoscopy. All this suggests that the Peak-End Rule is not useful as a normative guide to prospective choices.[10]

Furthermore, I doubt that a dying patient should significantly reduce the amount of time she still can live during which she has nonpeak adequate experiences just in order to make the very end point of her life better. For example, suppose a surgery were sure to make only her last few hours worse than they would otherwise be but would eliminate her nausea for weeks so she could get some

[10]   Daniel Kahneman did once suggest that since we spend more time remembering our experiences than having them, perhaps we should prospectively choose which ones to have on the basis of how we will remember them (in his 1994) For a criticism of this view see my (2007).

(mere) enjoyment in life before that worse end. She might reasonably choose surgery. One point here is that as Kahneman presents the Peak-End Rule it applies to the very end point of what is identified as an episode, and as such this Nausea Case shows that the end part of the rule does not work well as a prospective guide. However, Gawande most often thinks of 'the end' as the entire dying period of someone's life that could go on for months. This leaves it open that one might average goods and bads within that last period (or give priority to reducing the badness of any forthcoming worst point in life, whether it would come before or at the very end point of life). Furthermore, Gawande speaks of meaningful peaks that can occur within the extended ending period of one's life. Hence, the contrast between peak and end on which the Peak-End Rule depends is not maintained in his use of it if 'the end' refers to an extended dying period.

While it makes little sense for someone who will shortly die to focus on whether her memories of her dying period and very end point will be in accord with a retrospective use of Peak-End Rule, Gawande also mentions (e.g., 2017, p. 242) the effect on relatives of memories of a good end for their loved one. From the patient's intrapersonal point of view, this raises the issue of how it affects the meaning in her remaining life to know that she will affect the memories of her relatives in accord with the Peak-End Rule. It would certainly not be a sign of love on the part of those relatives to deny the dying person relief from nausea for weeks merely so that they have memories of a good peak (e.g., she can go to a wedding) and do not have memories of a very end point that is bad, caused by the procedure that would relieve earlier weeks of nausea.

Gawande's comparison of the end of a life with the end of a ball game seems particularly inapt. First, the end of the game really is the very end point by contrast to the longer dying phase. Second, since the point of the ball game is to win, there is a definite final goal toward which the players aim that (to a great degree) gives meaning to all the efforts made in the game. The same is not true with life; all the time before the end of a life (whether this is thought of as the very end point or the more extended dying period) is not lived for the sake of having the best possible end in terms of continuation of meaningful (or even enjoyable) activities. It would be particularly pernicious, I think, to use the ball game analogy to try to dissuade someone from using medical treatments that are the only way to get a small chance of truly lengthy survival on the ground that they will probably result in his life ending with a lot of physical suffering. This is especially so if there are means

F. M. Kamm

such as assisted suicide to escape the suffering. Gawande offers a life to the end with meaning in it as the alternative to physician-assisted suicide but it may sometimes be preferable to lose meaning near the end for a chance at much more life with the option of physician assisted suicide to avoid bad effects of not succeeding.

Finally, it is possible that many of the medical treatments that Gawande thinks interfere with having meaning in life at its end may provide opportunities for meaning in life. For example, suppose that someone chooses to pursue medical treatments because they have a small chance of extending his life, and these treatments introduce much pain and suffering in what is probably the last short part of his life. He certainly has a purpose of getting more life but this may not help him retain meaning while suffering. However, new discoveries that will gradually increase the efficacy of these treatments may depend on people like him trying them. Then helping to improve treatments may be an effect of what he does for other reasons and its having this effect may be enough, independent of his aiming to produce it, to make personally meaningful what he does in his remaining life. This is so even if he would not suffer treatment only for that effect and would suffer without it for his own sake (though suffering might then not be meaningful). Indeed, we might broaden the idea of an (optional) 'dying role' to include such ways of attaining meaning.

Nonetheless, suppose someone is offered some project that could give meaning to his suffering while dying and yet he prefers to use terminal sedation to avoid suffering though this gives no meaning to his remaining life. His choice to avoid the suffering rather than give meaning to his life seems entirely reasonable as well. In this case, having meaning in life would not be a decisive reason for going on in life in a certain way.

2. Ezekiel Emanuel's 'Why I Hope to Die at 75'

Ezekiel Emanuel's (2014) article 'Why I Hope to Die at 75'[11] is another discussion by a bioethicist that seems to me to be related to the issue of meaning in life though Emanuel does not specifically put the matter this way.[12] He discusses what to do after a 'complete

[11] He says he is not recommending suicide or physician assisted suicide and I will not here examine the moral status of these acts. I discuss his views of them in *Almost Over*.
[12] The discussion that follows is based on Chapter 6 of *Almost Over*.

life' by which he means the part of one's life that has the major achievements, great or small, that one will have in one's life. He thinks that the loss of capacities associated with life after (roughly) 75 make it at least not unreasonable, from a self-interested perspective, to refuse even easy and sure to succeed means that will keep one alive (e.g., a flu shot or antibiotic treatment).[13] This is so even if the life after 75 is not plagued by pain and suffering or disastrous mental and physical ailments, and one even finds happiness in pursuits open to those with ordinary diminished capacities brought on by old age. The exception to all this, he says, are those statistical 'outliers' who continue to be creative achievers.

Emanuel says that the life of even non-outliers beyond 75 is not worse than death. This could mean that value-wise it is either equivalent/on a par with death or else better than death. If it is the former, then resisting death or bringing it about might not make sense since neither would produce a change in value. But suppose the life is somewhat better than death. How can it make self-interested sense not to make minimal efforts to resist, or even bring about, the end of a life not worse than death? For example, Shelly Kagan in his book *Death* (2012) represents death as at the zero point on a graph, a life worse than death as below the x-axis and a life better than death as above the x-axis. He argues that from a self-interested perspective it 'makes no sense' to seek or accede to death if one's life could still be above the x-axis.[14] Suppose that one faces the prospect of losing all capacities for action and thought except for being given pleasurable sensations by way of neural stimulation. Assuming pleasure is an objective good above the x-axis, Kagan's view implies that it would make no sense to prefer death to this condition. By contrast, I think Emanuel would deny this.

Emanuel's reasons for his view primarily center on (a) the lack of worth of the activities one can expect to engage in past 75 and (b) one's lack of interest in engaging in such activities even if (c) one could predict that they would give one happiness. Focusing on the worth of activities and interest in them as well as the possibility of unworthy sources of happiness recalls the components of Susan

---

[13]   He starts with an even stronger claim that everyone (with a few exceptions) would be better off not living beyond 75. I will here only discuss the weaker claim that it is not unreasonable for some average post-75 people not to go on after 75.

[14]   However, I have argued that this judgment of his conflicts with other things he says in his book. See Kamm (2017) and *Almost Over*, Chapter 2.

F. M. Kamm

Wolf's account of meaning in life.[15] If so, we might construe Emanuel as thinking that it would not be unreasonable to refuse to continue living because further life will lack what can provide meaning in life.[16] Whereas Gawande is concerned with people retaining meaning in their life to its end even when the end is probably soon, Emanuel could be understood as concerned with not living beyond the point where meaning is possible even when the end needn't be soon.

Wolf's primary theory is that meaning in life is provided only by positive engagement with what one correctly believes are objectively valuable pursuits. She says that this means that there must be a union of subjective and objective value that she calls 'fitting fulfilment'. Fulfillment is a subjective condition broader than happiness since, Wolf thinks, being fulfilled can be present when there is concern and even anxiety as when a parent is fulfilled in devotion to a handicapped child. Importantly, feeling fulfilled in positively engaging with something is not enough on her view to produce meaning in life if the object of one's positive engagement is actually not worth engaging with. One example she gives is Fulfilled Sisyphus who finds fulfillment in endlessly rolling his rock up a hill only to have it fall down again. Even if he thinks there is meaning in his life, Wolf thinks he is wrong because what he is doing is objectively worthless. By 'objective' value or worth Wolf means no more than that believing that something has value is not enough to ensure that it has value; its value or disvalue is independent of belief and one could be wrong in one's beliefs. On the other hand, Wolf thinks that if one is doing something objectively worthwhile without being positively engaged with it (e.g., one is forced to do something worthwhile that one hates), there will also not be meaning in one's life, because the subjective component will be missing.

It seems to me that Wolf's concern about meaning in life should be distinguished from the question of the whether one's life overall has a meaning. Meaning in life can be present in particular activities and relationships without there being some meaning in one's life overall. One can have lived a meaningful life even if its particular meaningful elements don't hang together in a way that lets us deduce an overall meaning or narrative. (However, Wolf does specifically connect her view of meaning *in* life with what she calls 'the age-old question of the meaning *of* life' since the idea that we are 'actively

---

[15] See her (2010).
[16] At one point, Emanuel says that doing puzzles and reading all the time is not even a life.

engaged with projects of independent worth' beyond their value *for us* may put to rest worries about our insignificance that she suggests that age-old question is about) (Wolf, 2010, p. 29). On the other hand, 'meaning in life' suggests that at some point in her life the person will recognize the worth of what she is doing or has done. But it seems we can draw a distinction between 'meaning in life' and what I shall call 'meaningfulness in a life' where the latter could exist if someone has an objectively worthwhile component in her life but does not see it as such and hence does not feel fulfilled in it. (Wolf considers the distinction in response to Robert Adams' commentary on her work) (Wolf, 2010, pp 75–84).Wolf says that people want their lives to be connected to what is objectively worthwhile and her theory provides that. But that could also be provided by a theory that emphasizes what I'm calling 'meaningfulness in a life'. For example, imagine a case where ex ante one has to choose between (a) a life of greater meaningfulness (e.g., producing masterpieces but nevertheless feeling disappointed in them because one does not recognize their worth) and (b) a life with meaning in it (e.g., feeling fulfilled in producing artwork that is worthwhile but not at masterpiece level). At least someone who was truly passionate about art and willing to sacrifice his good mental state for it might choose life (a) rather than (b). This suggests that meaningfulness in life, not meaning in life as Wolf understands it, could sometimes be most important to us.

How does all this match with Emanuel's views? If he were right that the activities open to most post-75 (e.g., he cites doing puzzles and reading all the time) are objectively not worth doing for a sufficiently long remaining time alive, then there would be nothing with which those post-75 could positively engage that had sufficient objective value. If they were happy or fulfilled doing insufficiently worthwhile activities for a sufficiently long remaining life, they would be making the same mistake that Fulfilled Sisyphus makes. Those who are not attracted to this type of remaining life would be correct and more worthy of respect. Wolf implies something similar about Sisyphus when she says of Fulfilled Sisyphus, 'one might wonder whether the transformation that Sisyphus undergoes from being unhappy, bored, and frustrated to being blissfully fulfilled...actually makes his situation worse'. In not recognizing and responding correctly to the worthlessness of what he is doing 'he is either afflicted by mental illness or delusions or diminished in his intellectual powers' (Wolf, 2010, pp. 23–24).

Emanuel need not deny that puzzles and reading are (what Wolf calls) harmless pleasures when they are intermittent respites but it is problematic for him when they are one's entire life at least after a 'complete life'. The following two diagrams describe the first and second possibilities respectively where '____' represents worthwhile activities and '...' harmless pleasures.

1.   ____···____···____···____
2.   _____..........

Possibly, by contrast to Wolf, Emanuel's focus is more on what I called meaningfulness in life since his subjective lack of enthusiasm about pursuits open to diminished capacities is based on his view that they lack worth. He does not identify the lack of enthusiasm for something worthwhile as negative in itself (as it is for Wolf). Nevertheless, even he might argue against being forced to continue on in pursuits whose significant worth one does not recognize or to which one does not feel attracted.

I have focused on Emanuel's view of the worth of the activities available after a complete life rather than the radical change in activities pre- and post-75. Some think that a radical change in the nature of one's activities would create an 'identity crisis', in that in a certain sense one cannot continue being the person one has for the most part been, though of course one is not literally a different person. But suppose that post-75, Emanuel had to stop being a professional bioethicist and discovered that he had a previously unrecognized genius for pursuits even more worth engaging in (e.g., groundbreaking work in physics or painting masterpieces). I do not think he would reject a radical change in his 'identity' when it involved moving on to very different activities of greater (or even equal) worth.[17]

Emanuel's unwillingness to do what will help him continue on after a complete life if it lacks activities of sufficient worth can also be related to Williams' distinction between categorical and conditional desires if this distinction goes beyond mere desires and allows for objectively justified desires (e.g., reasonable ones). Conditional desires would be ones it is reasonable to have *if* one is going to go on living. These might include no pain and suffering. Categorical desires would be for things that one could reasonably want to go on living to get (e.g., seeing great art). It would usually not be reasonable to have a categorical desire to go on living merely in order not to be in pain or to avoid suffering even if one would reasonably want these things if one was going to remain alive. Hence,

---

[17]   These would not be like cases of ordinary 'outliers' who continue the sort of work they have already done and whose continued creativity therefore raises no comparable 'identity crisis'.

Emanuel might be understood to be claiming that there is nothing in the life of most past 75 that could be the basis for reasonable categorical desires and that in the absence of such desires, not doing what could easily save one's life could make sense. On the other hand, given that he is unwilling to commit suicide and so may remain alive when there is no threat to his life, he says he is willing to use palliative care to avoid pain and suffering. Presumably, he would also want to avoid boredom and get some enjoyment while alive, so he might do puzzles and read while waiting for death.

Hence, the satisfaction of conditional desires – including for negative objective goods like not being in pain and for positive ones like pleasurable sensations even caused by neural stimulation – could be what makes life not worse than death and so above zero on the x-axis Kagan uses. Yet the expected satisfaction of these desires would not ground reasonable categorical desires that make one want to go on living. This would provide an explanation of why, contrary to what Kagan suggests, life could be not worse and even (at least experientially) better than death and yet it could make sense from a purely self-interested point of view not to live on, even by refusing easy life-saving assistance.[18] In addition, Emanuel's particular view may be that one can have reasonable categorical desires only for things that can provide meaning in life (or meaningfulness in life) and that there are no such things in life past 75 (unless one is an outlier).

Emanuel might also (implicitly) tie the idea of meaning in life to the idea of dignity. It may be that one cannot lose one's dignity as a person simply because one has diminished capacities of the kind Emanuel has in mind. Nevertheless, living with diminished capacities may not befit someone who does retain his dignity as a person. (This is how I understand the complaint of those who say that they have 'lost their dignity' when they can no longer control their

---

[18]   That the positive zone above zero should not be identified with lives worth living does not entail radical skepticism about using such graphs. By contrast Thomas Schramme thinks no justification of their legitimacy has been given. (See his 'Can We Measure the Harm (or Benefit) of Death?' in this volume.) I think their legitimacy can be justified in part by their according with intuitive judgments about lives not worth living including what sort of lives it would be wrong to create out of consideration for the being created (e.g.,lives with nothing but great suffering in them). The same holds for particular views about what lives are worth living. Suppose some great modern artist was so engrossed in the use of color that she never examined life or her life in particular. Should we think that her life was not worth living? If not, this casts doubt on the view that the unexamined life is not worth living.

bodily functions, for example.) If one thinks that the dignity of the person requires that the life he leads have meaning in it, then the absence of what can give meaning in life could reasonably undermine categorical desires because further life would not be consistent with one's dignity as a person.

Before deciding whether a view like Emanuel's (as we have interpreted it) is correct, consider some contrasting views. We earlier discussed the idea of meaning in life given in the part of Gawande's book dealing with dying. In the section of his book dealing with those who are aged, Gawande offers a different idea of meaning in life that seems closer to Wolf's. He says this view is found in the work of Josiah Royce and it emphasizes pursuing goods outside oneself to which we attribute value (though, unlike Wolf, Gawande does not insist that the attribution must be correct). He also adds that these goods should be greater than oneself. However, the examples Gawande gives of pursuits that help the aged (even when demented) retain what he thinks of as meaning in life include taking care of a parakeet, maintaining plants, and interacting with children. A parakeet, plants, and children are not necessarily greater than oneself. Most importantly for the contrast with Emanuel, Gawande says that he is no longer afraid to grow old since he has seen how easy it is for the aged to retain meaning in life, for example by caring for a parakeet and interacting with others on this basis (2017, pp. 128–30). I think it is this very thing which eliminates Gawande's fear that frightens Emanuel, namely that he will become someone who will be experientially satisfied by pursuing something of as little worth as parakeet care and mistakenly (like Fulfilled Sisyphus) conclude that this provides meaning in his life. What Wolf says of Fulfilled Sisyphus (2010, pp. 23–24) would then apply to his own case: Going from 'being unhappy, bored, and frustrated to being blissfully fulfilled...actually makes his situation worse'. In not recognizing and responding correctly to the low or nonexistent worth of what he is doing 'he is either afflicted by mental illness or delusions or diminished in his intellectual powers'.

Wolf too considers a case of someone who feels fulfilled in devoting her life to the care of a small animal, in her case a goldfish. Wolf denies that this could provide meaning in the person's life. This conclusion could follow from considering only the properties of the activity itself and finding it lacking in objective worth. However, in response to comments by Nomy Arpaly, Wolf seems to revise her initial view of meaning in life that we have considered.[19] The woman in Wolf's

---

[19]   See Arpaly's comments and Wolf's response in Wolf (2010).

goldfish case had many other capacities that were not exercised in goldfish care and that could have led to doing other things of objective worth to ground fitting fulfillment. (Wolf also describes (2010, p. 24) Sisyphus in this way.) But Arpaly asks us to consider a mentally challenged child who exercises to the fullest all of his limited capacities in taking care of a goldfish and interacting with others around this interest of his. In response, Wolf agrees that this child does have meaning in life. She suggests that objective value may arise from objectively non-valuable pursuits (such as goldfish care or throwing a ball through a hoop) when they are done as rule-governed or other social activities.[20] An alternative interpretation of Wolf's view about the mentally challenged child is that she is relativizing the objective worth of an activity to the capacities of a person who engages in it and whether it fully exercises those capacities. On either interpretation she may agree with Gawande rather than Emanuel that an aged person whose capacities have diminished so far that they are fully exercised in parakeet care and social relations built around it can have meaning in life.

One problem is that neither interpretation of Wolf's response to Arpaly explains, at least in terms of having meaning in life, why we would want to have greater capacities and engage in activities whose intrinsic properties give them greater objective worth rather than have fewer capacities even if they are perfectly matched to intrinsically objectively less worthwhile activities (and are part of social and rule-governed enterprises). They also don't explain why, for the sake of the child or adult himself, we would want to improve his mental capacities, for example, by medical treatment. If we say that fewer capacities matched to intrinsically less valuable pursuits can provide no less meaning in life, we may again conclude that there is something else entirely than meaning in life (as Wolf understands it) that is important to us.

We have tried to better understand claims like Emanuel's and their relation to such (sometimes interrelated) ideas as meaning in life, categorical desires, and dignity. Now let us consider whether the claims are true. Do the pursuits open to people past 75 (excluding outliers) not have enough objective value to reasonably be objects of categorical desires? Considered on their own, it seems to me that reading, engaging in relationships, enjoying travel, and especially helping others with the skills one has developed in earlier work are worth doing and can provide reasons for going on in life. Can they always be the source

---

[20]   Nathaniel Serio argues that this interpretation would lead one to conclude that Nazi Party activities can provide meaning in life. See his (2020).

of meaning in life rather than mere enjoyment? Perhaps not, but even Wolf does not say that activities that provide meaning in life are the only ones that can give one a reason to go on living. In the case of people whose pre-75 life has failed to involve opportunities for enjoyable activities, it seems especially true that it is worth their living on to have these. In addition, living on merely for the sake of enjoyment taken in activities could be seen as something like a reward after a 'complete life' of high achievement.

Nevertheless, that whatever one does cannot provide meaning in one's life (in Wolf's sense) also seems to be a sufficient reason for not going on in life. This may be like the case of there being a sufficient reason to become a physicist and a sufficient reason to become an artist but some people are attracted to one sufficiently reasonable option and other people are attracted to another sufficiently reasonable option. Indeed for some getting satisfaction from goods of even considerable objective worth may not be possible after a complete life of extraordinary achievement. Suppose old Albert Einstein's loss of capacities leaves him only able to do bioethics at a high level. I assume that this activity is sufficiently objectively worthwhile to provide meaning in life on Wolf's account if someone can positively engage with it. However, given the (assumed) greater worth of his past activities, Einstein may not unreasonably be unable to positively engage with doing bioethics. Hence, doing bioethics would not provide him with fitting fulfillment.[21]

What of the relation of meaning in life to dignity of the person? It is not clear that only a life whose activities provide meaning in life (or meaningfulness in life) is consistent with the dignity of the person. This is so even if some pleasures are inconsistent with the dignity of the person (e.g., continuing on in life with only neural stimulation of pleasure centers in one's brain). In addition, Jeremy Waldron argues[22] that if conditions in old age arise that do not befit the continuing dignity of the person, a new form of dignity specific to old age can arise in confronting and coping with these conditions in a

---

[21] Perhaps even a radical change to something better from the type of person one has always been might sometimes provide a sufficient reason to not go on in what would still be literally one's own life. This is the so-called 'identity crisis' account of the reasonableness of not going on. For more on commitment to values that one is not rationally required to hold see *Almost Over*, Chapter 2.

[22] In his YTL Centre Annual Lecture, 'The Dignity of Old Age', at King's College London, July 8, 2021. My discussion here is based on my invited comments on that occasion.

clear-eyed way. This would allow one, he thinks, to have age-specific dignity unto death obviating the need to use death as a way to avoid indignity. Does Waldron's argument succeed?

Notice that the dignity specific to old age that concerns Waldron involves an achievement such a coping and being clear eyed about one's choices and prospects. This is by contrast to the core notion of human dignity which does not depend on personal achievements.[23] Hence, some people might fail to achieve old age-specific dignity, for example, by denying the diminished worth of their activities or reality of their approaching death. Then they would live on without old age-specific dignity and could avoid this only by not living on. However, suppose some do achieve this sort of old age-specific dignity. Could it give them a reason to go on living rather than omit easy life-saving means? This would be so if achieving this dignity could be the object of a categorical desire. But it seems to me that achieving this sort of dignity in one's life is only the object of a conditional desire – something one should want if one must remain alive – but it is not reasonably the object of a categorical desire. (Could it be conditional in a stronger sense in that it may be a condition – a side constraint – on staying alive which is not true of all objects of conditional desires in Williams' sense?[24] That would be so if lacking old age-specific dignity were not only a sufficient reason not to go on living but a decisive reason not to go on living. It seems unlikely.that it is such a decisive reason.) In the absence of other desires or reasons to stay alive, that one will be able to deal with limitations in a way that gives rise to old age-specific dignity is not a reason for going on living. Suppose refusing easy life-saving measures is itself consistent with dignity of the person. Then the reasonableness of remaining alive rather than refusing such measures might be supported by either a simple desire to be alive or by some categorical desire whose satisfaction is still possible in old age. These points may also bear on the adequacy of Waldron's argumentative strategy. That is, he considers how dignity specific to old age can arise while going

---

[23] The distinction between dignity due to achievements and as a status had by all persons just in virtue of being a person is analogous to the distinction Stephen Darwall draws between respect for someone's achievement and respect for him as a person. See his (1977). Whereas Waldron speaks in terms of dignity relativized to specific periods of human life, Havi Carel makes similar points by speaking of exercising virtues (an achievement) relativized to dealing with various imperfections in human life. See her 'Meaning, Value, and the Imperfect Life', in this volume.

[24] See footnote 3 on the two senses of 'conditional'.

F. M. Kamm

on living (e.g., by unblinkingly dealing with limitations and approaching death) before discussing the option of avoiding the limitations by ending one's life (e.g., by assisted suicide) which he thinks could also be consistent with the dignity of the person. But it is possible that what has dignity when it is the only option available, lacks dignity when another option exists that is also consistent with dignity. That is, insisting on coping in a way that achieves old-age specific dignity in the absence of reasonable categorical desires to live on may no longer be dignified when there is an alternative of ending one's life consistent with dignity. Analogously, living with paralysis when it involves adjusting to limitations can involve the sort of dignity Waldron sees as specific to old age. But suppose there is a simple pill that could cure the paralysis. Refusing to take it could not only be against self-interest; it could make achieving dignity by dealing with the infirmity not dignified. The opportunity to deal with a problem needn't be better than getting rid of it in a way that is consistent with dignity. Waldron's approach of attending first to what he thinks is the dignity specific to old age independent of considering it in the context where other dignified ways of avoiding a life with limitations exist may be a mistake.[25]

I conclude that if dignity were threatened by having only categorical desires whose satisfaction cannot provide meaning in life, achieving the old age-specific dignity that Waldron has in mind would not itself provide a suitable categorical aim.

3. Conclusion

In sum, in this article I have suggested that there could be sufficient reason to go on living without meaning in life (e.g., for football and chocolate ice cream). It is not necessarily inconsistent with one's dignity to do so. Furthermore, that one will retain one's dignity if one goes on living is not itself a sufficient reason to go on. There

[25] Suppose Waldron thinks that dealing with conditions of frailty, dependency, and mental decline can provide dignity that makes old age not undesirable overall. He could still agree that these conditions in themselves are undesirable and curing people of them while they still live on is a worthy goal even if it eliminates the opportunity for gaining dignity by dealing with infirmities. Suppose it would be better for these conditions of old age to be replaced in this way. This at least conveys that relative to a cure of infirmities old age specific dignity is undesirable even if choosing it when one could be cured of infirmities did not undermine the dignity of dealing with the infirmities.

could also be sufficient reason *not* to go on living (i) because of the absence of either meaning in life or conditions consistent with one's dignity and (ii) even though one could have meaning in life (e.g., when the latter arises from suffering in drug trials). Furthermore, many of the activities Emanuel takes to lack sufficient worth to ground either categorical desires or meaning in life may rather be activities with sufficient worth but with which someone with a particular past life may understandably not be able to positively engage.[26]

Rutgers University
frances.kamm@philosophy.rutgers.edu

References

Stephen Darwall, 'Two Kinds of Respect' in *Ethics* 88 (1977), 36–49.
Ezekiel Emanuel, 'Why I Hope to Die at 75', *The Atlantic*, (2014).
Atul Gawande, *Being Mortal: Medicine and What Matters in the End* (N.Y.: Henry Holt & Co, 2017).
Shelly Kagan, *Death* (New Haven: Yale University Press, 2012).
Daniel Kahneman, 'The Cognitive Psychology of Consequences and Moral Intuition', *Tanner Lecture on Human Values*, University of Michigan, (October 21, 1994).
F. M. Kamm, 'Moral Intuitions, Cognitive Psychology, and the Harming/Not-Aiding Distinction', reprinted in my *Intricate Ethics* (New York: Oxford University Press, 2007), 422–49.
F. M. Kamm, 'The Purpose of My Death: Death, Dying, and Meaning' *Ethics*, 127 (2017) 733–61.
F. M. Kamm, *Almost Over: Aging, Dying, Dead* (Oxford University Press, 2020).
D. A. Redelmeier and Daniel Kahneman, 'Patients; Memories of Painful Medical Treatments: Real-Time and Retrospective Evaluations of Two Minimally Invasive Procedures', *Pain* 66 (1996), 3–8.

[26] This paper draws on my discussion of Gawande and Emanuel in Chapters 3 and 6 of my (2020). Part of it was presented at the Royal Institute of Philosophy Annual Conference on Meaning in Life and the Knowledge of Death, July 2021. I am grateful to Prof. Michael Hauskeller for inviting me to speak. I am also grateful for the comments I received from other conference participants on that occasion and for written comments from Hauskeller and Peter Bauman.

F. M. Kamm

Thomas Scanlon, *Being Realistic About Reasons* (Oxford University Press, 2014).

Nathaniel Serio, 'If Goldfish Give Us Meaning in Life, What's Next?' *Journal of Philosophy of Life*, 1 (2020), 120–133.

Bernard Williams, 'The Makropulos Case and the Tedium of Immortality' in his *Problems of the Self* (Cambridge University Press, 1973).

Bernard Williams, 'Persons, Character, and Morality' in his *Moral Luck: Philosophical Papers 1973–1980* (Cambridge University Press, 1981).

Susan Wolf, *Meaning in Life and Why It Matters* (Princeton University Press, 2010).

Why Do People Want to Die? The Meaning of Life from the Perspective of Euthanasia

FREDRIK SVENAEUS

Abstract

One way to examine the enigmatic meaningfulness of human life is to ask under which conditions persons ask in earnest for assistance to die, either through euthanasia or physician assisted suicide. The counterpart of intolerable suffering must consist in some form of, however minimal, flourishing that makes people want to go on with their lives, disregarding other reasons to reject assisted dying that have more to do with religious prohibitions. To learn more about why persons want to hasten death during the last days, weeks or months of their lives, what kinds of suffering they fear and what they hold to be the main reasons to carry on or not carry on living, the paper offers some examples from a book written by the physician Uwe-Christian Arnold. He has helped hundreds of persons in Germany to die with the aid of sedative drugs the last 25 years, despite the professional societies and codes in Germany that prohibit such actions. The paper discusses various examples from Arnold's book and makes use of them to better understand not only why people sometimes want to die but what made their lives meaningful before they reached this final decision.

1. Euthanasia in the modern world

A possible way to examine the enigmatic meaningfulness of human life – what does it consist in, really? – is to ask under which conditions persons ask in earnest for assistance to die, either through euthanasia or physician-assisted suicide (PAS). Such measures are currently allowed in eight countries of the world – The Netherlands, Belgium, Luxemburg, Switzerland, Colombia, Canada, Spain, New Zealand and some states of the USA and Australia – and in many other countries changes in law to legalize euthanasia and/or PAS are being considered. What is currently allowed in many more countries to deal with pain is so-called terminal sedation, by which patients are allowed to sleep through the final days or hours of their life. An even more common practice, which is legally supported in most countries world-wide, is patients asking for and getting

doi:10.1017/S1358246121000333

Fredrik Svenaeus

granted withdrawal of life sustaining treatments, what is sometimes (rather misleadingly) referred to as 'passive euthanasia'.

The reason why death wishes in the final stages of life have come to the fore and why many countries and states are moving towards including euthanasia or PAS in their jurisdictions is not only or even mainly that citizens of these countries have become less religious. The main reason is that modern medicine has prolonged life with the help of new drugs and advanced technologies which not only make people live longer but also live under conditions in which their bodies are fraught and damaged by diseases. Before the second world war people generally suffered rather swift deaths whereas the modern death is prolonged and negotiated by way of therapeutic and life sustaining measures, such as antibiotics, insulin, pacemakers, CPR, feeding tubes and ventilators (Warraich, 2017). The pre-modern, swift death was often more painful than contemporary death in the sense that dying persons did not have access to palliative drugs, such as morphine, to the same extent that patients have today, but it was less painful in the sense that they did not survive long enough to experience all the forms of suffering I will explore below.

Although the rising demand for euthanasia and/or PAS cannot be explained only by secularization, it is clearly related to a late-modern life ideal, which is centered upon being in control of one's own life and choosing how to enact it (including how and when to die). To end up in a position in which one becomes more or less fully dependent upon other persons will increasingly be experienced as a meaningless and undignified in such a culture, whereas it will be easier to tolerate in societies that put emphasis on family-bonds and duties in relationship to collective strivings.

2. Suicide and physician assisted dying

Pleas for assistance to die in end-of-life care overlap with a much broader category of life situations, in which persons have suicidal thoughts or try to kill themselves for all sorts of reasons related to suffering, and may ask for support in doing so. However, the situations in end-of-life care are arguably rather different than the situations in which non-terminally ill persons attempt to kill themselves, so different that supporters of physician-assisted suicide rarely want to call this suicide but opt for other labels, such as 'physician-assisted dying' or 'self-determined dying'. I will stick to the term 'physician-assisted suicide' (PAS), since this description fits with what is literally taking place and also makes it possible to separate

298

PAS from euthanasia – in which the doctor is doing the killing – in contrast to labels such as physician-assisted dying, which sometimes refer to both practices.

There has been a strong tendency to medicalize suicidal thoughts and attempts to end one's life ever since such thoughts and actions slipped out of the prohibitive web of religious dogma. Presently, if a person who does not suffer from physically painful and disabling disease says she wants to die, not only doctors but also relatives and friends will most often think of this person as suffering from a depression. If the living conditions and recent life-history of the person in question are bad or unlucky enough we may deem the suicidal thoughts understandable under current circumstances. Nevertheless, if there is hope for a change, we will try to prevent the person from taking her life by measures such as compulsory psychiatric care. Perhaps we still find some room for philosophically motivated suicides in contemporary society, in which the persons who want to end their lives are deemed sane. However, suicides being looked upon as rational and for the best are very rare things outside the confines of end-of-life care and patients suffering from intolerably painful diseases. Depression and other severe psychiatric conditions could possibly in some cases be counted among such ailments, despite being categorized as mental disorders rather than physical diseases, but in such cases the suspicion that the person in question is not able to judge her own situation rationally is always lingering.

3. Some German stories about the wish to die

To learn more about why persons want to hasten death during the last days, weeks or months of their lives, what kinds of suffering they fear and what they hold to be the main reasons to carry on or not carry on living, I will offer some examples from a book written by a physician who has done much during the last 15 years to create a public discussion about euthanasia in Germany and who has pushed the opinion towards making PAS legal in this country. Uwe-Christian Arnold in the book *Letzte Hilfe: Ein Plädoyer für das selbstbestimmte Sterben* (Last Aid: A Plea for Self-Determined Dying) proudly confesses to having helped hundreds of people to die with the aid of sedative drugs made available by him in response to their requests and after having consulted their medical and personal history.[1]

---

[1] Arnold (2020, p. 9). All translations of quotes from this book in the following are my own.

Starting out secretly he increasingly ceased to hide these activities but rather made use of them in order to test the legal situation regarding PAS in Germany and create a public discussion.

The legal situation in Germany is complicated due to conflicting laws and professional codes of conduct on the national level and in the *Bundesländern*, but the base line according to the constitution is that assistance with suicide is not forbidden if carried out for altruistic reasons. This has recently (26 of February 2020) been confirmed after a period of five years during which a supplement to the constitution was in force, prohibiting professional assistance in attempts to kill oneself. The supplement was put in place to stop physicians – and the most well-known of them was clearly Uwe-Christian Arnold – from carrying out such business, but the *Bundesverfassungsgericht* (26 February 2020) found this 'Lex Arnold' to be unconstitutional.[2] Arnold himself did not live long enough to see the ban lifted, he died by his own hand in April 2019 after suffering from progressed cancer. It will be interesting to see how things will now develop in Germany and other countries – like Finland and Sweden – in which the legal situation regarding assisted suicide is more or less the same as in Germany and in which the public opinions are increasingly supporting PAS (Jersild, 2020).

I have chosen four cases out of Arnold's book which he claims to be typical and in which he has helped patients to die. His book contains a lot more than case studies: biographical details from his own life, a brief history of suicide and euthanasia, philosophical arguments to make PAS legal and criticism against those who resist this development and claim the only thing needed in Germany is improved palliative care.[3] Arnold supports palliative developments, but he also claims that in some situations, particularly in end-of-life care, the most humane thing to do is to help the patient to take his own life. Euthanasia is also discussed in the book, but Arnold thinks that institutionalizing PAS would be sufficient in the case of Germany and that the constitution of the country already supports this move (Arnold, 2020, p. 209).

4. Neurological diseases

So, what do such situations look like and what may we learn from them regarding the meaningfulness of human life?

---

[2] See: https://www.bundesverfassungsgericht.de/SharedDocs/Presse mitteilungen/EN/2020/bvg20-012.html

[3] For a different picture of the state of palliative care in Germany and what is needed in the future, see Reimer and Heller (2014).

My colleague Mr. S., a respected specialist in medicine, ran a successful private clinic in southern Germany. He was already looking forward to his retirement, during which he wanted to catch up with a lot of things that he had not been able to pursue due to his hectic working life, when, after having abruptly stumbled a couple of times, he was diagnosed with amyotrophic lateral sclerosis (ALS) at the age of 61. ...

What I witnessed when first visiting Mr. S. was shocking even for an experienced physician like me: the spindly patient sat strapped to a special nursing chair, his head was also fixed, otherwise it would have fallen to the side. The muscles of the arms and legs as well as the entire body had largely regressed. Mr. S. answered to my 'How do you do?' with an indefinable noise, causing a large amount of mucus to flow out of his mouth.

Mrs. S. asked me to read a letter that her husband had with the greatest effort of will laboriously tapped into the computer with one finger. ... Vividly Mr. S. in the letter described various aspects of his torments, such as the problems with the face mask that was supposed to make his breathing easier. The secretions that were constantly forming in the mouth, throat and lungs, and which had to be suctioned off every 45 minutes, caused him the greatest problems. 'Fight longer and longer under the mask against the bad slime'.

At night, Mr. S. continued in his letter, he lies awake every hour, he is in pain, and communication with others is becoming increasingly impossible. Every day his exhaustion is growing and he notices how his motor skills continue to dwindle – a state to which he no longer wants to be exposed: 'I can't do this anymore. I'm finished. Everything is just a great effort. I drag myself forward, hour by hour'. (Arnold, 2020, pp. 27–30)

What makes life no longer worth living for Mr. S are painful *feelings* pervading his entire existence. Not only bodily pains but also difficulties to breathe and the inability to move around, and even to move his arms or neck. These bodily inabilities include not being able to eat or drink – this is being managed by way of a PEG tube – or going to the toilet. On top of this, Mr. S suffers from insomnia because of the pains and breathing difficulties and because of anxiety and fear of more pains to come. He also, as the source of his suffering, mentions his increasing inability to make himself understood and communicate with others. This matters a great deal to him, since he fears this inability might make it impossible for him to communicate his wishes (including the wish to die) in the near future.

Fredrik Svenaeus

Neurological diseases such ALS or MS in some cases lead to very painful dying-processes if not shortened by way of sedating drugs. In the case of Mr. S, the drugs had to be administered via his feeding tube, since he did no longer have the ability to swallow. By having the patient turning a switch to let the drug infusion into the tube – in this case with the help of his finger – the case could be classified as PAS rather than euthanasia. Another possibility for Mr. S would have been to refuse the administration of liquid and nutrition via the tube altogether, but this would have led to a more protracted and probably painful dying-process.

So, to sum up the case, life is not worth living if negative physical experiences – pain, 'air hunger', the inability to move, itches or nausea (the last two not being mentioned in this particular case, but in many other cases of ALS or MS) – are making it intolerably painful and unbearable to continue. An interesting question is if positive physical experiences – various forms of bodily pleasures – could in such situations even out the physical suffering and make it more bearable. Probably not in the case of Mr. S, since the negative physical feelings tend to fill up every second of his life and leave no room for bodily pleasures. To press things further, one could ask if other forms of experiences than bodily ones could count as positive and turn the numbers in such accounts of life-meaning. I am not suggesting that a balance of negative versus positive future life experiences would be possible to carry out in practice, only that it might be an interesting philosophical project to pursue, since other things than bodily experiences matter a lot in a human life, although bodily sufferings characterized as intolerable or unbearable tend to make them significantly less important. In order to see this more clearly, let us turn to another case from Arnold's book.

5. Cancer

Helene C. did not want to live anymore. The metastases had spread throughout her body. It was difficult for her to breathe. For weeks, she had not been able to walk for long. In the meantime, she was so weakened that even the few meters from her bed to the toilet required an almost superhuman effort. Soon, she feared, she would not be able to get up at all.

The elegant but resolute elderly lady had long since come to terms with death, but to be tied to the bed and being diapered by others was a regular nightmare for Mrs. C., who had always valued a neat appearance. 'It is out of the question! I don't want to face my Creator in diapers!', she told me on the phone in her inimitable way shortly before our last meeting. ...

While I was chopping up the medication I had brought with me, Mrs. C. told me about her husband Paul, who had died of cancer 13 years ago – three years before she was diagnosed with the same disease. Mrs. C. had lovingly cared for him at home, it had been three months in total, which Mrs. C., as she said, never wanted to be without. But for her Paul the last few weeks, which he could only spend in bed, were pure torture. ...

I glanced at the daughter, who until then had listened to the conversation largely without contributing. When I asked how she felt about her mother's decision, she replied that it was a great shock to her when she found out about it. At first she was strictly against it. However, she knows all too well how difficult it is to change her mother's opinion once she has made up her mind. Since she also knows how miserably her father died, she can well understand that her mother wants to choose a different way. She might have made the same decision in her position. Unfortunately, this will not change the fact that it is now, at this very moment, incredibly difficult for her to let her mother go. ...

She didn't get any further. She started to sob horribly. Despite everything I've experienced in recent years, this scene touched me deeply. It is difficult to comfort those close to you. Fortunately, Mrs. C. responded right away. She stretched out her arms to her daughter: 'My darling, come here, everything is just as it should be!' (Arnold, 2020, pp. 19–23)

Mrs. C does not suffer intolerable pain – morphine and other drugs have made it possible to ease her pains despite the metastatic cancer spreading in her body. The vignette mentions difficulties to breathe – as in the case of Mr. S – but it is mainly other things than pain or 'air hunger' which make her ask for assistance to die. Important matters, that are further developed in parts of the story not included in the quote above, are that it is no longer possible for Mrs. C to get out for walks, meet with friends or take care of her own cooking. Everyday activities are becoming increasingly limited, something that was true also to an ever greater extent for Mr. S, who was no longer able to even eat or care for his own hygiene as an effect of the ALS. Being able to do everyday things matter a lot for our ability to experience life as meaningful, exactly what is important beyond basic things such as eating or taking care of one's own bodily hygiene may vary significantly between persons. If the most important thing in life is to read books or listen to music, the loss of sight or hearing may lead to depression and/or the wish to die. (It may also do so because these losses make it much harder to meet and communicate with other people.)

In the case of Mrs. C, reading and listening to music are things she still can do, but this is not enough for her in the current situation. She is bored. However, the main reason she wants to die appears to be neither physical pains nor being precluded from everyday meaning-inducing activities, but the threatening scenario of losing her independence and being nursed by others. This is something she provided for her own husband during his last three months in life, but she cannot imagine ending up in a similar situation herself, irrespective of being nursed by professionals or relatives (her daughter is more than willing to do this, but the mother will not allow it to happen).

The main reason for wanting to die in the case of Mrs. C is most adequately described as a threatening loss of *dignity*. She does not want to be nursed by others since this would make her appear in the eyes of others – according to her own impression – as a person she cannot bear to self-identify with. This includes her appearance in the eyes of the Almighty, who she, more or less jokingly, 'does not want to face in diapers'. Perhaps such things as wearing diapers matter more or less to different people, depending on how essential finding independence and self-control or appearing neat and tidy is to their self-image, but the experience of losing one's dignity *in the eyes of others* appears to be an important and rather common reason for why people with different life-constraining diseases ask for PAS or euthanasia (Rehmann-Sutter, Gudat and Ohnsorge (eds.), 2015). Dignity is not only reached or lost in the eyes of specific other people that the patient (fears to) encounter(s), but also in the self-understanding process established by way of *imagined* view-points of general others (not only their gazes but also their thoughts). This is brought out even more comprehensively in another case found in Arnold's book.

6. Paraplegia

Henning M. had suffered severe paraplegia due to a motorcycle accident. He had been in a wheelchair for ten years and could only move things with the help of his mouth. A diaphragmatic pacemaker enabled him to breathe. He was always in pain. But what bothered him the most was the constant, medically necessary care-taking of his body. Although it was done with extreme tenderness, the mere fact that he had to be handled and touched by others for several hours every day meant the 'loss of all privacy' for Henning.

Despite this stress, Henning was by no means depressed. ... Viewed from the outside, he lived with his disability under conditions that one could hardly have imagined more ideal: He had a loving and understanding family and lived at home in a comfortable room that was equipped with all technical refinements. Henning could operate his computer with a mouth control, and he spent a lot of time surfing the Internet and keeping up to date with developments in the world. ...

So why did he want to die? Henning justified his decision in his typical straight yet thoughtful way: 'I have lost my dignity, I have lost my sense of self, I hate my body, I hate my appearance. And being in the position of still accepting myself as a person, I want to go. I don't want to wait until I not only hate my body, but also my whole being'. (Arnold, 2020, pp. 103–104)

After having consulted with Henning and his family, Dr. Arnold ends Henning's life by first putting him to sleep and thereafter turning off the diaphragmatic pacemaker. This is legally classified as refusing life-saving treatment, but as Arnold admits himself, in disentangling the ethics, it comes very close to performing euthanasia (Arnold, 2020, p. 107). What the case of Henning may teach us, in addition to bringing up ethical issues regarding assistance to die for non-terminally ill patients, is to what degree a positive self-understanding is involved in experiencing one's life as meaningful or even bearable to live.

Chronic bodily pains represent a great challenge to finding meaning in life and so does the inability to perform everyday tasks that matter to the person in question. Pleasurable bodily experiences and meaningful daily activities make a person *flourish*, we could say with terminology borrowed from Aristotle and other virtue ethicists. But most important of all to the experiences of suffering or flourishing is probably the identity a person develops during her life in the process of various forms of self-understanding procedures (Svenaeus, 2017, ch. 2). Such self-interpretation is not mainly an intellectual matter, but rather the perceived, emotional quality of *appearing* as such and such in the eyes of others. Although Henning talks about hating himself, not about others hating him, it is clear that his hate stems from comparing his life to the lives of other people, and what he is able to contribute or rather not contribute to the good things that we may achieve in this world together. He is very interested in world politics, but also, more than others, unable to do anything that matters to the course of things in the world. The

Fredrik Svenaeus

project of developing a virtual identity by setting up a web page dedicated to some project and/or self-presentation is not mentioned in the
book, but it may increasingly be a possibility for people in Henning's
situation who want to ease their boredom and find new ways to flourish in and via the virtual world (achievements in the virtual world
may in many cases also matter to what happens in the real world).

Perhaps Henning's case is similar to Mrs. C's in the sense that he
feels to have 'lost all privacy' in being nursed by others. He hates
his paralyzed body, the situation it creates for him, and the person
it threatens to turn him into. It is clear that a person's bodily state
is deeply connected to their self-appearance, and, accordingly, to
the meaning they assign to their life. Not being able to move one's
body tends to be equated with being dependent upon and exposed
to other people, which is perceived as humiliating by Henning as
well as by Mrs. C. Henning faces this problem for all foreseeable
future, but even when we are talking about the final, perhaps rather
short chapter of a long life, becoming like an infant appears to be
difficult to deal with for those who are still adults in mind (cases of
progressed dementia are arguably different).

7. Long lives

Mrs. P. was 99 years old, her 100th birthday was just around the
corner, but with the best will in the world you would never have
thought that. ... Certainly, even Mrs. P. was plagued by a few
'little ailments,' as she called them: heart failure, deteriorating
eyesight, and osteoarthritis. But that wasn't something she complained about. However, walking really was a problem. Both hips
had been replaced by artificial joints many years ago. In the
meantime, these had loosened, but Mrs. P. did not want to go
through another operation with subsequent rehab at her age,
and her physician had also advised against it.

Mrs. P. lived on the ground floor of a rental building in a nice
area of Berlin with lots of green spaces. Despite her walking difficulties, she was still able to take care of her own basic housework
and she paid for additional cleaning help out of her own pocket.
... Overall, Mrs. P. was 'socially well integrated,' as she confirmed to me. ... So why did she want to die?

Mrs. P. told me that a few weeks ago she had stumbled again
and 'my whole body turned green and blue'. Fortunately, she
hadn't broken anything ... but the doctors in the hospital had
suggested she should go to a suitable 'facility' as soon as possible.

Mrs. P. categorically refused. Far too often, she explained to me, she had seen friends and acquaintances in nursing homes or care facilities approaching death under unworthy conditions: 'That is the fate of people who have lived as long as I have: we have to watch how everyone around us is dying'. Many of her friends had spent their last years in old people's homes – and that was almost always 'hell': 'Wild horses couldn't drag me there!' ...

That is why she interpreted the accident a few weeks ago as a sign that the time had come to draw a line. If she broke something next time she fell, her fate would no longer be in her own hands. And that, according to Mrs. P., would be 'absolutely unbearable' for her. So she wanted to go as soon as possible. I asked emphatically whether she was really quite sure. Given her excellent health, she would definitely have the chance to experience another ten good years of life.

Mrs. P. gave a short laugh: 'Mr. Arnold, you are still a young man. When you get to my age, you will understand that after a certain point life is no longer a gift, but a burden. The past seven years have been far from good, and the next are sure to be a lot worse. I can happily do without that. I have always attached great importance to being able to determine the course of my own life, and that should also apply to my death'. (Arnold, 2020, pp. 195–97)

The case of Mrs. P raises questions about how many people will in the near future end their lives by way of PAS if no qualifying condition of suffering from a disease that will lead to death within a foreseeable future is stated – the way it is legally organized in Oregon and eight other states of the USA (remaining life expectancy being specified to about or less than six months). As the life-ending medical practices in Benelux show – in which euthanasia or PAS has become a matter of choice for all patients who experience 'unbearable suffering' irrespective of prognosis – the number of deaths are more than tenfold when arranged in this manner compared to the situation in Oregon (4.6% of all yearly deaths in the Netherlands in comparison with 0.4% of all yearly deaths in Oregon).[4] What will likely increase the number of deaths through euthanasia even further in Benelux in the near future is the possibility of signing a living will declaring not only that one wants to abstain from life-saving treatment in case of contracting diseases (such as pneumonia), but also that one wants to

---

[4] SMER (The Swedish National Council on Medical Ethics), *Dödshjälp: en kunskapssammanställning* (Stockholm: Smer rapporter, 2017) 96, available at: https://www.smer.se.

Fredrik Svenaeus

be euthanized in the case of becoming severely senile due to dementia. Alzheimer's disease is an exploding problem in the Western world and will likely join cancer diseases and neurological diseases as the main reason for euthanasia in countries that make such living will solutions possible or that allow PAS or euthanasia measures in earlier stages of the disease by way of deeming the suffering in question "unbearable" (this is the defining condition in Benelux).

But the case of Mrs. P is different still, since she does not suffer from dementia in any stage, she is rather tired of living and, in addition to this, fears ending up in a nursing home. Such cases have also been discussed in the Netherlands and Belgium, but so far they have not been deemed cases of intolerable suffering. Dr. Arnold obviously means that PAS should also be allowed in such cases, since he helped Mrs. P to die under the current circumstances. He also does not think legalizing PAS will make old people feel pushed to die in order to not become a burden to others, a fear that many critics of PAS and euthanasia have expressed (Arnold, 2020, pp. 203–206).

Since the purpose of this paper is not to argue for or against making PAS or euthanasia legal with or without certain restrictions, I will not dwell further on Mr. Arnold's actions but rather ask why Mrs. P wants to die. It is not because of physical pains, such as in the case of Mr. S. It is not because of physical immobility, such as in the case of Henning (and Mr. S). It is also not because of not being able to do everyday things that matter for her in life, as it was the case with Mrs. C. (and Mr. S and Henning), although Mrs. P's life is developing in this direction and she fears that this will happen soon. It is rather that she feels her life is drawing to a close and she wants to take this matter into her own hands (with the help of Dr. Arnold's hands). She feels one, two or even seven more miserable years would make her *life as a whole* worse, not only in the sense that she would not enjoy the extra years, but that the extra years would increasingly transform her into a person which she does not want to include in her own and others' living memory.

8. The meaning of life in the shadow of death

Studying the reasons patients give when asked why they want to die, one can roughly divide them into three different yet connected *forms* of human suffering.[5] First, we have the feeling of pain and other bodily afflictions, such as difficulties to breathe, nausea, itches or

[5] Besides Arnold, *Letzte Hilfe*, see also: Gawande (2014); and Christoph Rehmann-Sutter et al. (2015).

308

the inability to move. Such *bodily suffering* could become constant and intense enough to invade the entire life of the person, making her life unbearable if it cannot be ameliorated. The body, in such situations, becomes a source of evil that brings torture to the person and alienates her from her own bodily being.

Second, we have the effects of bodily sufferings in terms of making activities that matter to the person in question impossible to engage in. We could discuss what to include exactly in such vital everyday doings, but I am thinking about basic actions necessary to tend to one's everyday needs and also what is favored by a particular person in terms of being pleasurable and important to her. Being alienated from carrying out such projects I would call *everyday suffering*.

Third, we have an alienating form of self-understanding, related to painful bodily feelings and being prevented from activities that matter, which articulates how these two other forms of suffering lead to becoming dependent upon or a burden to others, rather than representing a resource or source of joy for them. *Existential suffering* includes the pain of loneliness, lacking friends or close family members, who have died or disappeared during the course of one's life. Existential suffering can be phrased in terms of not having a valuable place and purpose in the world anymore. Existential suffering is brought to its height by the feeling of lost dignity in becoming bodily exposed and helpless and is further illustrated by the fears of losing one's memory and sanity, as it happens in cases of dementia. Existential suffering is a feeling of shame or vulnerability in the eyes of others, being exposed to their (imagined) gazes or appearing in their (imagined) thoughts as flawed, to be pitied and seen as better dead than alive.

In analogy to these three forms of suffering, the meaning of life brought to us by listening to people living in the shadow of death could be described as bodily, everyday and existential *flourishing*. To flourish means to develop one's potentials as a human being in being the particular person one happens to be. Flourishing is both passive and active in the sense that it falls back on experiences that are developed into accomplishments. Flourishing can be understood in terms of feelings, actions and thoughts. *Bodily* flourishing includes bodily pleasures and the enjoyment of existing as the kind of body that one is by nature. It does not exclude all pains, but merely includes them to the extent that they are necessary to intensify experience and make the contrast to pleasure more vivid. Pain and other bodily ailments may make a person more present in her own body, but beyond limits and self-control bodily suffering will also alienate a person from her own body. *Everyday* flourishing begins with the little things, doings and accomplishments connected to bodily

Fredrik Svenaeus

needs – hunger, thirst, physical exercise, hygiene, etc. – and after such needs have been satisfied may turn to play, education and working projects in and through which a person may develop her potentials during her lifetime. *Existential* flourishing engages intellectual capacities, thoughts and theories, but it is also, just as bodily and everday flourishing, rooted in feelings and a kind of activity in itself. To become the person one endeavors to be through the things that one accomplishes in the world, and in relationship to other people, is the goal of existential flourishing. This may include various forms of suffering, since experiences of lack and loss could sharpen the focus on the meaning of life and lead to changes in a person's way of living. But the hardships brought to us by the stories in Arnold's book should also teach us to cherish the moments when we do not suffer but merely enjoy being alive, bodily present in the world together with others engaged in everyday projects and attempting to be if not good, then at least decent to each other. Maybe such things as lasting love and making a difference in the world are the ultimate meaningful projects of life, but it is also nice merely to not be in pain and to be able to move around in the company of others doing little things. We should not forget such pleasures since we will surely be reminded of them and cherish them when they are eventually beyond our reach. They are also forms of human flourishing even though they do not include the existential quest we often intend when using the phrase 'meaning of life'.

Södertörn University, Sweden
fredrik.svenaeus@sh.se

References

Uwe-Christian Arnold, *Letzte Hilfe: Ein Plädoyer für das selbstbestimmte Sterben* (Hamburg: Rowohlt Verlag, 2020).

Atul Gawande, *Being Mortal: Illness, Medicine and What Matters in the End* (London: Profile Books LTD, 2014).

Reimer Gronemeyer and Andras Heller, *In Ruhe sterben: Was wir uns wünschen und was die moderne Medizin nicht leisten kann* (München: Pattloch Verlag, 2014).

P. C. Jersild, *Hur vill du dö? Om makten över livets slut* (Stockholm: Fri tanke förlag, 2020).

Christoph Rehmann-Sutter, Heike Gudat and Kathrin Ohnsorge (eds.), *The Patient's Wish to Die: Research, Ethics, and Palliative Care* (Oxford: Oxford University Press, 2015).

SMER (The Swedish National Council on Medical Ethics), *Dödshjälp: en kunskapssammanställning* (Stockholm: Smer rapporter, 2017) 96, available at: https://www.smer.se.

Fredrik Svenaeus, *Phenomenological Bioethics: Medical Technologies, Human Suffering, and the Meaning of Being Alive* (London: Routledge, 2017).

Haider Warraich, *Modern Death: How Medicine Changed the End of Life* (New York: St. Martin's Press, 2017).

Index of Names

Index of Names